Conjuring Asia

The promise of magic has always commanded the human imagination, but the story of industrial modernity is usually seen as a process of disenchantment. Drawing on the writings and performances of the so-called Golden Age Magicians from the turn of the twentieth century, Chris Goto-Jones unveils the ways in which European and North American encounters with (and representations of) Asia – the fabled Mystic East – worked to re-enchant experiences of the modern world. Beginning with a reconceptualization of the meaning of 'modern magic' itself – moving beyond conventional categories of 'real' and 'fake' magic – Goto-Jones' acclaimed book guides us on a magical mystery tour around India, China, and Japan, showing us levitations and decapitations, magic duels and bullet catches, goldfish bowls and paper butterflies. In the end, this mesmerizing book reveals Orientalism as a kind of magic in itself, casting a spell over Western culture that leaves it transformed, even today.

Chris Goto-Jones is Professor of Comparative Philosophy & Political Thought at Leiden University, where he was previously Professor of Modern Japan Studies. He is also a Professorial Research Fellow of SOAS, University of London.

Praise for Conjuring Asia

'If magic is the art of accomplishing the impossible, Goto-Jones
emerges as a scholar-magician: a wonderful book in every
sense.'

DERREN BROWN

'Goto-Jones opens with a surprise: far from killing magic,
modern science made it better. But his main trick is to follow
magicians on a cross-cultural chase to India, China, and Japan;
what began as a celebration of the Golden Age of Magic
becomes a treatise on global modernity. This is performance
research at its finest.'

MARTIN PUCHNER, HARVARD UNIVERSITY

'Modernity and magic are usually seen in opposition to one
another, as in early modern Europe. In Chris Goto-Jones's
extraordinary book, we see that they were in fact intricately
intertwined as modern Asia came into being. By combining
ideas about illusion and reality with the discourse of progress in
China, Japan, and India, Goto-Jones gives us a wholly original,
deeply thoughtful, and innovative approach to the history of
colonial and semi-colonial Asia, as well as representations of
Asia in the West.'

RANA MITTER, OXFORD UNIVERSITY

'Conjuring Asia is a wonderful book – yes, full of wonders – at
once erudite and entertaining, dazzling. It is full of marvelous
material gleaned from hard-to-come-by and all-too-overlooked
popular sources. This stupendous research has been judiciously
organized into Goto-Jones' eloquent, articulate, insightful, and
engaging critical analysis of a historical and modern transnational culture of magic.'

LEE SIEGEL, UNIVERSITY OF HAWAII

'With Chris Goto-Jones's Conjuring Asia, the academic study of
secular magic comes of age. Surprisingly enough, that is because

Conjuring Asia

Magic, Orientalism, and the Making of the Modern World

Chris Goto-Jones
Leiden University

CAMBRIDGE
UNIVERSITY PRESS

CAMBRIDGE
UNIVERSITY PRESS

University Printing House, Cambridge CB2 8BS, United Kingdom

Cambridge University Press is part of the University of Cambridge.

It furthers the University's mission by disseminating knowledge in the pursuit of education, learning and research at the highest international levels of excellence.

www.cambridge.org
Information on this title: www.cambridge.org/9781107433823

© Chris Goto-Jones 2016

First published 2016

Printed in the United States of America by Sheridan Books, Inc.

A catalogue record for this publication is available from the British Library

Library of Congress Cataloguing in Publication data
Goto-Jones, Christopher S., author.
Conjuring Asia : magic, orientalism, and the making of the modern world / Chris Goto-Jones, Leiden University.
New York : Cambridge University Press, 2016.
LCCN 2016020463 | ISBN 9781107076594
LCSH: Magic – Asia – History – 20th century. | Magic – China – History – 20th century. | Magic – India – History – 20th century. | Magic – Japan – History – 20th century.
LCC BF1622.A8 G68 2016 | DDC 133.4/3095–dc23
LC record available at https://lccn.loc.gov/2016020463

ISBN 978-1-107-07659-4 Hardback
ISBN 978-1-107-43382-3 Paperback

Contents

Figures

Acknowledgements

Many of us like to try to convince the people around us that writing is a horrible burden; we try to get our partners, our friends and family, and our students to feel sorry for us. But I have to confess right at the start that writing this book has been fun. In fact, I've been constantly worried that someone would find out how much fun it was and try to stop me doing it. These days, universities are not noted for embracing fun, and certainly not for funding it. So, it was little act of magic in itself that the Netherlands Organization for Scientific Research (NWO) generously supported this project in the context of a larger project: *Beyond Utopia – New Politics, the Politics of Knowledge, and the Science Fictional Field of Japan.* I cannot thank it enough. The support of the NWO enabled us to develop new research trajectories in the direction of performance philosophy and the political arts, and I'm especially grateful for the camaraderie of Cissie Fu and Florian Schneider.

When it comes to institutions, however, I also need to acknowledge the warmth and enthusiastic support offered by a number of magic societies in various parts of the world, some of which have asked not to be named (hopefully because of a desire to remain secret rather than out of any embarrassment about being associated with me). Chief amongst these must be the Magic Circle in London and the Conjuring Arts Research Center in New York; the staff and members of these societies have been tirelessly helpful with my questions, giving me access to their wonder-filled libraries and collections. A wide range of magicians and scholar-magicians have read all or parts of this book in various forms and at various times. All have provided invaluable feedback. There's no space to list them all here (I'm so sorry!), but I'd like to thank in particular Derren Brown, Teller, Eugene Burger, Stephen

Minch, Jim Steinmeyer, Edwin Dawes. In this company, I think I should also mention my brother Richard, who tricked me into an interest in magic when I was a little kid, simply by being my older brother and being interested in magic himself. If it hadn't been for him and the (now sadly defunct) Supreme Magician's Club, none of this would ever have occurred to me.

Just before the end, I'd like to thank Angela Zaeh, whose patience and persistent interest has been remarkable, and Simone Buitendijk, who has conjured time and space for my work. And finally there's Nozomi Goto, who has such an enduring and vital delight in magic that she has been an inspiration to me. Indeed, she demands magic of the world; no matter how disappointing reality might be, no matter how impossible things might seem, she always attempts to transform it with sheer force of will. Indeed, by impossibilizing the simple, she calls magic into the world. Here, in a tiny and mundane way, I'm trying to give some back.

Of course, no matter how much I have been supported and helped along this path, any and all mistakes and infelicities are my own. My editor in Cambridge, Lucy Rhymer, has been a star, so I can't even misdirect any blame onto her for any of the problems you encounter.

For the wonderful images that appear throughout this book, I'd like to acknowledge the Nielsen Magic Collection. And for the devilish 'whispering imps' that cavort between the lines, I'd like to acknowledge the illustrator Mark Stutzman and supplier Chris Chelko, who have generously allowed me to use this image from their iconic playing cards.

INTRODUCTION: MAGIC IN THE WORLD

First of all, I promise not to fill this book with puns about magic being tricky, or with a long series of bad jokes about things happening 'as if by magic'. But magic *is* a tricky business, and the extent to which this is true has become increasingly evident to me as I have worked on this project.

For one thing, it's not very clear what magic actually is. Even leaving aside the deceptively difficult (and completely incoherent) question of the difference between 'real magic' and 'fake magic' (which will preoccupy us for much of the first two chapters as I search for some form of unifying theory), it's even tough to know when a stage magician has just performed something that you recognize as magic. Of course, it's always clear when they've failed. And their failure often has nothing whatsoever to do with the success of whatever feat they were trying to accomplish: a magician can successfully pull a rabbit from a hat or a coin from your ear without your really knowing how he did it, but such accomplishments can be cringe-worthily mundane in the hands of Uncle Geek while being transportingly magical in the hands of Professor Sparrowhawk.

So, magic is not an object, not a prop or a mechanism, not even a technique or an accomplishment. As least, not *per se*. Magic flows from the hands of a magician only when an audience feels magic happening. It is an interpersonal and intersubjective phenomenon. And that, more than anything else, is the secret to magic: *a magician is one who causes you to feel that magic has transpired*, no matter what has transpired.

Yet, magic is more than a feeling; it's also a discipline, at least in so far as it includes an accepted canon of texts, techniques, and technologies aimed at the performance of impossibilities. Magic has methods and methodologies, theories, debates, and disagreements. It has history. It involves research and development and ideas about progress; it demands practice and performance. It has culture. Even while all of this learning seems to be targeted at enabling magicians to perform all kinds of secret techniques (which is also true), in the end, it is really all focussed on enabling a magician to make you *feel* that he (or she, but usually he) has done something magical. Magical knowledge concerns the ability to enchant somebody's senses, not necessarily the ability to ascertain their phone number or cut them in half.

Magic is a field of knowledge that is shrouded (and shrouds itself) in secrecy, constructing an epistemic community that is (at least to some extent) separate from the conventional world of the academy. It's no secret that the motto of the Magic Circle is *indocilis private loqui,* or that the first of Howard Thurston's inviolable rules of magic was: never reveal the secret. There are professors of prestidigitation, just as there are professors of nuclear physics. Yet they do not recognize each other; they rarely pass in the corridors of a university ... Actually, they pass each other surprisingly often in universities, but they pass in silence, unrecognized, without knowing that it has happened. Magicians are no more invisible than physics professors, but you can walk past either on the street and not know who they are. These days, the magician is probably not wearing a pointy hat or even a top-hat, just as the professor is probably not wearing a mortar-board; although either might sport a symbolic tie or a pin that would identify them to someone who knew what to look for.

Magic has multiple communities of people who identify themselves as magicians, some of whom are professionals in various different ways. Membership of these communities can be jealously guarded, requiring initiations or examinations or performances. Or not. Some are open and welcoming, even while others maintain strict codes of secrecy and silence between magicians and muggles.

For myself, one of my challenges writing this book was to find ways to bridge between these communities and their respective bodies of knowledge. I don't profess to be especially magical, but I am an Associate of the Inner Magic Circle in London and a member of the Academy of Magical Arts in Hollywood. And I'm also a professor at an old, European university that has no place for magic in its curricular offerings. In this context, it's mildly embarrassing to write an academic book about magic; people point and laugh (really). One colleague asked me if I could perform at his niece's birthday party. I declined.

And this is what I mean when I say it's difficult to pin magic down. My sensitive, open-minded colleague was not wrong to link magic with balloon animals. Indeed, some of the most wonderful magic imaginable happens in the hearts and minds of children. But it's astonishing to think that this category might also include transforming a piece of paper into a butterfly, walking through the Great Wall of China, or speaking to the dead. Just about anything *can be* magic, but almost nothing *is*. In fact, a lot magic isn't even magic; it generates feelings of embarrassment rather than wonder. It does not enchant, it riles.

For all of these reasons and more, the first part of this book, comprising the first three chapters, is largely concerned with trying to work out what magic is and how we can talk about it (analyse it and criticize it) in a clear and reasonably scholarly way. The first chapter focuses on the meaning and development of 'modern magic', which is often mistakenly understood as being different in nature from 'old magic'. One of the great lessons of modernity has been that the laws of nature are true at all times and in all places (with the possible exception of cosmological singularities), so old and new magic must (on some practical level) be the same, howsoever it is presented or performed. No matter how much we'd like to believe that the European Middle Ages were like Middle Earth, they were not.

The second chapter attempts to draw the outline of a theory of modern magic that will enable us to understand the approach adopted in the second half of this book. In particular, it is concerned with the historically, culturally, ethically, technically, and aesthetically slippery question: what is *good magic*? In these early chapters especially, but also later on, I make extensive use of texts written by and for magicians – texts that are usually not closely considered in the academy. My reason for doing this is simple: magicians are professional magic-makers (and often rather impressive scholars); they know more about how to make magic than anyone else, and so we should take them seriously (at least about this).

These first two chapters also explore the question of *modernity*. Unfortunately, the idea of the modern is almost as tricky as magic itself.

In this book, I am not using the terms 'modern' and 'modernity' in only their most everyday sense (to refer to a historical period proximal to the present). Indeed, the historical period I'm interested in is the so-called Golden Age of Magic, which extends roughly from the middle of the nineteenth century into the early twentieth. As well as temporality, modernity also brings with it a constellation of cultural, technological, and ideological issues that are usually associated with the European Enlightenment Project. We might think about the development of social rights and democracy, more pervasive educational provision, advancements of (and confidence in) rationality and science as the best (and only) way to solve mankind's problems and the riddles of the universe. These features are wrapped into a universal vision of history that emphasizes progress: mankind moves from barbaric to civilized, superstitious to rational, ritualistic to scientific, and so on. But we might also think about colonialism, empire, and the notion of the 'white man's burden' to chaperone the peripheries into the arms of civilization.

It is in this context that the Golden Age gives birth to something we might meaningfully call *modern magic*. While the force of modernity and modernization seems to push cultures away from magical thinking and magical belief, *modern magic* represents an attempt to maintain the experience of enchantment and the magical in the world. Hence, modern magic enjoys a deeply conflicted relationship with both modernity and magic, investing in them both despite their apparently contradictory tendencies. What kind of process can transform magic into something modern? Is that process magical in itself? This period sees modern magic develop an ethical mission to confront and expose what it sees as illegitimate magic or charlatanism – the Spiritualist movement, Theosophy, and other forms of new occultism that emerged during the so-called mystic revival.

It is this problematic and complicated connection between modernity and magic that takes us into the last chapter of Part I. Chapter 3 considers one of the cultural strategies deployed in Europe and the United States to square the circle: if the 'West' had really progressed beyond magic, and if people still wanted (or even needed) magic in their lives, then perhaps magic could be found (and imported from) outside the 'West'? In this context, Chapter 3 explores the various ways in which magicians constructed and exploited visions of the 'Mystic East' as the home of magic itself. This *Orientalism* was partially a genuine interest in India, China, and Japan, and partially an ideological and literary process of creating these distant lands as repositories of the West's magical fantasies.

Just as was the case with modern magic, magicians were deeply conflicted about the meaning and integrity of Oriental magic – they were torn between wanting to believe in a distant but still-living space of phantasmagoria and also wanting to assert the developmental super-iority and universal consistency of (Western) modernity. Western magi-cians wanted to find lost secrets of magic in the vastness of rural India, *but* they also wanted to expose such secrets as fraudulent when sub-jected to modern tests and inquiry. They wanted Oriental magic to be everything modern magic was not, yet they needed modern magic to be universally valid. For some, the idea of Oriental magic became a kind of flourish, like pixie dust, that could be cast over performances in London, Paris, and New York to help audiences find that precious feeling of enchantment. Orientalism became a kind of magic in itself.

Hence, Part I of this book is very much focussed on magic in the so-called West. Indeed, as we'll see in Part II, there is an extremely close affinity between the idea of 'modern magic' and the idea of 'Western magic', not only in Europe and the United States but also (and perhaps especially) in Asia. Like various other forms of Western culture and structures of knowledge that were exported to Asia during the processes of Western imperialism and colonialism, such as modern medicine, modern magic was largely seen as something distinctly Western. This was not only (but also) because modern magic seemed to require magi-cians to dress as a Victorian gentleman, not only (but also) because modern magic seemed to involve a specific repertoire of technologically advanced 'tricks', but also because it brought with it a certain normative and ethical framework that often challenged the principles of local magical practices. Indeed, just as modern medicine and modern military technology came into conflict with local practices and technologies in Asia, so too modern magic strove to establish itself as superior to local traditions. Even today the idea of 'modern magic' retains the basic form of this Golden Age ideal, leading to all kinds of new questions about whether contemporary magic (like history and art and literature) should now be considered post-modern.

So, while India, China, and Japan all have lively and rich tradi-tions of conjuring and magic that reach back for centuries, the first part of this book is mostly concerned with the formation and shape of something that we can meaningfully identify as *modern magic*, emerging out of a particular European tradition (including that tradition's interactions with Asia), engaging the particular conditions of industrial modernity at the turn of the twentieth century, and then being exported to Asia in gunboats and merchant ships. The rhetoric of modern magic is universal, but its history is particular and often imperial.

In this direction, the imperial history of magic draws stark attention to questions of racism and other forms of chauvinism (including sexism), from which magic is not miraculously free. Although there is significant resistance in the magical community to look back on the legacy of some of the great magicians of the period as racist, it is noticeable that very few white, European magicians today would even consider dressing in a silken kimono, speaking in pidgin English, and applying yellow make-up to make themselves appear 'Japanese'. While it's true that the parameters of acceptable behaviour are (at least partially) historically constructed, and so William Robinson or Theodore Bamberg (for example) probably didn't feel that they were being offensive when they presented themselves as Chung Ling Soo or Okito, it is also true that the cultural atmosphere and social practices of colonialism did all kinds of violence to people that is simply unacceptable. It would not be possible to write responsibly about these figures and practices today without taking such issues seriously. Hence, one of the things that this book explores in Part II is the way modern magic silenced the voices of magicians from Asia in the name of propagating the Western fantasy of Oriental magic. Indeed, this cultural strategy was so powerful that it even co-opted some of the most talented magicians from Asia into a form of self-Orientalism when they performed in the West. Just to be clear, it is not my intention to single out individual magicians as racist, but rather to understand the ways in which the culture of 'modern magic', as it developed in this colonialist historical context, incorporated and performed a kind of racism.

And so, Part II of this book, which includes Chapters 4 through 6, shifts the focus more directly towards the magic of the so-called Orient in this period. These chapters are rather more empirical than those of Part I and might be seen as a series of case studies that test out the theories and concepts developed earlier. For reasons discussed in Chapter 3, Part II interprets the 'Orient' to mean India, China, and Japan, and thus diverges somewhat from the usage of Edward Said (and others), who focussed mainly on the Middle East. For now, suffice

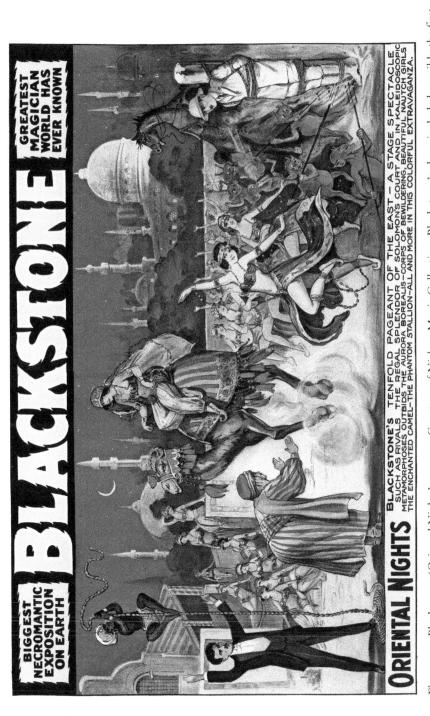

Figure 0.1 Blackstone, 'Oriental Nights', c. 1920. Courtesy of Nielsen Magic Collection. Blackstone's show included possibly the first vanishing camel in modern magic.

it to say that this triumvirate of Asian nations were the preeminent representatives of magical fantasies during the Golden Age. Each chapter of Part II considers one of these nations, exploring both how its magic was represented in the West (e.g., Indian magic) and then how magic was actually experienced and performed in that country (e.g., magic in India). In each case, special attention is given to the 'tricks' held to be most representative of that particular magical tradition, as well as to the personalities who enlivened that magic, and the interaction between all of these and the regime of modern magic.

I think it's important at the start to confess that this book makes no claims to being an ethnography or even a comprehensive history. This is especially important in the context of the intimidating, meticulous documentary historical work that is done within the magic community about the lives of magicians and the origins of particular tricks. Magicians are, as a group, deeply concerned about revealing who invented which trick and when it was first performed. The great Houdini set the tone for this by naming himself in testament to 'the father of modern magic', Jean Eugene Robert-Houdin, and then devoting himself to exposing Robert-Houdin for making false claims of originality.

In any case, it is not my primary purpose to expose anyone in this way, although my arguments sometimes require that I do this kind of documentary work. However, in some cases, I'll need to beg a little indulgence from these (rightfully) demanding readers, since it is quite often the case that my arguments are about the perception and misperception of magical history itself. Where I have omitted to mention some of the more esoteric or tortuous historical details that have been uncovered within the magic community, I apologize.

Indeed, I find myself full of sincere admiration for the historians of magic (who are often seen as 'amateur historians' in the academy) who have done astonishingly intricate work in this field. The quality of some of that work is second to none, and it really does emphasize the way that expertise in magic and in the university have tended to develop in parallel rather than in partnership over the years. Secret libraries and then balloon animals have contributed to making this so, but the situation is changing rapidly as magic societies and research centres go through the process of digitizing their assets in the age of the internet. I have benefitted immeasurably from the generous support of a number of such institutions as well as individual magicians in North America, Europe, and Asia.

Just to push this a little further, the place of the study of magic in the university is controversial and difficult. Of course, I'm not even talking about the controversies associated with the study of esotericism or the paranormal in university contexts, since these are only tangentially related to the magic discussed in this book. In general, the study of magic falls into cultural history or perhaps theatre studies. There has been work recently in psychology. Television shows attempt to convince us that magic could be studied in school as part of the science curriculum; tricks can be used to illustrate scientific principles. The admixture of Orientalism suggests that magic could be a topic in critical area studies, and work is beginning in this field. And I was gratified that the anonymous reviewers of this book also recognized the significance of this story of magic for global history, especially the history of knowledge and the formation of the great binaries of modern thought (East-West, reason-passion, old-new, etc.).

In recent years, we have also seen the development and recognition of a new field of knowledge called 'performance philosophy', which is allied to 'performance politics'. Given the conceptually radical nature of magic as well as its inextricable relationship with performance, it seems to me that this is a most fruitful and productive context from which to study magic. And, indeed, I have received great support from scholars in these fields, at conferences and elsewhere.

Before I finally step aside, I'd like to offer a couple of titbits of advice about how to proceed. First of all, the adventure of writing this book has required some juggling in its own right because it seems likely that readers from different backgrounds will come with different expectations. It is partly for this reason that the book is structured into two parts. While I hope many readers might want to read the whole thing, I'm conscious that the two parts meet rather different needs. It seems conceivable, then, that some readers looking primarily for Asia in these pages might prefer to skip the first part. With that possibility in the back of my mind, I think Part II can stand up on its own. It won't be altogether stable, but it should be at least teetering upright.

A second note regards notes. In the early stages of this project, I was encouraged to write with only minimal footnotes so that the book would appear as accessible as possible to non-academic readers. However, it quickly became apparent to me that, at least to the extent that these 'non-academic' readers are magicians, this is a false assumption. Indeed, as I've already intimated, if there is a single group of readers anywhere in the world that is more interested than academics in meticulous footnotes and curious tangents, it's magicians. So, I have not omitted notes, and I was delighted to be supported in this choice by the anonymous readers and my editor in Cambridge. However, taking my cue from Susanna Clarke, I have endeavoured to write in a way that does not make reading these notes essential or even important for all readers, but also not too painful. If chasing the white rabbit back into the hat sounds like fun to you, the notes are there. In a wonderfully generous turn of phrase, one of the anonymous reviewers suggested that readers might 'dip into them like humming birds seeking sweetness'. I hope you find some nourishment, at least.

And finally, this book includes a number of 'scenes', which are descriptions of performances of magic that I have found especially important or powerful in various ways. They are not all drawn from the Golden Age – indeed many of them are rather contemporary – but I hope they serve to illustrate some of the general points and arguments being made. They usually appear without much interpretation in the hope that they will resonate by themselves and serve as points of reference throughout. For slightly theatrical reasons (such as the need to perform some of the magic in question for readers who may not have been lucky enough to have witnessed it before reading), these scenes are more prevalent in Part I than Part II. The scenes are based upon historical accounts, interviews, and recollections, but they have been narrativized by me; their purpose is more performative than historical, so I take full responsibility for any oddities.

It is also in a slightly theatrical mode that I have adopted the convention of addressing the generic magician as 'she' (rather than 'he') in this book. The issue of gender is both powerful and important in the history of magic, and it is discussed in various places herein. With a number of important exceptions, the history of modern stage magic has been dominated by men, while the history of modern Spiritualism and occult magic has featured women very centrally. Rather than defaulting to the male pronoun (as is the usual practice in work about secular magic), to the grammatically clumsy 'they', or to the tiresomely cumbersome 'he/she', I have chosen to flag this issue with a consistent 'she'. I immediately accept that this fails to achieve gender-neutrality, but I'm not of the opinion that reality is gender-neutral.

Tokyo, 2015

PART I

1 MODERN MAGIC IN HISTORY AND THEORY

Modern magic in history (and magic in modern history)

This book is largely concerned with the so-called Golden Age of Magic, which is a grand expression often used to describe the period around the turn of the twentieth century. Useful signposts for this period might be the 'father of modern magic', Jean Eugene Robert-Houdin (1805–1871), who was (arguably) the first 'top hat and tails' magician of the modern period, and at the other end we have Houdini (Erik Weisz, 1874–1926), who named himself in tribute to Robert-Houdin but then systematically attempted to refute his place in history.[1] The precise historical parameters of this period are not extremely important. It is generally accepted that the early years of the nineteenth century were a low ebb for conjuring and magic, 'when conjuring proper was so eclipsed by ... ghost shows and mechanical contrivances', but then it was revived by the great innovators of 'modern magic'.[2] For many, the Golden Age continued at least into the

---

[1] Houdini's attempt to refute generally held claims that Robert-Houdin was the great innovator of magic at the dawn of the Golden Age was controversial, not only because of the uneven scholarship on both side of the debate but also because of the apparent violence with which he pursued his case against the legendary figure. Given the importance of Robert-Houdin as an icon in Houdini's early life, this seemed like a deeply personal issue. In any case, one important side-effect of this book was to destabilize the popular idea that modern magic began neatly with the French master. Harry Houdini, *The Unmasking of Robert-Houdin*. New York: The Publishers Printing Co. 1906/8.

[2] Sidney Clarke, *The Annals of Conjuring*. Seattle: The Miracle Factory, 2001, p. 185. This undisputed classic in this history of magic was originally serialized in *The Magic Wand*, 1924–1928. The decline of conjuring in the nineteenth century is generally

1930s and the outbreak of World War II. This chapter makes no attempt at a comprehensive history of this period, but rather seeks to sketch its basic shape and contours.[3]

What is important is that this era included many of the great names of stage magic. In addition to Houdini, these included (but were certainly not limited to) Johann Hofzinser (1806–1875), John Henry Anderson (The Great Wizard of the North, 1814–1874), William Palmer (Robert (or Joseph) Heller, 1826–1878), John Nevil Maskelyne (1839–1914), Ira Erastus Davenport & William Henry Davenport (The Davenport Brothers, 1839–1911 & 1841–1877), Harry Kellar (1849–1922), Shōkyokusai Ten'ichi (1852–1912), Zhu Liankui (Ching Ling Foo, 1854–1922), William Robinson (Chung Ling Soo, 1861–1918), Nevil Maskelyne (1863–1924), David Devant (1868–1941), Howard Thurston (1869–1936), Sigmund Neuberger (The Great Lafayette, 1871–1911), Horace Goldin (1873–1939), Harry Jansen (Dante, 1883–1955), Theodore Bamberg (Okito, 1875–1963), Harry Blackstone Sr. (1885–1965).

These men (for they were nearly all men)[4] ushered in the age of modern magic, building custom-made props and mechanical devices, appearing in the great theatres of the Western world, and travelling the world on steam ships in search of new audiences, new markets, new ideas, and fresh inspiration. This was magic on the grand scale – the genuine forebear of Las Vegas spectaculars and global TV specials. But it was also the magic of empire, with (especially) British and American

---

associated with its eclipse by the emergence of automata and other mechanical contrivances, as well as the popularity of so-called ghost-shows and phantasmagoria. Audiences visited the circus to view exotic creatures and trained animals. Hence, the skills of the magician in legerdemain fell out of favour for some time.

[3] Standard histories include: Clarke, *The Annals of Conjuring*; Christopher Milbourne, *The Illustrated History of Magic*. London: Robert Hale & Co. 1973; James Randi, *Conjuring: Being a Definitive History of the Venerable Arts of Sorcery, Prestidigitation, Wizardry, Deception, & Chicanery*. New York: St. Martin's Press, 1992; and the sumptuous Noel Daniel, Mike Caveney, Ricky Jay, and Jim Steinmeyer, *The Big Book of Magic*. Cologne: Taschen, 2013

[4] The vanishing of women from this story and their complicated place in the modern history of magic is wonderfully narrated by Karen Beckman, *Vanishing Women: Magic, Film, and Feminism*. Durham: Duke University Press, 2003. Conversely, a broader study of the central place of women in the new occultism is Alex Owen, *The Darkened Room: Women, Power, and Spiritualism in Late Victorian England*. Chicago: University of Chicago Press, 2004. The variance between the high status of women in occult magic (represented as marginal and spiritual) and their low status in modern stage magic (represented as technologically driven and relatively mainstream) is notable.

magicians traversing the (semi-) colonies, exporting a newly and mysteriously modernized version of magic to outposts in Egypt, India, China, and Japan. With creative and entrepreneurial flair, the great magicians transformed magic into an aspect of the so-called civilizing mission of Victorian society. Indeed, for some, it was a *duty* to take modern magic out into the world, just as it was a duty to take trade and moral virtue to the 'natives'. The complex ethics and cultural politics of the international political economy bubbled into the magic scene, not only emerging on stages around the world but also at the International Expositions, in the media, in literature, and eventually in film.

The *modernity* of modern magic was taken very seriously indeed. The Golden Age was the time of top hats and tails, of gentlemanly magicians who conducted 'experiments' and 'demonstrations' (rather than performing tricks). Positioning themselves as 'professors of magic', stage magicians seemed to embrace the positivism and empiricism of the scientific revolution. Not only entertainers, magicians sought to 'test' claims and to showcase the (still rather mysterious) capabilities of the emerging material and psychological sciences. Modern magic shows made ostentatious use of grand technology – new props and equipment that implied the power of science but coloured it with the notion that anything sufficiently advanced may *look like magic*.[5] They attempted to deploy science itself as a means to enchantment.[6] Magicians were educators and systematizers, organizing the field of magic into distinct disciplines for specialization and study, establishing societies to promote good practice. Starting with Robert-Houdin in France and Professor Hoffmann in England, magicians began writing

---

[5] Arthur C. Clarke's famous 'third rule' is today so well known as to seem axiomatic: 'Any sufficiently advanced technology is indistinguishable from magic.' It first appeared in Clarke's 1973 (revised) essay 'Hazards of Prophecy: The Failure of Imagination', in Arthur C. Clarke, *Profiles of the Future: An Enquiry into the Limits of the Possible.* Reprinted London: Orion Books, 2000. This essay also states his other two laws, which are also relevant to this: chapter: 1. When a distinguished but elderly scientist states that something is possible, he is almost certainly right. When he states that something is impossible, he is very probably wrong. 2. The only way of discovering the limits of the possible is to venture a little way past them into the impossible.

[6] This emphasis on technological advancement was such that, as Matthew Solomon explains, 'the relative importance of technology and the performer was a key issue, one that was vigorously contested in controversy about the purported death of magic at the turn of the century'. Matthew Solomon, *Disappearing Tricks: Silent Film, Houdini, and the New Magic of the Twentieth Century.* Urbana & Chicago: University of Illinois Press, 2010, p. 29.

long volumes of explanation and theory in order to educate their peers and public about how to practice and appreciate their art.[7] In other words, modern magic did not develop in confrontation with Victorian society's faith in progress and reason, but rather in tandem with it: modern magic brought us machinery that *performed for us*; technological creations that enabled us to cut a woman in half, levitate above the stage, or play chess against a mechanical automaton.[8]

Indeed, in some ways, modern magic resembled the kind of rationalization of pre-modern magic that Max Weber might have recognized as a fundamental feature of the modernization of society. This was certainly the conceit of many magicians of the period, who talked about clear distinctions between 'old magic' and 'new magic'. And yet, this Golden Age of Magic resides squarely in the period that Weber argued was characterized by the 'disenchantment of the world', so isn't the idea of modern magic oxymoronic? I think it's safe to assume that Weber's remark was not meant as a critique of the practices of stage magic at that time (although, as we will see, many critics of magic today would endorse the idea that modern magic has been disenchanted in practice). In his famous and influential speech, delivered at Munich University in 1917, Weber made the argument that 'the fate of our times is characterized by rationalization and intellectualization' in the Western world, where science and technology were effectively destroying ideas about mysterious powers and magical means.[9] No longer was man's relationship with the natural world to be based on mystical or incalculable forces controlled by divine or otherwise inexplicable interventions; instead, nature was to be mastered through reason, calculation, and technology. As a result, the enchanted meanings of things in the world were vanishing, and Western man was left only with a rational sense of the utility of things.[10]

---

[7] Jean Eugene Robert-Houdin, *Les Secrets de la Prestidigitation et de la Magie*, 1868, reprinted Paris: Hachette Livre, 2012. Professor Hoffmann, *Modern Magic: A Practical Treatise on the Art of Conjuring*. 1876, U.S. edition reprinted Philadelphia: David McKay, 1910.

[8] The place of automata on stage is dealt with comprehensively by Kara Reilly, *Automata and Mimesis on the Stage of Theatre History*. New York: Palgrave, 2011. The fabled chess-playing automaton is the subject of chapter 1 in James Cook, *The Arts of Deception: Playing with Fraud in the Age of Barnum*. Cambridge: Harvard University Press, 2001.

[9] Max Weber, 'Science as a Vocation', in H.H. Gerth & C. Wright Mills (trans. and eds.), *Max Weber: Essays in Sociology*. New York: Oxford University Press, 1958, p. 155.

[10] Landy & Saler note that the tendency of Western elites 'to define enchantment as the residual, subordinate "other" to modernity's rational, secular, and progressive

To some extent, then, we might place the development of modern magic *into* Weber's schema: perhaps its new emphasis on technology and mechanism represents the disenchantment of 'old magic' and the demonstration of scientific dominance over it. This is certainly a strong feature of the style of the secularized and professionalized 'professors of magic' at the turn of the twentieth century. However, it is difficult to reconcile this neat interpretation of the *mechanization of magic* in modernity with the fact that modern magic was still centrally, self-consciously, and essentially concerned with *magic*. Indeed, rather than contributing to the *dis*-enchantment of the world, we might suggest that (even modern) magic is fundamentally concerned with the enchantment (or perhaps the *re*-enchantment) of the world. This magic circle needs to be squared.

Of course, Weber's famous dictum was not an observation about the contemporary state of Europe at the *fin de siècle* – he was not claiming that Europe was already or completely disenchanted. Rather, he was addressing 'the fate of our times', our trajectory towards a radically disenchanted condition in the future. Hence, he was aware that disenchantment was a process not a state. In addition, he was explicit that this process was primarily a feature of Western societies, suggesting that it was proceeding at a different pace elsewhere in the world (or perhaps that entirely different processes were at work). Because of this, Weber's position is often seen as sympathetic with a modernist sense of developmental history, in which societies move from reliance on magic, through religion, and finally to science.[11] Different parts of the world may move at different speeds, but their trajectories are basically the same (not only but also because of increasing international interaction). This vision of historical development was

side' began in the seventeenth century. This drove 'enchantment' to the peripheries of society: children, women, colonies etc. Joshua Landy & Micheal Saler (eds), *The Re-Enchantment of the World*. Stanford: Stanford University Press, 2009, p. 3.

[11] A fascinating engagement with the relationship between stage magic, science, and religion is Fred Nadis, *Wonder Shows: Performing Science, Magic, and Religion in America*. New Brunswick: Rutgers University Press, 2005. Arguably the general field begins with the anthropologist Bronislaw Malinowski, whose influential 1925 essay, 'Magic, Science, and Religion' is a landmark (reprinted in Bronislaw Malinowski, *Magic, Science, and Religion, and Other Essays*. Illinois: Waveland Press, 1992). Two influential, recent texts from more historical perspectives have been Randall Styers, *Making Magic: Religion, Magic, & Science in the Modern World*. Oxford: Oxford University Press, 2004; Stanley Tambiah, *Magic, Science and Religion and the Scope of Rationality*. Cambridge: Cambridge University Press, 1990.

foundational to imperial Europe, undergirding the conceit of the 'civilizing mission' or 'white man's burden'.[12]

While this developmental idea allows some space for the continued presence of magic and enchantment in the world, one of the implications of this theory of history is that 'any lingering enchantment within Western culture must of necessity be a relic, a throw back, a corner of unenlightened atavism yet to be swept clean'.[13] Magic remains in the world only because the process of eradicating its regressive forms (whether in the West or elsewhere) takes time to complete. This means that any attempt to perform, sustain, or conserve magic in the world is morally dubious. In addition, ideologies that attempt to smuggle magical thinking back into the world through sleight-of-hand are probably instances of false consciousness designed to keep populations oppressed and in the thrall of capitalism.[14] Is the emergence of 'modern magic' such an instance?

Recent research has challenged the idea that the condition of modernity is necessarily one of disenchantment *per se*.[15] Rather than identifying modernity as an ahistorical ideal type, wherein enchantment

---

[12] Modernization theory (which suggests that economic development is naturally accompanied by cultural and political changes, pushing all societies towards similar systems of political economy to those currently extant in capitalist democracies) is controversial because of the way it seems to conflate the idea of modernization with Westernization, and thus it must defend itself against charges of Eurocentricism or cultural imperialism. The idea of the 'white man's burden' emerges from a poem (of the same name) by Rudyard Kipling, which appeared in *McClure's Magazine*, 5 February 1899. It describes the Victorian rationale for empire as a mission to bring civilization to those 'new-caught, sullen peoples, half-devil and half-child', expressing this as an act of beneficence and self-sacrifice by the British, showing that they had matured as a people. He calls on them to 'take up the White Man's burden, have done with childish days'. For reasons that are obvious today, this poem and its sentiments have been the subject of fierce criticism.

[13] Landy & Saler, *The Re-Enchantment of the World*, p. 3.

[14] This argument is most closely associated with Theodor Adorno, who argues that populations are encouraged to perceive some of the products of capitalism (including the market itself) as though they are themselves enchanted with a form of mystical aura, hence removing them from the realms of effective, rational critique. The idea that capitalism itself is enchanted becomes one of the mechanisms that serve the survival of capitalism. See J.M. Bernstein, *Adorno: Disenchantment and Ethics*. Cambridge: Cambridge University Press, 2001.

[15] An important, multi-disciplinary intervention in this respect is Birgit Meyer & Peter Pels (eds), *Magic and Modernity: Interfaces of Revelation and Concealment*. Stanford: Stanford University Press, 2003.

has no legitimate place, it could be more helpful to view modernity in its full historical richness, as the site of a struggle to embrace apparently contradictory tendencies in human nature, 'rationality and wonder, secularism and faith'.[16] Perhaps the idea of modern magic is neither oxymoronic nor a morally dubious and instrumentally defunct anachronism, but rather it is the idea of delight in simultaneous enchantment and disenchantment – the *performance* of magic even in the certainty that scientific laws of causation cannot be broken.

In this context, it is fascinating to consider the way in which the *fin de siècle* not only produced clear ideas about progressive and evolutionary history that enshrined rationality and science as the future of mankind, displacing ideas about magic into European antiquity or into the 'savage' societies that had recently become the subjects of anthropology, but also witnessed the rise of tremendous interest in magic, the occult, and mysticism.[17] Indeed, far from seeing an unproblematic endorsement of the dis-enchantment of the world,

---

[16] Landy & Saler, *The Re-Enchantment of the World*, p. 3. The idea that an unproblematic, linear history of development from magic to religion to science was already exploded as naively ideological in the 1970s with landmark works such as Frances Yates, *The Rosicrucian Enlightenment* (1972, reprinted as a Routledge Classic, London & New York: Routledge, 2001). Indeed, the synergy between Western esotericism and scientific advancement is no longer deeply controversial. As During observes, 'in the early modern period, science and magic were much more entangled than enlightened thinkers were willing to admit. Indeed, the scientific revolution developed as much out of so-called natural magic as against it.' Simon During, *Modern Enchantments*. Cambridge: Harvard University Press, 2002, p. 17.

[17] This period coincides with the emergence of professional, academic anthropology, which generally located 'magic' as an institution of so-called primitive societies and so depicted it as part of the process of dissolving it. See, for instance, James Frazer, *The Golden Bough: A Study in Magic and Religion*, 1890 (2 vols), reprinted London: Macmillan, 1911–1915 (12 vols); Bronislaw Malinowski, 'Magic, Science, and Religion', 1925, reprinted in *Magic, Science, and Religion, and Other Essays*. Illinois: Waveland Press, 1992; Marcel Mauss, *A General Theory of Magic*, 1902, reprinted London & New York: Routledge, 2001. Provocative work on the status of ostensibly 'primitive magic' in modern societies was done later by the philosopher Walter Benjamin, who was fascinated by the ways in which the processes of modernity and modernization generated opportunities and sites for the surfacing of the so-called primitive within modernity itself. As Christopher Stahl puts it, 'Benjamin believed that the modern imitative technologies staged fantastic images of the Other, drawn from the recesses of the cultural imagination, which had material and political effect.' Christopher Stahl, 'Outdoing Ching Ling Foo', in Francesca Coppa, Lawrence Hass, James Peck (eds), *Performing Magic on the Western Stage*. New York: Palgrave, 2008, p. 154.

this period witnessed the so-called mystical revival.[18] Rather than being seen as a simple anti-modern movement or 'revolt against positivism',[19] as has often been assumed, it's possible to see the mystical revival as an intrinsic feature of modernity, with elements of it attempting to mirror the scientific quest to gain knowledge and mastery of the physical world with the quest for (at least pseudo-scientific) knowledge and mastery of the non-material world. With the contemporaneous emergence of new scientific fields such as experimental psychology and psychoanalysis, the idea that the mind and the spirit were legitimate objects of inquiry and even manipulation was respectably modern for many.[20] That is, scientific advancements were the allies of technological and mechanical marvels as well as psychic experimentation. Perhaps the poster-boy for this unlikely alliance was the creator of the arch-rationalist Sherlock Holmes and leading exponent of Spiritualism, Sir Arthur Conan Doyle (1859–1930).

Emblematic of the mystical revival were institutions such as the Theosophical Society and the Hermetic Order of the Golden Dawn, which were established in the 1870s and 1880s. The Golden Dawn was an influential and high-profile magical order, focussed on arcana and the performance of ceremonial magic and rituals. It looked back through Western history and drew on a mixture of Rosicrucian traditions and the Hermetic Corpus attributed to the mythic figure of Hermes Trismegistus. Members were recruited to exclusive temples, where they would be trained in the magical arts and inducted into secret teachings. The so-called Higher Arts were only revealed to a select few within Golden Dawn, creating an elitist and hierarchical structure that emphasized the synergy of magic and power. This structure sat alongside the

---

[18] As Alex Owen observes, 'the term *mystical revival* was used across the ideological board to identify a range of spiritual alternatives to religious orthodoxy that sprang up in the 1880s and 1890s and gained momentum and prominence as the old century gave way to the new'. Owen attributes the phrase to Holbrook Jackson (1874–1948), the influential British writer and bibliophile. *The Place of Enchantment: British Occultism and the Culture of the Modern.* Chicago: University of Chicago Press, 2004, p. 20.

[19] This well-known phrase is attributed to H. Stuart Hughes, *Consciousness and Society: The Reorientation of Social Thought.* New York: Vintage Books, 1961. Cited in Landy & Saler, *The Re-Enchantment of Modernity*, p. 4.

[20] Sigmund Freud famously wrote that: 'If I had my life to live over again I should devote myself to psychical research rather than to psychoanalysis.' Quoted in Alex Owen, *The Place of Enchantment*, p. 6.

aristocratic and emerging middle-class demographic; members were generally well-educated and yet dissatisfied with existing mainstreamed, fashionable, and positivist explanations about the meaning of life, questions of metaphysics, and the spiritual dimensions of the world. They included doctors, lawyers, politicians, scientists, writers, artists, and Freemasons. Unlike the Freemasons, Golden Dawn admitted women, and women were a powerful driving force in the movement, often attaining to the highest levels. Other prominent members included the Nobel Prize–winning poet, W.B. Yeats (1865–1939), and the infamous 'black magician', Aleister Crowley (1875–1947), who eventually quit the Dawn in order to develop his own philosophy and cult, Thelema.[21]

It is noteworthy that many of the 'gentleman magicians' of the Golden Age carefully cultivated similar social and class identities, positioning their profession as a magnet for aristocrats and the new, educated middle-class, organizing themselves into secret societies where initiations and training could lead to progression into the inner circles of knowledge. Despite professing no supernatural powers (and indeed publically pronouncing a mission to debunk them), these exclusive societies still indulged in the romantic mystique of secrecy and thus the implication that they had dark secrets hidden in their libraries and clubhouses. The archetype might be the famous Magic Circle, established in 1905 in London, with its elite Inner Circle. Various other 'circles' or 'rings' were established around Britain and the British Empire, in varying states of 'linkage' with the prestigious society in London.

Like the Golden Dawn, initiates in the Magic Circle were also interested in at least the forms of arcana and the occult, often deploying their procedures and devices for performances of magic on stage, or using them as material for 'experiments' or 'demonstrations', while the adepts of the Golden Dawn would perform them with sincerity as magical ceremonies or rituals of power. In 1914, John Nevil

---

[21] The teachings of *Thelema* (will) first took institutional form in Crowley's own magical order, the *Argentum Astrum*, or Silver Star, which he established in 1907. An excellent account of the Golden Dawn is in Owen, *The Place of Enchantment*, chapter 2. The overall landscape around Golden Dawn, including the controversial contributions of Aleister Crowley, is colourfully evoked in Nevill Drury, *Stealing the Fire from Heaven: The Rise of Modern Western Magic*. New York: Oxford University Press, 2011. Crowley is comprehensively considered in Henrik Bogdan & Martin Starr (eds), *Aleister Crowley and Western Esotericism*. New York: Oxford University Press, 2012.

Maskelyne founded the Occult Committee of the Magic Circle,[22] which was specifically tasked with using the privileged knowledge of the Magic Circle to test scientifically the claims of mystics and other magical orders: nobody was better equipped than a magician to debunk another (kind of) magician.[23] So, despite positioning themselves against the occultists, it is interesting that the members of the Magic Circle insisted on calling themselves *magicians* – seeking to dissociate but also to associate themselves with the idea of supernatural power at the same time.[24]

[22] John Nevil Maskelyne (1839–1917) was, arguably, the most important figure in the emergence of modern magic in England. He is especially famous as an innovator and inventor of magical effects, as well for his ground-breaking work with George Alfred Cooke and then David Devant at the famous Egyptian Hall theatre in London. Maskelyne founded the greatest English dynasty of magic, with his son and grandson also becoming leading magicians. Gifted with a modern, mechanical frame of mind, Maskelyne also invented the penny-drop lock for public toilets, and hence originating the phrase 'to spend a penny' (to use the restroom).

[23] The career of Houdini as an exposer of Spiritualists attests to this. Indeed, he participated in a number of committees at various levels, and his campaign took him all the way to the White House, where his proposed bill (to criminalize fraudulent Spiritualism) was eventually defeated, apparently because of the number of politicians involved in the Spiritualist movement. He appears to have started his crusade while still president of the Society of American Magicians (whose cardinal rule was Do Not Expose!), when he published an article exposing some of the practices of so-called spirit-mediums in 1922. Kenneth Silverman, *Houdini: The Career of Ehrich Weiss*. New York: HarperPerennial, 1997, p. 285. Meanwhile, the Occult Committee of the Magic Circle very self-consciously participated in the legacy of Reginald Scot (1538–1599), who set out to prove that women being persecuted as witches by the Inquisition were not (and could not be) witches (because witchcraft is a fallacious accusation). In so doing, he discovered and exposed the mundane techniques and devices used by so-called witches to achieve their effects. At the time, his work was considered heretical and his books were burned. Unlike the Magic Circle in the twentieth century, which sought to prosecute charlatans who claimed supernatural powers, Scot sought to reveal charlatanism in order to save the lives of those accused of having such powers! Today, the first pages of Scot's famous book are reproduced a wall (under the spiral staircase) at the Magic Circle headquarters in London. Reginald Scot, *The Discoverie of Witchcraft*, 1584, reprinted New York: Dover, 1930/72. The best full-scale study of Scot is Philip Almond, *England's First Demonologist: Reginald Scot and 'The Discoverie of Witchcraft'*. London: IB Tauris, 2011.

[24] The label 'magician' was self-consciously a label of power in Victorian and Edwardian society. As Alex Owen observes, 'those who dedicated themselves to the study of occultism and the magical arts referred to themselves as magicians without either apology or irony'. *The Place of Enchantment*, p. 8. In the next chapter, we will see how Nevil Maskelyne and others preferred to use the term 'conjuror' to describe a stage magician but, for various reasons including the preferences of most such

One of the consequences of the coexistence of occult societies, like the Golden Dawn, and more mundane (but still secretive) societies of magicians, like the Magic Circle, was the ongoing public confusion about the meaning and content of the category of 'magician'. Magic seemed to blur between stage performances by David Devant in the Egyptian Hall, on the one hand, and the rituals of Aleister Crowley in the Abbey of Thelema, on the other. Both called themselves *magicians*; could they both be right?

One of the main differences, of course, was that Devant made no claim to supernatural powers (and indeed, as a dutiful modern, refuted their very existence) while Crowley professed genuine supernatural powers, drawn from ancient (pre-modern) origins. Hence, even with the plasticity and deep ambiguity of the term 'magic' that seemed to embrace them both, the idea that there was a substantive difference between something like 'pretend' (modern) magic and something like 'real' (ancient) magic became prevalent in the public discourse. The slippage between presentation and reality in these categories is a wonderful example of categorical sleight-of-hand: Crowley's *presentation* of himself as a real magician drawing on ancient supernatural powers becomes confused for the assertion that he *is* a real magician drawing on ancient supernatural powers. Even more confusing is the presentation of Crowley as a real *modern* magician, since this category seems genuinely oxymoronic if the term 'modern' is used in anything other than its purely chronological sense. While the modernity of Devant's status as a *modern* magician resides in his emplacement and participation in a rational, scientific worldview (albeit one that does not see this as contradicting the experience of enchantment), to say that Crowley was a modern magician is mostly to say that he lived across the turn of the twentieth century, even while he participated in a supernatural worldview with distinctly pre-modern characteristics.

Of course, this is a simplification, but the starkness of the comparison between these icons (whom I present here as 'ideal types') reveals a general picture: for it to have a coherent and non-contradictory meaning, *modern magic* must tend towards Devant and not towards Crowley; Crowley's claims to real magic are tantamount to an attempt to reside in a pre-modern magical worldview during the modern period.

performers, the term 'magician' persisted. The major magic societies all used this term: Society of American Magicians, International Brotherhood of Magicians, etc.

Such claims are features of this period; as far as we know, the powers claimed are not. Indeed, we might observe that it is a characteristic of the modern magician (as an ideal type) to see unsubstantiated claims to supernatural power as morally offensive. The modern magician, as an ideal type, is a sceptic.

Alongside the Golden Dawn were many other groups of occultists, mystics, and spiritualists that comprised the 'spiritual renaissance' of the late Victorian and Edwardian age. These included the 'Spiritualists' themselves, who rode a wave of séances, table-rapping, and mediumship out of the long Victorian period, following after the so-called Fox Sisters in the United States.[25] Leading rationalists such as the author Sir Arthur Conan Doyle were powerful advocates of the evidentiary basis of spiritualist phenomena, famously coming to blows with Houdini and other debunkers who saw such fakery as immoral and exploitative.[26] Indeed, Spiritualism was one of the magical arenas in which occultists and the stage magicians touched most closely, with the latter often slipping into performing séances in the parlours of affluent society with varying degrees of honesty and irony. It was quickly apparent to many stage magicians that they had all of the necessary skills and technologies to accomplish the same effects as the so-called mediums, and that there was more money to be made from these performances than from card tricks in the pub.

The pivotal differences between the Spiritualist and the mundane magician were, firstly, performance style, and, secondly, moral orientation. However, the tendency for magicians to hold séances as forms of entertainment based on exposé also contributed to blurring the lines between 'real' and 'pretend' magicians in the public imagination,

[25] Leah Fox (1814–1890), Margaret Fox (1833–1893), and Kate Fox (1837–1892) were pioneers of modern spiritualism and especially the use of table-rapping to communicate with the dead. Ironically, even after Margaret and Kate admitted to fraud and exposed their method in 1888, the spiritualist movement continued to gather strength.

[26] Houdini was relentless in his quest to expose the Spiritualists as frauds. Harry Houdini, *A Magician Amongst the Spirits*. New York: Harper & Bros., 1924, reprinted by Cambridge University Press, 2011. In Britain, John Nevil Maskelyne was similarly unforgiving, exposing the techniques of the Fox Sisters and the Davenport Brothers in writing, 'Modern Spiritualism', in Lionel Weatherly & John Nevil Maskelyne, *The Supernatural*, 1892, reprinted by Cambridge University Press, 2011. In fact, exposés of spiritualist techniques were already in print as early as the 1850s, with works such as Charles Page, *Psychomancy: Spirit-Rappings and Table-Tippings Exposed*. New York: D. Appleton & Co., 1853.

since some magicians (the apparently 'real' ones) claimed supernatural powers and others (the 'pretend' ones) did not. This pattern in the public discourse irritated magicians like Houdini and Maskelyne, for whom, if anything, the public had things precisely inverted: the only real magicians were the modern magicians who created enchantments and wonders in honest and respectable ways; the fake magicians were the Spiritualist charlatans who professed to have supernatural powers that they did not (and could not) have. For these socially engaged, sceptical magicians, the moral distinction between a real or 'legitimate magician' and a charlatan was foundational to the vocation of modern magic.

One of the fascinating features of this battle between the Spiritualists and the stage magicians was the spirit of modernity that pervaded it. The so-called new occultism of the *fin de siècle* participated in the fashion for scientific validation, constantly seeking to 'test' its mediums, to 'demonstrate' their efficacy, and to conduct 'experiments' to ascertain the limits of their effectiveness. Hence, debates with the sceptics (including with Houdini and Maskelyne) tended to pivot around a logical case: just because a stage magician could fake Spiritualist powers, that does not mean that there are no genuine mediums with authentic powers. It is an error of inference to claim that the exposure of one fraud means that everyone is a fraud; for the Spiritualists, this was just bad scientific method.[27] To the contrary, the existence of even one authentic medium should be enough to establish the authenticity of Spiritualism.[28] Taking this a step further, the

---

[27] The full form of this logical fallacy is something like this: *This banknote is a fake so, for all I know, all banknotes are fake.* The qualification 'for all I know' in this sentence is an invitation for scientific investigation not a statement of certainty. In addition, there is an internal impossibility to this claim: it is not possible that all banknotes are fakes, because if all banknotes were fake there could be no real banknote to copy; hence, this is tantamount to claiming that there are no banknotes.

[28] In addition to the famous work of Houdini (*A Magician Amongst the Spirits,* 1924) and Maskelyne (Weatherly & Maskelyne, *The Supernatural?* 1892) a fascinating salvo in this confrontation was Henry Evan's 'illustrated investigation into the phenomena of Spiritualism and Theosophy', in which he sought to test the claims of the 'two great schools of thought in the world – materialistic and spiritualistic'. In the preface, he immediately confesses that 'this age of scientific materialism' leaves him feeling 'barren, dreary, comfortless', and hence that 'in an age of such ultra materialism … it is not strange that there should come a great reaction on the part of spiritually minded people'. So committed to an open-minded stance, he proceeds to debunk and expose the mundane (material) techniques of Spiritualists and occultists. Henry Ridgely Evans, *The Spirit World Unmasked.* Chicago: Laird & Lee, 1902.

Figure 1.1 The Egyptian Hall, 'The Entranced Fakir', c. 1901, courtesy of Nielsen Magic Collection. John Nevil Maskelyne's classic Levitation.

Spiritualists, like the arcane magicians of the Golden Dawn, invested in the pervasive rhetoric of social evolution at the turn of the century, but argued that modernity would be incomplete if it restricted itself simply to material factors: the idea of evolution not only permitted but also required the consideration of the further development of the human spirit. Hence, it seemed that scientists who refused to countenance experiments in Spiritualism were denying the imperatives of science itself. In this way, the '"new occultism" ... co-opted the language of science and staked a strong claim to rationality while at the same time undermining scientific naturalism as a worldview'.[29]

Of course, not all the confrontations between modern magicians and Spiritualists or occultists were framed in such a rational way. There was plenty of simple mud-slinging. In some cases, particularly famous or successful magicians (including Houdini and Maskelyne themselves) were accused by Spiritualists of actually having authentic spiritual powers but of denying them for ideological or commercial reasons. That is, inverting the magician's criticisms of Spiritualists (for exploiting public credulity in order to make money), the Spiritualists argued that the magicians were attempting to trick the public into believing that their accomplishments were demonstrations of natural rather than supernatural powers in order to sell tickets to their shows. 'Scientism' was levelled as an accusation of immoral commercialism: modern magicians were held to be exploiting the fashion to explain the mysterious with faux science, relying on the credulity and ignorance of the public (who couldn't understand the 'real' causes).[30] The accusations of denial ranged from claims that these magicians were deliberately misleading their audiences to claims that the magicians themselves were ignorant of (or in genuine, pathological denial about) the origins of their own powers. On the other hand, the sceptics did not pull their punches either. Accusations of bad faith were pervasive. In his seminal essay of 1891, Maskelyne commences his attack on the 'giant imposture':

> In this year of grace eighteen hundred and ninety one, to write upon
> the deceptions which have been practised under the name of
> Modern Spiritualism is surely akin to thrashing a dead horse; but ...
> this pernicious doctrine has ever been productive of so much evil,

[29] Alex Owen, *The Place of Enchantment*, p. 13.
[30] The 'Great Wizard of the North', J.H. Anderson, published a little book that seems to encourage such accusations about the use of 'science' as a form of advertising: J.H. Anderson, *The Fashionable Science of Parlour Magic, Being The Newest Tricks of Deception, Developed and Illustrated, To Which Is Added an Exposure, of the Practices Made Use of by Professional Card Players, Blacklegs, and Gamblers*. Self Published, 1848.

and has done so much to fill our lunatic asylums.... The doctrine of
so-called Spiritualism embodies an abstract principle and a concrete
fact – the *principle* being that 'those who have plenty of money and
no brains were made for those who have plenty of brains and no
money'; and the *fact* is, that the ranks of the Spiritualists have ever
been largely recruited from these two classes. It is the old story re-
told – the story of Duplicity feeding upon Folly. It is a doctrine,
cradled in credulity and fostered by fraud.[31]

Given these levels of mutual distrust and hostility within the 'magical
world', it is no wonder that the idea and practice of exposé became so
central to modern magic in this period. Indeed, as we will see later, exposé
by magicians became constructed as a service to the modern public, educating them to recognize fraud for themselves and to appreciate the power
of natural science as well as the technology of 'props', while simultaneously
educating them to appreciate the skill and artistry of magic as a form of
theatre.[32] In this way, the development of 'new occultism' made space for
the development of 'modern magic' (or 'neo-magic') as its foil.[33]

There is no space or need to document all of the other magical or
occultist movements of this period. However, perhaps the most significant of these for our purposes was Theosophy. While Theosophy shared
in the *mystical revival* – participating in the culture of discontent with
the apparently alienating and dehumanizing dominance of material
science and industrial capitalism – one of its clearest features was its
interest in the 'East' as a source of spiritual salvation and power. In the
fin de siècle climate of resignation about the spiritual impoverishment of
Western modernity, the Golden Dawn looked back into the ancient
traditions of the West for magical inspiration, while Theosophists also
looked to the contemporaneous 'East' for practices, techniques, and
ideas.[34] In other words, for most occultists of this time, magic was

---

[31] Maskelyne, 'Modern Spiritualism', pp. 182–183.

[32] This association between exposé and modern magic has led some to see Reginald
Scot's (1584) *Discoverie of Witchcraft* as the first genuinely modern text in the canon
of magic.

[33] The term 'neo-magic' was coined as an alternative to modern magic by the great
theorist of modern magic, Sam Sharpe, *Neo-Magic: The Art of the Conjurer*.
Bradford: Clegg & Son, 1932.

[34] It is notable that key members of the Golden Dawn as well as the Spiritualist movement were also interested in the esoteric traditions of the so-called East. Members of
both travelled extensively in Egypt, India, and China. Some made it as far as Japan.
Aleister Crowley himself became a committed orientalist and developed a strong

something preserved elsewhere and/or elsewhen, enabling it to be recovered back into the modern West to help combat an apparent 'crisis of faith'.[35]

In this way, the 'new occultism' participated in a mixture of intellectual and cultural fashions of the *fin de siècle*, capturing popular (and scholarly) discontent with materialism, engaging with the idea of scientific rationality, but also entering into the discourse of Orientalism. The Western imagination had been riddled with references to the 'mystic East' and the 'mysterious Orient' for centuries,[36] and the fashion for Chinoiserie (in the eighteenth century) and Japonisme (in the nineteenth) fed into the Victorian romanticization of India as a place of enchantment and wonder. Drawn by the popular accounts of anthropologists and the new class of travel writers, who seemed to locate 'real' magic outside the modernity of the West, leading members of the Theosophical Society, including the ostensible founder, Madame Helena Petrovna Blavatsky (1831–1891) herself, told countless stories of their journeys of discovery around India, China, and Tibet, where they apparently studied secret, esoteric, and occult arts of magic with gurus, adepts, and mahatmas of various kinds. Although the veracity of many of these stories is open to question, Blavatsky's book, *Isis*

interest in Tantra, especially sexual Tantra, which took the form of sexual magic in the Ordo Templi Orientis (of which he was the head from 1922).

[35] The idea that the spiritual renaissance was a response to a crisis of faith in Victorian and Edwardian societies across the West is not controversial. It is powerfully maintained by Alex Owen, *The Place of Enchantment*, and also Janet Oppenheim, *The Other World: Spiritualism and Psychical Research in England, 1850–1914*. Cambridge: Cambridge University Press, 1985.

[36] In her wonderful *Stranger Magic*, Marina Warner explains how the advent of the Arabian Nights in Europe (in the seventeenth and eighteenth centuries) coincided with intense curiosity about Eastern culture, 'ranging from the Middle to the Far East', in which the 'disruptive incredulous bedazzlement' occasioned by the Orient was itself a form of enchantment. Marina Warner, *Stranger Magic: Charmed States and the Arabian Nights*. Cambridge: Harvard University Press, 2012, p. 24, citing the magnificent work of Raymond Schwab, *La Renaissance orientale*. Paris: Payot, 1950. Going even further back, Simon During reveals a type of 'Orientalist scorn' about the Eastern origins of magic and irrationality as early as the ancient Greeks. During, *Modern Enchantments*, p. 5. In fact, in his account of the Persian Wars, Herodotus attributed to the Persian Magi magical powers while calling the Greeks to embrace reason. The apparent Orientalism of Herodotus is later picked up by the twentieth-century anthropologist Malinowski, whose Argonauts are a clear reference to the Greek adventurers and bearers of rationality who discover the magical beyond the margins of civilization. Bronislaw Malinowski, *Argonauts of the Western Pacific*, 1922 reprinted London & New York: Routledge, 1978.

Unveiled, was centred around the esoteric teachings of India (including creative revisionings of Buddhism and Hinduism), suggesting that these combined with Western occultism to solve the problems of a spiritually impoverished Christian modernity.[37] In this way, Theosophy became synonymous with 'Oriental philosophy' and found a natural place in the Orientalism of the turn of the late nineteenth and early twentieth centuries in the West. This was also the period in which the great 'Sacred Books of the East' were first translated into European languages, adding to the mystique of the region and the Theosophy movement at the same time.[38]

Again, not to be outdone by the occultists, stage magicians of this period also participated in the creation, perpetuation, and exploitation of the 'Myth of the Mystic East'.[39] As we will see in later chapters, modern magicians travelled around the world in search of new magical effects, new audiences, and higher box-office returns. Many of the great magicians of the Golden Age wrote travelogues of their adventures, with varying degrees of reliability and fidelity.[40] These accounts found a natural readership in the Victorian and Edwardian thirst for travel writing, ethnography, and accounts by colonial officials and missionaries in Africa and Asia. They blurred into the stories of 'Eastern esotericism', flavouring the public perception of the 'East' as mystical, mysterious, and magical.

[37] Helene Blavatsky, *Isis Unveiled: A Master-Key to the Mysteries of Ancient and Modern Science and Theology.* 1877, reprinted by Cambridge University Press, 2012. Blavatsky's orientation toward the 'East' is well considered by Mark Bevir, 'The West Turns Eastward: Madame Blavatsky and the Transformation of the Occult Tradition'. *Journal of the American Academy of Religion*, 62:3 (1994), pp. 747–767. In *The Place of Enchantment*, Alex Owen suggests that Theosophy (and India) goes on to replace Egypt and the Middle East as the 'privileged "exotic" site of ancient wisdom so prevalent in the Western occult tradition', p. 29.

[38] Edited by Max Müller, *The Sacred Books of the East* series was published by Oxford University Press between 1879 and 1910. It includes translations of forty-nine key texts (and an index) of Hinduism, Buddhism, Taoism, Confucianism, Zoroastrianism, Jainism, and Islam.

[39] Robert Henry Elliot, *Myth of the Mystic East*. London: WM Blackwood & Sons, 1934.

[40] Examples of such magical travel include Charles Bertram, *A Magician in Many Lands*. London & New York: Routledge, 1911; H.J. Burlingame, *Around the World with a Magician and a Juggler*. Chicago: Clyde Publishing, 1891; John Watkins Holden, *A Wizard's Wanderings from China to Peru*. London: Dean & Son, 1886; Harry Kellar, *A Magician's Tour: Up and Down and Round About the Earth*. Chicago: R.R. Donnelley & Sons, 1886; Howard Thurston, *My Life of Magic*. Philadelphia: Dorrance and Co., 1929.

And yet, just as stage magicians had conflicted relationships with the aesthetics and practices of the Golden Dawn and the Spiritualists, seeking *both* to associate themselves with the imaginaries and their mystical power *and* to distance themselves from any implications of anti-modernism, so their relationship with the 'mystic East' was similarly conflicted. On the one hand, a number of magicians became so enwrapped in mystical Orientalism that they presented their entire shows in the guise of an 'Oriental' – dressing up as a fictive Arabian, Chinese, Japanese, or Indian magician – believing that this mode of presentation would communicate new levels of mystery and wonder to audiences in the West. The most famous performer in this tradition was certainly William Robinson (aka Chung Ling Soo).[41] On the other hand, however, just as they sought to expose the Spiritualists, modern magicians had a sense of moral mission to expose and debunk the spurious claims about the astonishing feats of impossibility that travellers reported having seen in the 'East'. Indeed, in his seminal work of exposé, Maskelyne focussed his fire onto three central topics: Spiritualism, Theosophy, and Oriental Jugglery.[42] In typically authoritative style, Maskelyne commences:

> It is probable that there is no subject on which man has ever written, which embodies so wide a field of investigation as the records of the many marvels of Oriental Jugglery. At the same time, there is no subject which, in so far as actual results are concerned, would be so very deficient in anything that may claim to be worthy of serious consideration, were it not for the alarming amount of misconception and falsehood to which it has given rise.[43]

While critics like Maskelyne were confounded by the persistence of the romantic idea of the 'mystic East' despite the lack of reliable evidence (and in the face of much evidence to the contrary, including a Magic Circle investigation into the Indian Rope Trick that proved it to be

---

[41] The definitive biography of Robinson is Jim Steinmeyer, *The Glorious Deception: The Double Life of William Robinson, aka Chung Ling Soo, the Marvelous Chinese Conjurer*. Philadelphia: De Capo Press, 2006.

[42] John Nevil Maskelyne, chapter VII, parts 1–3, in Weatherly & Maskelyne, *The Supernatural*.

[43] John Nevil Maskelyne, 'Oriental Jugglery', in Weatherly & Maskelyne, *The Supernatural*, p. 153.

a fiction), there was much less moral outrage in these attacks on Orientalist mysticism than in the attacks on Spiritualism.

Presumably this was partly because Western audiences usually encountered Oriental mysticism indirectly. That is, they read about it in the popular press or they witnessed Westerners performing in a supposedly Oriental manner. Because of the political and material disparities of imperialism, neither London, Paris, nor New York were flooded with Asian magicians attempting to convince the Western public of their incredible supernatural powers.[44] Instead, the main advocates of Oriental magic were Westerners themselves, often after their jaunts around the colonies. Hence, the nature of the deceit being practiced on the audience seemed to be different in the case of Spiritualism and Orientalism, at least partially because it was usually very clear that the magician was pretending to be an 'Oriental' for the purposes of entertainment, while it was usually not at all explicit that a charlatan Spiritualist was affecting a ruse in order to entertain. As we will see later, however, this was not always the case: some magicians went to great lengths to maintain the appearance that they really were 'Oriental' (or somehow transformed by their experiences in the Orient), and most of the public had no first-hand experience of what an 'Oriental' should be like (if indeed the category makes any empirical sense at all).

In any case, it was not until the 1970s that the ethical implications of Orientalism as an ideological disposition were clearly excavated,[45] so it is unsurprising that critiques in the 1890s were not fully formed in this sense. That said, the moral approbation of Maskelyne about Orientalism in 1891 was already rather serious; he disapproved of the way it indulged in the perpetration of falsehoods, misleading and regressing audiences in the West. He struggled to reconcile claims about the Orient with his identity as a *modern* magician.

---

[44] Of course, a number of Asian magicians and jugglers made their way to Europe and North America in this period, although the numbers are very small. Most famous are probably Zhu Liankui and Shōkyokusai Ten'ichi. In addition, troupes of performers from China and especially Japan went on world tours and appeared at the International Expositions. A small number of magicians from India were 'brought' to the West in the manner of curiosities. Nevertheless, the relative scarcity of such performers and the relative visibility of Orientalism in the West combined to leave a market niche for Western performers to take the role of Orientals.

[45] The force of Orientalism as a critical stance took its most coherent form in Edward Said, *Orientalism*. London: Penguin, 1979.

However, he was largely unconcerned about the epistemic and representational violence being done to the Orient itself (or to so-called Orientals) through these colonial imaginaries.

Modern magic in theory

Overcoming the difference between 'real' and 'pretend' magic

As both a historical and theoretical construct, magic is tricky. It's as though it doesn't want to be analysed, or perhaps that it wants to be analysed as something other than what it is. It is constantly oscillating between the romantic and the ridiculous, between the sublime and the mundane, between levitation and a rabbit in a hat. As we have seen, one of the basic ambiguities about the term even (and perhaps especially) in the modern period has been the assumed difference between 'real magic' and 'pretend magic', as though there are at least two kinds of magic, and one of them probably isn't really magic at all. 'Pretend magic' pretends to be magic, and so isn't magic. When we call it magic, we're just being polite and we're probably embarrassed about it.

This distinction, muddy and unclear as it may be, remains resilient and rather pervasive today. We hear it in the common accusation: 'that's not really magic, it's just a trick'. Sometimes the accusation is levelled in a more personalized way: 'She's not a magician, she's a fraud.'

In the context of debates and developments around magic during the so-called mystical revival at the turn of the twentieth century, it is fascinating to see that a basic question remains unanswered (or perhaps that the modern answer to the question remains unaccepted or unacceptable to the public at large). This question concerns the parameters of the concept (and practice) of magic itself: what is magic? When we say that something isn't really magic, what is the actual content of this claim? And, importantly, do we really understand what we mean when we claim that, for instance, the celebrated British performer Derren Brown is a fake?[46] Is this even a coherent thing to say?

---

[46] Even a cursory glance through online forums and response threads will immediately reveal the prevalence of such accusations about many professional magicians. I isolate Derren Brown as an example because he is explicitly involved in debunking so-called psychic phenomena and is always clear in his performances that he is not making use of any means of counter-physical supernatural causation, and yet there are invariably

If Brown were a fake, what would he be faking? Does he make claims about his performances that transpire to be fraudulent? When we accuse modern magicians of being fake, are we in fact accusing them of pretending to pretend to have supernatural powers when really they do have supernatural powers?[47] In fact, one thing that becomes clear very quickly is that our persistent and intuitive sense of a crisp distinction between real and pretend magic is itself a form of cultural illusion that emerges from centuries of representations of wizards, warlocks, and witches. Our attempts to see through this 'tissue of falsehoods'[48] rely upon ideational and institutional structures put in place only about a century ago. Rather than being able to maintain a clear and neat distinction between real and pretend magic, whichever way we draw the divide, we find ourselves in a nuanced landscape of magic containing various spectrums and continuums.

Building on the historical sketch in the last section, this section pays particular attention the theoretical work of modern magicians in an attempt to provide a coherent and unified vision of the meaning and integrity of 'modern magic' as a concept. The focus here (and in the next chapter) is on the work of these magicians themselves, on the basis that nobody knows (or cares) more about the parameters and quality of magic than magicians.[49] Nonetheless, it is noticeable that most

voices accusing him of being a fraud. Presumably, these voices are not claiming that he actually does have psychic powers (and so is fraudulently claiming he does not) – although such accusations have been levelled against performers in the past – so it is not clear what it would mean for him to be a fake.

[47] I'm particularly grateful to Derren Brown for a long, confusing, and completely unresolved conversation about this, 5 March 2014.

[48] Robert-Houdin, *Secrets of Conjuring and Magic*, p. 33.

[49] And yet, as early as 1876, Professor Hoffmann (Angelo Lewis, 1839–1919) wrote in the first English-language book on what he called 'modern' or 'white' magic, 'considering the great antiquity and the unfading popularity of the magic art, it seems at first sight a matter of wonder that its literature should be so extremely scanty'. Hoffmann's encyclopaedic treatment of modern magic really marked the beginning of a boom in publications about magic, both theoretical and practical in orientation. His book remains a classic to this day. Professor Hoffmann, *Modern Magic: A Practical Treatise on the Art of Conjuring*. Routledge, 1879, reprinted in USA, Philadelphia, David McKay, 1910, p. 1. Simon During suggests that there are three main textual resources for the study of what he calls 'secular magic', but which I construct as this kind of inclusive landscape of magic in general: '[1] critiques of real magic which present a detailed account of magic in the course of demystifying it; [2] descriptions of tricks or effects which have been designated magic in, for instance, how-to conjuring books; and [3] fictional narratives of magical events and performances'. During, *Modern Enchantments*, p. 34.

academic considerations of magic tend to overlook the theoretical work of modern magicians, preferring to treat them exclusively as performers or clowns.[50] Hence, modern magic is often analysed through the lenses of theories developed for other performance arts or for cultural history in general. While this approach has great value, it risks artificially bracketing off 'theatre magic' from the rest of the magical firmament for simply instrumental reasons. In addition, it risks neglecting the powerful and unique insights into magic produced by magicians, and so undervalues the way that magicians themselves have professionalized and organized magical knowledge over the last century, especially since the establishment of societies like the Society for American Magicians (1902) and the Magic Circle (1905).

To some extent, perhaps as a consequence of the culture of secrecy maintained by the international community of magicians, magicians and muggles (to borrow the now pervasive term from J.K. Rowling)[51] have developed separate bodies of knowledge about magic and separate systems of qualifications to recognize and grant access to them: as we have seen, in their 'Golden Age' professional magicians used to indicate their expertise by calling themselves *professors of magic*. As a result of these parallel structures, there is a degree of mutual indignation about the alleged expertise of either group of 'professors', and a level of suspicion about the quality and value of the work produced by both. While the academy recognizes the expertise of magicians as performers, their status as 'professors of magic' is usually ignored or viewed as a quaint quirk of an eccentric subculture; magicians are at best amateur scholars.[52] This is despite the fact that magical societies often

---

[50] The one major exception is consistent reference to the ideas of Jean Eugene Robert-Houdin (1805–1871), the so-called father of modern conjuring. Robert-Houdin's most influential book, *Les Secrets de la Prestidigitation et de la Magie* (1868) was quickly translated into English as *Secrets of Conjuring and Magic* (1877) and is now reprinted by Cambridge University Press (2011) in their Cambridge Library Collection, tasked with reprinting 'books of enduring scholarly value'. Ironically, Robert-Houdin's book is largely devoted to explaining how to accomplish specific feats of magic and does not include an extended or elaborate thesis on the theory of magic. The most common thesis attributed to Robert-Houdin is the idea that a modern conjuror 'is not a juggler; he is an actor playing the part of a magician' (1877/2011, p. 43).

[51] For the small number of readers unaware of *Harry Potter*, a muggle is a non-magical person.

[52] Anecdotally, conversations with university colleagues about magic books quickly (and consistently) reveal that any book containing a 'how to' section (how to vanish

include special processes, resources, and awards to honour the scholar-ship of their members. At least institutionally, magicians take scholar-ship about magic very seriously. Conversely, magicians may recognize the expertise of professional scholars in contextualizing magic from the outside, but their knowledge of magic itself (especially their knowledge of magic as a living art) is often viewed with scepticism. In particular, in a form of critique that resonates with contemporary movements in Performance Philosophy, magicians often complain that muggle-scholars don't properly understand the ways in which the practice of magic comprises its theory – the theory/practice division is not a living feature of the art. In short, the meaning and nature of magical knowl-edge is contested (epistemologically and politically) by the magic society and the university.

Thankfully, there are an increasing number of 'scholar-magicians' who have access to both types of material and are willing to write across the ostensible divide – many of them will appear in this chapter and the next.[53] Their challenge is to present their work in ways that seem both accessible and interesting to both sides, or least as not irrelevant to one side or the other. The audiences for such scholarship are diverse and complicated, requiring some performative elegance from the authors. This book seeks to supplement and enrich the existing work of cultural, literary, and theatre historians by focussing on the picture of modern magic that emerges from the magicians themselves.

a coin, saw someone in half, or walk through the Great Wall of China etc.) seems to be viewed with deep suspicion. This is despite (or because of) the fact that magical theory (for magicians) is valued primarily as a means to enhance the accomplishment of magical effects. The idea that theory is valuable in its own right (perhaps as a historical artefact) is somewhat alien to magicians, even as it is basic to the academy. In this way, the politics of the field borders the politics of the history of esotericism in the academy in general, where the magical, occult, and esoteric is frequently represented as the antithesis of scholarship.

[53] An important intervention in this regard is: Francesca Coppa, Lawrence Hass, and James Peck (eds), Performing Magic on the Western Stage. New York: Palgrave MacMillan, 2008. This book grew out of the programme in 'Theory & Art of Magic' at Muhlenberg College. Since then Lawrence Hass has worked hard to create a publishing forum for 'thoughtful magicians' called Theory & Art of Magic Press. Leading authors for this imprint include Eugene Burger, Robert Neale, Jeff McBride, and Hass himself. These are commercially oriented books, rather than academic per se; the website states that 'The mission of Theory and Art of Magic Press is to publish high-quality books and products for magicians that will feed their heads as well as their hands', http://www.theoryandartofmagic.com/information.php?info_id=6, accessed 31 March 2015.

As we have already seen, one of the first problems for the academic study of magic is the framing of a useful definition of magic itself. While it may feel obvious to a magician what resides inside and what outside the circle, this kind of intuitive grasp of the perimeter is not enough for a formal study. In their influential project, for instance, Coppa, Hass, and Peck made a working definition of magic as follows: 'magic is the artful performance of impossible effects'.[54] This definition (deliberately) provokes many more questions (and contains at least four additional concepts that need controlling), but it wonderfully captures the organic ambiguity of the term.

On the other hand, in his important book Michael Mangan acknowledges the conceptual ambiguity of magic as well as the importance of this ambiguity to the extent of magic, but he seeks to operationalize the concept in a much more controlled way: 'it is important to be clear from the outset that this is a book about tricks, staged illusions, prestidigitation and *legerdemain*, not about spells, charms or *grimoires*'.[55] This qualification enables Mangan to control the popular ambiguity about 'real' and 'pretend' magic by asserting that he is uninterested in the popular conception of 'real' magic from the start. However, as we have seen, it's not clear that it's possible to assert this distinction so neatly, convenient as it may be. As Cook notes, 'the distinctions between these meanings are not always entirely clear, as anyone who has witnessed a spoon-bending spiritualist on late-night television knows all too well'.[56] Yet, for understandable reasons, Mangan's strategy is shared by many academic researchers; Simon During opens his excellent cultural history with the qualification:

> The magic I mean is not the magic of witches or Siberian shamans –
> not, in other words, what one writer on the subject of the occult

---

[54] Francesca Coppa, Lawrence Hass, and James Peck (eds), *Performing Magic on the Western Stage*. New York: Palgrave MacMillan, 2008, p. 8. The authors suggest that this was derived from a more elaborate definition composed by Robert Neale: 'the performance exercise of imaginative mastery that grants symbolic power over life and death by means of ritual control over change in the artful play of impossible effects' (Robert Neale & David Parr, *The Magic Mirror*. Seattle: Hermetic Press, 2002, p. 55).

[55] Michael Mangan, *Performing Dark Arts: A Cultural History of Conjuring*. Chicago: Intellect Books, 2007, p. x.

[56] James Cook, *The Arts of Deception: Playing with Fraud in the Age of Barnum*. Cambridge: Harvard University Press, 2001, p. 164.

calls 'real and potent magic' – but rather the technically produced magic of conjuring shows and special effects. This magic, which stakes no serious claim to contact with the supernatural, I will call 'secular magic'.[57]

Hence, even though this current book is ostensibly interested in a similar sense of magic to that of Mangan and During, in this section I seek to explore the concept of magic in its full ambiguity to show that even this qualified sense of magic must include (at least the *performance* of) spells, charms, and grimoires. Indeed, these are instances of poor magic rather than 'real and potent' magic, since it's not clear that they accomplish any magical *feat* despite their performative *effect*. Instead of being neatly divided (even operationally) into real/pretend, white/black, ritual/stage, and so forth, I suggest that modern magic exists on a series of continuums that include each of these positions to varying extents.[58]

Modern magic as effect: performance and technique

At its best, modern magic provokes a potent sense of comprehension crisis. It confronts its audience with a claim to 'counterphysical supernatural causation'.[59] It makes things (appear to) happen that the audience believes are counter to the established laws of nature. We (seem to) witness occurrences that cannot or should not be true. In general, then, magic is not concerned with the improbable but rather with the impossible; and when it veers towards the merely improbable it seeks to suggest an impossible level (or means) of influence over it. For instance, when an audience member draws a card from a regular deck, there is a simply calculable possibility (1.9%) that the magician could guess the identity of that card. Such a guess would be remarkable, but it would not be magical: the idea of magic emerges partly because the magician has an occluded way to confound those odds in a manner so reliable that it

---

[57] During, *Modern Enchantments*, p. 1.

[58] This emphasis on spectra and continuum represents a different approach to the influential and important 'many magics' model of Robert Neale, who has begun the project of a magical typology. Robert Neale, 'Many Magics', in Eugene Burger & Robert Neale, *Magic and Meaning* (expanded). Seattle: Hermetic Press, 2009.

[59] This excellent phrase is use by Eugene Subbotsky, *Magic and the Mind*. New York: Oxford University Press, 2010, p. 5.

resembles the miraculous.[60] The modern magician gets the card right every time.

Much of the ambiguity about the term 'magic' resides in the parentheses of the last paragraph. Advocates of a clear distinction between 'real' and 'pretend' magic tend to claim a really existing difference between things behaving according to counter-physical supernatural causation and things *appearing* to behave in this way; the accomplishment of the impossible and the apparent accomplishment of the impossible. However, the actual accomplishment of the (apparently) impossible is only part of the story. Magic is not only a system of techniques of causation but also a *performance*. To be recognized as a magician, the would-be magician must persuade her audience that the power to achieve the impossible is somehow particular to her, where she might stand in for a fellowship of initiates into the necessary (and secret) knowledge, whether this is the Hermetic Order of the Golden Dawn or the Magic Circle. In other words, the socially recognized category of 'magician' owes as much, if not more, to the style and aesthetics of a performance as it does to the technical accomplishment of the (apparently) impossible. Indeed, it is a truism amongst magicians that (depending on their talent and presentation) the same 'trick' can be transformatively magical in the hands of one performer, mundanely mechanical in the hands of another, and sometimes dismally pathetic.

Hence, to some extent, the idea of magic also seems to refer to a special quality of experience. The great British magician, Nevil Maskelyne, son of John Nevil Maskelyne,[61] wanted his fellow

---

[60] In his wonderful book, *Hiding the Elephant* (Cambridge, Mass.: Da Capo Press, 2003), Jim Steinmeyer suggests that modern magicians have 'invented the impossible'.

[61] The Maskelyne Dynasty was influential in the magic world for at least three generations, beginning with John Nevil Maskelyne (1837–1917). John was one of the founders of the Magic Circle and an arch exposer of card sharpers and Spiritualists. Together with George Alfred Cooke (1825–1905), John invented many stage illusions that are still used today. He also began the association of the famous Egyptian Hall as a mecca of magical theatre, working with David Devant (1868–1941) after Cooke's death in 1905. John's son was Nevil Maskelyne (1863–1924), who took over the Egyptian Hall and the partnership with Devant, with whom he wrote extensively on the theory and practice of modern magic. Nevil was father of Jasper Maskelyne (1902–1973) and continued the family reputation as leading magicians, but he is most remembered for his role in the (possibly fictional) 'Magic gang' during World War II. Part of the Royal Engineers, Jasper was involved in helping to design camouflage, but the amazing stories of the 'war magician' that he recounted in his book, *Magic: Top Secret!* (London: Stanley Paul, 1949) are generally seen as fictional (David

magicians to recognize the difference between a *feat* of magic and a magical *effect*, where the former refers to a magician's accomplishment of her intentions and the latter refers to the result or human impact of this accomplishment.[62] A *feat* of magic is a technical accomplishment, but a magical *effect* relies upon performance. In other words, there is an important sense in which magic not only resides in the activity of magicians, but also in the experience of an audience. To some extent, a performance is magical if and when it transports its audience into an apparent realm of 'magical reality' in which, contrary to normal reality, events seem to progress in accordance with 'magical causation'.[63]

In modern society, we talk about the 'magical imagination' and 'magical thinking' as distinct from 'magical beliefs'.[64] While the former categories suggest that a sense of mystery and wonder are retained in the modern world through our imagination (without suggesting that we believe in magical causation *per se*), the latter implies belief that magical causality, events, and even characters actually exist in the normal world around us. As we saw in the context of the mystical revival, the quest for wonder and enchantment emerged as a structural feature of modernity that relied upon magical imagination, but the issue of magical belief was much more difficult to accommodate in modernity. Today, it is not controversial to observe that people in contemporary societies are still nourished by the experience of wonder in various ways, and that we search for such experiences amidst the generally rational parameters of contemporary, urban life.[65] Leaning on Nietzsche's assertion of the

Fisher, *The War Magician: The Incredible True Story of Jasper Maskelyne and the Magic Gang*. New York: Coward-McCann, 1983; Rick Stroud, *The Phantom Army of Alamein*. London: Bloomsbury, 2012). Jasper also wrote a creative biography of the dynasty, Jasper Maskelyne, *White Magic: The Story of the Maskelynes*. London: Stanley Paul, 1936.

[62] Nevil Maskelyne & David Devant, *Our Magic: The Art, Theory and Practice of Magic*. 1911. Reprinted by Wexford Press, 2008, p. 179.

[63] These invaluable terms are used by Subbotsky, *Magic and the Mind*, p. 5.

[64] Karl Bell, *The Magical Imagination: Magic and Modernity in Urban England*. Cambridge: Cambridge University Press, 2012; Stuart McWilliams, *Magical Thinking: History, Possibility and the Idea of the Occult*. London & New York: Bloomsbury Academic, 2012; Christopher Lehrich, *The Occult Mind: Magic in Theory and Practice*. Ithaca & London: Cornell University Press, 2007.

[65] There is a rich literature on the resilience of magical thinking, often at the intersection of psychology and anthropology. Particularly important is Stuart Vyse, *Believing in Magic*. Oxford: Oxford University Press, 1997. More recently Peter Lamont,

value of falsehoods over truths, Lawrence Hass has made the case for 'life magic' in a way that echoes Robert Neale's position that magical thinking can enhance our quality of life and well-being.[66] Indeed, for some, the search for wonder is equivalent to the search for meaning in the modern world.[67] Magical *imagination* and even magical *thinking* are alive and well. On the other hand, no matter how popular or apparently pervasive become the worlds of Harry Potter, Frodo, or Ged, it remains deeply controversial to *believe* in dragons, cloaks of invisibility, or raising people from the dead. Indeed, our ability to differentiate between the real role of magical imagination and the alleged reality of magical beliefs is an important cultural marker in Western modernity. Being enchanted by reading or watching magical fictions does not require belief in counter-physical supernatural causation.

In everyday life, certain forms of activity edge towards what we might term 'magical behaviour', in which we embody our tendencies towards magical thought or belief by performing (with various levels of ostentation and self-ridicule) rituals of luck or fortune: we tie our shoelaces in the same order each morning; we wear lucky underwear for a job interview or sports game; we avoid stepping on the cracks in the pavement or walking under a ladder. Most of us do not attempt to summon the rain with an incantation or to curse a rival with an intricate gesture, but such actions also reside along the continuum of magical behaviour. While a little magical *imagination* is enough to encourage us to perform superstitious or magical rituals in an everyday manner, knowing (with varying levels of

Extraordinary Beliefs: A Historical Approach to a Psychological Problem. Cambridge: Cambridge University Press, 2003. A more cognitive interpretation of the resilience of magical thinking from childhood into adulthood is Subbotsky, *Magic and the Mind*. And recent work in neuroscience includes Stephen Macknik & Susana Martinez-Conde, *Sleights of the Mind: What the Neuroscience of Magic Reveals about our Everyday Deceptions*. New York: Picador, 2011. From the standpoint of a magician, we have Robert Neale, *The Mirror of Magic*. Seattle: Hermetic Press, 2002. A delightful literary treatment is Marina Warner, *Phantasmagoria*. Oxford: Oxford University Press, 2006.

[66] Lawrence Hass, 'Life Magic and Staged Magic', in Coppa, Hass & Peck, *Performing Magic on the Western Stage*. Robert Neale, *The Mirror of Magic*. Seattle: Hermetic Press, 2002.

[67] See for instance the kinship between the enterprise of philosophy and the search for wonder. Raymond Tallis, *In Defence of Wonder and Other Philosophical Reflections*. Durham: Acumen, 2012. Mary-Jane Rubenstein, *Strange Wonder: The Closure of Metaphysics and the Opening of Awe*. New York: Columbia University Press, 2008.

confidence) that they will not really make a difference (although some of them may be psychologically beneficial to our sense of well-being), significant levels of magical *belief* are needed for us to attempt to cast a spell in good faith.

A successful 'magical performance' challenges a modern audience to examine the boundaries between the limits of their own magical imagination and the frontiers of magical belief. Indeed, a good performance is itself a type of magical behaviour, in so far as it takes the *form* of an action within an apparently magical reality, conforming to the audience's expectations about causality in such a reality rather than within the normal reality of everyday life. At the very least, the magician seeks to create the impression that the normal rules of causality do not apply in her sphere of influence (i.e., in the space of the performance – on the stage or wherever). Depending upon the nature and skill of the performance, however, the effect on the audience might permeate beyond the boundaries of the stage and begin to challenge their understanding of everyday reality itself. This approaches what Eugene Burger means when he argues that good magical performances connect the audience with wider worlds of meaning.[68] The ethics and politics of these 'wider worlds' are controversial. On the one hand, for some performers, this kind of radical re-enchantment of the everyday is their explicit purpose – we might consider the controversial, pseudo-religious work of so-called Spiritualists or mediums in this way. To some extent, we might also consider other forms of IMB (institutionalized magical beliefs), such as organized religion, in this category.[69]

---

[68] Burger's thesis on meaning and magic has been very influential. Eugene Burger & Robert Neale, *Magic and Meaning* (expanded). Seattle: Hermetic Press, 2009. At about the same time, Darwin Ortiz argued that the meaning of magic need not be tied to specific narratives, rituals, or dramatic devices, instead suggesting that meaning emerges from the magical experience itself; magic is inherently meaningful. Darwin Ortiz, *Strong Magic*. Ortiz Publications, 1994/5, pp. 131–132. Likewise, Derren Brown makes the case that magic should not be a means of encoding a social, political, or spiritual vision: the meaning should be the magic itself. Although he also cautions against believing that there is a fixed, inherent meaning to magic: 'Magic is not inherently anything', but changes in the dynamics of the moment in which it is performed. Derren Brown, *Absolute Magic: A Model for powerful Close-Up performance*. Humble: H&R Magic Books, 2003, p. 94, 50.

[69] Subbotsky makes a distinction between IMB (institutionalized magical beliefs), including those that form part of established religious ideologies, and NIMB (non-institutionalized magical beliefs) that are unrelated to any official doctrine. *Magic and the Mind*, p. 12.

At the other end of the scale, a magical performance that fails to take the form of magical behaviour at all might succeed only in creating the impression of a puzzle for the audience to solve using their existing knowledge of the laws of nature – in which case, one might suggest that there has been no magic at all. In between, the modern magician is content to acknowledge (and cultivate) the stage itself as setting the effective parameters of her magical behaviour.

In other words, the magical behaviour exhibited by a magician on stage (or in some other kind of performance) is a subtle and complex problem. It is not the case, despite the prevalence of this way of framing the question, that such behaviour is either *real* or *fake*. Magic is not an absolute category, but rather a spectrum of representational and performative possibilities. Hence, we have to be careful with the commonplace accusation that a magician's performance was not *really magic*. It's not immediately clear what this accusation means.

And yet, of course, it *is* immediately clear what is commonly meant by such accusations. Accusers seek to indicate that they do not believe that the magician is making privileged use of 'counterphysical supernatural causation'. Instead, they believe they are being *tricked*; indeed, this is why (in the modern period) we conventionally refer to a *feat* of magic as a 'magic trick' (despite the protestations of Nevil Maskelyne and others, who found the term 'trick' to be muddle-headed, misleading, and even offensive). But this accusation of fraud (i.e., that magic is not or should not be a trick) is incoherent precisely because *magic is a trick*. Ironically, hidden behind this accusation (that magicians are trying to trick us) is belief in a magical worldview in which 'counterphysical supernatural causation' is genuinely possible, and where some magicians have authentic access to it while others do not: *this* magician does real magic, but *that* magician is tricking us.

Yet, as Maskelyne explains it in 1911, 'we who live in the Twentieth Century are, or should be, aware that the laws of nature cannot possibly be contravened', at least not at the level of human action. No matter how a performer represents her magic to the audience, the audience knows (or should know) that any appearance of counterphysical supernatural causation is merely 'the *apparent*, not *actual* defiance of natural laws. Modern magic, therefore, deals exclusively with the creation of mental impressions'.[70] That is, while magical *performance*

---

[70] Maskelyne & Devant, *Our Magic*, p. 175.

may be a type of magical *behaviour*, this is only in its *form* and *effect*, not in terms of the *feat* itself. There is nothing magical about the *techniques* of magic. Nobody can *do* magic, we can just facilitate others to experience it. In the words of Derren Brown, it is the 'unique nature of magic . . . that it *only* happens in the minds of spectators'.[71] The trick is not magical; the feeling engendered should be magical.

At the turn of the twentieth century, enwrapped in the relentless march of industrial modernity and shrouded in the haze of the mystical revival, Maskelyne and others struggled to develop a coherent vocabulary to talk about these slippery and contradictory distinctions by drawing a line between the so-called Old and New Magic, where the idea of the 'Old Magic' participated in a magical reality permeated with magical *belief* and new magic was a form of *imagination* embedded within the rational, scientific worldview of modernity.[72] In each case, 'magical' referred to the *effect* of a performance – to a quality of the audience's experience – and not to the means of causation employed. As we have seen, one unanticipated consequence of this argument was the perpetuation of the romantic idea that magic (rather than merely the *performance* of magic) was different in the past than in the present – indeed, that the past was somehow more (and more authentically) magical than the present, and that modernity had somehow disenchanted the world (not only by changing the way magic was performed and signified but by actually eradicating the technologies, practices, and feats of magic itself). This was basic to the stance of the so-called new occultists at the *fin de siècle*. Given the intensely and deeply Eurocentric Victorian worldview, this enchanted view of the European past very quickly slid over into an enchanted view of the non-European present, as though travelling away from the European metropoles was tantamount to travelling back in time: just as magic was somehow more potent in history than in the present, so it seemed more potent in Africa and Asia – in the so-called Orient – than in the rational and scientific realm of Europe. This was basic to movements such as Theosophy.

However, the fact remains that the laws of nature that could not be broken in Paris, London, or New York in 1911 were exactly the same in 1211 or in India in 2011; they were not invented or created

---

[71] Brown, *Absolute Magic*, p. 50.

[72] A classic work from this period is Henry Evans, *The Old and The New Magic*. Chicago & London: Kegan Paul, 1906.

by modern Europeans, but rather discovered. Indeed, the idea that they could have been created would itself be a vestige of magical thinking. Hence, no matter how 'Old Magic' was *performed*, its practices, processes, methods, and devices must also have been 'tricks', deploying principles similar to those on which 'New Magic' relies to create the *mental impression* that the laws of nature have been overcome (without actually violating them). Of course, the effective and affective mental impressions will vary in different historical, cultural, and institutional settings.

Even allowing space for invention and progress in the techniques and technologies that enable magicians to perform *feats* and create magical *effects*, it seems sensible to assume that the actual distinction between Old and New Magic, like the distinction between ostensibly real and fake magic, resides chiefly in the manner of its performance and its relationship with the cultural norms of the audience in a particular time and place.

In other words, we know (now) that it is not the case that there was some mystical period in the past in which magic was real in any technological sense other than the sense in which it is real today, just as we know that there is no distant place (in Asia, Glubbdubdrib, Rivendell, or Tatooine, for instance) where magic is real in any technological sense other than the sense in which it is real in Europe, North America, or anywhere else. The medievalism of modern fantasy fiction is analogous to the Orientalism of the 'mystic East'.[73] So, we know that, at least in so far as we're talking about magical techniques, feats, and processes, the distinction between 'real' magic and 'pretend' magic is false. All magic is effect – successful pretence – so we might instead say that it's all real in a particular and consistent way.[74] And it is in this

---

[73] The Medievalism of fantasy fiction refers to the ways in which so-called high fantasy after J.R.R. Tolkein (1892–1973) deploys medieval European settings for tales of magic, filling the public discourse with representations of the European Middle Ages that are akin to Middle Earth and thus associating this period with the 'reality' of magic in the popular consciousness. Tolkein's landmark novel, *The Hobbit*, appeared in 1936.

[74] This enables an inversion of the anthropological dissolution of magic at the turn of the twentieth century, as expressed in classics such as Mauss' *A General Theory of Magic*. These anthropologists demonstrated that even the magic of so-called primitive societies beyond the boundaries of modernity was little more than a series of simple and mundane techniques of deception and so concluded that it wasn't really magic but instead simply an institution with social functions. Hence, magic just disappeared. The inverse seems equally true: discovering that all magical feats are produced by mundane technologies, and that whatever enchantment they generate is a result of a

context that we must try to understand the meaning of the accusation: *That magician is a fraud!* The accusation itself reveals a great deal about the cultural matrix of a particular time and place, as well as the relationship between the magician's style (and success) of performance and the audience's degree (and style) of magical imagination and belief. But it doesn't tell us anything about the devices or techniques of causation being used by the magician.

Rather than being concerned with devices and techniques, then, some of the most influential voices in the era of modern magic have been more interested in the *ethical* and *social* force of performances and of accusations about charlatanism. For instance, in their landmark publication, *Our Magic* (1911), David Devant and Nevil Maskelyne freely (albeit controversially) exposed the techniques and technologies behind a number of magical feats and attempted to establish *moral parameters* around the category of the 'legitimate modern magician'. Between them, Devant and Maskelyne were presidents of the famously secretive Magic Circle from its establishment in London in 1905 through to 1924, so this was a momentous step.[75] For them, the difference between a legitimate or modern magician and a charlatan does not reside in the processes they use or the feats they accomplish, but rather in the manner of their performance and in (what the Victorians liked to call) their character. While both modern magicians and charlatans seek to communicate the 'mental impression of supernatural agency at work ... a legitimate magician never deludes his audience as to the character of his performance. He makes no claim to the possession of powers beyond the scope of psychical science'.[76] In the lovely phrase of Simon During, it is 'self-consciously illusory magic'.[77]

In other words, 'legitimate magic' (or what they sometimes call 'white magic', 'modern magic', or 'authentic magic') works exclusively to misdirect the *senses* of an audience, while illegitimate magic or charlatanism works to misdirect and defraud the *intelligence* of an

magician's performance, reveals that this is what real magic means! Continuing to hold this real magic up against a fantastical image of magic that has never existed (and then actually giving the fantasy ontological priority) is like claiming that horses aren't really unicorns, so therefore horses don't really exist.

[75] Famously, Devant was expelled (and reinstated) from the prestigious magicians' society three times, as punishment for breaching its motto: *Indocilis Privata Loqui* (not apt to disclose secrets).

[76] Maskelyne & Devant, *Our Magic*, p. 176.

[77] During, *Modern Enchantments*, p. 27.

audience. While legitimate magicians sought to communicate the experience of wonder about accomplishing the impossible (without attempting to refute its impossibility), charlatans sought not only to impart a sense of wonder, but also to normalize that wonder by convincing their audiences that the laws of nature were malleable or misconceived (i.e., the impossible was possible). Devant and Maskelyne are unforgiving about the moral standing of performers who seek to prey on the intellectually vulnerable, calling them 'unscrupulous adventurers' and excluding them (at least conceptually) from the fraternity of modern magicians.[78] The modern magician is not a con man; a con man should not be entitled to call himself a magician. Devant and Maskelyne, like Maskelyne's father and Houdini in the United States at the same time, had the so-called Spiritualists in their sights, the exposure of whom became a matter of honour for 'legitimate magicians' in the early twentieth century. Moreover, their argument about the importance of virtuous character rapidly became a general one: Devant's advertising billboards often carried his slogan, 'All done by kindness'; Maskelyne's work on the theory of magic repeatedly stressed the importance of being gentlemanly. As we will see in later chapters, however, this ethical stance became rather plastic when magicians were travelling outside the Western world.

While there were very few voices of dissent about the need for modern magic to be morally upright and honest about its sphere of operation (on a real stage in the real world),[79] the idea that this emphasis made it acceptable to expose the techniques and processes of the art was (and remains) deeply controversial. Exposing fraudulent Spiritualists and exposing other 'legitimate magicians' seemed like very different activities, even if the techniques and devices being exposed were often the same. As we will see in the next chapter, the debate about the

---

[78] Maskelyne & Devant, *Our Magic*, p. 177. Maskelyne goes even further, suggesting that it is also charlatanism when performers 'refrain from committing themselves to any definite statement on the subject of their powers' and instead inform the audience that they will know the performer has the power to perform miracles if the audience cannot explain his methods for themselves. Maskelyne adds dryly that the majority of people cannot explain the working of even the simplest devices.

[79] This excepts the many voices that defended the Spiritualism movement during this period. However, advocates of Spiritualism were not (in general) trying to have its mediums counted amongst the magicians, but rather were trying to separate mediums (with 'real' powers) from magicians (with 'fake' powers).

scientific, artistic, and ethical merits of exposé is one of the defining concerns of modern magic.

Whatever the case, the idea of a domain of legitimate magic brings magic out into the open and reveals it clearly as a form of performance art, whatever the context of that performance. While it remains conceivable that legitimate magic could be performed in various settings, the imperative for honesty about its inevitable adherence to natural laws tends to push modern magic more and more firmly into the realm of entertainment. Indeed, locating the performance of magic as a form of entertainment (rather than as a ritual of supernatural power) is itself a way to emphasize its artifice. It is when magic edges off the stage and into the domains of religion, politics, and other activities (such as Spiritualism, occultism, witchcraft, or gambling) that the moral dilemmas of an art of sensory deception become most clear and most stark, requiring delicate and nuanced moral manoeuvres by the magicians in question. Likewise, locating legitimate magic as an entertainment places an imperative on the magician to understand the cultural context in which her performance takes place, where this imperative is not only ethical but also commercial. What happens on a stage may be symbolically sealed within the magic circle of the floodlights, but the membrane of that circle is permeable; performances there can have effects outside the theatre as well.

So, to some extent, 'legitimate modern magic' is the story of how magic has attempted to define an artistic space of entertainment for itself by differentiating itself from 'other' forms of magic (which may be technically the same, but which are performed in other contexts and with other forms of intentionality that render them 'illegitimate'), such as ritual magic (including witchcraft), religious magic, and various types of charlatanism (including Spiritualism and cardsharping etc.). Ironically, however, part of the entertainment value of legitimate magic is precisely its association with these marginal, liminal spheres of activity, with which it is technically unified. Indeed, for many, magic seems least magical when entirely divorced from these 'illegitimate' versions of itself – magic seems to need these associations in order for it to have *meaning* and for its *feats* to have magical *effect*.[80] To some extent, 'new magic' needs to entertain the illusion of 'old magic' in order for it to participate in the public understanding of the

---

[80] There are very few people in the modern world who have not experienced the horrendously un-magical 'magic' of a birthday clown or the irritatingly puzzling 'tricks' of a card-magician at a corporate convention or club: *pick a card, any card.*

representation of magic *per se*. Indeed, in the absence of these associations with magical beliefs, modern magic seems to become dis-enchanted.

It seems that this was what the 'father of modern magic', Jean Eugene Robert-Houdin, meant when he famously declared that a modern 'conjuror is not a juggler; he is an actor playing the part of a [real] magician'.[81] Indeed, Robert-Houdin goes even further than this, calling on the conjuror himself to participate in this representational fantasy as an essential element in the transformation of a mundane show into a show of magical behaviour. The modern magician must enter into a form of magical belief:

> Although all one says during the course of a performance is – not to mince the matter – a tissue of falsehoods, the performer must sufficiently enter into the part he plays, to himself believe in the reality of his factitious statements. This belief on his own part will infallibly carry a like conviction to the minds of the spectators.[82]

[81] This quotation from Robert-Houdin is often seen as marking the commencement of *modern* magic, as it asserts a critical difference between the *conjuror* (i.e., the modern performer of magical effects) from the figure of the *magician* (i.e., the fantasy from folklore, myth, and fiction). It is important to note that this is actually a conceptual rather than a historical distinction: magicians in the past were also conjurors playing the part of [real] magicians. The codification and endorsement of this principle is modern, but its critical applicability is universal. Robert-Houdin, *Secrets of Conjuring and Magic*, p. 43. Alongside this strong endorsement of conjuring as a performance, Robert-Houdin is emphatic that the most important quality of the good conjuror is not persona but skill: 'to succeed as a conjuror, three things are essential – first, dexterity; second, dexterity; and third, dexterity' (p. 29).

[82] This is the eighth of Robert-Houdin's fifteen 'General Principles'. Robert-Houdin, *Secrets of Conjuring and Magic*, p. 33. This appears to be an anticipation of Stanislavsky's school of Method Acting. Sam Sharpe endorses this position in 1936, noting that a magician 'can only convince his audience that the results are due to forces beyond natural science by believing in such fiction himself for the time being'. *Neo-Magic*. Bradford: Clegg & son, 1936/45, p. 60. This stance has remained central to the idea of good conjuring to the present day, especially in fields such as mentalism. It acts as a modifier on Robert-Houdin's famous dictum that a conjuror is an actor playing the part of a magician, since he must do this without (giving the impression that he is) acting. Derren Brown remarks: 'Most importantly of all, I will believe in what I am doing. This is the vital point. When the generic mentalist stands before an audience and writes things on a board or pad, he is probably not acting in congruence with himself. By this I mean that he will be asking you, through his patter, to accept that he can read minds. This conscious level of communication is giving one message. Yet his body language and visible manifestations of his internal states do not suggest that anything of the sort is happening. Indeed, at this level, he is acting like a magician. Therefore, we are not convinced. Again, we are not watching mind reading: we are

Summary and terminology

This book is concerned with magic during the so-called Golden Age of Magic, which approximately coincides with the period Max Weber identified as being characterized by the 'dis-enchantment of the world' and also with the *fin de siècle* movement known as the mystical revival. Both of these cultural trajectories are essential to our understanding of the nature of 'modern magic', which participates in the ideals and technologies of modernity while cultivating an ambiguous association with other forms of mystical and occult belief, including the arcane and the Orientalist. *The idea of 'modern magic' is thus deployed as an 'ideal type', fully cognisant that there were magicians in the period (and many contemporary magicians) who would not subscribe to it, either consciously or otherwise.*

One of the conceptual innovations of modern magic is the recognition that the commonplace distinction between real and pretend (or, sometimes, old and new) magic has no substantive meaning when it comes to the techniques and devices of a magician. That is, the technologies and processes of magic, even the *feats* accomplished, are more-or-less a unified field, providing for no clear-cut technical distinctions between the various forms: modern magical theory maintains that magic describes a quality of *affect* and *effect* – it resides in the *experience* of the audience – and is not a qualifier for the means of causation itself. Modern magic holds that causation is always subject to natural laws that are the provenance of scientific inquiry: real magic deals with communicating the impression of counter-physical supernatural causation but cannot employ supernatural causation itself (since that is impossible). Contrary to common opinion, modern magic holds that it is the only real magic possible; it is a residue of pre-modern or fantastical magical beliefs to maintain that 'real and potent' magic involves supernatural powers.

To be clear, this theory of magic makes no claims that scientific knowledge of the laws of nature are static or always correct. But rather involves an investment in the scientific method precisely because magic is concerned with performing the *impossible*. So, if it were the case, for example, that the possibility of communicating with the dead or reading

watching a man write down information on a pad.' Derren Brown, *Pure Effect: Direct Mindreading and Magical Artistry*. Humble: H&R Magic Books, 2000, pp. 115–116.

minds were scientifically established, then the apparent performance of these *feats* would cease to be magical *effects* (and presumably they would also become part of the arsenal of *techniques* that magicians would use to apparently accomplish other impossible things). In this way, we can see that modern magic relies upon magical *imagination* to conceive of the impossible and on science to bring about its apparent accomplishment; and hence it remains within the interests of modern magic constantly (and scientifically) to test magical *beliefs* and claims about magical *behaviour*.[83]

So, while the techniques and skills of magic are important, modern magic requires a theory of *performance* in order to understand and appreciate its impact and value. The development of a theory of 'good magic' in this aesthetic sense will be the focus of the next chapter. In this chapter, we saw that 'good' also operates as a moral quality in the critique of magic, with modern magicians drawing a distinction between *legitimate magic* and *charlatanism*, where the former refers to an attempt to evoke wonder through the deception of an audience's *senses* and the latter refers to an attempt to deceive the audience's *intellect* in order to exploit them. Central to discussions about how to differentiate between legitimate and illegitimate magic in modernity is the difference between engaging an audience's magical *imagination*, perhaps by encouraging magical *thinking* in a space bounded by a stage, rather than attempting to evangelize specific magical *beliefs* that then spill over into everyday life. These factors are features of the magical *behaviour* of the performer, and in their manipulation resides the means to differentiate between the different forms of magic that are (otherwise) technically unified. In the next chapter, we will consider a theory of modern magic that enables appreciation and criticism of 'good' magic in its moral and aesthetic sense.

I'd like to end this chapter with an illustration of how these various issues coalesce in a modern performance. I will not comment on it, since I think it is provocative in its own terms.

---

[83] Perhaps it's not inappropriate to repeat Arthur C. Clarke's first and second laws of science at this junction, since they eloquently describe the fluidity and dynamism of scientific knowledge that is being discussed: '1. When a distinguished but elderly scientist states that something is possible, he is almost certainly right. When he states that something is impossible, he is very probably wrong. 2. The only way of discovering the limits of the possible is to venture a little way past them into the impossible.' Arthur Clarke, 'Hazards of Prophecy: The Failure of Imagination', in *Profiles of the Future*.

Scene one: magician or maniac?

David Blaine sits with Ricky Gervais in a restaurant booth. There are brightly coloured balloons attached to the white walls and bobbling against the ceiling. While they sit, Blaine licks the back of a playing card and then blows from underneath it, so that it spins ten feet into the air and sticks against the ceiling. Gervais watches with suitable admiration; he takes a card playfully and has a go himself. After a few abortive attempts, Gervais concludes that what Blaine has done was not possible. For some reason, this doesn't seem unusual.

Even after having convinced his dinner companion that he has accomplished the impossible, Blaine seems to decide that more is needed. He wants Gervais to *feel* the force of his magic, as though simply *wondering* how he could blow a card ten feet into the air was not enough. So, Blaine takes a long steel skewer from the waiter's trolley and proceeds to push it very slowly and deliberately through his own arm. No fuss, no magic wands or top-hats, no longer any balloons in view, just a simple 'do you see how the needle *looks like* it's going into the arm?'

That *is* what it looks like.

Gervais watches in increasing discomfort, ready for a trick but not sure he's seeing one. He looks rapidly between Blaine's face and his arm, clearly exposed by the plain black T-shirt Blaine is wearing. Blaine grins.

'Do you see how the needle *looks like* it going into the arm?'

'Yes ... yes, it does ... '

Gervais tries to make a joke, clearly feeling uncomfortable with what he's witnessing. Blaine doesn't laugh. Silence descends over the table as both Blaine and Gervais focus all their attention on the metal skewer now apparently two inches deep in Blaine's bicep. After a few more moments, Gervais breaks the tension with a sudden but inarticulate exclamation: 'Agh ... what the f&*k?!' The tip of the skewer appears to be pushing out the skin on the opposite side of the arm.

Blaine repeats his mantra calmly: 'See how it really *looks* like – '

'—this is mental!' Gervais can't let him say it. 'Seriously, David, this is nuts. This is not a trick, you're just sticking a f&*king needle through your arm. What are you doing?'

Calm with focus, Blaine responds: 'See how it *looks*, Ricky, like it's *really* going through my arm?'

Gervais pushes himself away, revolted, keen to get some distance from the horrible sight. 'You're a maniac!'

'See how it *looks* like –'

'—that's the worst thing I've *ever* seen in my life. What are you doing?!'

Despite himself, Blaine's implacable calm cracks briefly and a smile flickers across his face; this couldn't be going better. 'You see how it *really, believably looks* like –'

The end of the skewer breaks the surface of the skin on the opposite side of his arm, visibly impaling his bicep. Gervais grasps the arm and studies it with a mixture of horror, disbelief, and indignance. There is no blood.

'How are you doing it? What do I mean how are you doing it – you've just stuck f&*king a needle through your arm!'

'It looks pretty real, right?'

'Sorry, I don't understand, how is that *not* real? What do you mean it *looks* pretty real?' Gervais prods and pokes at the arm. 'How is *that* not real? I don't understand . . . how is that a *trick*? How is that *not* a needle going through your arm?'

After a moment to let the battle with belief rage a little more, Blaine finally asks Gervais to pull the needle out of his arm for him, 'so that you can see the magic trick'. It's pretty clear that Gervais is not very comfortable doing this. He tugs experimentally and then stops. 'Right', he says, fixing Blaine with a serious expression as though telling him to stop fooling around now and tell him the truth. Enough is enough: 'Is that *really* stuck through your arm?'

Blaine smiles. 'Just pull it out. Then you'll see how it works.'

Gervais freezes, unsure whether to go on, apparently thinking through the implications of what could happen if he pulls out a skewer that is really stuck through an arm and how that would be different from pulling out a skewer that isn't really stuck through an arm. Eventually, decision made, he pulls firmly on the skewer and becomes certain that it's real: 'This is real, this is real – you're a maniac.' He's almost fitful as he slowly withdraws the giant needle.

Blaine grins, stands up, and walks off, leaving Gervais sitting alone at the table with his head in his hands clearly unable to process what has just happened. The effect on Ricky Gervais is itself deeply affective. He's genuinely struggling with how to understand something that challenges a core belief, trying to work out whether or how this breach with his sense of the world can be *real*. As we watch Ricky Gervais, his struggle is our struggle: I am Ricky Gervais.

'That's real', he says to the camera. 'You saw it – It's not a trick, it's real. He stuck a needle through his f*&king arm ... but he couldn't have, because nobody would do that. So *how* did he do it?' Gervais pauses, evidently trying to think of the answer himself. Then a new question occurs to him. '*Why* would you, why would you do that?'

After a while, Blaine is back at the table and Gervais is still trying to understand what has happened. 'It's amazing either way: either that was the best illusion I've ever seen close up, or you're a maniac.' Blaine laughs boyishly, clearly happy with this feedback. 'Either way, well done. Well done!' Had he been wearing a hat, he would have tipped it, *chapeau*!

Gervais thinks some more, searching for a conclusion. 'It's not a trick – it's a double bluff. You just did something and you want people to think it's an amazing illusion like your card tricks, but really you just stuck something through your arm. That's brilliant. If that's true, it's brilliant. It's the best con ever because it's not a con. It's like someone pretending to cut their own foot off, and then they hobble off without a foot. And they say, "Do you see that, didn't it look like I cut my foot off?"'[84]

---

[84] This scene is from the David Blaine ABC special, *Real or Magic*, first aired on 19 November 2013.

2 A THEORY OF MODERN MAGIC

Good, bad, and ugly magic

In the last chapter, we explored the varied landscape of the magical terrain at the turn of the twentieth century, testing the conceptual duplicity of 'real' and 'pretend' magic to reveal a technically unified space differentiated mainly by aesthetic and performative issues. Building on that basis, this chapter seeks to develop a way for us to differentiate between good and bad magic in order to enable a language of criticism and appreciation.

As was the case with the idea of 'real and potent' magic, it becomes evident very quickly that the idea of 'good magic' triggers all kinds of intuitive responses from people today. In particular, it emerges as another way to talk about so-called white magic – that is, supposedly supernatural magic that is seen as morally upright and ethically good. Here, good is juxtaposed with evil, white with black magic.[1] For the general public, such distinctions seem to rely upon notions about supposedly diabolical *means* (techniques and devices) and/or diabolical *feats*; yet, as we saw in Chapter 1, such distinctions actually tend to rest upon the *appearance* of diabolical *effects*, as in the macabre of Bizarre Magic

---

[1] The idea of 'black magic' emerges from modern European expansion into Africa and the (re)encounter with pagan or diabolical magics. 'A patina of racism intruded into the blackness of "black" magic, which now also connoted skin color' (Simon During, *Modern Enchantments*. Cambridge: Harvard University Press, 2002, p. 10). The linguistic coincidence of necromancy (conjuring the dead) and negromancy (black conjuring) enabled a racist political culture.

(where an atmosphere of horror is vital to the performance of horrific *effects*, but where nothing horrific is really accomplished).

It is important to note immediately, however, that the modern period has not seen the complete disappearance of (what we might call) *diabolical means* – that is, the use of morally offensive techniques or devices that are intended to accomplish magical feats. We might include in this category techniques that involve doing harm to animals or people: at one extreme, the technique might involve sacrificing an animal in the belief that doing so will serve as counter-physical supernatural causation for an otherwise impossible outcome (i.e., sacrifice is a type of *magical behaviour* that embodies specific *magical beliefs*), and at the other extreme we might think of the use of a collapsible birdcage to 'vanish' a dove, which actually kills the poor animal by squashing it flat. It is important to keep in mind that, in our schema for modern magic, these techniques are only techniques of magic if they produce apparently impossible *feats* that communicate magical *effects*. Otherwise (and perhaps even so), they are simply acts of wanton cruelty and there is nothing *magical* about their moral dubiousness at all. In the case of these two examples, for instance, it seems so unlikely (to the point of impossibility) that killing a rabbit will make it rain (or even give anyone the impression that it has made it rain) that while it may be a diabolical act, it is not really diabolical *magic* in our sense.[2] On the other hand, stuffing a dove into a mechanical device and then apparently producing it from inside the coat of a mystified spectator does seem like a magical effect, and, even if this *effect* is not diabolical, we may want to ask whether the *technique* was morally deficient.

As we will see later in this chapter, a more contemporary movement in magic known as 'Bizarre Magic' will aim at the production of horrific magical effects by giving the impression of the deployment of diabolical techniques, perhaps allowing an audience to believe that the magician has killed a rabbit in order to make it rain, or giving them the impression that the dove is squashed to death when it vanishes (perhaps,

---

[2] It seems only fair to note here that some rainmakers have succeeded in producing the 'magical effect' of producing rain by performing their rituals just before they (but not their audience) know that it is going to rain. Nonetheless, following Keith Thomas, whose monumental *Religion and the Decline of Magic* (New York: Charles Scribers & Sons, 1971) remains seminal in the field, we must resist collapsing magic into 'the employment of ineffective techniques to allay anxiety when effective ones are not available' (p. 668). If magic is not effective, what is magical about it?

but not necessarily, revealing later that it was actually unharmed). Hence, intriguingly, this kind of horrific magical effect could be a prime example of good magic. In Maskelyne's terms, which we considered in Chapter 1, this is legitimate (white) magic precisely because of the way in which the moral horror experienced by a modern Western audience occasioned by what appears to happen functions as a form of performative confession that it is not really happening: by pretending to do something egregiously unacceptable (and possibly illegal), the magician is confessing that her magical effects are not produced by counter-physical supernatural causation, but rather by some (explicable) process that has been dressed to give this impression.

In other words, the common idea of 'white magic' as a term for morally upright magic has at least two dimensions. First, it can refer to the moral acceptability of the devices and techniques used to accomplish a feat, or perhaps to the nature of that feat itself. Second, following Maskelyne's sense of 'legitimate' magic, it can refer to a magician's performative honesty about the deployment of mundane technologies to produce miraculous effects.[3] This suggests that it makes little sense to describe a magical *effect* as white or black, except in a purely aesthetic sense; adopting the appearance of black magic could be an aesthetic

---

[3] The literature of modern magic has a general consensus that 'white magic' describes the second of these dimensions. This is partly because of the work of the Maskelynes, who framed themselves clearly as 'white magicians' (Jasper Maskelyne, *White Magic: The Story of the Maskelynes*. London: Stanley Paul, 1936), but the case is also made in the earliest texts of modern magic (Professor Hoffmann, *Modern Magic: A Practical Treatise on the Art of Conjuring*. 1876, U.S. reprint, Philadelphia: David McKay, 1910, p. 1), especially the early French classic by Jean Nicholas Ponsin (1801–1863), *Nouvelle Magie Blanche Dévoilée: Physique Occulte Et Cours Complet De Prestidigitation* (Reims: A. Huet, 1853). Published fifteen years before the much more famous book of Robert-Houdin (*Les Secrets de la Prestidigitation et de la Magie.*, Paris: Michel Lévy, 1868), Sam Sharpe argued that Ponsin's book was the single most important book on the techniques of conjuring since Reginald Scot's *The Discoverie of Witchcraft* (London, 1584) and Henri Décremps' (1746–1826) *Magie Blanche Dévoilée* (Paris, 1784), and the first *modern* text. Ponsin seems to have drawn heavily on Décremps' work, including on the tradition of referring to scientifically accomplished magic as 'white magic'. Sam Sharpe, *Ponsin on Conjuring*. London: George Johnson, 1937. In the context of Western imperialism at the turn of the twentieth century, it is difficult to overlook the intrusion of a 'patina of racism' around the idea of 'white magic', just as Simon During observes racism in the notion of 'black magic' at the time.

choice to help create a magical experience, but this is not in itself necessarily a moral choice.[4]

Hence, in the end, 'good magic' is not only a moral judgement but also an indicator of *quality*, sometimes of *artistic quality*, which suggests that we need some form of theory of magical appreciation in order to be able to judge and critique it. We may be able to recognize that an Indian street magician who pushes a skewer through his throat is doing something more (or at least differently) disturbing than David Blaine when he pushes a skewer through his bicep in front of Ricky Gervais in a restaurant (as in Scene one), but can we really say why? We may be able to see that the cringe-worthy, awkward close-up performer in a bar or the embarrassing clown at a child's birthday party is a worse magician than David Copperfield, but are we really able to explain why this is the case?

If we're willing to accept that some magicians are better than others (and perhaps that some magic is better than others, or indeed that some 'magic' just isn't magic at all), we need a vocabulary and theoretical apparatus of criticism and appreciation. Furthermore, precisely because the imagined distinction between *real* and *pretend* magic is incoherent and the lines between white and black magic are not simple, we need a theory of magical appreciation that integrates (rather than excludes) issues of ethics and morality into the concept of the good. A particular performance of magic might be technically excellent but morally dubious in non-simple ways, or *vice versa*, even today.

As in Chapter 1, this chapter makes extensive use of the theoretical work of magicians themselves in an attempt to build a theory of magic appreciation. This is on the basis that nobody is better equipped

---

[4] I immediately accept that it is overly simplistic to claim that aesthetics have no moral significance. My point here is simply that is possible that a successful dramatic performance of a fictional daemonic rite that involves the inexplicable production copious tomato ketchup is not *per se* black magic. It is worth noting that the fifteenth century witch hunter Heinrich Kramer (1440–1505), author of the infamous *Malleus Maleficarum* (The Witches' Hammer, 1487) was ultimately uninterested in the style of performance or even the devices employed to accomplish apparently magical effects. For Kramer, the issue with magic and witchcraft was not simply whether a witch had real supernatural 'black' powers, but was also whether she perpetrated deceit *per se*. For Kramer, stage and street entertainers such as conjurers and ventriloquists were also sinning: tricks, illusions, and 'prestiges' were the very business of the Devil on earth. In Kramer's framework, then, all magic, even so-called white magic, is black.

to judge (and justify) the quality of magic than a magician. This is especially the case because our framework for judgement requires not only an appreciation of its aesthetic impact on an audience, but also technical and performance expertise regarding the means deployed and their artistic transformation into a magical effect. It is important to acknowledge the quantity of high quality theoretical work produced within the magic community in the modern period, which is rarely considered from the 'outside'.

I am very much aware that my own construction of 'magical theory' will be controversial to many, not only (but also) because talking about a 'theory of magic' is already deeply controversial for magicians, many of whom feel alienated by the very idea that there can be (or should be) an abstract framework of appreciation and criticism. For many, magic is a hobby or an obsession or a game, and attempts to treat it as something serious (or as 'art') just risks destroying the fun or appearing pompous. For others, it is a belief system or a life philosophy, and attempts to analyse it as a mundane entertainment or craft are simply insulting.

It is not my intention to destroy the fun or to cause offence. I offer my thoughts on a possible theory of magic as a way to frame a technical and ethical appreciation of magic and its place in modern society. My goal is not to suggest that people should stop enjoying themselves with whatever they take to be magic, but only to indicate that if/when we are talking about the social responsibility of performers then we need to have a language in which to have this discussion. By its very nature, a performance involves an audience of other people, not only the magician herself, so it is always already pregnant with social significance. Magic is real, and so it has a real place in the world and real effects on individuals and cultures.

So, rather than being an attempt at a comprehensive history of the theory of magic, this chapter aims towards establishing a framework of tools and terms that can be used in the rest of the book to talk about magic in the modern period.[5] In this context, this chapter considers the state of magical theory today; it draws heavily upon texts and thinkers

---

[5] I can only agree with the wisdom of Juan Tamariz when (in his own invaluable contribution to the theory of magic) he notes that he can only follow the stepping stones of modern magical theory laid by the 'authentic geniuses' of magic: 'Robert-Houdin, Maskelyne, Sharpe, Ramsay, Fitzkee, Vernon, Slydini, Fu-Manchu and Ascanio'. Jan Tamariz, *The Magic Way: The Method of False Solutions and the*

of the Golden Age, who defined the contours of the field, and links them into a story of the development of magic theory into the present. In other words, in this chapter, we are concerned with developing theory that is modern, while the last chapter was occupied with excavating magic that is modern.

By the end of this chapter, we will see a picture of modern and contemporary magic that is deeply self-conscious and riddled with existential angst. Since at least the turn of the twentieth century, magicians have striven constantly to redefine their field in ways that negate its associations with various theoretical and practical constructions: religion, Spiritualism, witchcraft, charlatanism, and so on. One of the central dilemmas has been the desire of modern magicians to take the idea of magic seriously in an era that ridicules it. The results of this basic tension have included the development of numerous styles of performance, some of which theorists have found counter-productive or even offensive, while other styles are lauded. The ground is constantly moving beneath our feet.

We will see that being able to talk sensibly and clearly about magic turns out to require us to be able to differentiate between good and evil, between manipulation and jugglery, between props and performances, between puzzles and mysteries, between feats and effects, and between confusion and magicality. Furthermore, we need some terminological consistency about these things in order to make sure that criticism is understood. For instance, when we say that something is a *trick*, what does this imply? Where are the lines supposed to be drawn between feats that are magical and those that are not? When does a particular performance contribute to the further development of magic, and when does it seem damaging? Is this 'further development of magic' a socially responsible goal? When should a magical performance be considered art? When is it honest, and when a sham? How do we know when we experience good magic? And is good magic an ethical or an aesthetic category, or both? If we accept that the crucial characteristic of magic is that it involves the production of a *magical* experience for its audience, in what precisely does the quality of *magical* consist? To what extent is 'magical' a historical, cultural, or even political variable?

Magic Way. Seattle: Hermetic Press, 2014 (originally in Spanish as *La Via Magica*, 1987).

Scene two: mentalist or medium?

The applause subside, and Derren Brown looks into Matt's eyes. He seems to reach a decision. 'I'm going to hang onto you for a minute,' he says, 'because I think you are *very* good at this. You have a *natural affinity* for this.' Matt blushes a little, flattered but also self-conscious in front of the theatre audience. Boyish. 'It means you have high levels of empathy, and also bravery ... it's tied in with being *brave*.' Brown pauses as though weighing up the evidence. 'So yes, we'll do it tonight', he calls into the wings. 'We'll do it tonight with Matt. Can we get a couple of chairs, please, and the table?' Evidently, whatever they're about to do is not something that can be done with just anyone on just any night.

Matt has already been chosen from amongst the hundreds of people in the audience following a series of induction and sugges-tion tests, which were focussed on the eerie automaton that Brown has named Svengali. Svengali resembles a young boy from the nineteenth century, complete with blue velvet suit, ruffle-collar, tussled blond hair, and large, unfocussed blue eyes. He sits on a stool, stage left, broodily lit in the atmosphere of careful darkness. At the start of the show, Brown had elaborated the story of this Svengali, explaining to the audience that the famously sinister character of the same name in the 1894 novel, *Trilby*, by George Du Maurier, was actually based upon this automaton. Evidently, this Svengali had been infamous for its apparently physic powers, including for its ability to possess people. Brown explains that he is an instance of a 'true automaton' – a free-standing device that runs on its own without interference or control of human agency. There is a complicated story about the journey of Svengali through the occult underworld, where he was obviously highly prized, before Brown himself apparently purchased him (anonymously) at an auction in Philadelphia. It had then taken him four years to refurbish the automaton (which apparently contains more than 150 yards of brass tubing and 3,000 cogs), to bring it back into its original condition. Svengali is powered by clockwork, so Brown had to spend 6 minutes winding the mechanism before the show; opening Svengali's chest to reveal his clockwork interior, he just does the final 'tightening' on the stage. Out of consideration to the audience, Brown has installed a mic inside Svengali so everyone can hear the mechanisms as they whir and grind. He is going to demonstrate the feats that nineteenth century audiences mistakenly attributed to occult or supernatural causation.

'So, sit yourself down, Matt', invites Brown as the chairs arrive from offstage. 'You'll enjoy this; I don't get to do it very often. Now, what do I . . . ?' He looks around, apparently not quite sure how to proceed because this is such a rare occurrence; the moment of confusion is charmingly offset against Brown's immaculate formal attire. 'Ah yes, I need this', he picks something off the table, stage right. 'It's also rather handy that we're filming this tonight . . . ' Yes, what a fortunate coincidence. Brown heads over to Svengali, removes the automaton's right hand, and then returns to sit with Matt, placing the dismembered, wooden hand on the table between them.

In the previous segment, Matt had proven himself to be readily sympathetic with Svengali. Facing it, he had found himself unable to resist mimicking the automaton's motion while it raised and lowered its hand. Facing the other way, Matt had seemed to feel on his own body the touches that Brown gently laid onto Svengali. And then blindfolded, after Brown had explained that Svengali was the first (and only) doll ever to have been exorcised by the Catholic Church (in 1873, following the demonstration Brown was about to perform), Matt had written out the initials that the automaton indicated on a Ouija board (with his left hand).

'Could you just put this on your right hand for me?' asks Brown, handing Matt a surgical glove. 'Now put your right hand in your lap and your left flat on the table.' Matt obliges, showing signs of nervousness. 'Now, I just want to check something. I need to check that you don't feel anything when I do this.' Brown prods and pokes at Svengali's detached hand on the table, as it lies, lifeless next to Matt's hand. 'You can't feel that can you?'

'No.'

'Nope, good. No reason you should, of course. This is a *dead* bit of wood. It *feels nothing*. It's an *inanimate* bit of wood. *No sensations* in there at all; it's *dead*.'

Everyone nods and smiles, slightly nervous.

'Now,' continues Brown, 'I just want you to look at *this* hand here.' He touches a finger on the back of Matt's left hand, flat on the table next to Svengali's right hand. 'And one last time I want you to let him take full control of that hand . . . As you watch the back of the hand, he's going to make it completely numb . . . Now, bring up your other hand and just touch yourself on the arm first – you can feel that can't you, quite normal?' Matt prods at his bicep and nods. 'Now touch the back of that hand, what's that feel like?'

Matt taps repeatedly on the back of his left hand. He shakes his head and laughs uncomfortably. 'I can't feel it at all.'

'You can't can you? It's completely dead. Can you just show them? Pinch a bit of skin and twist it right round – yank it right round – show them that you can't feel it at all. You could bash it, you could pinch it, you could *stick a needle through it*, and you really wouldn't feel a thing would you?'

Matt just shakes his head.

'Would you be prepared to do this for us? You are *very good* at this ... If I promise you that you won't feel a thing, would you be happy if we just pushed a sterilized needle right through the skin on the back of the hand?'

Matt takes a breath, unsure whether he's happy to do this. 'OK.' In the audience, people are whispering, 'No way.'

'Great, thanks, Matt. So, just a couple of health and safety points for me to adhere to as well', explains Brown as he puts on some surgical gloves and removes the 'sterilized needle' from its surgical packaging. He points out that the needle is a bit bendy so offers to stabilise Matt's skin by holding it for him while Matt sticks the pin through.

There is a moment of shock. '*I'm* going to do it?' asks Matt. The audience laughs with him and at him, sharing the discomfort.

'Yes, of course you are', replies Brown matter-of-factly. 'But I'll steady it, just because it's a bit bendy.'

Brown proceeds to pinch up a fold of skin on the back of Matt's hand, which Matt then impales with the needle, pushing it through himself without any signs of pain or physical discomfort. He's laughing quietly and nervously. The audience is full of cringing, repulsed faces.

Brown releases the pinch and the needle pulls flat against the back of Matt's hand, clearly impaling the skin, stitched through about two centimetres of flesh.

'What goes through your head as you look at that? What is it like?' asks Brown eagerly.

'I just can't feel anything.'

'Is it like looking at someone else's hand?'

'Yeah, I can't take it off the table or anything.'

'And of course, in a sense it is someone else's hand at the moment. This is also interesting, look, if I pinch it again ... ' Brown folds the skin on either side of the needle to allow Matt to withdraw it in the same way as it was inserted. 'Just slowly pull that out, and you'll see that doesn't bleed. Just slowly. Because a wooden hand does not bleed.'[6]

A modern theory of magic

The death and fear of magic

In 2005, the eccentric American magician Max Maven (Philip Goldstein) published a little book called *Protocols of the Elders of Magic*. Because of the extremely limited print run (only 500 numbered copies), the book became an instant collector's item for magicians around the world. In his own words, it is an 'unpleasant little book'.[7] It contains a century of obituaries for magic itself, beginning in 1894 with the judgement of the French illusionist Edouard-Joseph Raynaly (1842–1918) that '[modern magicians] have dealt [magic] certain blows which have thereby made it somewhat sick'. And it ends in 1992 with the death of the great Canadian 'professor' Dai Vernon (1894–1992), who had lived as 'magician in residence' at the Magical Castle in California since the 1960s. In between, it contains myriad notices and warnings about the death of magic in modern times. Writing in *The Sphinx* in August 1912, G.G. Laurens observes that 'it is the opinion of many ... that the first half of the twentieth century will witness the passing away of the conjurer'. And this seems to remain the opinion of many for nearly a hundred years. Former close-up magic world champion, Richard McDougal voices a representative view in the *Magic Circular* in January 1990: 'Magic is wonderful – but magicians let it down.'

It is certainly the case that magic has faced some serious challenges in the modern period. These are not only (and perhaps not even

---

[6] This scene is from the acclaimed Derren Brown UK production, *Svengali* (2011–2012), which won the 2012 Laurence Olivier Award for Best Entertainment Show. The show was filmed by Channel 4 and first broadcast on TV on 18 September 2012. As we saw in Chapter 1, Brown is participating in a well established fantasy about automata from the turn of the twentieth century.

[7] Max Maven, *The Protocols of the Elders of Magic*. Seattle: Hermetic Press, 2005 (unnumbered pages).

chiefly) the challenges represented by new stages for performance that ushered in the end of the Golden Age (television, film, etc.), although the impact of these has been lamented by some.[8] Rather, even as technological advances in the material and psychological sciences made ever more ambitious feats possible, so these advances simultaneously seemed to undermine the atmosphere of mystery and wonder on which the magical experience relies.[9] Not only that, but, as we saw in Chapter 1, magicians themselves were in the vanguard of social forces calling for the exposure and debunking of so-called old magicians and Spiritualists, seeking to uphold the ethical standards of Western modernity. To paraphrase Ricky Gervais, magicians seemed desperate to chop off their own feet.

However, rumours of the death of magic have been exaggerated, even if anxiety about it persists into the present day. As we saw in Chapter 1, a number of important works of cultural history have emerged in recent years, marking a resurgence of scholarly interest in the field.[10] But one of the major developments in magic in the contemporary period has been the beginning of serious attempts to understand it and to model it as a performance art in the context of Theatre Studies or

[8] An excellent account of the controversies around magic in/ and film is Matthew Solomon, *Disappearing Tricks: Silent Film, Houdini, and the New Magic of the Twentieth Century*. Urbana: University of Illinois Press, 2010, especially chapter 2.

[9] The association of modern magic with technological advancement was clear in important works such as Albert A. Hopkins, *Magic: Stage Illusions and Scientific Diversions, Including Trick Photography*. New York: Munn & Co., 1901. This book was partially drawn from a regular series of articles by Hopkins that appeared in the influential science magazine, *Scientific American*. The importance of technology and scientific devices to the pioneer of modern magic, Jean Eugene Robert-Houdin, is specifically discussed by Joshua Landy, *How to Do Things with Fictions*. New York: Oxford University Press, 2012, chapter 3, part 1. And as Matthew Solomon notes, 'the relative importance of technology and the performer was a key issue, one that was vigorously contested in controversy about the purported death of magic at the turn of the century'. *Disappearing Tricks*, p. 29.

[10] Landmarks include Simon During, *Modern Enchantments*. Cambridge: Harvard University Press, 2002; James Cook, *The Arts of Deception*. Cambridge: Harvard University Press, 2001; Matthew Solomon, *Disappearing Tricks*. Urbana & Chicago: University of Illinois Press, 2010; Karen Beckman, *Vanishing Women*. Durham, NC: Duke University Press, 2003; Fred Nadis, *Wonder Shows*. Piscataway, NJ: Rutgers University Press, 2005; Joshua Landy & Michael Saler (eds), *The Re-Enchantment of the World*. Stanford: Stanford University Press, 2009; Jane Benett, *The Enchantment of Modern Life: Crossings, Attachments, and Ethics*. Princeton: Princeton University Press, 2002. Also noteworthy is the remarkable work of popular historian (and eminent magician) Jim Steinmeyer.

Performance Studies.[11] Inspired by practitioner-theorists like Eugene Burger, Robert Neale, and Lawrence Hass, universities are starting to develop programmes in the study of performance magic. A landmark case might be the Theory and Art of Magic programme at Muhlenberg College, in the United States.[12] Given its conceptually provocative nature, magic is also finding a natural home in the context of the growth of the field of Performance Philosophy.[13] At the crossover between the academy and practice itself, there are also educational and training initiatives such as the Magic & Mystery School.[14] We are now better equipped to analyse and critique magical performances than ever before.

According to Burger, however, one of the toxic legacies of the intellectually and ethically confused history of magic in the West that we saw in the last chapter is that modern magicians – even 'legitimate magicians' – tend to be *afraid* of magic. As a consequence, they behave (and perform) in ways that compromise or even destroy the magical.[15] Burger suggests that we see this fear in a performance when, following the successful completion of a wondrous feat, the performer suddenly makes 'an exceedingly stupid joke' that completely

[11] A valuable contribution from the standpoint of Performance Studies is Michael Mangan, *Performing Dark Arts: A Cultural History of Conjuring*. Chicago: Intellect Books, 2007.

[12] An important product of this programme is Francesca Coppa, Lawrence Hass & James Peck (eds), *Performing Magic of the Western Stage*. New York: Palgrave MacMillan, 2008.

[13] Effective instances include a number of the contributions to Landy & Saler (eds), *The Re-Enchantment of the World*, especially those by Andrea Nightingale ('Broken Knowledge'), Linda Simon ('Bewitched, Bothered, and Bewildered'), and Michael Saler ('Waste Lands and Silly Valleys'). In this context, we might also consider Chris Goto-Jones, 'From Burden to Blaine: The Way of Endurance as Performance Philosophy' at *Theatre, Performance, Philosophy*. University of Paris, Sorbonne, June 2014; Chris Goto-Jones, 'Mentalism and Magical Thinking: Performance Philosophy as the Overcoming of Reason' at 2nd *Biennial Performance Philosophy Conference*, School of Art Institute of Chicago, April 2015.

[14] Founded in 1992 by Jeff McBride and supported by Eugene Burger (dean), Lawrence Hass, Robert Neale and others, the Magic & Mystery School is a progressive attempt to train magicians to be more thoughtful and effective about (and in) the art of magic. It is serious about its mandate as an institution of learning, and some of its courses give university credits. An interesting book emerging from this school is Todd Karr (ed.), *Eugene Burger, Jeff McBridge: Mystery School*. Seattle: The Miracle Factory, 2003.

[15] Eugene Burger's arguments about this appear in numerous places. Perhaps the most sustained version is in Eugene Burger & Robert Neale, *Magic and Meaning* (expanded). Seattle: Hermetic Press, 2009. (first edition, 1995).

shatters the atmosphere, reducing the potentially miraculous into something 'tacky'. This common device seems to be a response to fear or embarrassment about the possible impact a magical *feat* might accomplish if allowed to become a magical *effect*.

On the one hand, we might interpret this recourse to the comedic as one possible strategy to address the ethical imperative of 'legitimate magic'; the magician cannot easily be accused of propagating superstitions and supernaturalism if her performance is ridiculous. The ridicule undermines the stature of the magician and any potentially serious claims. But on the other hand, it hardly seems necessary to go as far as self-ridicule to convince a modern audience that a staged theatrical performance is not attempting to persuade them of the reality of counter-physical supernatural causation. Instead of being a strategic response to moral panic, then, this move looks like a simple confession of embarrassment. Which suggests to the audience that the magician herself believes her feats are 'trivial, insignificant, silly, not important'.[16]

As early as 1911, theorists of magic were already cautioning magicians against representing themselves and their art in trivial and debased ways. In the same breath as calling on magicians to embody 'legitimate magic' by avoiding giving the impression that they claimed any supernatural powers, Maskelyne warned of the dangers of 'japes' and 'wheezes' that risk debasing the profession: 'what respect can the public have for men who do not respect their own work?'[17] He wanted to draw a distinction between the legitimate use of humour to enhance an effect or its entertainment value (which he applauded) and trivial patter that 'not only degrades himself and his performance, but reflects discredit on the whole magical profession'. Such degrading patter included 'making fun of his art' itself, making any allusion to the social class (or poverty or education) of either magicians or their audience, or asserting any alliance between magic, 'humbug, swindling or chicanery of any kind'. Instead, the modern, legitimate magician should be aspiring towards *artistry* in her performance, and thus contributing to the elevation of performance magic as an art.

In his influential commentary on the theory of Maskelyne & Devant, *Through Magic-Coloured Spectacles* (1976–1981), Sam Sharpe endorsed this basic view of the role of humour in magical performance,

---

[16] Burger & Neale, *Magic and Meaning*, p. 2.
[17] Maskelyne & Devant, *Our Magic*, p. 146.

arguing against the use of cheap or 'derisive' jokes and insisting that 'true comedy in conjuring arises from the magical situations themselves, not from extraneous matter in the form of funny patter or clowning'.[18] All magic, he adds, is 'funny peculiar' in the sense that it deals with the unusual and incongruous, but 'funny ha-ha' has to be carefully managed. The humour of magic should properly reside in the discomfort of the eerie and uncanny.

As recently as 2003, in his 'Note on Perverse Spectator Handling', Derren Brown has lamented the tendency for fellow magicians to dress their performances in crass or rude behaviour, presumably on the basis that they believe (patronizingly) that this will generate some form of rapport with their audience: 'Am I missing something obvious, or is there something deeply perverse about interrupting people while they are enjoying themselves, demanding that they trust you when we do nothing to communicate that trustworthiness, and then make insulting comments ... I hope that a magician has made an insulting comment about someone's shirt and then been punched in the face.'[19] Brown goes on to elaborate why this 'may be the stuff of comedy, but it is not the stuff of magic', theorizing that the reason for this situation is the insecurity and embarrassment felt by most magicians in contemporary society, where their 'art' is seen as (at best) rather geeky.[20] 'When the performer works from a base-point of embarrassment at his own material or presence, the performance becomes inherently embarrassing.'[21] Brown's own acclaimed performances are notable for their confident wit and carefully controlled humour, as well as for their architectural irony. As he freely admits, 'there can be no nerdiness in our model of magic'.[22]

What Brown sees as a performer's *embarrassment* about magic tends towards what Burger identifies as the magician's *fear* of magic. It appears to be a feature of the performance culture of modern magic, but also seems to have been a continuous concern in the field

[18] S.H. Sharpe, *Through Magic-Coloured Spectacles*. Originally albeit intermittently serialized in the Magic Circular (1976–1981). Reprinted in *Art and Magic*. Los Angeles: The Miracle Factory, 2003, pp. 309–310.

[19] Derren Brown, 'A Note on Perverse Spectator Handling', *Absolute Magic: A Model for powerful Close-Up performance*. Humble, TX: H&R Magic Books, 2003, p. 204.

[20] In his *Performance of Close-Up Magic* (KAUFMAN & Company, 1987), Eugene Burger talks about the role of 'Uncle Geek' in the trivialization of magic.

[21] Brown, *Absolute Magic*, p. 207.   [22] Brown, *Absolute Magic*, p. 131.

since early modern theorists like Maskelyne. Hence, when Victor Sansoucie asks Burger whether the horrible joke that shatters a magical effect is the result of 'a traditional magical upbringing', he really means to ask whether this is a consequence of a *modern* magical upbringing. Modern 'magicians have been taught that people do not believe in magic, so don't insult them by professing to have any magical power'.[23] The fear and embarrassment about performing magic thus leads to derision of self, other, and magic. Crucially, magicians fail to convey their own belief and conviction in their magic, and this absence of 'belief on his own part will infallibly carry a like conviction to the minds of the spectators'.[24]

As Burger observes, most of us in modern societies have grown up watching magicians behave in this self-recriminatory way, which not only reinforces this pattern of behaviour as the norm but also sullies our exposure to the experience of the *magical* itself. That is, many people will have seen dozens of magicians and witnessed many *feats* or *tricks*,[25] but most of these people will never have felt a magical *effect*, witnessed magical *behaviour*, or had a magical *experience* at a performance. In other words, self-conscious, cynical, derisive comedy (resulting from embarrassment about the concept of magic in modernity) risks destroying even the ethically 'legitimate' experience of magic in contemporary societies.[26] The performances of many so-called magicians (however entertaining they may be) serve mainly to sever the connection between magic 'tricks' and the experience of the *magical*. When the magician is afraid of magic, the audience holds it in contempt.

Hence, despite being performed everyday on stages (including TV, movies, and the internet) all over the world, often to massive audiences, legitimate modern magic retains some of the features and powers of a *taboo* – the compulsion to speak 'entirely ridiculous sorts of sometimes-humorous "lines" or "patter"' is society's way of

[23] Victor Sansoucie in conversation with Eugene Burger, in Burger & Neale, *Meaning and Magic*, p. 2.

[24] Jean Eugene Robert-Houdin, *Secrets of Conjuring and Magic* (English edition, 1877, reprinted by Cambridge University Press, 2011, p. 33.

[25] Like Maskelyne and others, Burger believes that 'the word "trick" is also part of this conditioning'. *Magic and Meaning*, p. 2.

[26] It is in this context that we must understand Burger's complaint that it is so 'unfortunate that so little is written about why ninety percent or more of all conjuring is wrapped up in comedy. And, if I may say so, low comedy at that!' (*Magic and Meaning*, p. 4).

neutralizing the taboo of *feeling* something magical. On this view, both the magician and the audience are complicit in an attempt to disenchant magic because of the modern *fear of experiencing the quality of 'magical'*.[27] This is importantly and radically different from a pre-modern fear of experiencing counter-physical supernatural causation in 'old magic'. That is, the fear in question is not focussed on the potential collapse of the laws of nature (and the chaos that might ensue), but rather is the fear of having an experience (which doesn't break those laws) that makes you feel (or causes another to feel) genuinely mystified and enchanted.[28] To twist Maskelyne's terms a little, for the audience, it is not the fear that our *intelligence* is being defrauded, but rather the fear that our *senses* are being defrauded.[29] From the standpoint of the audience, this form of the fear of magic might approximate the fear of *intoxication*; from the standpoint of the magician, the fear is of *intoxicating*.

Modern magic appreciation and criticism

It is not the case that cheap jokes and buffoonery are the only responses to a fear of magic. Contemporary critics have also been keen to draw a distinction between the experience of magic and the experience of *confusion*. Indeed, as the great Dai Vernon was known to repeat,

[27] The precise parameters of what kind of experience is meant by 'magical' is discussed delicately by Simon During, who seeks to differentiate it from other related concepts such as wonderful, miraculous, fantastic, and uncanny. During, *Modern Enchantments*, esp. pp. 27–32. However, for our purposes, it is important to recognize the way in which the flavor of magic (and hence its affective qualities) ranges across these various meanings depending on the context and style of a given performance.

[28] As we will see, the experience of 'magic' is importantly different from the experience of being puzzled, which is a cognitive state in which we seek to calculate and reason the solution. The idea of the magical is that it an experience that feels beyond the reasonable. Burger notes that 'comedy can so easily change the magical experience into the experience of a puzzle' (*Magic and Meaning*, p. 4).

[29] It's not clear that this distinction is consistently maintained in the critical literature, where, for instance, Burger seems ambiguous about these two types of fear when he talks about the origins of a magician's fear and embarrassment: 'I suspect that it is that dim realization, lurking behind our "civilized" consciousness, that the very idea of *magic* suggests a worldview surprisingly and breathtakingly *different* from that suggested by our "common sense," from the picture most of us were conditioned to believe' (*Magic and Meaning*, p. 3).

'confusion is not magic'.[30] Vernon lamented the tendency amongst his peers to obscure their feats behind muddle and confusion, rather than dressing them with respectability or as elevated mysteries, leaving their audience unsure about what they have witnessed and thus unsure about what kind of experience they were supposed to have had. In such circumstances, there is no magical *effect*, and the audience is left feeling *tricked* or even annoyed. It feels like a *con*. As Burger observes, 'once the audience becomes confused, their confusion destroys the magical experience. If I am confused, I have the sense that something (anything) might have happened that I didn't notice because of my confusion. To be in such a state is not to experience something magical.'[31] When a card magician obscures her hands from view or does something that looks very unnatural, the audience becomes alert to the likelihood of a counter-intuitive outcome – they may not know what the magician did (they may be confused by it), but they know she did something to bring about this feat (that they didn't see or understand).

In other words, the experience of magic – the magical affect – relies upon a performance that makes the proceedings seem clear, straightforward, and *fair*. The astonishment that we associate with the magical arises only when the accomplishment of the feat seems impossible given the stages that preceded it. If the preceding stages had no logical (or otherwise predictable) trajectory, this sense of astonishment is jeopardized and we are left with confusion. In his later work, Sam Sharpe was careful to differentiate between confusion and complexity, arguing that while complexity in concept and performance can result in confusion when badly handled, at the opposite extreme there is the danger that 'oversimplification inevitably leads to a lack of charm or enchantment'. For Sharpe, the idea of complexity is related to the accomplishment of subtlety, finesse, and artistic routining; he sees it as a way to combat a tendency towards lowest-common-denominator audiences 'whose attention and intelligence must not be strained'.[32] Hence, he cautions magicians not to abandon artistic ambitions towards complexity of feat, effect, and performance solely because of a desire to avoid confusing an audience; complexity must be handled with finesse and clarity, but oversimplification risks patronizing the audience as well

---

[30] This is known to have been a pet phrase of Vernon. It is recorded in Dai Vernon, *Expanded Lecture Notes*. Chicago: Magic Publishing, 1964.

[31] Burger, *Magic and Meaning*, p. 14.

[32] Sharpe, 'Magic-Coloured Spectacles', pp. 277–280.

as undermining the possibility of achieving a magical effect.[33] The potential rewards of complexity in terms of creative expression must always be weighed against the risks of confusion at the expense of the magical experience.

Connected to the dangers of confusion is the experience of *puzzlement*. Again, many contemporary thinkers about magic are critical of performances that seem designed to provoke (or even not to discourage) the audience from trying to puzzle out how the feat was accomplished. Of course, this is not to deny that most audiences (not only modern audiences) will respond to the experience of witnessing something apparently inexplicable by trying to work out how it was done; the inexplicable invites explication. The point rather, is that this should not be the principal response – the experience of the magical should involve the thrill and pleasure of being mystified, not merely provoke an inquiry into the possible mechanisms deployed.[34] A truly magical performance should be transporting; it should tap into the magical imagination of an audience and tease the frontiers of their magical beliefs. Pushing too far could provoke resistance and backlash (or moral dilemmas); not pushing far enough is simply to turn a trick or perpetrate a con.[35]

For this and other reasons, some modern theorists of magic have suggested that the best possible audience for a magician is one composed entirely of other magicians. This is not only because, presumably, the accomplishment of a feat of magic (without being 'caught out') in front of such a well-informed audience is already a professional accomplishment of some magnitude. Rather, it is also because an audience of magicians will already be predisposed to view a performance analytically – treating it as a puzzle to be solved by inspecting how apparatus is deployed and which techniques are used – and hence achieving a magical *effect* (by communicating the experience of the

---

[33] In his earlier work, *Neo-Magic* (Bradford: Clegg & Son, 1932/46), Sharpe made a hierarchy of merit for conjuring effects, in which the deployment of complexity can be seen to be a high-risk, high-reward strategy: 1. Good complex; 2. Good simple; 3. Poor simple; 4. Poor complex (p. 21).

[34] This 'magic way' is beautifully illustrated by Jan Tamariz as his 'method of false solutions'. Juan Tamariz, *The Method of False Solutions and The Magic Way*. Seattle: Hermetic Press, 2014 (previously in Spanish, 1987/2011).

[35] As Derren Brown puts it, 'your aim as a magician is to create and manipulate wonder and astonishment while avoiding confusion and mere puzzle solving on the part of the spectator'. *Pure Effect*, p. 23.

magical) for this audience is a singular challenge. Indeed, the audience will be uniquely well qualified to understand, critique, and appreciate the extent to which a magician's *performance* has transformed technical competency into magical behaviour.[36]

One fascinating implication of this approach is that it opens the possibility for a magical performance in which the techniques deployed are not hidden at all, since the quality of 'magical' resides in the performance and not in the secret technologies that undergird it. This enables our consideration of so-called manipulation as magical, if it is performed appropriately. For instance, one of the most influential magical feats to emerge from Japan in the nineteenth century was the so-called Butterfly Trick, in which the performer keeps one or more paper butterflies in flight around him through the device of a simple folding fan. Although the device being deployed is clear to everyone – there is little *trickery* – the effect can be so enchanting that the experience is magical nonetheless.[37] Indeed, audiences are sometimes so enchanted by the effect that they question whether it could really be accomplished using such a simple device; the experience of the magical becomes a critique of technology. In the same vein, in the twentieth century, we might consider the astonishing work of the British magician Cardini (Richard Valentine Pitchford, 1895–1973) as an instance of an explicit card manipulator whose performances were uncontroversially magical, and perhaps contrast his performances with those of contemporary 'extreme card manipulation' (XCM) or 'cardistry' in which the display

---

[36] In their preface to their *Our Magic*, Maskelyne and Devant declare a 'well known fact, viz.: – that the very best audience a skilled magician can have is one composed entirely of magicians.... Such an audience will very seldom be perplexed by what is exhibited, and will never attach great importance to "how it is done." Every member of such an audience will have his mind engrossed, almost exclusively, in noting the art with which the performer uses devices, known or unknown, to produce an intended effect. If his art be meritorious, the expert spectators will appreciate the performance highly, no matter how old, how new, how ingenious or how simple may be the technical devices employed' (pp. vi–vii). Later in the book, Maskelyne explains that magicians might also develop entirely new techniques to enable them to deliver performances to other magicians that will confound them technically as well as artistically. Yet he cautions magicians not to presume that these techniques would also be superior for a general audience: the magician must match her choice of technique and performance to the tastes and capacities of her audience to ensure maximum magical effect (pp. 32, 60–61).

[37] In fact, there is often a 'trick' to this effect that involves the use of a fine thread (or human hair) to prevent the 'butterflies' from simply flying away.

Figure 2.1 Dante, 'Oriental'. Courtesy of Nielsen Magic Collection. Danish magician Harry August Jansen, 1883–1955, was given the name Dante by his mentor, Thurston, in 1922.

of incredible manual dexterity is the goal in itself. XCM resembles a sport as much as a discipline of magic. Here we approach the always marshy and disputed borderlands between magic and jugglery, recalling Robert-Houdin: 'a conjuror is not a juggler: he is an actor playing the part of a magician'.

As we saw in Chapter 1, the extent to which a magician should want to draw an audience's attention to her technical expertise has been hotly debated in the modern period: an audience's appreciation of a magician's skill is often inversely proportionate to their experience of the magical. Nonetheless, contemporary societies place a high premium on the display of skill, so there is considerable commercial pressure on magicians to put it on display it – many magicians work for years to be able to perform certain feats of sleight of hand or mental dexterity. For some critics, the ostentatious display of skill, like 'stupid jokes or a condescending, superior attitude', is one of the 'greatest culprits in moving audiences towards the analytical experience' rather than the magical experience.[38] In addition to the clumsy emphasis on technological devices, it is because of concerns about the prevalence of these kinds of attitudes and behaviours that Max Maven was able to assemble his 'unpleasant little book', foretelling the doom of magic at the hands of modern magicians.

At the other end of the scale, we might consider performances that make no claims to produce a magical effect on their audiences but which make open and clear use of the techniques and devices of magicians. In the common parlance, we call such performances *exposés*. Historically, as we have seen, the exposé has been used for all kinds of social, political, and ethical purposes: confronting the injustices of the witch-trials; debunking the claims of charlatan spiritualists; inspiring the public about the emancipatory potentials of science, and so on. Indeed, for a period at the turn of the twentieth century, debunking claims to supernatural powers through exposé was seen as one of the core tasks of the 'legitimate' magician.

However, the development of the slightly unusual, commercial genre of 'magical exposé' (in which the devices and techniques of stage magic – which the contemporary audience already knows are not supernatural – are revealed to an audience as a form of entertainment in itself) is of more recent origin. In many cases, such performances rest

[38] Burger, *Magic and Meaning*, p. 24.

on the conceit that, despite living in a cultural context in which belief in counter-physical supernatural causation (i.e., magical belief) is at best marginal, it remains a service to the public to systematically debunk the performances of stage performers.[39] Whether or not this is really the case, it is clear that performances of magical exposé have a commercial place in modern societies. Rather than participating in a social or ethical mission to overcome superstition, such exposés seem to capitalize on the decline of magic into a form of puzzle – providing the solutions for audiences whose experiences of so-called magic have merely served to provoke the analytical question, 'how did she do that?' In turn, the exposé industry fuels public perceptions that the appropriate way to engage with a magician is to attempt to work out how she is accomplishing her feats.

In other words, the exposé industry emerges from and then consolidates what Maven laments as the death of magic. However, it is important to realize that the contribution of exposé to this decline in magic is not (or at least not chiefly) because the devices, techniques and skills of magicians are revealed to the general public. To some extent (although the actual extent is controversial), it doesn't matter if the audience knows how a feat is accomplished since the quality of *magical* is not contained in the devices or techniques but in the performance and the subsequent effect. In the modern world, we know that *magical* is a performative quality or a quality of experience, not another name for supernatural causation. So, the damage done by exposé is, primarily, the public dissociation of magical feats from the experience of wonder and their association with puzzlement instead. No matter how entertaining an exposé performance might be, there is nothing magical about the experience of watching it – its purpose is antithetical to the magical experience. Although, if the critics are to be believed, there is also nothing very magical about the performances of many magicians either,

---

[39] One of the additional differences between the contexts of early and late twentieth century is the widespread (and often free) availability of information about how magical feats are accomplished in contemporary societies. It is not longer the case that either an exposé or even a legitimate magic show contains many 'secrets' unavailable to a curious member of the public with an internet connection. Indeed, as early as 1876, Professor Hoffmann had already noted that 'there is hardly a trick performed upon the stage which the amateur may not, at a sufficient expenditure of shillings or guineas, procure at the conjuring depôt. There being, therefore, no longer the same strict secrecy, the literature of magic has improved a little'. Professor Hoffmann, *Modern Magic*, p. 2.

rendering the main difference between the 'magician' and the 'exposer' simply whether or not they *attempt to trick* (not even yet enchant) their audience.[40]

From this counter-intuitive standpoint, it seems that modern magicians actually support and participate in the business of exposé when their performances communicate puzzlement rather than magic. If audiences really experienced these performances as instances of magical behaviour that buoyed their magical imaginations, and hence were mostly interested in their artistry and beauty, they would be no more likely to pay to watch an exposé of magic than an exposé of the secrets of painting or dancing after a visit to the Tate or the Royal Ballet.[41] Exposé is as much a symptom of the failure of magic as it is a cause of its decline.

As early as 1911, magicians were themselves already debating the relative merits of exposing their techniques to the public. For instance, despite the motto of the Magic Circle (*Indocilis Privata Loqui*), of which they were successive presidents, Maskelyne and Devant proclaimed that there was nothing wrong with revealing the secrets of the trade, precisely because magic did not reside in those secrets but in the artistry of the performer.[42] As we saw in the last

[40] Following the innovative performances of Penn & Teller, who dressed brilliant magic in the guise of exposé, it is now a well-established convention for magicians to attempt to combine the persona of exposer with the ambitions of the magician – using fraudulent exposé as cover for magical feats and effects. A nice discussion of this aspect of Penn & Teller is Robert Neale, 'Illusions about Illusions', in Coppa, Hass, & Peck, *Performing Magic on the Western Stage*.

[41] Claims to this magnitude of artistic importance for magic are controversial and, to some, ludicrous. While Maskelyne certainly pushed in this direction, leading voices after him have been reluctant to take things this far. Even S.H. Sharpe cautioned against being overly laudatory about the artistic potentials of magic. In recent years, reflecting on Paul Harris' affectionate magic books, *The Art of Astonishment* (3 vols., MURPHY'S Magic Supplies, 1996/2007), in which Harris suggests that the experience of astonishment is a glorious return to a primal state of mind, Derren Brown cautions that 'it is dangerously flattering to ourselves to believe that we are putting people in touch with something primal and perfect through the very act of performing magic'. *Absolute Magic*, p. 49.

[42] This position is echoed today by the great inventor of illusions and magical equipment, Jim Steinmeyer, who puts the matter beautifully: 'Magicians guard an empty safe. There are few secrets that they possess which are beyond a gradeschool science class, little technology more complex than a rubber band, a square of black fabric or a length of thread. There are no real principles worthy of being cherished, only crude expediences. But magicians have learned to appreciate how such simple devices can be manipulated into illusion, how a piece of thread can, through feints and contrivances,

chapter, with characteristic investment in Victorian values of education as key to a progressive civilization, these famous magicians framed exposé as part of their moral responsibility to educate the public into better understanding of the arts. Exactly as it was necessary to educate people about music and painting (so that they may be better able to judge and appreciate them), so it would be good for society to be educated about the techniques of magic – not to debunk it, but to enable its proper, elevated appreciation.[43] Indeed, for Maskelyne and Devant, taking magic seriously as a performance art *required* this kind of pro-gramme of public education – they had a moral obligation to expose their *craft* in order to enable it as an *art*. They fantasized about the levels of art that might be reached if all magic performances were akin to performances in front of an audience of discerning magicians.

Of course, seminal and influential as Maskelyne and Devant's work was, it was (and remains) controversial. A generous critique might be that of Sam Sharpe, who notes simply that *Our Magic* was overly enthusiastic about exposé (and about art). Sharpe notes that Maskelyne and Devant pushed their case too far when they argued that 'in order fully to appreciate the acting and presentation of the conjurer' and thus the magical effect, 'they consider (in theory) that it is necessary to divulge his secrets'.[44] While Sharpe is highly sympathetic to the idea that modern magic can be (and should be) an art, he is clear that exposé is not a *necessary* feature of art or of the experience of the magical. An accomplished magician himself, he talks of the wonder-ful feeling of enchantment he experiences when a talented magician performs a feat using techniques he does not know (as long as that feat is performed in a manner appropriate to the communication of a magical effect). Even if he agrees that exposé does not of itself destroy the possibility of a magical experience, Sharpe's point is simply that exposé is not a *necessary* preparation for the experience of magic – it is not a condition of the possibility of enchantment, although *qua*

for the centerpiece for five minutes of entertainment. The art of the magician is not found in the simple deception, but in what surrounds it, the construction of a reality which supports the illusion.'*Art & Artifice and Other Essays on Illusion.* New York: Carrol & Graf, 1998/2006, pp. 7–8.

[43] 'So far from feeling any reluctance towards letting the general public into the secrets of our procedure, we are most anxious to educate the public in such matters, in order that a proper understanding of our art may be disseminated among its votaries and patrons.' Maskelyne & Devant, *Our Magic*, p. vi.

[44] Sharpe, 'Magic-Coloured Spectacles', p. 237.

education such knowledge might sometimes enhance it. An ignorant audience can still experience (and appreciate) mystery, wonder, and magic.

For some, one of the consequences of the modern concern for techniques and devices that undergirds interest in exposé has been the shift in emphasis away from the artistry of performance and towards a more direct presentation of props, as though the material equipment used on stage were itself the subject and purpose of the performance. As we've seen, this was a major feature of 'modernity' in the stage magic of the Golden Age, with spectacular props and stagings doing much of the work themselves. This tendency has been disparagingly referred to as transforming modern magic into the 'adventures of the props in the performer's hands'. Symptoms of this apparent malady are still evident at every level of the art, from the children's 'magic set' that promises to enable the performance of magic (with various props) within minutes of opening the box, through to grand stage illusions in which the performer (and his assistant) is almost irrelevant to the show. As early as 1897, a *New York Times* reviewer lamented how much of a performance was 'given up to the exhibition of mechanical tricks' because 'in these mechanical illusions the principal performer is really of no use at all. The trick would proceed to its startling climax even if he remained in his dressing room'.[45]

However, as Burger states very flatly, 'magic ... isn't about the props. Magic is about life.' Props do not create the experience of magic by themselves: putting a volunteer into an odd-looking box that then gives the impression he has been cut in half or vanished altogether does not provoke the feeling of magic by itself, but rather provokes an audience to wonder how the box works. Where is the mirror? Where is the second person hiding? To the extent that it's present, a magical aura is cast over the props by the personality and style of the performer and the presentation. Hence, the box is decorated in a particular way; the performer explicates its functioning in a special manner. Patter matters. A magical *performance* should transform the props into symbols of a larger mystery, of a larger world in which the magical imagination and magical effects are valued. To the contrary, however, in the spirit of the death of magic, Burger laments that 'the props have lost

---

[45] This is a review of Dixey, who was an emerging star of the magic scene (much praised by his peers and the trade press). Cited in Solomon, *Disappearing Tricks*, p. 29.

their symbolic value and power, and so they have become the end in themselves' on the contemporary stage.[46]

Magical restoration

In addition to all the angst and soul-searching that we have been exploring in this chapter, the modern era has also seen various movements in magic that have attempted to reinvigorate the field in practice. In the last chapter, we saw how magicians in the so-called Golden Age of magic around the turn of the twentieth century attempted to respond to the death knells of magic by organizing themselves into professional associations (such as the Society of American Magicians, the Magic Circle, and then the International Brotherhood of Magicians) in order to promote education and good practice. These fraternities cultivated a self-consciously modern style in order to enchant audiences with the mysteries and accomplishments of technology. Performers also exploited the ways in which the aesthetics of Orientalism could be deployed as mechanisms to communicate the idea of mystery and wonder, apparently from a timeline historically 'other' than that of Europe. In the second half of the twentieth century, though, the most powerful movements have been 'Bizarre Magic' and 'Street Magic'. As we'll see, these styles owe much to earlier developments in the mystical revival, even as they *appear* so different.

So-called Bizarre Magic found its origins in the counter culture of the 1950s and 1960s. Its proponents were deeply influenced by the work of Howard Phillips Lovecraft, whose brand of supernatural horror became tremendously popular only after his death in 1937.[47] In many ways, Bizarre Magic was a direct response to the perceived disenchantment and death of magic; in the face of ever more impressive technological accomplishments and spectacular props, it was an unapologetic and flamboyant attempt to refocus the performance of magic on the performance itself. And in the context of increasingly spectacular special effects on TV and in the movies,

---

[46] Burger, *Magic and Meaning*, p. 6.

[47] Leading proponents in this early wave included Charles Cameron, Tony Shiels, Tony Raven, and Tony Andruzzi. More recently, leading voices have included Max Maven, Eugene Burger, Stephen Minch, and Jeff McBride. The movement had its own periodical, *New Invocation*, edited by Andruzzi (aka Masklyn ye Mage), which ran from 1979 to 1996.

together with the grand, camp spectacle of Las Vegas magic shows, Bizarre Magic represented a symbolic return to an idea of magic that was not glossy and shiny, but instead was macabre and dirty. Supporters of Bizarre Magic added a 'k' and called it magick.[48] In the words of Matthew Field, proponents worried that 'to many people, magic is a lesser craft, holding the same position in the arts that a pie in the face does when one is discussing Shakespeare'. He considered 'the possibility of bizarre magick restoring the sense of awe missing from the magic of today'.[49]

The notion of a *magical restoration* (and not only in the sense of a torn banknote) is appropriate, since the Bizarre Magicians looked back romantically to an age in which magic was seen as sacred, eerie, and frightening, finding the appropriate imaginary in the dark fantasy of H.P. Lovecraft and Thomas Malory. Indeed, in his famous 'Undelivered Lecture', the theorist Sam Sharpe prevails on magicians to think about the glamour of mystical and foreboding figures such as Merlin. He suggests that 'one of many definitions of magic might be: Illusion plus Glamour', where 'Glamour is a deceptive mask of enchantment or allurement of the emotions for the purpose of overcoming the powers of observation and reason'.[50] Sharpe goes on to explain the essential connection between the performance of *ritual* and the accomplishment of glamour, linking both to the magical dramatization of apparatus, costume, gesture, and movement.

Sharpe observes that 'we have suburbanized the enchanter Merlin and made him respectable by stripping him of his glimmering robe of legend-fairy lore, and dolling him up in a boiled shirt'. He laments the replacement of incantations with wisecracks and the taming of a 'poetic giant'.[51] Then, having reduced this heroic Magus to an

---

[48] 'Magick' is an early modern English spelling of 'magic'; it was consistently used in seventeenth century translations of occultist texts. In the twentieth century, it was re-evoked by new-occultists such as Aleister Crowley as a way to differentiate between what they considered 'real and potent' magic and the new, 'fake' magic of stage performers. In the context of his Thelema (will) beliefs, Crowley defined magick as the science and art of accomplishing change to accord with one's will. Aleister Crowley, *Magick: Liber ABA, Book 4*. London: Wieland & Co., 1913.

[49] Matthew Field, 'Foreword'. Eugene Burger, *Strange Ceremonies*. Kaufman & Company, 1991, p. 9.

[50] S.H. Sharpe, 'Acted Magic: An Undelivered Lecture (cont.)'. *Magic Circular*, 69 (1975), p. 204.

[51] Sharpe, 'Acted Magic', p. 205. In fact, Sharpe has an elaborate theory about the ideal affinities between magic and poetry, which is developed in his earlier works, *Conjured*

'insignificant stature, we somewhat naively turn to wondering where his magic has gone'.

The point Sharpe is pursuing is very simple: when we (in the West) think about great icons of magic, we think about Merlin or Gandalf or Sparrowhawk (and now Dumbledore). These *are* our cultural fantasies of magicians; they have *glamour*.[52] We do not (in general) think of Bobo the Clown or our Uncle Geek as exemplars of magical greatness. And, since the performance of magic is also a fictional enterprise (like any other piece of theatre), why should magicians shy away from associating themselves with these fantastical wizards rather than with a particular group of amateur hobbyists who make us cringe? Allusion allies with illusion. Performers take themselves and their art too seriously and not seriously enough at the same time.

To be clear, Sharpe is not advocating an anachronistic return to a pre-modern framework for magical performance in which the magician exploits the credulity of the magical beliefs of her audience. This is not a call for a return to what Maskelyne called charlatanism. Sharpe does not believe the magicians of today (or of any day) are real Merlins, nor does he believe in this level of public credulity. Rather, Sharpe wants to draw our attention to the magic of symbolism and cultural tradition: participants in an 'ancient art' should build upon and enrich its tradition, not ignore or obscure it, not be embarrassed by or frightened of it. 'It were folly to suggest that we in our day return to magic of the magician's sanctum and the wizard's dip. That would be decadent and retrograde. Each generation of artists must find a way of presenting the eternal magical symbols in its own fashion in order to survive.'[53] Modern magicians should not throw out their cultural heritage just because the Victorians and Edwardians found it distasteful: making creative use of the past is not the same as attempting to return to it, indeed it is a sign of artistic maturity. In his commentary on the theoretical work of Maskelyne, Sharpe phrases this faith in magical

Up (1935), and *Good Conjuring* (1936) (now reprinted in S.H. Sharpe, *Neo-Magic Artistry*. Seattle: The Miracle Factory, 2000), where he establishes the idea of 'Poems in Illusion' as the most appropriate label for beautiful and effective magical performances. His sense of the poetic relies on Plato: 'Poetry is a general name signifying every cause whereby anything proceeds from that which is not into that which is, so that the exercise of every inventive art is poetry; and all such artists, poets' (p. 195).

[52] It is noteworthy that 'glamour' is also an archaic word for the magic of the faerie folk, which was held to change the appearance of things, especially of the faerie themselves.

[53] Sharpe, 'Acted Magic', p. 205.

iconography as an endorsement of Maskelyne's position: 'it was, we believe, Robert-Houdin who said that a conjurer is in reality "an actor playing the part of a magician." There is only one fault in that statement. He should have said "a great [magician]." Because, as we all know, there are many conjurers who only play the part of some other conjurer.'[54]

In other words, in his 'Undelivered Lecture', Sharpe is calling on the members of the Magic Circle to recognize that the most prevalent styles of performance seem to be stagnant and mediocre, lacking in the language (and experience) of magic, mystery, and wonder. He ends his lecture with an emotional and emotive call to action:

> And why do none dare to include in their programmes a single effect presented with all the high solemnity of Magic in the Grand Style? Is there not one among us with the courage and dynamic drive of magical genius behind him to set a new pace? Surely our ranks cannot for much longer remain in their present state of conglomerated mediocrity, awaiting the fire of an inspired arch-magus with whom we can identify our ancient art, so that his spirit shall liberate us from our petty bonds of cynicism and doubt, and guide us in our quest to new magical horizons.[55]

This kind of manifesto for a new magic appears dramatically at odds with the manifestos developed at the turn of the twentieth century, when magicians since Robert-Houdin, the Maskelynes, and then Houdini implored their compatriots to avoid Medievalisms and pointy hats at all costs: 'the most probable result of assuming the conventional garb of a wizard will be to make the wearer an object of derision'.[56] As Professor Hoffmann recommends as early as 1876, 'the costume de rigueur of the

---

[54] Maskelyne, *Our Magic*, p. 5. Sharpe cites this in *Magic-Coloured Spectacles* (p. 263). While he endorses the idea that a conjuror should play the part of a *great magician* (like Merlin) rather than just another conjuror, he further notes that Maskelyne places too much faith in the idea that only acting will be enough to accomplish this. In reality, a conjuror can only play the role of a great magician if he/she has superior dexterity and skills in the techniques of magic as well as superior acting ability (including the capacity to believe in the role being played). Great magicians let alone great conjurors are those of rare ability, just as great actors and great musicians are rarer than merely good, competent, or terrible ones.

[55] Sharpe, 'Acted Magic', p. 205.

[56] Robert-Houdin, *Secrets of Conjuring and Magic*, p. 36. This is Robert-Houdin's fifteenth and final 'general principle' of modern magic.

magician of the present day is ordinary "evening dress".'[57] However, what Sharpe shares with these famous voices is the idea that the experience of the magical resides in an artistic sensitivity to the spirit of the times and to the public representations of 'real magic' in those times – the archaic concept of faerie *glamour* is non-trivial. While Robert-Houdin avoided pointy hats, his compatriots enthusiastically dressed up as Indian fakirs, Japanese princes, or Chinese 'celestials' in the belief that these imparted *glamour* to their performances.[58]

Hence, as critics continue to talk of the death of magic, what is needed above all else (above new techniques and devices) is for a new generation of performers to develop new styles of dramatization and performance that resonate with the audiences of the day. As we've seen, at the turn of the twentieth century, this meant 'experiments' by gentlemanly 'professors of magic' or 'mysterious illusions' by fakirs from the 'mystic East'; today, it means the urban-themed street magic of David Blaine and Dynamo, or the complex blends of retro-theatrical hypnosis, suggestion, and magic associated with Derren Brown.

Sharpe's manifesto echoed through the clubhouses of England during the middle of the emergence of the Bizarre Magic movement, which was already embracing many of these ideas about glamour and drama. Indeed, for Stephen Minch there was a sense in which the Bizarre was really a literary or theatrical movement, not only because it emerged so clearly from Lovecraftian horror but also because of its emphasis on drama and aesthetics (rather than technologies and devices *per se*). His 1979 book, *Lovecraftian Ceremonies*, was an elaborate fiction tailored for magicians. He carefully described how to set up and perform various magical rituals (that had never existed), based on the conceit that Lovecraft's fictional universe was a real historical setting. Hence, the book contains instructions on how to perform the 'Stigmata of Cthulhu' and the 'Ceremony of the Eye'.[59] At about the same time, under the

---

[57] Hoffmann, *Modern Magic*, p. 9.

[58] It is noteworthy that the pointy hat, so closely associated with Western wizardry, is also likely to have been of 'Oriental' origin. Marina Warner explains that the 'magician's steeple hat [was] inspired by the dress of dervishes'. *Stranger Magic: Charmed States and the Arabian Nights.* Cambridge: Harvard University Press, 2012, p. 26.

[59] Stephen Minch, *Lovecraftian Ceremonies: Seven Occult Dramas for the Magickal Performer.* Bob Lynn, 1979. Now reproduced in Stephen Minch, *The Book of Forgotten Secrets.* Seattle: Hermetic Press, 2009. Simon During could have been talking about Bizarre Magic when he wrote: 'given its suffusion in fantasy, there

ironic pen name Masklyn ye Mage, Tony Andruzzi published a series of beautifully handmade books that culminated in the *Legendary Scroll of Masklyn ye Mage* (1983).[60] The scroll was completely handmade in 'traditional' style and even hand lettered. It was carefully aged to resemble popular fantasies of ancient scrolls, and production numbers were so small as to make ownership exclusive. The scroll describes a dozen effects and rituals.

Performances of the fictional rituals from the canon of Bizarre Magic constituted deliberate attempts to fantasticalize magic once again – to associate the performance of magic with our cultural fantasies about magic – in the hope that doing so would help to achieve magical effects and experiences for the audience, albeit in a darkly ironic (Bizarre) dramatic framework.[61]

In many ways, in its quest for arcane *glamour*, the Bizarre Magic movement was the inheritor of the Orientalist Magic movement that we'll explore in the next chapter. The Orient that was depicted in such performances often had no greater historical veracity than the world of Cthulhu, even if its imaginary aesthetics contributed to the creation of a magical atmosphere for performers during the mystical revival. Both Orientalism and the Bizarre deployed fantasy fictions as elements in the creation of magical effects. And in both cases there were people (both magicians and their audiences) who missed the literary pretensions of these aesthetics and sincerely believed that they were engaged in historically authentic activities. Perhaps taking Robert-Houdin's methodology too seriously, they believed in the actuality of their own magical

---

exists no clear distinction between fictional or trick sources and books committed to real magic'. *Modern Enchantments*, p. 34.

[60] The name Masklyn ye Mage is clearly an attempt to make an arcane version of Maskelyne the Magician. Andruzzi's three books that preceded the scroll were *The Negromicon of Masklyn ye Mage* (Chicago: Self Published, 1977); *The Grimoire of the Mages* (Chicago: Self Published, 1980); *The Daemon's Diary* (Chicago: Self Published, 1982). All of the books were produced to resemble ancient magickal texts, complete with elaborate calligraphy and illuminations.

[61] Some audiences, especially (but not only) devoutly religious ones, seemed unimpressed by the irony of this movement and instead recognized it as an attempt to restore the evils of ritualistic magic. Responses to this charge that involved confirming that the magic of Bizarre Magick rituals is indeed as real as the magic in the medieval rituals of Witchcraft (i.e., not real in the sense feared) do not seem to help. In addition, it is not always clear that the performers recognized that they were (or should have been) participating in an ironic fantasy fiction. Accounts of Satanists co-opting the rituals as their own are now the stuff of urban legend.

performances.[62] Rather than being a modern movement, then, we might consider Bizarre Magic a postmodern development.[63] However, also like Orientalist Magic, Bizarre Magic (and perhaps Oriental magic) gradually lost its glamour and developed into a camp parody of itself; as its impact on audiences began to shift away from mystification, the predictable decline into 'japes and wheezes' began.

Scene three: magick or magic?

The door was shut. It looked heavy and inclined towards remaining shut. Black ironwork ran over its oaken surface, elaborate yet sturdy. There were dents and patches of ash in the wood, where the door remembered resisting an assault, unmoved.

Looking around at my friends for support, I knocked again, more gingerly this time. It was beginning to look like a door that *should* be shut, as though it had been made so menacing to keep people out, or to keep something else in. Either way, it was shut.

'Is it the right time?' asked Natalie, checking her watch in the dim light of the corridor. She peered at it, unable to read it clearly. 'I can't really tell. Jake, can you see what time it is?'

Jake sighed. 'It's 20.27.' The green glow from his digital watch faded immediately. But for some reason that didn't sound like a real time. It didn't fit in the same space as the oak door.

'He said twenty-five past, right? He was quite particular about it.' Natalie was nervous. She didn't like the dark, and she didn't like waiting either. The combination made her anxious in a way that was contagious. I turned from the door to see whether she was all right – we'd only just met, but she was kind of cute.

[62] Hence, Orientalist magicians were perhaps amongst the first (and most literal) Westerners to attempt to indulge the fantasy of *becoming* Asian. The most famous case was probably William Robinson (1861–1918), who became Chung Ling Soo both on and off stage. This incredible case will be explored in later chapters. Readers interested in the intersection between this case and Orientalism can also see Chris Goto-Jones, 'Magic, Modernity, and Orientalism: Conjuring Representations of Asia'. *Modern Asian Studies*, 48:6 (2014), pp. 1451–1476.

[63] To some extent, we might also locate the innovatively ironic theatricality of Derren Brown in this postmodern category. Brown deliberately recreates the atmosphere of the magical Golden Age in many of his performances (as seen in his Svengali show), using this atmosphere both sincerely (to create the feeling of authentic magic that an audience might suspect to be 'old magic') and as a parody of itself (since the audience is fully aware that the show is taking place in the twenty-first century).

Just then there was the crack of a heavy bolt sliding into its brace. The sound echoed in the hallway. We jumped. Two more bolts and then the iron handle twisted from the other side, and the door creaked open. It retreated heavily and slowly, revealing a dark room and the figure of a tall, slim man in a hooded cloak.

'Greetings', came a deep voice from under the hood. 'I am Rincewind. You may enter, if you chose.' The figure stood to one side and swept out his arm to indicate that we should move into the room. With only a slight hesitation, we filed in, one at a time, looking around at the small chamber as our eyes adjusted to the light of three candles that were clustered into the centre of a large round table in the heart of the room. There was a noxious and overpowering scent in the air, and something bubbled on the edge of hearing, as though a cauldron roiled behind one of the vaguely visible velvet curtains that hung over two of the walls. The third wall, opposite the door, was completely covered in bookshelves. There must have been hundreds of old, leather-bound books lining the shelves. But there were too many for the space, so some had been stuffed horizontally into the gaps above the other books. Interspersed, here and there, were some objects that I couldn't see clearly and didn't recognise. Perhaps little statues of animals or people, or something else. It was too dark to make them out properly.

'I see there are seven of you', intoned Rincewind as he moved between us slowly. He seemed to be gliding in his cloak and, looking down, I saw that its hem obscured his feet. For a moment, I found myself wondering whether he even had any feet. After a moment, he took up a position on the far side of the table, with the candles like a barrier of light between us. Only hazily visible, I saw him gesture once again. His cloak billowed to both sides, indicating the armchairs that were carefully arranged into a crescent around the table. We sat deliberately. There were seven chairs.

After a long and silent pause, which made us shift nervously in our seats, Rincewind sat at the other side of the table. In the dark room, he was almost completely obscured behind the light haze of the candles. I squinted to see him, trying to make out his face.

'We are gathered here this evening to call up to our plane one of the Old Ones, dread ruler of the seas and oceans, mighty Cthulhu, from his slumber in the sunken ruins of R'lyeh.' Rincewind's gentle voice echoed unexpectedly in the small room. He wasn't loud, but he was pervasive. It was as though he were whispering and shouting at the same time. 'There must be complete quiet as I summon dread Cthulhu and prepare to open the way. Any disturbance made during the ritual will close the gates and doom our purpose.'

I pursed my lips, not quite sure about this. It didn't feel quite right. Looking over at Natalie, whom I was pleased to see in the seat next to me, I saw her blue eyes glittering with concentration in the candlelight.

Rincewind rose from his seat and loomed up above the candles in his hood. With great care, he moved the candles from the centre of the table, placing them precisely around the perimeter so that they formed the points of an equilateral triangle. For the first time, I glimpsed the face under the hood, but there seemed to be something wrong with it. I couldn't quite grasp it.

Walking back to the bookshelves, Rincewind removed an old iron box and returned with it to the table. With the long, ornate dagger that he withdrew from the box, he started to carve a pattern into the surface of the table. After about a minute, a pentagram was etched deeply and clearly across the expanse of the wood. Finally, holding out his palm, he carved the tri-horned ring of Cthulhu into his skin right in front of us, letting the blood drip into the centre of the pentagram before laying the dagger onto that point.

I realised that I was holding my breath. Glancing to the side, I saw Natalie's eyes bulging. Even Jake seemed transfixed.

'Ph'nglui mglw'nafh Cthulhu R'lyeh wgah'nagl fhtagn.' Rincewind's hands were clenched against his chest as he whispered the diabolical chant.

Nobody moved. Nothing happened.

'Ph'nglui mglw'nafh Cthulhu R'lyeh wgah'nagl fhtagn', repeated Rincewind, slightly louder. This time he looked up towards the ceiling, and his hood fell back. But I was watching the dagger on the table. It seemed to tremble. The faint noise of noxious bubbling grew louder, as though the cauldron had become impossibly hot. The stench was overwhelming.

'Ph'nglui mglw'nafh Cthulhu R'lyeh wgah'nagl fhtagn', he demanded, throwing his arms out to his sides beseechingly.

Suddenly, Natalie lurched from her chair and collapsed forward across the table, sending the dagger spinning off onto the floor. Instantly, silence fell in the room. In the faint light of the candles, we could see that Natalie was not moving.

'No!' cried Rincewind, 'it is broken! He was near but you have shut the gates between us. He is once more lost.' He paused and slumped, as though broken himself. His scarred face flickered in the faltering light. 'But wait', he began, noticing something important. He lifted his head once again, looking from one of us to the next. 'Mighty Cthulhu was with us for a time. Look! His mark is upon us all!'

For a moment I was just frozen in my chair, not quite sure what to do. Natalie was still sprawled across the table, but Rincewind was pointing directly at my face with an intense gleam in his black eyes. I glanced over towards Jake for a clue about how to proceed, but found that everyone was staring at me.

'What?' I said, strangely indignant.

'Dude, you've got the mark on your forehead!' said Jake, his eyes wide.

'What?' I said again, lifting my finger to my face as though they could see the mark. But then I noticed that Jake also had the mark on the side of his neck. Jumping up, I dashed past him to the others, checking their faces, necks and arms. Without exception, everyone carried the mark.[64]

Contrary to Bizarre Magic, Street Magic appears to represent a self-conscious move away from theatricality and dramatization. As a creative response to the widely perceived (and strangely lingering) death of magic, Street Magic (re)emerged into the mainstream at about the same time as the Bizarre, arguably under the charismatic leadership of Jeff Sheridan in the streets of New York City in the late 1960s. Sheridan's later book, *Street Magic: An Illustrated History of Wandering Magicians and Their Conjuring Arts* (1977), was notable for being a sensitive cultural history of magic performed on the streets.[65] Its affectionate tone and lyrical imagery helped to establish an approach to Street Magic that distanced it from common perceptions about charlatans and mountebanks turning tricks and performing gambling routines in seedy alleyways. Instead, the revival of Street Magic was framed as a romantic restoration of Orientalist fantasy and the

[64] This scene is describes a performance of the 'Stigmata of Cthulhu', the guidance for which originally appeared in *Invocation*, October 1974. It is based on my experience of a performance in Cambridge in the 1990s. Direct quotations from the rite are from the reprint in Stephen Minch, *The Book of Forgotten Secrets*, pp. 17–18. My thanks to Stephen Minch for permission to use this and for confirmation that I got this right. In case anyone is worried, nobody was hurt in the making of this scene!

[65] Edward Claflin & Jeff Sheridan, *Street Magic: An Illustrated History of Wandering Magicians and Their Conjuring Arts*. New York: Dolphin Books, 1977.

democratic ideals of the so-called Golden Age of Magic, with the latter personified by Houdini as the 'people's magician'.[66] Sheridan himself became famous for his avant-garde aesthetics and his silent card manipulation routines in Central Park, where he apparently earned enough money to live as a professional Street Magician, transforming him into a pioneer and poster-boy for this approach.

In some ways, then, Street Magic was inheritor to a very particular trend in modern magic that is closely associated with Houdini, especially in the later years of his career. Already for Houdini, one of the problems with mainstream magic performances in the early twentieth century was their social pretension: performed by self-proclaimed 'professors of magic' in dinner jackets and top hats in grand auditoriums using elaborately complexifying apparatus, magic was not only inaccessible but also alien to most people. In combination with the failure of many performers to communicate anything genuinely magical in such contexts, Houdini took this as a reason to take magic directly to the people. Hence, he performed his feats in public spaces amidst thousands of spectators and fans, often exposing his own methods (and thus the methods of others) in a self-conscious bid to educate people about the legitimate (and frequently remarkable) powers of the human body (rather than allowing them to believe that supernatural causation had to be considered).[67] For Houdini, then, Street Magic was an antidote to what he perceived as the social irrelevance of theatrical stage magic, as well as being a step on his quest to combat superstition and supernaturalism in modern America.

However, while contemporary Street Magic retains this aesthetic challenge to theatrical stage magic at its core, its ethical charge is much less clear today than it was for Houdini. Indeed, just as Bizarre Magic can be seen as a critical and ironic postmodern evolution of 'old magic', so contemporary Street Magic has developed into a more ironic representation of its own modern Golden Age. Instead of being a relatively spontaneous alternative to elaborate stagings, Street Magic

[66] Claflin and Sheridan devote the first third of their book to a representation of the Oriental origins of Street Magic, and later characterize the emergence of modern Street Magic as 'The Age of Houdini'.

[67] In his later career, Houdini increasingly focusses on performing feats that could be done openly without undermining public awe at his achievements. Hence, he performed exposés of mediums and spiritualists, and linked these to feats of escapology and endurance (which often deployed some of the same devices and techniques).

is now (also) a way of staging an elaborate television special.[68] This means that even though many practitioners still strive to follow the example of Sheridan, high-profile performances by figures such as David Blaine and Dynamo are those that impact on the public discourse. So, contemporary Street Magic also includes levitations, dramatic transpositions, grand illusions, and walking on water – anything that takes place on a street, no matter how elaborate, commercial, or contrived.[69] In these instances, Street Magic simply describes the location of the stage, not necessarily a counter-hegemonic approach to magic. As Blaine himself observes, 'magic is powerful drama and the world is its stage'.[70]

One of the most intriguing issues to have been re-invigorated by contemporary Street Magic is the idea that magic should be seen as a *power* inherent to a person rather than a feature of a performance. As we have seen, even though Houdini is sometimes known as America's 'first superhero',[71] this is exactly the opposite of the position being proffered during the Golden Age of modern magic, when theorists, critics, and 'legitimate magicians' were keen to emphasize that magic resided in the performance not in the performer. Modern magic is an experience of the audience not a feat of the magician. The symbolic distance of the theatrical stage from the experiences of everyday life together with the professorial mode of 'demonstration' helped to bolster this position. However, following the emergence of David Blaine, the contemporary Street Magician seeks to represent herself as the 'mysterious stranger' who can spontaneously engage in magical behaviour in the street, where the street stands in for everyday life in an urban society; this type of Street Magician resembles a magical creature that directly engages with the frontiers of magical belief. The audience is not only encouraged to experience magical effects that toy with their magical imagination, but is also encouraged to believe that these effects were made possible by the innate mysteriousness – the enchanted *being* – of

---

[68] It is for this reason that Lawrence Hass prefers the term 'staged magic' to 'stage magic'. Hass, 'Life Magic and Staged Magic', p. 19.

[69] Of course, Houdini also performed grand feats in the streets, but in general those were not feats of magic or mystery. Instead they were demonstrations of endurance or escapology, designed to expose rather than obscure the demanding techniques employed.

[70] David Blaine, *Mysterious Stanger*. London: Pan Macmillan, 2002, p. 7.

[71] William Kalush, *The Secret Life of Houdini: The Making of America's First Superhero*. New York: Atria Books, 2007.

the magician, the *Magic Man*.[72] A landmark in this process of representation was Blaine's acclaimed 1997 NBC special, *Street Magic*.[73]

As we have seen, this mode of presentation was deeply controversial at the turn of the twentieth century, but it should presumably be understood as an ironic position in the contemporary context.[74] Hence, like the contemporaneous Bizarre Magic movement, this 'magic man' development becomes an ironic commentary on the development of modern magic, inviting the audience to participate in an existential mode of enchantment that is self-consciously fictional on the part of both the performer and the audience. If Bizarre Magic participates in the literary conventions of Fantasy Fiction, Street Magic is a species of Magical Realism.

In this way, like Bizarre Magic, Street Magic also exists as an inheritor of the Orientalist Magic tradition. Indeed, when Blaine said that he wanted to 'bring magic back to the place it used to be 100 years ago', the public generally understood this to be a reference to an ambition to become the 'new Houdini', but Street Magic is also a reprisal of the idea of the everyday magic man.[75] It engages with the themes and tropes of the 'old magic' and 'low magic' associated with Medievalism and Orientalism at the turn of the twentieth century, which saw peripatetic magicians from Europe and North America travelling around the world to test out their magic in various cultural contexts (that they

---

[72] David Blaine, *Magic Man*. NBC, 20 August 1999.

[73] David Blaine, *Street Magic*. NBC, 19 May 1997.

[74] In fact, Blaine also plays with the question of whether or not his work should be seen as ironic. In later shows, such as the 2013 special, *Real or Magic*, he explicitly invites the audience to engage with this question, challenging them to make a leap of faith into magical belief. In earlier shows, including notably in *Magic Man* itself, Blaine showcases the controversial figure of Uri Geller, who has made a career out of not-admitting that he uses readily explicable techniques and devices to accomplish magical feats (even after apparently being exposed as doing so by, amongst others, James Randi in *The Truth about Uri Geller*. Prometheus Books, 1982). One of the fascinating things about Geller is that, while he makes a lot of modern 'legitimate' magicians very angry, his studied silence on the question of how he accomplishes his feats immediately engages him in this more general question of whether his performances are participating in a postmodern, ironic milieu (in which, like the Bizarre Magicians, his pretence about having supernatural powers is maintained as a form of fantasy fiction to transform mundane feats into magical effects, and hence the pretence relies upon the fact that his audiences are aware of and complicit in this fictional experience).

[75] James Ryan, 'If He Can Conjure Magical Ratings, That's Some Trick'. *New York Times*, 11 May 1997.

considered less developed) where they encountered impoverished conjurers in the streets of Cairo, Delhi, and Hong Kong.[76] Such performers
seemed to *embody* magic rather than to *perform* it; they were magic
men – not performers of tricks – their feats were magical because it was
they who performed them. To express this slightly differently, their
glamour was intrinsic not extrinsic. As we will see in later chapters,
they were the fakirs and yogis who were represented in the travel
writings of Western magicians as 'low magicians' (as opposed to 'high
magicians' in theatres and temples) who simply lived lives of magic in
the streets. They were drawn as analogous to 'wise men' and 'witches' of
European history – not performers of magic but magical beings capable
of (for instance) performing the mythical Indian Rope Trick.[77]

[76] One of the most difficult ethical issues about contemporary Street Magic is its occa-
sional use of similar patterns of travel in order to showcase audiences with different
sets of (or proclivities towards) magical beliefs.
   A criticism of some of David Blaine's Street Magic, for instance, has been that
rather than using the street as a way to bring an empowering (and enlightening)
experience to a wider, more disadvantaged population (à la Houdini), he has focussed
on showcasing the credulity of less well educated audiences as a way to bolster the
impression that he might have real supernatural powers. The shows of disbelief and
incomprehension, together with a willingness to confess the possibility of magical
belief, add significantly to the magical *effect* that is communicated by the television
special. When a live audience (howsoever that has been selected), especially a live
audience that appears impromptu (in the street), expresses confidence that it has had a
magical experience, the television audience is much more likely to experience Blaine's
feats as magical effects rather than as tricks or simple feats. In other words, it is
conceivable that the audience is selected precisely so that its reaction to Blaine can be
folded into the entertainment of the mainstream audience. When the audience is
selected from a population that appears unusually disposed towards magical belief,
such as when Blaine (but also other contemporary magicians) performed Street Magic
in Haiti (in *Magic Man*), these issues become even more controversial, evoking the
ways in which European missionaries once made use of conjuring as part of their
endeavours to demonstrate the superior power of Christianity to local populations
steeped in magical imagination and belief. See the next chapters for more on this.
   Of course, all performers have an audience of some kind, and I don't mean to imply
that David Blaine is unusual in this respect. It is certainly not the case that his audience
always fits this description or serves this function. However, the transition of Street
Magic to become staged magic in the street enables (and thus provokes) these kinds of
ethical dilemmas, just as did the 'Oriental adventures' of European magicians in the
so-called Golden Age.

[77] In this context, it is interesting to reflect on the way that David Blaine has sometimes
represented his endurance acts as only coincidentally about performance but as chiefly
about self-cultivation. That is, there is a sense in which Blaine represents (or perhaps
performs) the recovery of magic as a way of being in the world, modelled on a
romantic vision of the disciplined asceticism of Oriental Street Magic and spiritual

This romantic fiction quickly became an aesthetic form for the performance of magic in the West – a mode of glamour, if you like – providing modern magicians with theatrical opportunities that seemed to evade the strictures of 'legitimate' magic in the modern West. Oriental Street Magic displaced the idea of 'illegitimate old magic' into the realms of another contemporaneous place rather than another period in history – this magic was both ancient (here) and current (there) at the same time – which provoked deep anxieties for the concept of modernity.

The world of Street Magic today retains elements of this existential orientation: the magic man on the street is the postmodern fakir, just as the Grand Magus of Bizarre Magic is the postmodern High Priest or Arhat. The (ironic) conceit is that magic resides bodily in the magician herself rather than being located in the experience of an audience that witnesses her performance: what she does is magic because *she* does it, even if she's not performing at all. She would be magical even if there were no audience at all. Bizarre Magic and Street Magic (and Oriental Magic) are attempts to re-engage with the faculty of popular magical *belief*, even in the face of a hegemonic modernity that refutes it. And both toy with the existential line drawn by Robert-Houdin, who called on modern magicians to *believe in their pretence of being a 'real' magician*.

Summary and terminology

As we have seen, there remains much contestation and confusion about the terminology appropriate to the analysis of magic, not least because the term 'magic' itself retains a level of ambiguity. Indeed, it seems to suit the interests of magicians to maintain this ambiguity since it enables a range of dramatic and artistic performances. Precisely because we (now) know that magic resides largely in the quality of its performance (and in the experience of that performance), this ambiguity is itself basic to the definition of magic.

practice.Chris Goto-Jones, 'From Burden to Blaine: The Way of Endurance as Performance Philosophy' at *Theatre, Performance, Philosophy*. University of Paris, Sorbonne, June 2014.

The literature contains an unstandardized vocabulary, which promotes this kind of ambiguity and risks exacerbating it into confusion. As we saw in Chapter 1, one of the fundamental definitional issues concerns the commonplace assertion that there is a meaningful difference between 'real magic' and 'pretend magic', which is also sometimes expressed (or nuanced) as the difference between 'old magic' and 'new magic', 'sacerdotal magic' and 'secular magic', 'ritual magic' and 'stage magic', 'natural magic' and 'artificial magic', 'life magic' and 'entertainment magic', 'magick' and 'magic', or perhaps 'ancient magic' and 'modern magic'. Allied to these pairings is the idea that there is a clear distinction between a 'magician' or 'black magician' (who works 'real magic') and a 'conjuror' or 'conjurer' or 'white magician' (who works 'pretend magic').

Adding to the terminological complexity is the way in which some of the terms can be paired differently, at which point they seem to invert their meaning. For instance, 'natural magic' (which appears juxtaposed with 'artificial magic' to indicate magical causation that arises from the manipulation of nature itself rather than the deployment of man-made devices designed to give this impression) can also be juxtaposed with 'supernatural magic' or sometimes 'preternatural magic' (at which point 'natural' refers to the deployment of predictable, rational laws of nature and man-made devices that manipulate these rather than any pretence towards the supernatural manipulation of the laws of nature themselves).

Likewise, the term 'conjuror' is inconsistently deployed in contrast to 'magician' to refer to performers who admit to their artificial (i.e., natural!) means of producing magical effects, but when placed in juxtaposition with 'prestidigitator' (which indicates expertise in manual dexterity) it is used in its more mystical sense to refer to someone involved in the conjuration of spirits – something closer to a thaumaturge. On the other hand, if juxtaposed with 'juggler' (which indicates someone who *displays* great manual dexterity), both 'magician' and 'conjuror' suggest someone with great dexterity that they seek to obscure. In general, the modern theoretical literature prefers the terms *conjuror* and *modern* or *legitimate magician* as indicators of someone honestly engaged in a performance art – eschewing *white magician* for racialized reasons in contemporary societies; this is contrasted with *arcane* or *illegitimate magician* as the term for someone living life as a magical creature – eschewing *black magician*. However, popular literature and public institutions are much less clear about these distinctions, and even evaluate them in completely inverted ways.

Sam Sharpe laments that the 'terminology has become so loose that conjurers [continue to] call themselves magicians, wizards, necromancers, or anything else suggestive of magic'.[78] In other words, the label used by modern magicians for themselves must serve a double function: it is not only an analytical category for the theorists to manipulate but also an element in their performance that must evoke their *glamour* – their label must be *suggestive of magic*. Hence, 'magician' remains pervasive for almost everyone.

So, rather than being crisply distinct categories that signify meaningful differences in kind, it is clear that these clusters of pairings indicate trajectories, tendencies, and stylistic choices along various continuums in the same landscape – they are themselves devices to cultivate or decay the *glamour* of a magician – and so this is how the terms will be employed in this book. It is noteworthy that *glamour* in its magical sense (as well as in its everyday sense) is culturally and historically determined, and that its cultivation is central to the idea of magical artistry.

Where there does seem to be a clear analytical difference is between the ethical categories of 'legitimate magic' vs. 'illegitimate magic' or 'white magic' vs. 'black magic'. Rather than indicating any tampering with heavenly or devilish powers (except perhaps as a stylistic or aesthetic choice in performance), these point in at least two directions: first, they refer to moral judgements about the techniques and devices used to accomplish a feat of magic; second, they attach to the idea of the modern magician and the charlatan respectively. To reiterate, the difference between these roles is not that the one possesses supernatural powers and the other does not (since neither do), but rather resides in the honesty (or dishonesty) of the performer regarding her deployment of trickery. Hence, the modern magician should be clear with her audience that she is not making use of counterphysical supernatural causation, while the charlatan may attempt to convince the audience that he does have such powers. The modern magician should be clear that she is misleading the audience (to create

---

[78] Sharpe, 'Magic-Coloured Spectacles', p. 251. He proceeds to note that 'in my view, the definitions of *magic* and *conjuring* would remain constant if conjurers did not themselves create confusion by calling themselves magicians'.

a magical effect), while the charlatan may attempt to convince the audience that they are not being misled (for the charlatan's own gain). The modern magician misleads an audience's senses, while the charlatan misleads their intellects. In practice, there appears to be a grey zone in between these positions that enables some performative creativity, such as the artistic deployment of irony by magicians who act as though they are magical creatures (i.e., they masquerade as charlatans). Indeed, the idea that a modern magician is a performer who plays the part of a fantastical magician relies upon (and enables) the possibility of this ironic standpoint.

In terms of the composition of magic as an activity, the literature is clear about the need to differentiate between the *devices* employed by magicians (which might range from material props through physical dexterity to mental gymnastics), the execution of any *techniques* required to deploy those devices, and finally the artistry of the *performance* itself. In general, modern theory tends to privilege devices, techniques, and performance in ascending order of power, with performance being the most important. The theory of performance that emerges from the modern literature approximates that of Stanislavsky, whose method involved *becoming* the character being portrayed in order for that character to live in the performance; likewise the modern magician must believe she is a fantastical magician if she is to play this role convincingly. However, this theoretical prioritization of performance appears as a response to the fear that, in practice, modern magicians have got things downside up by focussing too heavily on the *mechanics of trickery* (the devices and techniques) and not enough on the *communication of magic*. In any case, the modern appreciation of magic involves a combination of understanding the quality and innovation of devices, techniques, and performance, including the artistry (and sometimes poetry) of the assembled result.

Finally, when it comes to describing the activities associated with a magician, the critical literature is wary of the word 'trick'. This is ostensibly because the word 'trick' becomes confusing when it is used to mean both the *feat* or *effect* being performed *and* the secret means by which it was accomplished. However, since the word 'trick' has become so synonymous with what a magician does (i.e., the *magic trick*) rather than how she does it (i.e., the *trick of the magic*), it is increasingly difficult to sustain this objection. The other objection to the word 'trick' is that it is subtly derogatory about the activities of magicians because its implication is of triviality. Hence, following the lead of early twentieth century magicians, modern theorists tend to talk of *experiments* or sometimes *demonstrations* instead of *tricks*.

In sum, at its base, good modern magic is the artistic and non-harmful performance of apparent counter-physical supernatural causation, resting on the honesty of its pretence amidst a shared complicity in the denial of that pretence. This is not a million miles from Sam Sharpe's concise definition: magic = illusion + glamour.

3 ORIENTAL(IST) MAGIC

Scene four: the tragedy of orientalist magic

The audience gazes in admiration at the lush, silken curtains, resplendent with the image of a giant green dragon, apparently the sacred emblem of the Manchus. The silk ripples slightly as the curtains settle, having dropped over the stage after the antics of a Japanese acrobat – colourful yet ascetic – who had astonished everyone by walking across the naked blades of swords with bare feet. Truly it seemed that there was nothing an Oriental magician could not accomplish.

Silence falls, and an air of expectation gradually fills the auditorium of the Wood Green Empire in London. The audience shifts in anticipation of the show's headline feature. And just as the tension seems to become unbearable, a faint note of gentle, eerie music wafts out from behind the curtains. The instrument is exotic, unrecognisable, and unearthly. Strings play at bizarre intervals forming a melody that seems both alien and beautiful. Silence falls into the theatre once again, as the audience hold their collective breath. The heady scent of incense insinuates itself into their lungs. The beat of a drum sounds, as though from far off. But it gathers in strength and power, beating the methodical march of an approaching army.

As the curtain rises suddenly, the audience gasps involuntarily, as though taken by surprise. But the stage is empty. While the drums pound louder and more emphatically, the sound of marching feet seems to blend into the beat until, just as the audience thinks the invisible army can't get any closer, two files of magnificent Chinese soldiers parade onto the stage. Their demeanour is austere and awe-inspiring, while their ornate, antique armour glistens like gold in the stage-lights. They are a vision of another world, conjuring the audience's imagination of the legendary Boxers and the spirit warriors of ancient China.

The soldiers stamp to attention in two crisply parallel lines across the stage. The snap of their salute silences the drums and the audience's eyes widen, waiting. From the silence, a glorious fanfare of trumpets. From off stage emerges a gloriously colourful palanquin, glittering with gold and studded with jewels. It is borne by a gorgeous coterie of Chinese attendants, bedecked in flowing silks, each bearing the legendary crest of the Mandarin of the One Button.

The palanquin comes to rest in centre stage, and the attendants scatter into sundry preparations. One waits proudly for the activities to be completed, then sweeps open the ornate doors in a grand gesture of revelation. Stepping out from the palanquin into an eruption of applause and gasps, Chung Ling Soo – the Marvellous Chinese Magician – strides to the front of the stage. The ovation resounds for several minutes as Soo bathes in the limelight. His partially shaven head glints slightly and his long queue whips around as he turns his glance around the auditorium appreciatively. The smooth features of his face communicate a calm composure and Oriental mystique, and his fabulous silken robes highlight his status as a celestial of the highest imperial order. In his eyes the audience sees the dance of impossible powers; never uttering a word, his silence seems full of mystery.

As the applause finally fades, the chief attendant moves alongside the celestial magician and addresses the audience in the best English he can muster. His words are strongly accented, and the audience concentrates on trying to understand what he's saying. They know that Chinese people in Hong Kong and Shanghai speak a form of pidgin English, and this sounds as exotic as they had expected. The attendant stands proudly and patiently next to the magician, waiting for two volunteers to join them on stage. After a few moments of bustle in the stands, two British soldiers emerge, climbing the steps onto the podium. The contrast between the neatly uniformed British soldiers and the fabulously attired Orientals echoes like poetry around the theatre.

Soo's assistant explains in his unnatural English that the great magician had once been forced to make use of his powers to escape from the clutches of the (anti-British) Boxer rebels. He goes on to say that the Celestial Soo would like to demonstrate this feat to his friends here in London – the greatest feat of Chinese magic that had defeated the enemies of England. He asks whether the audience had heard about the ability of the Boxers to make themselves invulnerable to bullets and blades. A muttering of confirmation ripples around the auditorium, and a few voices whisper references to the Japanese sword-walker from the earlier set. Someone shouts out that he had once visited Hong Kong and had seen a Chinese magician levitate high into the sky and then vanish completely. Another murmured voice seems to confirm this by explaining that he'd seen an Indian fakir make a young boy vanish from the top of an unsupported rope. Truly it seemed that there was nothing an Oriental magician could not accomplish.

The British soldiers, dazzled into the lights and by the reflected glory of the Mandarin Magician, are presented with two muzzle-loading rifles, which they examine carefully to confirm that they are just normal guns. They nod their confirmation smartly and crisply: yes, these are standard rifles.

The lights on the stage go up a little more, and a petit Chinese lady is seen shuffling and skipping energetically towards the soldiers. She darts across the stage as though impossibly light on her dainty feet, carrying a cup full of lead bullets, which she offers to the British Tommies. Somewhat distracted by the tiny, exotic beauty, the soldiers do their best to appear dignified and dutiful, inspecting the bullets and marking them with their initials. They watch attentively as the great Chinese Magician takes the bullets and loads them carefully into the rifles, ramming them home with firm determination. Finally, in a moment of spectacular cultural communication, Soo offers his elegant hand to the incongruous British soldiers, who shake it firmly with a mixture of admiration, respect, and disorientation. As they return to their seats, the audience applauds warmly, appreciating the contribution of the British Empire to confirming the legitimacy of proceedings.

But now the audience settles into expectation. Offering the house an enigmatic smile, Chung Ling Soo turns and strides purposefully to a marked spot at stage right. Meanwhile, the diagonal lines of Chinese warriors spread out to the left, with two of their number standing forward of the others to receive the loaded rifles. Attendant at Soo's side, the delicate Chinese lady clasps a pristine china plate to her breast, waiting while Soo smooths his robes and adjusts his elaborate head-dress, checking to make sure he's standing on the right spot. Finally, Soo takes the little plate from the bowing lady, smiles mysteriously – perhaps to the girl or perhaps to the audience – and then holds the plate out in front of him, like a tiny brittle shield between himself and the riflemen.

Absolute silence falls in the theatre, like a guillotine dropping. The stage seems to freeze into gorgeous Chinese painting. And the audience dares not even breathe. Then Soo nods almost imperceptibly, signalling the riflemen to fire. Instantly, they pull the triggers; a puff of gun smoke clouds the report of two shots firing.

For a fraction of a second, the only motion is the waft of smoke from the barrels of the guns. Chung Ling Soo stands motionless, the little plate held out before him. Then, suddenly, he seems to crumple. A second later he slumps forward, collapsing under the layers of his silken robes onto the stage. Somebody screams as a pool of blood emerges from the magician's unmoving body. Just as the commotion starts, the sacred green dragon on the stage curtains billows down to obscure the tragic scene.

Two days later, the *Daily Express* reports: 'Chung Ling Soo, the Chinese magician, was accidentally shot at Wood Green Empire on Saturday night, and died from his injuries yesterday morning. The fatality occurred during the second house at about 10:45 during the performance of his chief trick, which consisted of deflecting by a plate bullets from rifles fired by two assistants from the side of the stage and was due to the faulty mechanism of one of the rifles.... Chung Ling Soo, who was an American, aged fifty-nine, possessed a wonderful faculty of "make-up" and was generally accepted as a genuine Chinaman. He had performed before the King on several occasions' (25 March 1918).[1]

---

[1] This account of the death of Chung Ling Soo (William Robinson) has been assembled from a number of sources, including newspaper reviews. The trick being performed was the (in)famous Condemned to Death by the Boxers. It is noteworthy that the 'Chinese' assistant who requested volunteers from the audience was probably Frank Kametaro (a Japanese American who spoke no Chinese), and the 'Chinese' lady was probably Olive Path (aka Suee Seen), both of whom affected 'Chineseness' as part of the act, like Robinson himself. Of course, most (if not all) of the staging was similarly inauthentic.

Figure 3.1 Chung Ling Soo, 'Stage Shooting', c. 1918. Courtesy of Nielsen Magic Collection. Soo died while performing the bullet catch in London, 1918.

Orientalism and magic in modernity

Throughout history, magic has occupied a special place on the margins of society, defining the contours of experience that are in some way exceptional or outside the normal and everyday. In the modern period, magic has also become intertwined with powerful political and cultural discourses around the existence of a colonial periphery and the romance of 'Others'. At least since the 1970s, with the landmark publication of Edward Said's *Orientalism*, controversy has raged about the extent to which Western societies have sought to represent non-Western cultures as lingering exemplars of pre-modern, esoteric, and spiritual practices. Today, it is impossible to read nineteenth- and twentieth-century accounts of encounters with Asia without consciousness of this post-colonial politics of knowledge.[2] Indeed, for many commentators, Said has effectively transformed the meaning of the word 'Orientalist' from its nineteenth-century usage (someone who studies the Orient or Asia broadly defined) into its (post)modern usage (someone who attributes romantic or fantastical qualities to the non-Western world, or who deploys a quasi-fictional Orient as a representation of these qualities). That is, while *Oriental* may be a descriptive reference to areas of the globe, *Orientalist* has become an ideological standpoint.[3]

One of the core ideological issues that has arisen from this discourse is the question of whether Orientalists are genuinely interested in understanding the Orient at all, or whether they are more interested in understanding themselves and hence make use of the Orient as a canvas on which to paint their own fantasies of alien societies (or magical domains) as a mechanism of self-reflection (i.e., the invention of a society that represents the instantiation of values opposite to those

---

[2] Edward Said, *Orientalism: Western Conceptions of the Orient*. London & New York: Routledge & Kegan Paul, 1978. The dimensions of the debate sparked by Said's thesis are well captured in Alexander Macfie (ed.), *Orientalism: A Reader*. New York: New York University Press, 2000.

[3] There is also much debate about whether the term 'Oriental' can legitimately be used as a geographical signifier, since its referent is inconstant, depending on the period and agenda of those using the term. Its association with the negative category of 'non-Western' renders its place in the politics of knowledge subordinate to the idea of the 'West', which is also a region of dubious and contested geographic and cultural parameters. In this chapter, I am using the term 'Oriental' in a manner consistent with the sources being consulted, where it refers to the Middle and Far East, with an emerging emphasis on South and East Asia.

that the Orientalist would like to see as characteristic of his or her own society). Hence, in the case of Orientalism and magic, we see the demonstration of two competing trajectories: first, as we've seen in previous chapters, the self-identification of the modern West as rational, scientific, and post-spiritual; second, the persistent desire of the West to exist in a world replete with magic, mystery, and spiritual vitality, even (or perhaps especially) if that magic is located in a non-Western site. Of course, this tendency towards the instrumentalization of the Other (where instrumentalization and fantasization tend together) also raises deep moral and ethical questions about appropriate conduct towards people who are recognizably different from ourselves (whosoever we might be).

Representations of Oriental Magic

In the context of the history of magic, as we've already seen, it is fascinating to observe how the precise period highlighted by Said (the late nineteenth and early twentieth centuries) was also one in which Western magicians showed a marked interest in representations of the Orient. In the words of John Nevil Maskelyne in 1892: 'Oriental jugglery! The very words call up a thousand thoughts and fancies associated with all that is weird and mysterious. For Asia was the birthplace of magic.'[4] For Elbiquet in 1917, 'the conjurers of India are world-famous, and many are the wonderful feats that have, for ages, been associated with them'.[5] As Henry Evans observes in 1928, 'wonderful stories are told about the necromancers of the Orient. From the time of Sir John Mandeville to the present day, travellers have related the most miraculous tales of the feats performed by the fakirs, bonzes, and dervishes.'[6]

This period of industrial modernization may have been characterized by the disenchantment of the world, but we've already seen that it also featured the mystical revival, and here we see that Orientalism is associated with the same historical moment. In Chapter 1, we saw how new-occultists and Theosophists travelled to Egypt and India in search of secret magical knowledge; in the next chapters, we will see how

[4] John Nevil Maskelyne, 'Oriental Jugglery', in Lionel Weatherly & John Nevil Maskelyne, *The Supernatural.* 1892, reprinted Cambridge: Cambridge University Press, 2011, pp. 155–156.
[5] Elbiquet, *Supplementary Magic.* London: Routledge & Sons, 1917, p. 99.
[6] Henry Ridgely Evans, *History of Conjuring and Magic.* Kenton: IBM, 1928, p. 181.

modern magicians went on tours of the 'Far East', bringing back new knowledge, new tricks, new costumes, and fantastical written accounts of their journeys for the consumption of Western audiences.[7]

To some extent, we might simply see magic as an aspect of a more general cultural appreciation of the Orient in this period. While Said focuses his attention on representations of the Near and Middle East – where Marina Warner identifies a form of 'stranger magic' – here I am interested in how the logic and critical force of Orientalism also extended to the public imagination of the Far East.[8] Indeed, as we have already seen, India, China, and Japan gradually replaced Egypt and the Middle East as loci of the magical imagination during the mystical revival, at least partially because private travel to new colonial holdings in the Far East was becoming commercially viable for the first time in history. The symbolic and epistemic politics of distance and accessibility was powerful; Robert Elliot pushed things another step in 1934:

> Has it ever occurred to you to wonder why it is that India and China, once the very homes of mystery, have yielded the palm to Tibet and the Snows of the Himalayas? I will venture to predict that when we know as much about Tibet as we do to-day about India, some other more remote spot – if indeed one can be found – will be selected to replace the land of the Lamas as the hiding ground of the occult and the mysterious.[9]

The *fin de siècle* interest in East Asia emerged from the cultural context of *Chinoiserie* (which began in force in the eighteenth century) and *Japonisme* (which took Europe by storm in the nineteenth century, after Japan finally opened its doors to foreign trade).[10] These aesthetic

---

[7] For the influential theorist and performer Coco Fusco, the colonial practice of bringing back to Europe various 'specimens' for display and entertainment rendered the fringes of empire into 'living expressions of colonial fantasies', fuelling a contorted image of the non-Western world in the popular imagination of Europeans and Americans. Coco Fusco, 'The Other History of Intercultural Performance', *TDR: The Drama Review*, 38:1 (1994), p. 149.

[8] Marina Warner, *Stranger Magic: Charmed States and the Arabian Nights*. Cambridge: Harvard University Press, 2011.

[9] Robert Henry Elliot, *Myth of the Mystic East*. London: W.M. Blackwood and Sons, 1934, p. 7.

[10] From the early seventeenth century until 1853, Japan remained under a formal policy of *sakoku* (closed country). It was only after the forcible opening of its borders that open trade and communication from Japan recommenced in the mid-nineteenth

movements in Europe and North America reflected a more general public enchantment with the colourful cultures of distant lands and colonies. This is the period of the great World's Fairs and International Expositions, where nations such as India, China, and even the rapidly industrializing Japan would routinely represent themselves in traditionalist, quasi-mystical ways, deploying performances that emphasized the aesthetic elements of their culture (rather than emphasizing the tremendous technological or industrial developments) – this tendency has come to known as 'self-Orientalism'.[11]

The impact of this cultural environment at the turn of the twentieth century was potent in Europe and the United States. For instance, this period witnessed a transition in the nature and style of travel writing: while travelogues of the nineteenth century tended to 'be produced by missionaries, explorers, scientists, or Orientalists (Livingstone, Darwin, and Burton, for example)', who sought to use the medium to disseminate factual knowledge to the public, by the twentieth century travel writing had 'become a more subjective form, more memoir than manual, and often an alternative form of writing for novelists. The period from 1880 to 1940 saw this change take place.'[12]

This shift towards recognizably modernist travel writing precisely coincides with increased travel to (East) Asia; one of the first travellers to write an account of Japan (after it finally opened its doors to the West in the 1850s) was the remarkable woman, Isabella Bird (1831–1904), whose *Unbeaten Tracks in Japan* (1880) caught the public imagination of this previously unvisited land.[13] The tendency to blend travel writing with fiction and fantasy in this period, however, is most clearly represented by the work of Lafcadio Hearn (1850–1904), who was famously enchanted by Japan. Hearn's Japan was 'wise, calm,

century, although evidence also suggests that *sakoku* was neither perfectly nor uniformly observed prior to that point.

[11] In recent years, the power of self-orientalism is often associated with the imperatives of the tourist industry. It is also visible in the cinema and other commercial activities, where the importance of being recognizably (i.e., stereotypically) from a particular country or tradition is a market asset. Famous examples would include the explosion of 'Chinese' films modeled after Ang Lee's *Crouching Tiger Hidden Dragon*, 2002.

[12] Helen Carr, 'Modernism and Travel, 1880–1940', in Peter Hulme & Tim Youngs (eds), *A Cambridge Companion to Travel Writing*. Cambridge: Cambridge University Press, 2002, p. 74.

[13] In fact, Isabella Bird also travelled through China, Korea, and Tibet, publishing travelogues throughout the 1890s. Isabella Bird, *Unbeaten Tracks in Japan*. London: John Murray, 1880, reprinted New York: Dover, 2005.

beauty-loving, and mysterious', full of magical stories and hope for a West disenchanted by modernity. As Carr observes, Hearn's influential and popular writings created a '"fictive nation" that *became* Japan for a generation in the West'.[14] Indeed, one of Hearn's great fears was that increasing traffic between Japan and the West would ruin the enchanted land he loved.

The importance of travel writing in the formulation of public perceptions of the Orient in this period should not be underestimated, not only because (as we'll see in the next chapters) modern magicians produced their fair share of such accounts but also because these magicians wrote in the context and company of a wider literature. As Said himself noted about representations of the Middle East in the travelogues of this period, travel writing rarely consists 'simply of individual or disinterested factual accounts. Rather, travellers have already been influenced, before they travel, by previous cultural representations that they have encountered.'[15] In other words, as a literary form, the travelogue of this period works against a clear differentiation between 'scientific observation and fiction'; it works towards 'problematizing any clear-cut distinction between these two poles'.[16] Given the characteristic dramatization of the engagement between self and other, and between self and the world, travel writing seems to tend towards (and privilege) fiction.[17] In is in this context that we must understand the public imaginary of the 'Mystic East' during the Golden Age of Magic. Some magicians, such as Howard 'The King of Cards' Thurston (1869–1936) even went so far as to publish excerpts from his memoirs,

[14] Carr, 'Modernism and Travel', p. 78. As travel writing, Carr cites Lafcadio Hearn, *Glimpses of Unfamiliar Japan. Leipzig*: Berhard Tauchniz, 1907. However, perhaps Hearn's most enduring work was his retelling of Japanese myths and fairy stories in Lafcadio Hearn, *Kwaidan: Stories and Studies of Strange Things*. Boston: Houghton Mifflin & Co., 1930. A fascinating account of Hearn's construction of Japan is in Carl Dawson, *Lafcadio Hearn and the Vision of Japan*. Baltimore: Johns Hopkins Press, 1992.

[15] Tim Youngs, *The Cambridge Introduction to Travel Writing*. Cambridge: Cambridge University Press, 2013, p. 9.

[16] Charles Forsdick, 'French Representations of Niagara', in Susan Castillo & David Seeds (eds), *American Travel and Empire*. Liverpool: Liverpool University Press, 2009. I'm grateful to Tim Youngs for pointing me towards this essay.

[17] The priority of fiction as an element in the heterogeneous character of travel writing is emphasized by Michael Kowaleski, *Temperamental Journeys: Essays on the Modern Literature of Travel*. Athens: University of Georgia Press, 1992. This position is also evident in the work of Tim Youngs, *The Cambridge Introduction to Travel Writing*.

'Further Adventures in India', in periodicals such as *Tales of Magic and Mystery*, which deliberately blended fact and fiction.[18]

It is worth remembering that this cultural pattern was not limited to the entertainment industry or to the general population. This was also the great age of anthropology, in which classics of that emerging discipline were read eagerly by scholars and the educated classes. Within this picture, then, we might include the seminal (if by now deeply controversial) works of Frazer, Malinowski, Mauss, and others, for each of whom (albeit in different ways) the margins of European empires were sites of encounter with 'primitive' or even 'savage' peoples still steeped in the unearthly powers of 'real and potent magic'.[19] Through these scholarly accounts, high society, as well as the general population, was exposed to the idea that potent kinds of magic lost to the modern West persisted in places beyond the everyday experience of Europeans or Americans; the idea that geographical distance from the metropolitan centre acted as an analogy for historical distance into the darkly mysterious history of esotericism in the West became prevalent.

In this context, a number of modern magicians chose to participate in the West's enchantment with the so-called East, taking on the persona of the Arabian genii, Indian yogi, Chinese mystic, or Japanese

[18] Howard Thurston, 'Further Adventures in India', in *Tales of Magic and Mystery*, 1(3):25–28 (1928). *Tales of Magic and Mystery* was a pulp magazine that published only five issues between 1927 and 1928. It's mandate was to publish stories about magic, both fictional and non-fictional. Thurston was commissioned to write a monthly feature. The editor, Walter Gibson, was a friend of Harry Houdini, on whom he wrote in the magazine ('Daring Exploits of Houdini' in 1(3): 43–48). Perhaps the most significant story was 'Cool Air' by H.P. Lovecraft (1(4), March 1928). The innovative format, blending fantasy stories with accounts of modern magic, was indicative of the mood of the time, and also helped to established the conditions of Bizarre Magic later on, as we saw in Chapter 2.

[19] See, for instance, James Frazer, *The Golden Bough: A Study in Magic and Religion*. 1890 (2 vols), reprinted Macmillan, 1911–1915 (12 vols); Bronislaw Malinowski, 'Magic, Science, and Religion', 1925, reprinted in *Magic, Science, and Religion, and Other Essays*. Illinois: Waveland Press, 1992; Marcel Mauss, *A General Theory of Magic*, 1902, reprinted in London and New York: Routledge, 2001. As we saw in previous chapters, the general force of these anthropological inquiries was to dissolve the category of magic by demonstrating that it was really a social institution rather than a supernatural force. Nonetheless, the prevalence of anthropological writings about magic in the non-Western world kept the idea of 'real and potent' magic alive in the public imagination.

Figure 3.2 Carter, 'Chinese Magician', c. 1926. Courtesy of Nielsen Magic Collection. Californian Charles Joseph Carter, 1874–1936, owned the famous magic store Martinka in New York before it was purchased by Houdini in 1919. Legend has it that he kept his lion in the shop's famous 'back room'.

sorcerer. In his early years, even Houdini participated in this practice, appearing as a 'Hindu fakir' in a turban to perform 'Indian magic' at the 1893 Chicago Fair. Taking this symbolic step into the colonial peripheries of Europe enabled performers to appropriate the language, tropes, and *glamour* of 'fantastical magic' without contradicting the dominant narrative of Western modernity. By locating magic in distant and apparently mystical or spiritual territories that most audiences had never encountered directly, magicians were able to develop fantastical stage personas – they were conjurors playing the role of great (Oriental) magicians, as advocated by Robert-Houdin. In so doing, they affected a grand style of misdirection, displacing the problem of magic in the modern world to the 'pre-modern' peripheries, or drawing on an origination in such peripheries as a means to claim authentic magical potency. Hence, Western audiences could retain faith in their own progressive, industrial modernity while enjoying the fantasy that magic continued to thrive in the 'mysterious East'.

As a form of critical cultural theory, Orientalism is allied to other fields in the politics of knowledge. For instance, work at the intersection of Gender Studies and Orientalism is often concerned with questions of marginality, liminality, and the kinds of epistemic violence that can be perpetrated against those who reside in such sites. One of the main concerns about this complicated period at the turn of the twentieth century, then, is the contradictory place of women. On the one hand, they appear to be marginalized in an emerging modernity that ostensibly privileges industrial technology and scientific reason, in a cultural context that associates these features with masculinity. Hence, there appears to be an affinity between women and the Orient.[20] On the other hand, in the field of magic, the persistent idea of 'real and potent' magic appears to reside in a non-technological and irrational domain; hence, the marginality of women in modernity also makes them central to the field of occult magic during the mystical revival.[21]

[20] The association of women with the Orient and the Orient with the feminine has been central to the discourse. In recent years, new perspectives on this issue have been presented by thinkers such as Reina Lewis, *Gendering Orientalism: Race, Femininity and Representation*. London & New York: Routledge, 1995.

[21] An excellent account of women and the occult in this period is Alex Owen, *The Darkened Room: Women, Power, and Spiritualism in Late Victorian England*. Chicago: University of Chicago Press, 1989.

That said, the notion of 'modern magic', which, as we have seen, invests in the technological and rationalist orientation of modernity, marginalizes women from participation and privileges modern magic as the legitimate sphere of activity for male magicians. The implications of this theory are that women could have a high profile in occult and Spiritualist circles but not in societies of modern magicians, and that men would dominate modern magic while appearing transgressive in occult circles. As we have seen, this is more or less what the mystical revival reveals to us.[22]

This gendered context casts new light on the significance of Orientalism in the period. In particular, the geo-cultural displacement represented by Orientalist fantasies of 'real and potent' magic elsewhere in the world adds another dimension to the historical and cultural parameters of magic in the West. That is, because the Orient had been constructed in Western culture as a site of mystery, sensuality, spiritual awakening, and irrationality (which were all associated with femininity in the modern West), the Orient was also a place in which men could still be authentically magical. While the Western male was supposed to be rational and devoted to technology, the Oriental male was represented as somehow retaining his connection with the more mystical and spiritual forces of the cosmos. Hence, Orientalism became a kind of magic in itself, enabling male Western magicians to displace themselves from Western modernity and to transform themselves into a fantastical magician. For the modern magician, Orientalism was a form of *glamour* in the full sense of the faerie. It involved powers of transportation and

---

[22] The disparity in the profile of women in occult circles and in modern magic is stark. Many of the leading Spiritualists and Theosophists were women, including the founder Madame Helena Blavatsky. Stage magicians, however, have been overwhelmingly male, especially in the West. Indeed, women were not even entitled to full membership of the famous Magic Circle until 1991. In 2015, only 80 of the 1500 members are women. The breakthrough magician, Katherine Mills (the first female to front a TV magic show in the UK, *Mind Games*, in 2014) laments constantly being mistaken for the magician's 'glamorous assistant' (cited in James Rampton, 'Katherine Mills Dazzles in new Magic Show', in *stuff.co.nz*, 15 March 2015). The place of women in stage magic is admirably analysed by Karen Beckman, *Vanishing Women: Magic, Film, and Feminism*. Durham, NC: Duke University Press, 2003. Conversely, while it is true that men dominate modern magic, it would be untrue to say that they are insignificant in the arena of the occult. Having said that, it is certainly the case that such men are generally considered transgressive in various ways and, in the high-profile case of Aleister Crowley, in almost every way.

transformation. It can be no coincidence that, at the turn of the century, America's first dedicated magic periodical (later to become the organ of the Society of American Magicians) was named *Mahatma*.[23]

Responses to Orientalist Magic

In keeping with the previous chapters, in this chapter we will explore the ways in which modern magicians themselves have thought about and theorized the idea of Oriental(ist) magic; they have devoted considerable energy to the interrogation of the 'Myth of the Mystic East', 'Oriental Jugglery', and 'Oriental Conjuring and Magic'.[24] In some ways, we will see that the engagement of modern magic with Orientalism echoes its relationship with the new occult: while many magicians strove to debunk the most outrageous claims about the 'real and potent' magic of the East, it is also possible to detect a reluctance amongst magicians to accept their own conclusions about this. That is, despite consistently exposing the mundane and often simple reality of the 'tricks' being performed by so-called Oriental magicians, modern Western magicians remained at least partially enchanted by the glamour of the Mystic East. Even though modern magicians have been able to see through the technical devices and processes (recognizing many of them as familiar to the Western tradition), there persists something in the aura of the 'Orient' that makes these simple feats into enchanting effects. Orientalism is itself a kind of magic.

As we will see in the chapters that follow in Part Two of this book, during the so-called Golden Age of Magic this complex relationship between modern magicians and Asia was played out in various different ways; some of the great magicians of the West travelled to Asia to investigate the reality of Oriental magic for themselves, while at the same time taking a distinctively modern style of magic with them. In some cases, these modern magicians succumbed to the temptations

---

[23] Mahatma (the Hindi and Sanskrit title of honour given to a 'great soul') was published in New York City from March 1895 until February 1906.

[24] Robert Henry Elliot, *Myth of the Mystic East*. London: WM Blackwood and Sons, 1934; John Nevil Maskelyne, 'Oriental Jugglery', in Weatherly & Maskelyne, *The Supernatural*, 1892; Will Ayling & Sam Sharpe, *Oriental Conjuring and Magic*. Exeter: The Supreme Magic Co., 1981.

of charlatanism in these distant lands, using their art to convince superstitious local populations that they had genuine supernatural powers.
While this constitutes a betrayal of the legitimacy of modern magic in an
era of imperialism, it also reveals something important about perceptions of the geo-cultural and ethical parameters of 'modernity' at the
time.

In his memoirs of travelling in India, for instance, Howard
Thurston relates how 'native journals of Calcutta' attributed his
stage performances to genuine supernatural powers. Rather than
seeking to dispel this superstitious rumour in the responsible manner
of a legitimate, modern magician, Thurston appears to have indulged it
and even exploited it. He describes how he extricated himself from a riot
by threatening the local people with his magical powers:

> I repeated that I was an American; that I was the great magician
> who could make people float in the air; who could pass living
> persons from one place to another; who could cut off a duck's head
> and place it on a rooster.
>   I mentioned that I could cast strange spells of good luck or of
> misfortune; and that as I had the power to bring happiness to them,
> so could I cast evil spells upon them.[25]

This story is reminiscent of many similar stories told by magicians and
missionaries who travelled around Africa and South America during
this period, where they attempted to show the superiority of Western
civilization and Christianity over local religions by demonstrating their
own magical potency. The blurred lines between magic, religion, and
imperial politics in such situations runs counter to the aspirational
moral clarity of 'modern magic' that we saw in the last two chapters.
In fact, Thurston's allegedly supernatural powers in India were attributed to his Christianity: 'One newspaper described me as an angel sent
down from heaven to indicate to all believers some of the powers that
would be theirs if they remained true to their religion.'[26] Some years
earlier, Harry Kellar, 'The Dean of American Magicians', related how
Mexican newspapers had attributes his magical powers to diabolic
means: 'He is in league with the devil; he is *el mismo Demonio*, who is

---

[25] Thurston, 'Further Adventures in India', p. 28.
[26] Thurston, 'Further Adventures in India', p. 25.

permitted to walk the earth for a season.'[27] And then, when he reached
Punta Arenas at the extreme southern tip of South America on
3 February 1875, Kellar reports that he was asked by a government
official to 'impress the natives with the power of civilized man ... to try
his arts on the half-naked savages'. More than willing to acquiesce to
this request, Kellar:

> surprised and started [the natives] by a variety of sleight-of-hand
> tricks; then, assuming a fierce look, he told them he could burn the
> earth, if he so desired, and to prove it he would set the ground on
> fire. Now, the land of Punta Arenas is covered to a considerable
> depth with white sand. While Kellar had been mystifying the
> natives, his assistant had mixed some chlorate of potash and white
> sugar in equal parts, and filled a deep hole in the sand with it,
> without attracting attention. When all was ready, Kellar secretly
> produced a small bottle of sulphuric acid, and dipping the end of his
> wand in the liquid, waved it about his head and shouting, 'Burn,
> O Earth!' thrust the dampened end of the stick into the mixture in
> the sand. Instantly a column of flame, white and dazzling, shot into
> the air, and with screams of dismay, the natives broke for the hills.
> Not one of them stopped until completely out of sight, and they
> could not be induced by any means to return.[28]

Meanwhile, back in London, Paris, and New York, many Western
magicians were inspired by these imperial fantasies of *being* magical in
faraway places and by romantic representations of the power of

[27] Harry Kellar, *A Magician's Tour: Up and Down and Round About the Earth.*
Chicago: RR Donnelley & Sons, 1886, p. 32.

[28] Kellar, *A Magician's Tour*, pp. 51–52. Kellar's use of chemistry here is a wonderful
illustration of Arthur C. Clarke's third law ('Any sufficiently advanced technology is
indistinguishable from magic.'). In fact, there is a long history of Christian missionaries making use of conjuring and magic to demonstrate the power of Christianity in
colonial holdings around the world. For instance, H.J. Burlingame relates how
Professor Seeman was encouraged to use his performances in Cape Town as 'a sort
of indirect mission to induce the natives to join the Christian church'. H.J.
Burlingame, *Around the World with a Magician and a Juggler.* Chicago: Clyde
Publishing, 1891, p. 47. This tradition of magic has not been entirely lost. In the
contemporary period, however, so-called Gospel Magic is now largely employed as a
way to illustrate and enhance a sermon rather than to suggest supernatural powers of
God or angels. Hence, Gospel Magic has entered into the paradigm of modern magic
as a form of 'visual aid'. Andrew Thompson, *Gospel Magic: How to Use Magic Tricks
as Visual Aids.* Cambridge: Grove Books, 2001; Andrew Thompson, *Gospel Magic
for Preachers: Theology and Praxis.* Saarbruchen: Blessed Hope Publishing, 2013.

Oriental magic. Some attempted to participate in its glamour by presenting their shows in (what they took to be) Oriental style. These fantastical Orientalist aesthetics often bore little semblance to the manner of performances or costume in Asia itself, but they successfully captured the imagination of the European and American public. As we'll see in Chapter 3 for instance, in a famous incident in London in 1905, the ostentatiously fake 'Chinese magician' Chung Ling Soo (William Robinson) was judged by the public to be the authentic Chinese performer in a 'magic duel' with the authentic Chinese magician, Ching Ling Foo (Zhu Liankui), on whom Robinson had actually patterned his persona! 'Chineseness' had become a category of popular fiction, not of authentic cultural origination, and it was deployed as a means to enchant a performance.[29]

Other magicians were less interested in the aesthetics of *Orientalist magic* and more interested in the mechanics of *Oriental magic* – that is, in the *feats* being performed *in the Orient*. Hence, various of the 'tricks' that had been witnessed by travellers in Asia were adapted and appropriated into the programmes of modern magicians in the West. For some, as we've seen, this meant an embrace of new ideas about Street Magic. For others it meant modernizing these 'primitive' tricks by dressing them in top hat and tails as part of a self-consciously modern set. Props such as the 'Chinese linking rings' or the Japanese 'Kuma tubes' became staples of modern magic without any particular significance being awarded to their origins in Asia. It is at least debatable that levitations and decapitations were also imported from Asia.[30] In these cases, the modernity of modern magic seemed to trump geo-cultural difference; modernity was implicitly recognized as a universal category, and thus the Orient was just another source of techniques and devices like any other.

On the other hand, the Asian magicians who travelled to Europe and North America from China and Japan presented Western audiences

[29] The full story of Chung Ling Soo is told in William Dexter, *The Riddle of Chung Ling Soo*. London: Arco, 1955, and in Jim Steinmeyer, *The Glorious Deception of Chung Ling Soo*. New York: Carroll & Graf, 2005.

[30] The question of the origin of levitation is still debated, with many historians accepting that its modern origin lies in the workshop of Robert-Houdin. However, this was one of the (many) devices challenged by Houdini in his *The Unmasking of Robert-Houdin*, where he cites the possibility that techniques required for performing levitation were learned from an 'Oriental annual' obtained from officers in the Indian army in the early 1840s.

with similarly complex dilemmas of interpretation, challenging the relationship between ethnicity, culture, and modernity. For example, there were performers who committed to an aesthetic representation of their ostensible 'Japaneseness', such as Shōkyokusai Ten'ichi. But such performers often intermixed familiar classics of Western magic into their programmes, performing these feats in Japanese robes and flavouring them with something of 'Oriental glamour'. Just as Western magicians appropriated a number of Oriental feats (dressing them into the aesthetic of modern magical effects), so the opposite was also true.[31] Implicit in this kind of performance is the idea of 'alternative modernities', in which a technologically unified modernity can adopt myriad cultural forms depending on its location or origination: a modern Japanese magician could be both authentically modern and authentically Japanese at the same time, on equal footing with a modern Western magician.[32]

Some Asian performers, especially those from Japan like Ten'ichi, often performed in top hat and tails on stages in the West and/or in Japan itself, sometimes even performing traditionally Japanese magical feats in this ostensibly modern, Western style. Representing themselves as (and actually *being*) modern magicians in the same Western manner as Devant or Maskelyne, these magicians discovered that a form of 'Occidentalism' could be just as enchanting (especially to audiences in Asia) as Orientalism was to audiences in the West.[33]

[31] As Sidney Clarke notes in the 1920s: 'It is to be observed that while the troupes, whether from India, China, or Japan, generally confine themselves to juggling and balancing feats of the sort usually associated with those countries, the individual performers have to a large extent abandoned tricks of an Oriental character in favor of the exhibition of tricks of the same class as those presented by European and American conjurers.' 'Oriental Conjuring', p. 400.

[32] The idea of 'alternative modernities' was very fashionable in the 1990s, but has subsequently been strongly criticized for its latent Eurocentricism. It was originally developed as a response to criticisms that the idea of modernization was tantamount to Westernization, in cultural and political as well as economic terms. The idea of an 'alternative' modernity allowed for the possibility of decoupling technological and economic modernization from cultural convergence. Recent critiques, however, seek to challenge the basic assumption that even material modernization should be seen as an inevitable phase of development in every culture. In short, the idea of 'alternative modernities' is another way of circumscribing universal historical development within the parameters of modernity itself, howsoever that is expressed in particular cases. A provocative intervention in this debate is Dilip Parameshwar Gaonkar (ed.), *Alternative Modernities*. Durham, NC: Duke University Press, 2001.

[33] The idea of Occidentalism (ideologically charged envisionings of the West) is much less prevalent in the literature than Orientalism, partially for reasons of the politics of

To some extent, as we'll explore in Part Two of this book, these modern Asian magicians represented and performed a political challenge to the common assumption that modernity was the special preserve of the imperial West in the early twentieth century. The agency of contemporaneous Asian magicians was often inconvenient to those who sought to represent Orientalist magic in romantic ways: indeed, we will see that 'magic duels' were actually fought over ownership of cultural 'authenticity'. The 'Orient' functioned like a powerful incantation or spell that different magicians wanted to harness to their own desires.

It was in this complex and dynamic cultural environment that modern magicians struggled to understand the significance and practice of Oriental(ist) magic. As we'll see in the second half of this chapter, some of the leading theorists of magic in the Golden Age were already developing a critique of Oriental magic that anticipated the emergence of Orientalism as a ideological standpoint in the 1970s. In a manner that might have been recognizable to Said later, they wrestled with their own frustrations about the misrepresentations of the Orient in the West and tried to understand how such misinformed opinion could persist in the face of clear evidence about its erroneousness. Just as the modern magician saw it as his moral mission to debunk charlatanism, his engagement with Orientalism also took on an ethical dimension.

De-glamouring Orientalist Magic

Although beyond the historical focus of this book, it's interesting to reflect that in the second half of the twentieth century the glamour of Orientalist magic faded dramatically. In the context of the emergence of Street Magic and Bizarre Magic, which we considered in Chapter 2, Orientalist magic looked increasing camp and ridiculous. And in the context of post-colonialism and, indeed, critical recognition of Orientalism as an ideology after the 1970s, stereotyped and exaggerated representations of the Orient began to look regressive and offensive.

knowledge in the Western-dominated academy, but also because its function as a critical theory mirrors that of Orientalism itself. That is, its logic and structure is the same, while its referent is the opposite. In recent years, Occidentalism has resurfaced as a powerful and politically charged concept in the context of the so-called War against the West. Attempts to deploy this term as a label for representations of the West in the Islamic world include James Carrier, *Occidentalism: Images of the West*. Oxford: Clarendon Press, 1995; Ian Buruma & Avishai Margalit, *Occidentalism: A Short History of Anti-Westernism*. London: Atlantic Books, 2004.

Rather than being enchanting, the image of a middle-aged, white man pretending to be a fantastical Chinese or Indian magician veered between the ridiculous and the repellent. Perhaps the last magician to attempt this kind of role was Ali Bongo (William Wallace, 1929–2009), whose act was a kind of comedic parody of its own representational politics, with dubious incantations such as 'uju buju suck another juju'.[34] In his affectionate account of Bongo, James Randi sums him up: 'There is an Englishman who sports a monstrous turban and ridiculous shoes with turned-up toes, and who for his burlesque of an Arabian wizard should be put to every imaginable Persian pain and torture. Except for the fact that children all over the United Kingdom adore his madness, that is … Long may he delight us.'[35]

At about the same time as Bongo, we saw the rise of a number of 'authentic' Oriental magicians on the world stage, such as Luxor Gali-Gali (Mahguob Mohamed Hanaf, 1902–1984) from Egypt and P.C. Sorcar (Protul Chandra Sorcar, 1913–1971) from India, who performed magic in 'traditional' style for audiences in the West and elsewhere in Asia. However, in general, the most successful Asian magicians of the twenty-first century, such as the renowned Taiwanese magician, Lu Chen, or the 'Magic Boys' of Japan, are unselfconsciously 'modern' in

[34] William Oliver Wallace was actually born in Bangalore, India, into a serving military family (his father, also William, was a Sergeant Major). His family returned to England when he was seven years old. His stage persona, the Shriek of Araby, was elaborate to the point of pantomime: flowing robes, curly-toed slippers and a hybrid hat that combined turban with fez. He chanted nonsensical incantations that combined sounds that were vaguely reminiscent of the 'stranger magic' of the Arabian Nights and contorted everyday words. He was a popular children's entertainer for the BBC in the 1970s. In many ways, his act represents the limit-case for Orientalist magic in the West; even its raucous self-deprecation and ridicule could not prevent more politically correct audiences from cringing away. Certainly, the aura of Orientalism no longer acted as magical glamour, but instead as comedic parody. After the 1970s, such an act was almost unthinkable (with the exception of some acts in Vegas – where anything is apparently thinkable – which still adopt such modes of Orientalism with varying degrees of irony).

In fact, Bongo was an extremely talented and knowledgeable magician, much loved and appreciated in the magic community, where he was eventually elected as president of Magic Circle in 2008. He worked tirelessly as a writer, innovator, and inventor of new techniques and devices, helping many of the leading magicians of the second half of the century and winning awards in Europe and the United States.

[35] James Randi, *Conjuring: Being a Definitive History of the Venerable Arts of Sorcery, Prestigitation, Wizardry, Deception, & Chicanery.* New York: St. Martin's Press, 1992, p. 238.

Figure 3.3 Thurston, 'East Indian Rope Trick', c. 1927. Courtesy of Nielsen Magic Collection. Howard Thurston's staging of the Rope Trick was the most famous modern version of this mythical trick.

their aesthetics.[36] Rather than representing an Orientalist fantasy of a mystical past, Lu Chen is a child of the technologically cutting-edge and uber-modern megacities of East Asia.

With some exceptions in the deliberately camp world of Las Vegas, audiences today who expect to see 'Orientalist magic' from an Asian magician will generally be disappointed, just as audiences who expect Asian musicians to play the sitar or the shakuhachi will quickly discover world-beating pianists and violin virtuosi. Given the rapid and spectacular modernization of East Asia over the last century, none of this should be surprising. However, it does reveal some intriguing questions about the imperialism of modern magic itself, as the performative diversity of mainstream magicians around the world seems to converge around an apparently hegemonic model from the West.[37]

One of the reasons for this convergence around 'modern magic' that can be seen in the literature of the history of magic in Asia is the way that the category of modern magic is generally seen as a creation of the West in the Golden Age. That is, modern magic arrived in Asia with the gentleman magicians (and the gunships) of the Victorian and Edwardian periods: their manner and style, not to mention their techniques and devices, came to define what it means to engage in modern magic. Indeed, the aesthetics of Western modernity were themselves part of the glamour of modern magic for an Asian audience – the top hat and tails and the mechanical props were exotic and intoxicating. As we'll see in Part Two, while India, China, and Japan all had their own traditions of magic and conjuring, it was not immediately clear to the practitioners of those arts that they had anything to do with this new 'modern magic' of the grand theatre.

So, while Europeans and Americans agonized about the differences between occultism and modern magic in the West, in Asia there

---

[36] Ōkubo Kazumi, *Magic Boys: majishantachi no shōzō*. Tokyo: Kintoun, 2010.

[37] Inquiring into the reasons for this magical convergence would require a study in itself, including by reaching an understanding of the global economy of the entertainment industry and transnational cultural trends in general. Is magic simply another feature of cultural convergence in global modernity? We would also have to consider issues of emerging hybridity, both in techniques and styles: is Street Magic actually a form of Oriental magic? And then there would be the question of figures of multiple descent, such as the American-Japanese magician Cyril Takayama (who was born in California to a Japanese father and a French-Moroccan mother in 1973). Finally, there is the additional factor of the international magic competitions, which are very popular in East Asia in particular, which prescribe certain technical and aesthetic regulations. The Las Vegas model is hegemonic in such circles.

were similar debates about the differences between indigenous traditions of conjuring and jugglery and this new 'modern magic'. Furthermore, in Asia there was the added complication of being forced to consider this new 'magic' as being in tension with some form of supernatural realm, which may not even have been a coherent idea in those cultures. Indeed, already in 1912, Emile Durkheim was challenging the idea that the dichotomous notions of natural/supernatural could be natural categories rather than historical constructions of modernity itself. Durkheim explains that the idea of magic and the supernatural relies upon a cultural conception of the *impossibility* of certain feats – after all, magic is the accomplishment of the (apparently) impossible, which means something 'irreconcilable with an order which, rightly or wrongly, appears to us to be implied in the nature of things'. For Durkheim, this necessary order of the world has been constructed by the positive sciences in modernity.[38] Without this modern sense of scientific causality, the idea of magic as the supernatural becomes incoherent. This does not mean that we cannot recognize acts as magical from the standpoint of Western modernity, but it does mean that such acts may not be recognized as such by the people involved. The categorization itself is a act of modernization. In other words, the idea of supernatural magic relies upon modernity, which means 'it is unfortunate that the natural-supernatural dichotomy has been so persistently invoked ... in describing the outlook of peoples in cultures other than our own'.[39]

In other words, while modern magicians in London, Paris, and New York were preoccupied with the 'Mystic East' and the promise they recognized for new modes of enchantment, these same modern magicians were evangelizing a particular model of magic and exporting it around the world, blissfully unaware of the cultural turmoil that doing this would cause in the places they visited. Precisely because of

[38] Emile Durkheim, *The Elementary Forms of the Religious Life*. 1912, reprinted in English, London: Free Press, 1965, p. 43.

[39] Irving Hallowell, 'Ojibwa Ontology, Behavior, and World View', in Stanley Diamond (ed.), *Culture in History*. New York: Columbia University Press, 1960, p. 28. Hallowell also argues that 'a thoroughgoing "objective" approach to the study of cultures cannot be achieved by projecting upon those cultures categorical abstractions derived from Western thought' (p. 21). Hallowell's point is to demonstrate that labelling specific characters from the myths of Ojibwa as 'supernatural persons' is misleading and inappropriate from the standpoint of the Ojibwa themselves. Cited in Benson Saler, 'Supernatural as a Western Category', *Ethos*, 5(1):31–53 (1977), p. 32.

their success in fashioning a modern magic in Europe and the United States, modern magicians became instruments and symbols of Western modernity in Asia. Perhaps there could be no greater indication of the success of the ideological project of modern magicians like John Nevil Maskelyne (and their attempts to distance modern magic from the occult, which we saw in the last chapters) than to see the export of modern magic as part of the package deal of Western modernity at the turn of the twentieth century. Modern magic arrives in Asia just as did modern medicine, Western music, or Western philosophy.

A consequence of this situation in the contemporary period is that the decision of, say, a Japanese magician to perform traditionally Japanese effects is also an act of cultural politics. Rather than (or as well as) devoting himself to producing magical entertainments, such a magician is engaged in preserving national heritage. In China, we think of the Peking Opera or the State Circus, and in Japan there is the field of *Wazuma*, a traditional style of 'magical' performance that includes Japanese classics such as the Butterfly Trick and the Magic Fountain – in 1997 the Japanese Agency of Cultural Affairs recognized *Wazuma* as an Intangible Cultural Property of Japan, citing a tradition stretching back to the eighth century.[40] Performing *Wazuma* is a way to defend traditional Japanese artistry from the overwhelming global dominance of 'modern magic', just as performing *Kabuki* or *Noh* affects a juxtaposition with Western theatre. In other words, modern magic has become a field of contestation for cultural integrity in the globalized world.

Scene five: the Orientalist rope trick

Deep in the heart of Delhi, secluded in an artfully atrophied courtyard, Penn and Teller carefully arrange their equipment. They have traversed the subcontinent in search of Indian magicians who could perform the fabled Indian Rope Trick in its complete form, but they

[40] *Wazuma* is often presented as allied to two other Japanese traditions: *daikagura* (a form of juggling that also involves feats of balancing, acrobatics, and the lion dance) and *rakugo* (a form of story-telling). In the past, these arts had various ceremonial functions, sometimes as magical rites at temples and shrines. Although describing a tradition of many centuries, the term *wazuma* (Japanese conjuring) was coined in the Meiji Period (1868–1912) specifically to differentiate two different kinds of *tezuma* (conjuring/sleight-of-hand): *wazuma* (Japanese conjuring) and *yotsuma* (Western conjuring).

have found themselves disappointed. And now, as the sun begins to orange over the dusty buildings and the strange gentleness of evening settles into the long shadows of the narrow streets, they are going to perform it themselves in the authentic manner.

A few evenings before, we were privileged to see an Indian magician perform a version of the Rope Trick at sunset, with the glorious Taj Mahal looming up behind the rope. The setting was as perfect as could be, and the scene cried out for magic. However, the effect had been somewhat spoiled by a few technical problems, and in the end we had been disappointed because it was not *really* the Indian Rope Trick. Playing his flute and drum, the magician had made the rope rise slowly out of a basket, at which point it had stiffened and a boy climbed it to the top, with the Taj Mahal fading into the twilight behind. But, as Penn explained, the *real* Indian Rope Trick requires a magician to throw the end of a rope into the air, where it miraculously stays, allowing a young boy to climb up it. The boy then vanishes. So the magician climbs up after him with a sword, also vanishing. After a few moments, the severed limbs of the boy rain back down to the ground, where they are eventually reassembled and reanimated by the magician. As far as we know, nobody has ever filmed the complete trick, although there are any number of accounts by people who claim to have witnessed it.

The difficulty of this ancient trick should not be underestimated. The courtyard in Delhi is bustling with preparations and people eager to see the trick performed properly at last. The rope is tested for length, making sure that it reaches all the way past the upper balconies when stretched out. The basket is carefully positioned on the chequered and tiled floor, in the last pool of golden sunshine, caught in a beam of light that is riddled with dancing motes of dust. Scattered around the courtyard are the trappings of life in Delhi: broken furniture, piles of papers, and stacks of old, crumbling books. The balconies are strewn with laundry, as the residents make use of the last rays of sun to dry their bedding. The young boy is brought into position, ready to climb at the perfect moment. An audible murmur of excitement and anticipation whirls around the space like an eddy, swirling through the dust.

Everything is ready, although the magician himself is yet to appear. At the last moment, Penn and Teller decide that they want to ensure that some tourists see the effect as well. So they dash out

into the labyrinthine streets, rushing through the fading light and
the bustling of people until they finally encounter two Brits. In all
haste, they explain that they are making the first-ever film of the
authentic Indian Rope Trick and ask the couple whether they'd be
willing to come and witness it. The British man reveals that he's
seen the Indian Rope Trick before, but that he'd love to see it live in
India. Just then, the call comes through that they're starting the
trick before the light fails.

With time running short, the little group dashes back through
the streets, desperate to get to the secluded little courtyard in time.
More agile, the cameraman runs on ahead, making sure that he
doesn't miss even a single moment of the magic.

As they approach the courtyard, we can hear the magician's
flute and drum. The audience sounds excited. There are audible
gasps. Penn and Teller charge into the courtyard with the British
tourists just in time to see the rope fall into a coiled pile on the
ground, collapsing down from its full height near the ceiling.
The magician is pacing, clearly exalted and exhausted. At his feet
is a black sheet that has been thrown over the body of the young
boy. A bloodied blade is discarded nearby. The audience is wild
and wide-eyed.

'Oh no! We've missed –' begins one of the tourists.

'Shhhhh!' Penn silences him as they notice that the magician is
stooping down and beginning to chant a mantra. He reaches his
hands under the black sheet and lets his voice resonate and oscillate.
As the sheet begins to tremble, the magician reawakens his flute and
the drum, casting them over the fabric as though scattering the
sound like magical dust.

Abruptly, the sheet is thrown back and the young boy springs to
his feet from underneath it. There are bloody seams around his
shoulders and legs, where his limbs have been reattached to his
body. A trickle of blood runs from the corner of his mouth.

There is a moment of stunned silence while the audience, Penn,
Teller, and the British tourists struggle to understand what's hap-
pened. And then there is an explosion of cheers and applause.
The courtyard goes wild.

Within hours, the streets of Delhi are alive with stories of the
successful performance of the real Indian Rope Trick. Days later,
people who had been in the audience were still telling their friends,
taxi-drivers, and tourists about the amazing trick they'd witnessed.
About a week later, a couple of British tourists returned to London

and told their families that they met Penn and Teller in Delhi and seen the first-ever filming of the real Indian Rope Trick.[41]

A modern theory of Oriental(ist) magic

Revealing the Oriental in the Orientalist

Just as they were obsessed with exposing the charlatans involved in the Spiritualism movement, magicians of the Golden Age were similarly preoccupied with confronting public credulity about the apparently miraculous feats of magic that were routinely performed in the Orient. It is noticeable that moral critiques of Spiritualism and Theosophy by modern magicians were focussed against the charlatans themselves; indeed, to some extent, the idea of modern magic was forged as an ethical confrontation with these 'illegitimate' performances. Ethical critiques of Orientalist magic, on the other hand, tended to sidestep the performer and instead to focus on the credulity of the (Western) audience itself; rather than blaming the Oriental(ist) magician for attempting to mislead the intellect of her audience, the modern magician simply expressed astonishment at the resilience of miscomprehension in the face of robust scientific data. Orientalism seemed to provided a window in the walls of modernity, with a view of a magical kingdom outside. In short, the modern magician was torn between disdain for public foolishness and admiration for the magical effectiveness of Oriental glamour. Orientalist magic, in other words, enchanted modern magicians almost as though it was a device of their art.

With characteristic assertiveness, John Nevil Maskelyne begins his 1892 dissection of 'Oriental Jugglery' with sentiments that would later be shared by most of his peers:

> It is probable that there is no subject on which man has ever written, which embodies so wide a field of investigation as the records of the many marvels of Oriental Jugglery. At the same time, there is no

[41] This scene is from the three-part miniseries, *Penn & Teller's Magical Mystery Tour: Episode 3, India* (CBC/Channel 4, 2003). Of course, the Penn & Teller version of the Indian Rope Trick is simply not to perform it, but to give two tourists the impression that they might have witnessed its finale, and thus the impression that it was accomplished. The rumours about the success of the Rope Trick appear to have been legitimate. I'd like to thank Teller for further information about this scene.

Figure 3.4 Kellar, 'Levitation with Indian', c. 1904. Courtesy of Nielsen Magic
Collection. Harry Kellar's famous 'Levitation of Princess Karnac', was probably an
adaptation of the Levitation performed earlier by John Nevil Maskelyne.

subject which, in so far as actual results are concerned, would be so very deficient in anything that may claim to be worthy of serious consideration, were it not for the alarming amount of misconception and falsehood to which it has given rise. In the history of Mankind, nothing has ever been productive of so much cry and so little wool. In fact, no more fitting subject could be found to illustrate the prevalence of 'sense deceptions' among those whose faculties are intact.[42]

More than forty years later, Robert Henry Elliot found it appropriate to open his semi-autobiographical account of encounters with 'The Myth of the Mystic East' with very similar sentiments: 'There is a widespread belief in this country [Britain] that the East is the "Home of Mystery". It may be suggested that such an idea is only prevalent amongst ignorant people and that it is limited in its currency, but this is quite incorrect ... I have talked to men who have occupied high and responsible positions in our Empire who are by no means clear on this subject of "mystery".'[43]

As both a medical doctor and an amateur magician, Elliot is a classic representation of the gentlemanly modern magician. He is interested in exposing the juxtaposition between magical beliefs and the scientific worldview, which he takes to be self-evident by 1934. He states categorically that the mystery to be solved is not whether or how Oriental magicians can manipulate supernatural powers, but rather why it is the case that educated, modern citizens of the Empire are willing to invest their belief in this kind of nonsense. He's unreserved in his scorn for people who suggest that supernatural magic is possible: 'No intelligent person can believe for one moment that natural laws are habitually altered at the whim of a strolling performer.'[44] And he is equally scornful of those who suggest that natural laws are somehow differently applied to different groups of people around the world: 'The fact that a man has a brown, yellow or black skin, and lives in far-away parts of the earth little known to the majority of us, gives him no claim to mystery. Man is man, wherever you find him. His powers are as limited in China as in Chiswick, in Tibet as in Tooting.'[45] In short, as a modern magician, Elliot stands behind the facticity of universal laws of nature.

[42] Maskelyne, 'Oriental Jugglery', p. 153.
[43] Elliot, *The Myth of the Mystic East*, p. 3.
[44] Elliot, *The Myth of the Mystic East*, p. 57.
[45] Elliot, *The Myth of the Mystic East*, p. 5.

And yet, the idea of the mystic East persisted. To begin with, Elliot hypothesized that the reason for this persistence in the public imagination was simply because the majority of imperial travellers to Asia were untrained as magicians, and so they did not watch the magic being performed with an adequately critical eye. As Maskelyne observed, 'the writers of these distorted histories have been, as a rule, entirely lacking in any knowledge of magic whatsoever'.[46] They were tricked. And, after all, since it is precisely in such trickery that resides the art of the magician, this should be no great surprise. To some extent, this is a call for greater public acknowledgement of the skills and knowledge of the modern Western magician as a kind of hero of modernity: with his superior education in such matters, he is able to reveal charlatanism in Delhi or Shanghai just as easily as in London or New York.[47] In previous chapters we saw similar calls in the context of the public duty of magicians to expose Spiritualists.

To illustrate his point, Elliot contrasts the public understanding of magic with their understanding of medicine, implying incidentally that the category of 'Oriental' seems to operate towards the convergence of magic and medicine. He discusses various romantic ideas about Oriental medicine and also various claims made by Indian medics that he encountered during his stay in India. As in the case of magic, he suggests that 'there are people who to-day talk about the mystery of Eastern medicines, which they claim are still unknown to Europeans', noting that 'it is frequently said that Western prejudice prevents us from using these'.[48] He discusses particular cases in ophthalmology, explaining how he was open to the possibility that local treatments could be efficacious but sought to test them scientifically. He witnessed the use of the 'dung of the sacred cow, human milk and virgin's urine' as treatments for eye infections, explaining that in one case the use of urine as an eyewash had led to permanent blindness 'by venereal disease'.[49] Furthermore, having revealed the ineffectiveness of these medical procedures, Elliot explores the magical thinking used to explain the failures (and successes) of such treatments: 'a certain drug did not act because it

---

[46] Maskelyne, 'Oriental Jugglery', p. 159.
[47] Indeed, Elliot goes to some pains to ensure that his readers are aware of his credentials as a scientist (a medical doctor) and as a magician (a member of the Magic Circle).
[48] Elliot, The Myth of the Mystic East, pp. 27, 26.
[49] Elliot, The Myth of the Mystic East, p. 28.

was not gathered in the right phase of the moon, or because a suitable mantra had not been said at the time of its ingestion'.[50]

Medicine, which has been traditionally allied to magic in many cultures around the world, including in Europe, is commonly seen as one of the strong-cases for universal modernity.[51] Whatever else may be our feelings about the imperialism of Western modernity, it is hard to argue with the demonstrable effectiveness of penicillin.[52] In comparison, bathing an infected eye in a virgin's urine does indeed seem to deserve the appellation 'primitive'. For Elliot, it was 'difficult to imagine anything more degrading, more ridiculous, or more primitive' than the medical treatments he witnessed and tested in India. As a doctor himself, his exasperation with the local doctors and with Western romanticism about these doctors is clear: 'To depict them or their knowledge as something wonderful, which we of the West should copy, is an absurd travesty of the true position which only gross ignorance of the facts can explain.'[53]

In other words, Elliot makes use of Orientalist fantasies about medicine in Asia to demonstrate the importance of expert, educated witnesses and scientific testing. In the context of the 1930s, after the horrors of the Great War in Europe, his account of Indian medicine would indeed have been repulsive to his readers, forcing them to reconsider their romantic view of the 'East'. The analogy between Western fantasies of Oriental medicine and similar fantasies of Oriental magic is powerful. And Elliot is clear that both rely at least partially on 'defective observation' by travellers who lack the necessary expertise and education to make 'a reliable judgment'.[54]

---

[50] Elliot, *The Myth of the Mystic East*, p. 27.

[51] This affinity is explored in the seminal, James Randi, *The Faith Healers*. New York: Prometheus Books, 1989.

[52] Alexander Fleming discovered penicillin in 1928. While it may be hard to argue with the effectiveness of such drugs, it is noteworthy that attempts to make arguments against the use of modern 'Western' medicine have been made in the name of cultural and ethnic purity. Although the historical veracity of stories about the Viet-Cong amputating the arms of children who were vaccinated by American doctors is dubious (the story probably emerges from the movie *Apocalypse Now*), the fact that such stories have entered the public discourse demonstrates that they are thinkable. Indeed, Slavoj Zizek (and others) have referred to this atrocity as historical fact, Zizek, *Iraq: The Borrowed Kettle*. London: Verso, 2004.

[53] Elliot, *The Myth of the Mystic East*, p. 28.

[54] Elliot, *The Myth of the Mystic East*, pp. 47, 51. Having established his credentials as a medical doctor (which his readers would immediately accept as evidence of superior

However, Elliot's argument is only partially about education; it is also about the cultivated common sense of the modern world: even if a specific Englishman cannot see through the trick of a particular local Indian magician, he should still *know* that he is simply being tricked by an effective performance. Anticipating his son's argument about the need to educate modern citizens in the techniques and devices of magic, Maskelyne quipped only half-jokingly in 1892: 'Truly, a little common sense and a five-shilling *Hoffmann* would save some people a world of disquietude.'[55] Whether he knows how the trick was accomplished or not, the Englishman who fails this test of common sense fails to participate in the modernity of the British Empire. Understanding the mechanisms of a particular trick is only a way to reinforce what should already be known as common sense in a modern society: there is a readily explicable, scientifically normal mechanism behind the *feat*; the magical *effect* is due to artistic *performance* and *glamour*.

Romancing the Orientalist

Almost without exception, the magicians who wrote on Oriental magic during the Golden Age (and many who have written on it since) have done so with a sense of the tragic. Interwoven with the pride of a modern magician exposing nonsense, there is clear sadness in the tone, as though by exposing the Orient as a place just as mundane as the Occident, they are removing something valuable and beautiful from the world. For instance, in the 1920s, Sidney Clarke began his classic study with a lament: 'From very early times, amazing stories have been told of marvels said to have been performed by the jugglers, or conjurers, of India and China, which have been accepted as true by the uncritical for so many generations that it is a rather

understanding of medical science), Elliot carefully explains his expertise in magic, including his efforts to establish a Magic Circle in Madras and his membership of the Magic Circle in London, where he 'had the opportunity of seeing Western conjuring at its very best and from the inside. I think I may claim that this has enabled me to form a reliable judgment of the true nature of Indian magic.'

[55] Maskelyne, 'Oriental Jugglery', p. 172. *Hoffmann* is a reference to the classic manual of conjuring, Professor Hoffmann, *Modern Magic: A Practical Treatise on the Art of Conjuring*. 1876, U.S. edition reprinted Philadelphia: David McKay, 1910.

thankless task to enquire into their authenticity.'[56] In a similar vein, Maskelyne expresses the dilemma of an iconoclast tasked with destroying something he loves: 'since it has ever been the fashion to eulogise the wonders of the East, there are few who can find it in their hearts to do otherwise than to follow in the footsteps of those who have gone before them'.[57]

For Elliot, then, it is clear that something other than a modern magical education and faith in science is operating. Anticipating Said by more than forty years, he suggests that Europeans have grown up in a cultural environment riddled with representations of the East as a place of mystery and magic, and that even though the modern European knows that these representations must be fantasies 'the impression produced on him of the unusual and the mysterious never quite leaves him'.[58] In fact, Maskelyne takes this even further by suggesting that Europeans are not only passive recipients of this web of representations, but that they also *desire* these fantasies to be true: after all, a fantasy is a form of desire. He writes that even 'those who pride themselves upon their advancement in knowledge, and their freedom from all that may savour of superstition, are yet led, by an innate love of the marvellous, into the belief that some remnant of the power which built Aladdin's Palace still lingers in the lands of the rising sun'.[59]

There is an obvious double standard about the romance of this desire, since the theorists of modern magic offer no such confessions of nostalgia or understanding towards the Western Spiritualists.

[56] Sidney Clarke, 'Oriental Conjuring', in *The Annals of Conjuring*. Seattle: The Miracle Factory, 2001, p. 185. This undisputed classic in this history of magic was originally serialized in *The Magic Wand*, 1924–1928.

[57] Maskelyne, 'Oriental Jugglery', p. 154.

[58] Elliot, *The Myth of the Mystic East*, p. 11.

[59] Maskelyne, 'Oriental Jugglery,' p. 155. Elsewhere, Maskelyne recognizes this same tendency in the reception of fantastical tales about the Orient: 'It occasionally happens that some writer of fertile imagination evolves from his inner consciousness a romance embodying suppositional incidents and fictitious miracles. This, on being published, is seized upon with avidity by those in search of the marvellous, and repeated as a record of something which has actually occurred' (p. 161). In this spirit, it's revealing to note, for instance, after lamenting his general misery at the chaotic mess and stink in Macao, Howard Thurston cannot resist adding: 'But I had never been happier in my life, and to me the Orient will always be Arabian Nights.' *My Life of Magic*. Philadelphia: Dorrance & Co., 1929, p. 158. We have already seen the way in which the Far East gradually replaced the Near and Middle East as the preferred location of Orientalist magic in the public imagination. A wonderful study of the 'stranger magic' in the Arabian Nights is Marina Warner, *Stranger Magic*.

Presumably, the difference in stance is for ethically motivated reasons, although the ethics of this kind of Orientalism, which would be readily recognizable to Said in the 1970s, are also controversial. However, the literature exhibits no double standards about the difference between magicians and muggles with regard to this Orientalist desire: just like the general public, and perhaps even more so, the modern magician wants to believe that 'the lands of the rising sun' are magical kingdoms. A fascinating example might be found in the writings of the American magician Harry Kellar, a giant of the Golden Age, whose 1886 memoirs include colourful stories of his tour around Asia. Even before Maskelyne, Kellar states very clearly that 'most of the wonders attributed to Oriental jugglers have never existed anywhere outside of the imagination of those who tell them'.[60] In fact, he goes even further and claims that 'the ability of the entire fraternity of Indian jugglers is beneath contempt'.[61] However, about seven years later, after his return to the United States, Kellar writes in *The North American Review* of the fabulous stories about Oriental magicians and concludes that, *based on his own experiences in Asia*, some of them are true.[62]

Kellar's remarkable about-face needs to be understood carefully, since he does not appear to abandon his principles as a modern magician in a fit of hopeless romanticism. For instance, he does not claim that Oriental magicians can manipulate counter-physical supernatural causation. Instead, apparently desiring to (re)enable a vision of the Orient where the inexplicable and the mysterious thrive without leaving himself open to the scorn of modernists, Kellar makes two rhetorical moves, neither of which is unreasonable *per se*, but both of which reveal more about his desire than about his commitment to science. Not a hopeless romantic, but a hopeful magician.

First, in an argument used commonly by the Spiritualists, as we've seen, he suggests that it does not necessarily follow that the exposure of fraudulent or simply mediocre Oriental magicians means that all Oriental magicians lack superior powers of magic. Furthermore, he suggests that hundreds (perhaps thousands) of years of fantastical

---

[60] Kellar, *A Magician's Tour*, p. 115. [61] Kellar, *A Magician's Tour*, p. 114.
[62] Harry Kellar, 'High Caste Indian Magic'. in *The North American Review*, 156:434 (1893), pp. 75–86.

rumours about Oriental magic are not in themselves evidence that Oriental magic is entirely fantastical rather than factual. 'Yet, through a thousand years of rumour, the high caste fakir has succeeded in preserving the secret of his powers, which have on more than one occasion baffled my deepest scrutiny, and remained the inexplicable subject of my lasting wonder and admiration.'[63] Kellar's use of the romantically aristocratic category of 'high caste magician' seems to have been a deliberate move to distance these figures from the apparently 'low caste' performers that he had previously disparaged. The idea of superior castes in Asian societies was itself rather enchanting for Westerners in this period, and numerous magicians would claim association with (sometimes entirely fictional) castes of sorcerers, aristocrats, and celestials.

His second argument is more original and shows his attempt to remain within the spirit of an emerging scientific modernity. Again, as we saw in Chapter 1, echoes of it can be heard in the debates between Spiritualists and modern magicians. Rather than claiming that these inexplicable powers are somehow supernatural, Kellar argues that 'fifteen years spent in India and the Far East have convinced me that the high caste fakirs, or magicians, of Northern India have probably discovered natural laws of which we in the West are ignorant. That they succeed in overcoming forces of nature which to us seem insurmountable, my observation satisfies me beyond doubt.'[64]

In other words, despite having been (by his own account) deeply disappointed by his experience of Indian magic, Kellar still finds a way to preserve and actually to re-enchant the magic of India by claiming for it the status of advanced technology. What he calls 'high caste' Indian magic, he suggests is magical in exactly the sense

---

[63] Kellar, 'High Caste Indian Magic', p. 75.

[64] Kellar, 'High Caste Indian Magic', p. 75. In fact, Kellar was far from alone in attempting to maintain this position. In his largely unromantic account of Oriental Magic, for instance, Henry Evans declares that while 'fantastic accounts of Oriental wizardry are mostly gross exaggerations ... there are certain feats of clairvoyance, telepathy, hypnotism and imitation death, performed by the Yogi, that have a scientific basis'. *History of Conjuring and Magic*, p. 181. Perhaps the most astonishing assertions in this direction came from C. Alexander, 'The Crystal Seer', who wrote extensively on why Oriental magic was super-normal and not supernatural. C. Alexander, *Oriental Wisdom: Its Principles and Practice*. Los Angeles: Alexander Publishing, 1924.

Figure 3.5 Chung Ling Soo, 'Ancient and Modern Mysteries', c. 1906. Courtesy of Nielsen Magic Collection. Soo made revolutionary use of posters to associate himself with ancient and Orientalist mysteries.

that Arthur C. Clarke envisioned magic in his famous third law.[65] The irony of a modern Western magician using this argument to explain the magic of a colonial territory is powerful and tantalizing, even as it runs exactly counter to the hegemonic discourse of development and modernization of the time. That Kellar was willing to entertain this kind of radical thinking, even in the face of his own contradictory observations, is testament to the power of his Orientalist desire.

Oriental glamour

If it's really the case that modern magicians systematically and consistently debunked ideas about Orientalist magic, the question remains of how the public imagination regarding the association of magic with the 'lands of the rising sun' could be retained and why various magicians, otherwise so committed to the modernity of their art, were eager to re-enchant these faraway countries. Magicians themselves offered various explanations.

Since we have already explored the idea that magic is a form of intoxication, it is worthwhile to note that a relatively common way to explain the accounts of early travellers in the 'mystic East' is that when they thought they were witnessing inexplicable feats of magic they had in fact been chemically intoxicated by their hosts. For instance, Sidney Clarke suggests that 'another matter which should not be overlooked in endeavouring to find an explanation for Eastern marvels is that they may ... have been the result of a dose of opium or other drug'. At the very least, argues Clarke, such intoxication could explain the 'grossly exaggerated accounts of the quite commonplace tricks of Eastern performers'.[66]

However plausible it might be that some travellers were indeed intoxicated, it is difficult to accept that this can explain the wide range of accounts. One of the most fantastical explanations,

---

[65] Arthur C. Clarke's famous 'third rule' is today so well known as to seem axiomatic: 'Any sufficiently advanced technology is indistinguishable from magic.' It first appeared in Clarke's 1973 (revised) essay 'Hazards of Prophecy: The Failure of Imagination', in Arthur C. Clarke, *Profiles of the Future: An Enquiry into the Limits of the Possible*. Reprinted London: Orion Books, 2000. It is discussed in Chapter 1 of this book.

[66] Clarke, 'Oriental Conjuring', p. 389.

which was more prevalent during the Golden Age than we might be comfortable believing today, involved the assertion that Western observers of apparently inexplicable feats of Oriental magic had been hypnotized. In the words of John Maskelyne, there is 'a theory that the wonderful achievements of the Indian jugglers are not the result of any great manipulative skill which they possess, but are produced by the aid of Hypnotism. That is to say, the spectators do not really see what they suppose, but are mesmerised into the belief that certain things happen which are in reality only the outcome of the imagination.'[67] In other words, while it may not be true that an Indian fakir had really performed the mythical Indian Rope Trick, it was explicable that various Western travellers (and any number of local people in India) were under the impression that they had witnessed it. They were not witness to supernatural causation, but they were victims of a form of mass suggestion.[68]

In the context of the nineteenth century boom of interest in the work of the German physician Franz Mesmer (1734–1815) and then the development of 'hypnotism' as a technique by the Scottish physician James Braid (1775–1860) in 1843, the controversial ideas of mesmerism and hypnotic suggestion were alive in scientific debates of the Golden Age.[69] Indeed, while mesmerism was caught up into the discourse of Spiritualism and the new occult,[70] Braid worked very hard to separate hypnosis and hypnotherapy from the more spurious associations of

[67] Maskelyne, 'Oriental Jugglery', p. 161. A couple of years earlier, 8 August 1890, the *Chicago Daily Tribune* carried a (now notorious) story, 'It is only hypnotism', which became one of the founding texts in the modern myth of the Indian Rope trick, in which the author attributed the appearance of great magical powers to mass hypnosis (p. 16).

[68] Elliot refers to this possibility, *The Myth of the Mystic East*, p. 83. Hypnosis and mesmerism appear as relatively common explanations in the literature of the time.

[69] One of the key texts in this regard was the work of Chauncy Hare Townsend (1798–1868), who was famously a friend of Charles Darwin (1809–1882). Townsend's book, *Facts in Mesmerism with Reasons for a Dispassionate Inquiry into It* (1840, reprinted Cambridge: Cambridge University Press, 2011), was influential in England, not only (but also) because of Townsend's attempts to test the claims of mesmerism scientifically. While Braid was the first to make use of the term 'hypnosis' in English, the term was already in usage in French since the 1920s, usually attributed to Etienne Félix d'Henin de Cuvillers (1755–1841) who, like Braid, was more interested in mental processes than in Mesmer's ideas about animal magnetism.

[70] A number of influential works in the late nineteenth century directly tied Mesmerism to Spiritualism, especially with regard to the phenomenon of 'table turning', which was a popular parlour-trick in Victorian society. For instance, William Benjamin

mesmerism (such as the claims about magnetic fluids enabling clairvoyance and psychic control). By the turn of the twentieth century, hypnosis (or 'neuro-hypnology', as Braid called it) was gaining a respectable place in the emerging science of psychology. At the same time, as we'll see in the next chapter, Indian magicians were closely associated with snake charming, which was frequently attributed to a form of animal mesmerism. Hence, the argument that Westerners were being hypnotized into believing that they had witnessed great feats of Oriental magic was not as fantastical as it might sound.[71]

Nonetheless, this argument is unsatisfactory for many different reasons. Lionel Branson puts his finger on one of them in 1922:

> 'It is done by mesmerism.' How many times have I heard this futile remark when discussing the Rope trick. What always defeats me is this. Supposing it could be done by mesmerism, why does this wonderful mesmerist, hypnotist, or suggestionist limit his powers, marvellous as they are, to making people believe that they see a boy climb up a rope? . . . His limitations are unbounded, yet he sticks to this absurd rope and the boy climbing up it.[72]

The most obvious reason is that it is simply untrue that even a very talented hypnotist could accomplish this form of mass suggestion, let alone that the Orient was full of magicians who could accomplish this feat with complete reliability. Unless this theory is accompanied by an elaborate conspiracy, in which each foreigner is individually kidnapped and subjected to intense and systematic psychological conditioning to make them believe in Orientalist magic, then we have to accept that mass hypnosis is probably not the explanation.[73]

Carpenter, *Mesmerism, Spiritualism, &C.: Historically & Scientifically Considered.* (1877, reprinted, Cambridge: Cambridge University Press, 2011).

[71] In fact, the association of India with mesmerism and hypnosis has persisted into the contemporary literature. The 'Dean of American Hypnotists' Ormond McGill (1913–2005), to whom the field of stage hypnosis owes much of its architecture today, was fascinated by the possibility that India was the (historical and spiritual) home of hypnotism. He wrote persuasively, eruditely, and controversially on this in three volumes in the late 1970s: Ormond McGill, *Religious Mysteries of the Orient.* New York: Gazelle Books, 1976; Ormond McGill, *The Mysticism and Magic of India.* New York: A.S. Barnes & Co., 1977; and Ormond McGill, *Hypnotism and Mysticism of India.* New York: Westwood, 1979.

[72] Lionel Hugh Branson, *Indian Conjuring.* London: Routledge & Sons, 1922, p. 84.

[73] In 2012, Derren Brown screened a two-part TV special (Channel 4, 26 October, 2 November) in which he apparently tested the plausibility of deep hypnotic suggestion

In case it is needed, a second reason for the unconvincingness of the hypnosis theory is that it simply replaces one form of supernatural power with another. In order to explain why audiences erroneously believe that Oriental magicians have superior magical powers to their Western colleagues, this theory asks us to believe that Oriental magicians have superior magical powers to their Western colleagues. 'They' may not be able to perform the Indian Rope Trick (because that's impossible), but they are able to perform mass hypnosis (even though that's also impossible): perhaps they cannot control the material world with any form of supernatural manipulation, but they can control our minds.

Having said all this, modern magicians have been very interested in exploring the possibility that Orientalism is itself a form of mass suggestion, even if not hypnosis *per se*. John Nevil Maskelyne explains that 'we must allow for the mental bias inseparable from the legends, the traditions connected with everything Eastern, all of which tend to throw a halo of meretricious glamour around the subject and lead the mind astray from the real facts'.[74] In a similar way, Elliot talks about the importance of 'the psychology of suggestion' as a factor that explains the resilience of romantic perceptions of Orientalist magic.[75] To be clear, he is not only talking about the ways in which popular representations of the 'Mystic East' in Western societies predispose Western audiences to witness Oriental magic as supernatural (although, as we've seen, he also believes this with Said). In addition, he's making a professional critique of the performance of Oriental magicians, who deploy their staging and their glamour in creative and powerful ways in order to transform mundane *feats* into magical *effects*.

to convince just one person that he was experiencing the *Apocalypse*. Brown also attempted to replicate an alleged CIA hypnosis programme by deep-conditioning an individual to shoot a specific celebrity (Stephen Fry) on command (Episode 1 of the series, *The Experiments*, Channel 4, 2011. The amount of preparation and collusion to accomplish this for one individual is certainly sufficient evidence to discredit the idea that it could be simply and easily accomplished for an entire audience or every foreigner!

[74] Maskelyne, 'Oriental Jugglery', p. 160. In even more poetic language, Maskelyne talks of the way in which Westerners have 'drunk of the Asiatic Soma provided for them by their predecessors', which has made it impossible for them to believe the truth when it conflicts with the contagious fantasies (p. 154).

[75] Elliot, *The Myth of the Mystic East*, p. 38.

It is this combination of generic, cultural Orientalism in the West and the performative skills of the Oriental magician himself that is so enchanting for a Western audience. In a wonderful phrase, Elliot suggests that 'the glamour of the mystic East is upon them'. He describes the difference between the conditions of performing magic in the West (on the stage of a modern theatre) and those in the East, where:

> the atmosphere is different. The men seem in deadly earnest; the cobra-baskets alongside of them intensify the pervading sense of mystery.... Above is the deep blue sky; beneath this the luxuriant foliage of Eastern plants; and lastly, there is the red earth of India intensely lit by hard tropical sunlight which outlines the men and silhouettes their shadows with a clear-cut sharpness that once seen is never forgotten. The summation of effects is arresting. It is perhaps not surprising that under this combination of psychic forces very many go away deeply impressed.[76]

Orientalist magic and modern magic

At this point, it should be worthwhile to pause to consider our theory of modern magic more explicitly. In particular, it is possible to reconstruct the frustrations of modern magicians about the spuriousness of Orientalist magic as a mode of professional appreciation. If we recall Sharpe's condensed theory of magic as 'illusion + glamour', it is clear that Oriental magicians had found a deeply effective mode of glamour in which to cloak their tricks in order to transform them from the puzzling into the enchanting. Given the appreciation of modern magicians for the vital importance of performance as glamour, indeed as the defining feature of modern magic itself, it should come as no surprise that these magicians were fascinated by the myth of the mystic East.

Clothed in layers of frustration and indignation about the alleged superiority of these non-modern magicians, this appreciation is reflected in the way that critics identified the contrast between the tremendous magical *effect* generated by performances and the great simplicity of the *feats* being performed in Asia. Elliot could be speaking for any number of his peers when he describes the feats as merely 'a few shallow tricks of legerdemain', and he asserts that a Western magician

[76] Elliot, *The Myth of the Mystic East*, p. 60.

who attempted the same simple feats in London would be 'laughed off the stage'. However, showing considerable sensitivity to the theory of modern magic as well as the cultural conditions of his time, Elliot adds an important proviso, emphasized in his own italics: 'he would be laughed off the stage, *unless he dressed up in Eastern robes*'.[77] In other words, Elliot recognized that the magic of the performance was not contained in the feat itself, but rather in 'glamour of the mystic East'. As Henry Evans observes:

> Of late years Occidental magicians have manifested a decided *penchant* for masquerading as Orientals. They have got themselves up as Chinese, Japanese, Hindoo, and Arabian necromancers, with gorgeous *mise-en-scène*, often imposing upon a credulous public as to their real nationality. But nothing is so effective as an Oriental background for an illusion.[78]

In fact, a significant number of Western magicians attempted to don this Oriental glamour as though it resided in costume and pantomimicry. Taking Robert-Houdin at his word, these conjurors were attempting to play the part of a (great, Oriental) magician, investing themselves in the aura of mystery and wonder that accompanied this imaginary, thus hoping to transform mundane tricks into magical effects. And yet, as a strategy for magic, this Orientalist investiture was deeply flawed and ethically dubious.

On the one hand, a modern Western magician who was clearly adopting the costume of an 'Oriental sorcerer' was just as clearly not an Oriental sorcerer at all. This was partly because of the conditions of staging a modern magical performance in London, Paris, or New York, where the show would invariably be in a theatre and not under the deep blue sky or within the luxuriant foliage of the jungle. There were no baskets of cobras nearby. No darkly serious intent. However, it was also partly because the Western performer was usually a white, middle-class man who had arrived at the theatre in a top hat. It's difficult to overstate this: *he was not an Oriental magician*, and no member of his audience could realistically think otherwise. Hence, no matter what his own ability to *affect becoming* an Oriental sorcerer for a few minutes, the level of suspension of disbelief required of the audience was already

[77] Elliot, *The Myth of the Mystic East*, p. 37.
[78] Evans, *History of Conjuring and Magic*, p. 182.

considerable even before any magic was attempted. Just as Robert-Houdin and Hoffmann warned the modern magician away from the pointy hats of fantasy wizards, so they also cautioned about the turban and the fez. A possible consequence of the attempt to co-opt Oriental glamour in this way was the reduction of a performance to pantomime, 'japes and wheezes'. This might have been entertaining for an audience at the time, despite the troubling issues of racialism involved, but it was unlikely to heighten the sense of magic *per se*. In other words, as a strategy for modern magic, the adoption of Oriental costume seems flawed. We will explore this in more detail in the next chapters.

On the other hand, perhaps recognizing this flawed approach, there were a few Western magicians who took the question of *becoming an Oriental* a step further. Rather than dressing themselves into Oriental robes (of varying degrees of authenticity) simply to perform particular tricks or shows, some endeavoured to sustain their assumed identity both on stage and off. That is, they attempted to live as though they were *really Oriental*, so that the audience would not be forced to navigate between their incredulity about a white man pretending to be Asian and their enchantment in the face of assumed Oriental glamour. Presumably the conceit of this position is that being a real Oriental (as an ethnic category) is a significant element in the glamour of Oriental magic. That is, Oriental magic is experienced as a racialized category (even though the 'Orient' is a diverse, politicized, and semi-fictional cultural category). Even leaving aside the troubling question of what it might mean to live as an 'Oriental' (and especially what people might have thought this meant in the early twentieth century), this deeply committed act of pretence generates myriad moral dilemmas.

As we will see in Chapter 5, by far the most famous case of a Western magician who adopted this strategy of *becoming Oriental* in order to manipulate the glamour of Oriental magic was William Robinson (Chung Ling Soo, 'The Marvellous Chinese Conjurer'). Robinson made a serious attempt to live his life as though he were really Chung Ling Soo. He couldn't speak or read Chinese, so he spoke a strange form of gibberish that was then interpreted by his 'translator' (who was actually Japanese and didn't speak Chinese), and his bill-boards sported Chinese text that was either nonsense or full of mistakes. He appeared as Chung Ling Soo off stage as well as on, giving the impression that Chung Ling Soo was a normal public person. In fact, Robinson managed to convince a great many people that he was

Chinese and that his magic was authentically 'Celestial'.[79] Despite being entirely inauthentic, Robinson managed to participate in the popular imagination of the Orient so successfully that his magic was enriched by Orientalist glamour.

The case of Chung Ling Soo raises all manner of questions that we will consider in detail later on. However, for now, it's important to draw out at least two ethical issues. The first, which was a live issue at the time even if it was not fully acknowledged in the literature, is the question of the extent to which William Robinson fails to meet the ethical standards of what Maskelyne and Devant called 'legitimate modern magic'. We have already seen how the idea of modern magic involved maintaining a line between performances that sought to mislead the *senses* of an audience and those that sought to mislead their *intellects*. The intended consequence of this standpoint was the delegitimization of charlatanism, specifically in the form of Spiritualism, and the clear differentiation of modern magic from these spheres of activity. It is at least debatable that Robinson/Soo resides on the wrong side of this line, since his intention was to mislead the public into believing that he was Chinese on the basis that being Chinese gave him privileged access to magical effects. So, even leaving aside the details of his performances on stage, we have to ask whether his performances off stage were already a form of charlatanism designed to mislead (and regress) the intellect of the people. By indulging and reinforcing the idea of Orientalist magic, was Robinson/Soo working against the advancement of rationality and the public interest, and thus against the ideals of modern magic?

To some extent, Chung Ling Soo represents the limit-case of the tendency of modern magicians to adopt stage personas that imply great magical potency. In the so-called Golden Age, the devices of this kind of self-identification ranged from simply adding 'The Amazing' before a magician's name, through claims about being the official magician of a king or sultan, to the attribution of honorific titles or qualifications such as 'Professor'.

[79] There were, of course, rumours that Robinson was not really Chinese, but such rumours predispose a level of acceptance that he was really Chinese. In addition, such rumours should be understood in the general context of rumours about all kinds of 'Orientalized' magicians in Europe and the United States at that time, some of whom made no pretence of being Oriental, while others adopted the pretence much less successfully. Hence, there was genuine public confusion about the authenticity of apparently Oriental magicians, so such an extent that even genuine magicians from Asia were frequently rumoured to be genuinely Asian!

The second ethical issue, which would not have been on the agendas of many people at the opening of the twentieth century, is a question that seems blatant to us today: is it morally acceptable fraudulently to appropriate an ethnic identity from a position of privilege and power, let alone to use this position to manipulate the meaning and representation of that identity? Perhaps a more nuanced version of this question would be to ask whether there are conditions under which perpetrating such fraud would be acceptable?

It seems plausible that there are conceivable theories of ethics that would identify conditions under which representing oneself as a member of a different ethnic group and then acting to represent that group to others could be acceptable.[80] However, it is difficult to imagine that these conditions could include material self-interest, the accomplishment of celebrity, or the perpetuation of superstition and misrepresentation. After Said, it becomes very difficult to discuss the politics of representation without considering the possibility that attempts to represent an Other always involve doing violence to that Other. For Said and others, it was one of the lamentable features of the period of imperialism at the turn of the twentieth century that representations of the Orient were created by and for Westerners. In this respect, too, Robinson/Soo seems to serve as a limit-case.

Real Oriental magic, bad magic, non-modern magic

While it may now seem that the notion of 'real Oriental magic' is oxymoronic or at least a form of faerie glamour to be deployed by magicians themselves, the magicians of the Golden Age did not restrict themselves to debunking Orientalism. Indeed, they gave some considerable attention to unearthing what they took to be the real characteristics of magicians in Asia.

In general, while modern magicians were unusually sensitive to the ideological charge of Orientalism in the realm of magic, they seem

---

[80] At about the same time as Robinson/Soo, for instance, we have the famous and controversial case of T.E. Lawrence (Lawrence of Arabia, 1888–1935), who sought to identify himself with the Arab cause in the Middle East and then to represent that cause to the British. There are many reasons why the cases of Lawrence and Robinson are different (Lawrence did not claim to have become an Arab, only to represent the Arab cause etc.), but the comparison is instructive.

to have been relatively naïve about its force in society as a whole. As a consequence, their depictions of 'real' magicians in the Orient serve to reveal the multi-layered nature of Orientalism as a cultural force: debunking one layer does not necessarily free you from another. Hence, from the standpoint of the present day, the magicians of the Golden Age seem to have been deeply embedded within Western cultural prejudices about the so-called non-Western world, even if they were keen to show that this peripheral world was not a magical kingdom.

Once again, Elliot's expansive account of his time in Asia helps to illustrate the point, although, as we'll see in the next chapters, his orientation towards the Orient was typical of magicians rather than exceptional. His views range from what we might now see as vulgar racism (such as his observation that 'to European eyes so many Indians look alike') to more nuanced cultural critique.[81] In general, it might be said that Elliot resided in the cultural framework of Kipling's 'O East is East and West is West, / And never the twain shall meet'. Indeed, he quotes these famous lines of the 'great poet of Empire' approvingly, arguing that 'very few who quote these words realise the depth of meaning that lies beneath them; they look on them as a catchword or as a happy quotation. They are nothing of the kind; they are the expression of a great truth ... one which constitutes an impassable gulf between the European and the Indian.'[82]

In this overall framework, Elliot and others were interested in drawing contrasts between West and East at such levels of abstraction and generality that they resemble fictions. For instance, Elliot observes that while in the West 'it has been said that language is a means of concealing our thoughts', he asserts that this is even more the case 'out East', where 'no Oriental will blurt out his thoughts' because 'his whole nature is secretive'.[83] In addition to a natural disposition to be secretive,

---

[81] Elliot, *The Myth of the Mystic East*, p. 64. In fact, Elliot suggests that the racial similarity of Indian people allows them to perform certain magical effects (such as transportations) that would otherwise be difficult. Instead of transporting one person to another location, an entirely different person is revealed without anyone noticing that they are not the original person. Of course, the racist position here also suggests that all Indians look alike even to other Indians, whom Elliot assumes were also tricked by this effect.

[82] Elliot, *The Myth of the Mystic East*, p. 15.

[83] Elliot, *The Myth of the Mystic East*, p. 15.

Elliot also suggests that the Oriental is *naturally* callous[84] and *naturally* deceitful:

> It has often been said that there is a great deal of graft, and very bad graft too, even in England. I am quite well aware of this, but it has always seemed to me that there is one difference in this matter between the East and the West. The West condemns graft and dishonesty whenever it is made public. I do not think the East does so. The West holds that to deceive one's neighbour is a heinous offence; while the East only disapproves of being found out in deception and considers success in that line rather a credit than a discredit.[85]

When it comes to witnessing magic, one of the consequences of this apparently secretive, deceitful, and callous nature is that 'the observer can never really exclude the possibility of collusion' between the magician and the local people, which further undermines the likelihood that European travellers can trust their own experiences of magic in the Orient.[86]

Given Elliot's documented commitment to universal laws of nature and the equality of the capacities of man everywhere (when he was arguing the ridiculousness of any claim that Oriental men could have magical powers that European men could not), it is remarkable that he is willing simultaneously to assert the *natural* secretiveness, callousness, and deceitfulness of the Oriental. That said, this incoherent position in cultural and racial politics enables the modern magician both to debunk the allegedly privileged access of Oriental magicians to magical power *and* to assert the failure of these Oriental magicians to meet the ethical standards of modern magic itself. It will be recalled that 'legitimate magic' requires a level of honesty about the perpetration of deceit, and that 'white magic' requires that no human or animal be injured during a performance. Hence, the result of Elliot's paradoxical stance is a complete inversion of the imagined magical hierarchy through selective application of ostensibly modern principles: the

---

[84] Elliot observes that the callousness of the Oriental is a result of a combination of nature and nature: 'the Oriental is largely indifferent to suffering, whether human or animal; such indifference is part of his make-up, and is the outcome of the conditions in which he has been brought up'. *The Myth of the Mystic East*, p. 32.

[85] Elliot, *The Myth of the Mystic East*, p. 37.

[86] Elliot, *The Myth of the Mystic East*, p. 55.

modern Western magician emerges as the internationally superior magician, technically and ethically; Oriental magic crashes down from being the emblem of magic itself to being a mediocre delusion of dubious moral standing.

Having dispensed with the glamour and the ethics of performance, Elliot and his peers also turn their attention to the techniques and devices of magic employed by their Oriental confreres. In fact, they readily acknowledge several practical characteristics of Oriental magic, many of which appeared to be praiseworthy. In particular, Western magicians were willing to concede that 'on the manipulative side of conjuring the Oriental is extremely skilful; indeed, he is probably unrivalled anywhere'.[87] Given the weight placed on sleight of hand, prestidigitation, legerdemain, and dexterity by modern magicians, this tribute is significant.[88] However, even this acclamation is quickly qualified: 'this [level of skill] must not be placed unreservedly to his credit when he is being compared with his Western confreres'.[89] Pushing it a little further, Evans cautions that 'the *natural* magic of the East is not comparable to that of the West'.[90]

The reason Elliot thinks that we should hold back our praise for the great skill of Oriental magicians in legerdemain (when placed in comparison with the skills of Western magicians) is because such skills emerge only after relentless and persistent practice, and 'the Oriental has time in plenty, and his patience is proverbial'.[91] Presumably, this contrasts with Western magicians in modern societies, who are proverbially industrious and busy, without the time or opportunity for the amount of practice available to the Oriental. This argument appears to amount to saying that the Oriental magician has superior skills of manipulation only because he practices more. Since this argument

---

[87] Elliot, *The Myth of the Mystic East*, p. 52. In a similar way, Henry Evans asserts that 'there is no denying the fact that Oriental conjurers possess considerable digital dexterity', *History of Conjuring and Magic*, p. 182.

[88] It should be remembered, for instance, that Jean Eugene Robert-Houdin was emphatic that the most important quality of the good conjuror is not persona but skill: 'to succeed as a conjuror, three things are essential – first, dexterity; second, dexterity; and third, dexterity'. *Secrets of Conjuring and Magic*, p. 29.

[89] Elliot, *The Myth of the Mystic East*, p. 52.

[90] Here, Evans uses *natural* magic to refer to feats accomplished by non-psychic phenomenon such as the devices and inventions of technology and science, but also including the physical manipulation of these. *History of Conjuring and Magic*, pp. 181–182.

[91] Elliot, *The Myth of the Mystic East*, pp. 52–53.

seems merely to be a description of how to become better at any skill, it is reasonable to assume that there is an ulterior meaning. That is, Elliot is keen to avoid giving the impression that there is something inherent to the Oriental magician (i.e., something ethnic or racial) that makes him superior in dexterity to the Western magician. Once again, we see the residue of racialist thinking even in the context of an overall argument that attempted to debunk such thinking by rooting itself in universal natural law.

In fact, Elliot's argument gradually evolves into a cultural comparison, which ends in the position that Oriental magicians may appear to be talented in feats of dexterity, but this is only because they fail to participate in the magic of the modern world and hence spend all their energies duplicating tired old feats rather than developing exciting new innovations that drive the field into the future. They are good at some techniques and devices, but not those that are worthy of the attention of a modern magician. Indeed, this is what Evans meant by the poor level of *natural magic* in the Orient: 'the wonders of modern science, utilized by the prestidigitators of Europe and America, have not penetrated, to any great extent, into the Orient'.[92]

In passages that would be familiar to many of his peers in London, Paris, or New York, Elliot explains how the Oriental magician 'learns his tricks from his father or grandfather, and passes them on to his sons and grandsons', which means that 'his repertoire is extremely restricted' and invariant since time immemorial. Indeed, 'this changelessness of habit' is drawn as a characteristic of Oriental cultures in general, especially in juxtaposition with the dynamism and constant quest for innovation in the West, where 'there is a constant demand for "something new", whether in ideas or methods. That, to my mind, is the glory and great strength of Western magic. The changeless East is utterly unconscious of any such demand.'[93]

---

[92] Evans, *History of Conjuring and Magic*, pp. 181–182.

[93] Elliot, *The Myth of the Mystic East*, pp. 53–55. It is noteworthy in this regard that the first great textbook of modern magic in English, Professor Hoffmann's *Modern Magic* (1876/1910, p. 3), set out two essential rules that have defined modern magic ever since, both of which militate against the kind of predictable and repetitive effects that Elliot identifies with Oriental magic. First, 'never tell your audience beforehand what you are going to do'; second, 'you should never perform the same trick twice on the same evening'.

In this way, the Oriental magician is depicted as an icon of traditional, non-modern structures of knowledge and skills acquisition, in which skills are passed on to the next generation in order to preserve them rather than as a step towards advancing them to new heights. This means that the magician's apprentice is a repository of cultural heritage, like the aforementioned *Wazuma* artists in Japan. 'From childhood to the grave he does the same few tricks under the same conditions and in exactly the same way, all day long and all his life long, until he could almost do them when he is asleep.'[94] While this approach ensures that the performers embody their art perfectly, it also means that they are participating in something radically different in purpose and meaning from modern magic. Indeed, on this model, the Oriental magician is engaged in a form of self-cultivation or of ritual to preserve a set of cultural artefacts, while the modern magician is aspiring towards technological and artistic creativity in order to communicate magic to a modern audience.[95]

> Here, then, we have the really strong point of Eastern magic; it is the possession of the unusual skill which these men acquire by long and constant practice in a strictly limited number of purposive manipulations – a skill made more unconscious by being first acquired in infancy and then perfected by dint of lifelong practice. Here, too, lies the great weakness, at least as I see it, of Eastern magic. If you become a member of the Magic Circle or any similar body in the West, the first thing that will strike you will be the constant demand amongst your colleagues for something new, or for a new way of doing an old thing. A trick which you learn one day, and which is, for the moment, all the rage, has in a few weeks been altered or improved in some ingenious manner until it looks almost new again.[96]

---

[94] Elliot, *The Myth of the Mystic East*, p. 53.

[95] It in interesting to reflect here that, as we saw in Chapter 2, the contemporary magician David Blaine appears to participate in this conception of magic as a form of self-cultivation. Rather than engaging in magic and feats of endurance principally as a means to entertain and mystify others, his performance is often represented (at least by him) as being a form of conditioning and test – part of a quest towards self-perfection. To the extent that this is a recovery of an Oriental conception of magic, this represents its intriguing reinsertion into modernity.

[96] Elliot, *The Myth of the Mystic East*, pp. 53–54.

Summary and terminology

The turn of the twentieth century witnessed a sustained and critical engagement with the idea and practice of Oriental magic by modern magicians, many of whom travelled to India, China, and Japan and experienced the magic of those countries at first hand. As travel to the so-called Far East become more viable, the public imagination was fired by fantastical accounts of Asia as the historical and spiritual home of magic, contributing to a pervasively romantic vision of what we might call *Orientalist magic*. At the same time, both affronted and enchanted by this Orientalist vision, modern magicians sought to uncover the truth about magic from the Orient, or what we might call *Oriental magic*. In the end, modern magicians from the West revealed some of the ways in which Orientalism functioned as a form of magic in itself – they showed how an 'Asiatic Soma' or the 'glamour of the Mystic East' worked on the minds and imaginations of Western audiences to communicate the impression of impossibly grand and aspirational magical effects. Furthermore, modern magicians discovered that these enchanting visions, which were supported by popular representations of Asia in Western cultures, were belied by the mechanical and technical simplicity of the limited repertoire of feats actually performed by Asian magicians. In the end, far from being gloriously superior to modern magic, Oriental magic was disclosed as non- modern and 'bad magic' in the dense and complex sense of this phrase.

Nonetheless, modern magicians found themselves confronted by the persistence of the public vision of the Orient as inherently magical. Indeed, there is ample evidence that many Western magicians shared in a sense of nostalgia for the (ostensibly dying) idea of the Mystic East, and there was some frustration about the inability of Western magicians to access this romantic font of magical power. With varying levels of commitment and irony, a number of Western magicians adopted a form of Orientalist or perhaps *Orientalized magic*, performing in the guise of an (imagined) Oriental magician in order to participate in the glamour of the Mystic East – we might call these *Orientalist* or *Orientalized magicians*. The technical, affective, aesthetic, and ethical success of these performers was uneven. The politics of ethnicity and race was often handled in clumsy or offensive ways, with some magicians apparently unaware that a Western male playing the role of an Indian fakir had a different ethical status from playing the role of Merlin.

At the same time, various magicians from the Orient (*Oriental magicians* or, perhaps, *Asian magicians*) travelled to Europe and North America, where they performed in various styles. Some chose to represent themselves in a manner that resembled the Western fantasy of Orientalist magicians, leading to what we might call *Self-Orientalist magic*. Others attempted to perform in styles that more closely resembled their actual traditions from Asia rather than playing to the romantic ideal; in some cases, this 'authentic' *Oriental magic*, which was counter-hegemonic, was seen as less glamorous (and less magical) than *Orientalist* or even *Orientalized magic*. And still others adopted a modern, Western style of performance and thus challenged the representational hegemony as *de-Orientalist magicians*.

Finally, it is important to keep in mind the fact that neither Asian nor Western magicians performed only in the West, but also in Asia itself, where the performance of modern Western magic was an exotic element of *Occidentalism*. To some extent, the introduction of modern magic into Asia was also the introduction of a new category of knowledge and performance, which critics and audiences had to locate within (and differentiate from) pre-existing traditions of conjuring, juggling, ceremonial magic, and so forth. In fact, 'modern magic' has come to have the same technical and aesthetic meaning and implications in Asia as in the West, which has left space for other forms of *magic-like* performance arts to be maintained as elements of Asian cultural heritage. This complex space of cultural politics risked rendering Western magicians into evangelical modernists, and simultaneously presented serious challenges for the identity politics of Asian magicians in Asia.

While this chapter has attempted to frame a critical theory of Oriental(ist) magic at the level of regional abstraction, fitting magic into the overall discourse of Orientalism, in the next three chapters, we will take a closer look at magic in (and of) India, China, and Japan during the Golden Age.

PART II

4 INDIAN MAGIC AND MAGIC IN INDIA

Indian magic

Travellers have been reporting on the incredible magic of India for centuries. As we saw in the last chapter, these astonishing accounts built on and reinforced each other, gradually yet persistently establishing a popular representation of the subcontinent as a land of mystery, darkness, and wonder. Such accounts formed part of the cultural context of the Golden Age of Magic in the West, informing the public imagination of India and guiding the expectations of travellers who ventured in the footsteps of Marco Polo (1254–1324), Ibn Battuta (1304–1377), or the East Indian Company. Although China and then Japan also emerged as fantasies of enchanted lands during the Golden Age, it was India that remained firmly in the magical spotlight. When America's first specialist conjuring magazine was published in 1895, it was titled, *Mahatma*.[1] While the first cover story was about Robert-Houdin, the 'father of modern magic', the image that swirled around the journal's title was of an India fakir or *jādūwālā* with a drum and a cane, charming a hooded cobra; a Western explorer sits partially obscured behind the banner he's holding (on which MAHATMA is written), gazing at the Indian magician.[2]

Disgruntled by their own apparent marginality in this story, sceptical modern magicians of the turn of the twentieth century

---

[1] *Mahatma* (the Hindi and Sanskrit title of honour given to a 'great soul') was published in New York City from March 1895 until February 1906.

[2] The *jādūwālā* is featured this way on the cover of each issue, while the image of the Western conjuror changes periodically.

endeavoured to disenchant these romantic stories of Indian magic by appealing to the unreliability of pre-modern witnesses when compared with the scientific perspective of the modern eye. With characteristic confidence in the power of modernity, John Nevil Maskelyne declares that 'as a rule the more modern the authority, the less improbability there is in the story; the less predominant is the element of romance, and the more nearly it approximates to the facts as we know them to be. We are, on the whole, keener observers nowadays, and we are more sceptical.'

As we saw in Chapter 3, however, Maskelyne and his confreres in magic were also deeply dubious about the ability of the average member of the modern public to see through Orientalism to the bare facts of what they witnessed. Indeed, Orientalism seemed to function as a kind of magic in itself, clouding the minds of travellers with mysterious mists through which even the simplest and most mundane of feats took on the proportions of fantastical wizardry. Not even the educated and trained modern magician was inoculated against the Asiatic Soma; those who should know better were sometimes the most spectacular patsies of all. Maskelyne concedes, then: 'It is seldom … that an author is found who can free himself entirely from the spirit of romance which hovers around the earlier writings.'[3] The character of travel writing this period – suspended somewhere between documentary and fantasy fiction – served only to compound the difficulties.

It was in this period that many Western magicians started to perform in the guise of Indian magicians. It is a little-known quirk of history that one of the first British conjurors known to have performed in this manner was Charles Dickens (1812–1870). 'In 1849, Dickens, a keen amateur conjuror, blacked up his face and hands, dressed himself in exotic robes, and presented himself as "The Unparalleled Necromancer Rhia Rhama Rhoos," the name presumably derived from the Indian jugglers, Ramo Samee and Kia Khan Khruse.'[4]

Dickens was only slightly ahead of his time, as more and more professional magicians also adopted this kind of role. One of the most famous was the British magician Isaiah Harris Hughes (1813–1891),

---

[3] John Nevil Maskelyne, 'Oriental Jugglery', in Lionel Weatherly & John Nevil Maskelyne, *The Supernatural*. 1892, reprinted Cambridge: Cambridge University Press, 2011, p. 162.

[4] Peter Lamont & Crispin Bates, 'Conjuring Images of India in Nineteenth Century Britain'. *Social History*, 32:3 (August 2007), p. 320.

who moved to the United States and attempted to convince the public that he was from Ava in Burma, performing as 'The Fakir of Ava, Chief of Staff of Conjurors to His Sublime Greatness the Nanka of Aristaphae.' His claim was supported by black make-up, exotic silken robes, and elaborate stage aesthetics of dubious authenticity. Despite his choice of stage persona, Hughes performed a set of almost entirely conventional Western magic, simply dressing it as Indian – *Orientalizing it* – in the hope that this would add to its effective enchantment.[5] At about the same time, Joseph Stoddart (1831–1866) was performing at the Egyptian Hall in London, where his 'Indian Magic' was tremendously successful. Unlike Hughes, Stoddart did not pretend to be Indian; instead, he adopted the person of 'Colonel Stodare', intending to suggest a life of travel and mystery in the British Raj, where presumably he had learned the esoteric secrets of Indian magic. His performances included some classics of that genre, such as the Mango Trick and the Basket Trick, but his methods were almost entirely different from those used in India.[6]

Between them, Hughes and Stoddart represent a number of issues in the politics of knowledge that we explored in Chapter 3. For Hughes, for instance, the magic of Orientalism resided almost entirely in the *glamour* of India. That is, his performance was premised upon the notion that even familiar, conventional *feats* of magic could be re-enchanted by dressing them as Indian *effects*. To some extent, he invests in an ethnic conceit, since he wants his audience to believe in his own *Indian-ness* as a condition of his *magical being*. We will consider this sense of ethnic identity in the next section on the Indian Rope Trick and then later in the context of 'street Levitations'. However, there is also a sense in which his pretensions towards ethnic transformation are themselves merely glamour: he is simply glamourizing with the (inauthentic but popularly accepted) trappings of the Western imagination of India. In this way, Hughes is a clear representation of the

---

[5] An accomplished performer in his own right, Hughes is most famous for having been the mentor of the 'Dean of American Magicians', Harry Kellar, who was deeply influenced by Hughes' romantic vision of India, as we'll see.

[6] Stodare began his Indian Magic set at the Egyptian Hall in April 1865. Later that year, he also introduced the effect for which he would become most famous, the Sphinx Illusion. Towards the end of that year, he performed at Windsor Castle for Queen Victoria. The standard study of Stoddart is Edwin Dawes, *Stodare: The Enigma Variations*. Washington: Kaufman & Co., 1998.

tendency to pair the idea that India is the home of magic with the idea that Indian magic is superior to Western magic.

In fact, this tendency was recognized by many modern magicians, often with chagrin and indignation, and became one of the chief motivations for the debunking of the 'myth of the Mystic East'. As Major Lionel Branson (1879–1946) explains at the start of his 1922 book, *Indian Conjuring*, 'This little volume is written in the hopes that it may prove of interest to the thousands who reside in India, and those other thousands who, visiting its coral shores from time to time, often discuss in wondering amazement how the Indian conjuror performs his tricks. *It is also written to uphold the reputation of the Western conjuror against the spurious ascendency held by his Eastern confrere.*'[7]

Contrary to Hughes, Stoddart makes no claims to Indian-ness either ethnically or aesthetically, and instead presents himself as an imperial officer able to reproduce all of the allegedly superior magic of the colonies in superior ways, using modern Western techniques. As Lamont & Bates observe, 'the press praised such European exponents of Indian magic over "their more simple-minded Indian congeners, who practise with bare arms." Playing the part of an officer and a gentleman, Stodare's version of Indian magic was presented as both authentic and better than the original.'[8]

---

[7] In the context of the fake 'colonel' Stodare, it might be noted that Major Lionel Hugh Branson was a real major in the British Indian Army. Indeed, Branson's profile very closely fits the fictional profile created by Stoddart: a military explorer, officer, and magician (Member of the Inner Magic Circle). L.H. Branson, *Indian Conjuring*. London: Routledge & Sons, 1922, p. 2 (emphasis added). Branson's was only one of many books published in this period with the same goal (i.e., to show that Indian magic was readily explicable to modern magicians). See also John Nevil Maskelyne, 'Oriental Jugglery', in Weatherly & Maskelyne, *The Supernatural*; Samri Baldwin, *The Secrets of Mahatma Land Explained*. New York: TJ Dyson & Sons, 1895; Herewood Carrington, *Hindu Magic: An Exposé of the Tricks of the Yogis and Fakirs of India*. Kansas: The Sphinx, 1913; Elbiquet, *Supplementary Magic*. London: Routledge & Sons, 1917; Robert Henry Elliot, *The Myth of the Mystic East*. London: W.M. Blackwood & Sons, 1934. There is some debate about whether or not Elbiquet was a pen-name of Lionel Branson.

[8] Lamont & Bates, 'Conjuring Images of India', p. 320, citing (without page number) Edwin Dawes, *Stodare*. Later, Lamont & Bates contest the claim of Simon During that the ability of European magicians to impersonate Oriental magicians and to perform European repertoirs as well 'established for European audiences the supremacy of Western over Oriental magic' (Simon During, *Modern Enchantments*. Cambridge: Harvard University Press, 2002, p. 112). Instead, they suggest that 'it seems more

As we see in this chapter, many other magicians adopted various elements from Indian magic, with varying levels of explicitness, honesty, and effectiveness. Some, like Robert-Houdin himself, sought to duplicate *feats* of Indian magic that had appeared in the press, designing mechanisms and devices to accomplish these illusions. Perhaps the most famous of these was the Levitation, which was inextricably associated with India at that time. While Robert-Houdin appears to have attempted to produce a 'modern Levitation', as though the feat were somehow culturally neutral, it seems naïve to suggest that his audiences would not have associated the notorious trick with the 'Mystic East'.[9] Others, like Maskelyne & Cooke at the Egyptian Hall, created revolutionary new ways to perform ostensibly 'Indian magic' and then dressed them in dramatic sketches that self-consciously played with the question of ethnic and cultural origination. Perhaps the most successful of these (certainly from the standpoint of the history of magic itself) was the 1901 premier of the play, 'The Entranced Fakir', which saw George Cooke (1825–1905) in the guise of Dryanard Boo Sing (an Indian fakir with a long, white beard), Maskelyne as the Western showman, Dan'l Daw, and the German Paul Valadon (1867–1913) performing as a Chinese magician. The performance was an aesthetic *tour de force*, with the bewilderingly eclectic glamour, but it was also a technical triumph, leaving the audience (and other magicians) completely baffled about how it had been accomplished. In his evocative account of this show, Jim Steinmeyer explains that '"The Entranced Fakir" found magicians stumbling onto the pavement of Piccadilly and blinking at each other in stunned silence.'[10] It was a superb instance of *good magic*.

Conscious of this complicated politics of knowledge and identity politics at play during the Golden Age, in this chapter we will consider the various ways in which modern magicians sought to engage

likely that western conjurors' appropriation of the eastern image was an attempt to take advantage of the growing impression of quite the reverse, that Indian magic was more mysterious, and therefore superior to, western magic'. Lamont & Bates, 'Conjuring Images of India', p. 321.

[9] Lamont & Bates are correct to observe that Robert-Houdin adapted the Levitation and other tricks 'without any reference to their Indian roots' ('Conjuring Images of India', p. 319). However, it would probably be incorrect to say that the appropriation of this Indian *feat* would not be associated with India by his public, even if the *effect* were re-dressed into the glamour of modernity rather than Orientalism.

[10] Jim Steinmeyer, *Hiding the Elephant: How Magicians Invented the Impossible and Learned to Disappear*. Philadelphia: De Capo Press, 2003, p. 165.

with myths of *Indian magic* (such as the fabled Rope Trick), with the realities of *magic in India* (such as the Mango Tree and the Basket Trick), and finally with aspirational effects that seemed inspired by ancient India but which were only fully developed by modern magicians (such as Levitation). In the end, we will see that 'India' functions at various levels of identification: as a fantasy of magic itself; as an aesthetic style designed to enhance glamour and enchantment; as an ethnic conceit that positions magic as a form of embodiment; and finally as a de-racialized Way of Life.

The legendary Indian (or Chinese) Rope Trick

Perhaps the most famous, certainly the most notorious, example of the cultural politics of the 'mystic East' in this period is the so-called Indian Rope Trick. Indeed, this legendary illusion still casts its spell over magicians and would-be audiences all over the world today, as we saw in Scene four (in Chapter 3). So, before moving on to discuss some examples of magic actually performed in India, we should spend some time considering this powerful example of magic that has never been performed anywhere. In particular, the Indian Rope Trick can be seen as a fascinating example of the interplay of issues of race, ethnicity, culture, and modernity during the Golden Age.

One of the issues for the modern magicians of Europe and the United States was that they could (in general) explain and replicate most of the feats they witnessed or heard about in India. But they could offer no explanation for the workings of the Indian Rope Trick. If it were a genuine feat, then modern magic was at a loss. As Teller observes, the idea of an inexplicable magical feat in 'a far-off place filled a void in the West', feeding the fantasy that India was a place of 'real and potent' magic. 'Hungering for the unexplainable, but eager to consider themselves enlightened', Western societies tended to reason thus: 'We know the natives are too primitive to fool us; therefore, what we are witnessing must be genuine magic.'[11] This kind of public reaction mobilized and provoked modern magicians into aggressive defensiveness. In his treatise on *Indian Conjuring*, for instance, Lionel Branson explains various feats of magic in India and then laments:

[11] Teller, 'The Rise of the Indian Rope Trick: The Gift of the Magi', *New York Times*, 13 February 2005.

> Having complete the average programme of our Jadoo-wallah,
> I feel sure that people will say to each other 'Yes' but what about the
> Rope trick? He cannot explain that and has avoided the best known
> trick of all Indian conjuring tricks.
>   *In self-defence therefore*, we will deal with the Great Rope
> trick.[12]

This defensive stance was entirely typical of the writings of modern magicians during this period, as they strove to debunk *both* the idea that the Rope Trick was a result of genuinely counter-physical supernatural causation *and* the idea that it was a regular instance of conjuring that they simply didn't understand. Given the unified theory of modern magic that we explored in earlier chapters, it can be seen that this position was tantamount to claiming that the Rope Trick was simply a fantasy. Hence, while Branson goes on to explain the effect as it was reported to him, he then notes that he has been in India for twenty-three years, 'during which period I would gladly have travelled from one end of India to the other to [see the Rope Trick, but] I have never yet met anyone who has definitely told me that he with his own eyes had seen the trick.... I have met innumerable people whose aunt's sister's cousin saw it done, but never have I had the pleasure of meeting anyone directly deceived by it.'[13] Branson was certainly not the only travelling magician to offer a large financial reward (in his case, a year's pay) to anyone who had seen the trick and could direct him to an able performer, and was likewise not the only one to keep his money.

Branson's vision of the feat is consistent with the version we saw in Scene four:

> The performer, in one's own compound, throws up the end of an
> ordinary rope into the air. By some mysterious means this end
> remains suspended in mid-air, without any visible means of sup-
> port, so much so that the little boy assistant climbs up the rope to its
> very highest point, whence, after an interval, he entirely disappears.
> The performer then takes a sword and waves it in the air, when the
> legs and arms, disjointed, and finally the trunk and head of the little
> boy fall with a profusion of blood upon the ground at the foot of the
> rope. By means of an incantation these resume their natural

[12] Branson, *Indian Conjuring*, p. 78 (emphasis added).
[13] Branson, *Indian Conjuring*, p. 80. Branson notes that the Irish bandmaster of a Gurkha regiment once claimed to have seen it, but he was 'trying to pull my leg'.

positions, and the little boy gets up and walks off, apparently none the worse for his most trying ordeal.[14]

If we can accept that none of the modern Western travellers around India ever saw this feat accomplished and never even met anyone who had seen this feat accomplished, perhaps the most interesting question becomes that of why the Western world came to believe in it. In this regard, it is fascinating to see that Maskelyne doesn't even mention the Rope Trick in his 1892 debunking of 'Oriental Jugglery'. For him, the highlights of Indian magic included three main feats in addition to Levitation: the Basket Trick, the Mango Tree Trick, and the Buried Alive Trick. In other words, the Indian Rope Trick only emerges into the public consciousness later in the 1890s, quickly establishing itself as one of the emblems of Orientalist magic. In fact, Maskelyne himself confronts it in 1912, when he ties it to the Orientalism of Theosophy as the 'greatest imposture ever perpetrated under the cloak of religion'.[15] By the time of Branson's book (1922) and Elliot's book (1934), it was by far most controversial and discussed feat of Indian magic; indeed, both authors devoted special sections in their manuscripts to explaining why the failure of modern magic to replicate it was not because Indian magic was superior but simply because it was an elaborate fiction that nobody anywhere had ever accomplished.[16]

So, what happened in the 1890s? The important recent work of Peter Lamont suggests that the Indian Rope Trick first came to the attention of modern Western readers in an article in the *Chicago Tribune* on 8 August 1890.[17] The journalist, John Elbert Wilkie, wrote the article under a pseudonym (Fred S. Ellmore = Fred Sell More) and then (four months later) published a retraction in the same newspaper,

---

[14] Branson, *Indian Conjuring*, pp. 78–79.

[15] John Nevil Maskelyne, *The Fraud of 'Theosophy' Exposed, and the Miraculous Rope-Trick of the Indian Jugglers Explained*. London: Routledge, 1912.

[16] Branson, *Indian Conjuring*, chapter 9; Elliot, *Myth of the Mystic East*, chapter 3.

[17] A full and interesting account is given in Peter Lamont, *The Rise of the Indian Rope Trick*. London: Little, Brown, 2004. This book builds on important earlier work by Lamont: Richard Wiseman & Peter Lamont, 'Unravelling the Indian rope-trick'. *Nature*, 383 (1996), pp. 212–213; Peter Lamont & Richard Wiseman, 'The Rise and Fall of the Indian Rope Trick'. *Journal of the Society for Psychical Research*, 65 (2001), pp. 175–193. The article in *Nature* was a landmark in the contemporary discussion of the Indian Rope Trick as a hoax.

saying that the original article had been an experiment that had gar-
nered far more attention than he had expected.[18] In fact, the article
created a storm that has still not completely subsided. It was translated
and republished all across Europe (usually without the retraction),
provoking a number of people (especially in Britain and France) to
claim that they too had witnessed the illusion while in India,[19] creating
a potent mix of imagery about the mysterious colonial margins of
Empire, which itself seemed to provide an enabling condition for people
to believe in the story.

In addition to the article in the *Chicago Tribune*, which suggests that the Rope Trick is a modern invention, a cluster of other
sources appeared at about the same time that enabled the invention of
the Rope Trick as an *ancient* accomplishment. For instance, as we'll see
later, the end of the nineteenth century also saw the translation and
publication of the travels of Ibn Battuta, who relates having witnessed
something very similar to the Indian Rope Trick in 1346, but in
Hangzhuo, China. Evidently, the Chinese magicians used a chain
instead of a rope. Furthermore, it is less well known that the classic
of Chinese literature, *Strange Tales from a Chinese Studio* (1740), by
Pu Songling, was also translated into English for the first time in
1880.[20] Coincidentally or not, Pu Songling wrote in Hangzhuo and
professes to have seen the White Lotus Rope Trick.

As we'll see in the next chapter, Pu Songling's collection of
supernatural tales of magic and mystery in ancient China became
much cited by Western scholars and journalists in accounts of the
White Lotus Society and the Boxer Rebellion, contributing significantly

[18] The illustrated article describes the journey of two Yale graduates on their journey
around India. It explains that they saw a street fakir throw a ball of twine into the air,
letting it unroll from his teeth until the other end vanished into the clouds, at which
point a young boy of six climbed the twine and vanished from the top of it. The
photograph taken by the Yale alumni shows no twine or boy, presumably because the
former had collapsed back to the ground and the latter had vanished. The fakir is
sitting on the ground calmly. The author of the piece concludes that the fakir probably
hypnotized the entire crowd.

[19] Perhaps the first European to claim to have seen the Rope Trick first hand was
Sebastian Burchett in 1904, who reported his sighting to the Society for Psychical
Research, which found his story unreliable. In addition, various fake photographs
were published in the press.

[20] Herbert Giles (trans.), *Pu Songling: Strange Stories from a Chinese Studio*. London:
T. De La Rue, 1880.

to the aura of China as part of the 'mystic East' even in the modern age of warring empires.[21] Most significant for us is tale number twelve, 'Stealing a Peach', which contains a description of the Rope Trick with nearly all of its vital features: a man throws a rope into the air, which a boy then climbs until out of sight in the clouds; the boy throws down a peach, but then the rope collapses, and the boy's bloody limbs rain down to the ground; after some fuss, the boy re-appears unharmed from a basket.[22] Pu Songling comments: 'To this very day I have never forgotten this extraordinary performance. I later learned that this "Rope Trick" was a speciality of the White Lotus sect. Surely this man must have learned it from them.'[23]

Leaving aside for the moment the likelihood that the legend of the Indian Rope Trick is actually the legend of a Chinese Rope Trick, the invention of this feat as the emblem of Indian magic at the *fin de siècle* resulted in intense public discussion. Given its powerful sense of public responsibility and the moral mission of legitimate, modern magic, it should come as no surprise that the Magic Circle in London intervened forcefully in this debate. At a public meeting in 1919, investigators and members of the Magic Circle concluded that the Rope Trick was a hoax, notwithstanding the fact that a number of prominent magicians were already performing (rather crude) versions

[21] Judith Zeitlin, *Historian of the Strange: Pu Songling and the Chinese Classical Tale.* Stanford: Stanford University Press, 1993. The White Lotus was originally a millenarian Buddhist movement which re-emerged in later imperial China as a label for various different popular uprisings with magical, spiritual, and/or millenarian associations. Some commentators link the White Lotus Society to the rise of the Triads in modern China. The Boxer Rebellion was a protonationalistic, anti-imperialist uprising in the late Qing dynasty – the rebels were represented as martial artists who practiced spirit possession and Daoist magic in order to make themselves invulnerable to weapons and bullets.

[22] One of the first modern accounts of a sighting that approximates this macabre version came in 1904 (shortly after Sebastian Burchett's failure with the Society for Psychical Research). She adds to the version of the fictional Yale graduates some details about the boy who 'vanished from sight, and a few minutes later bits of his (apparently mangled) remains fell from the sky, first an arm, then a leg, and so on until all his component parts had descended'. Thankfully, the fakir was able to make the boy whole once again by covering him with a sheet. Lamont, *The Rise of the Indian Rope Trick*, p. 98.

[23] Pu Songling (trans. John Minford), *Strange Tales from a Chinese Studio.* London: Penguin, 2006 (ebook version). Intriguingly, the anonymous woman who claimed to have seen the same feat in 1904 remarked that the performance aroused no particular response from her at the time.

of it in their stage shows, most famously Howard Thurston.[24] Importantly, the verdict of the Magic Circle was not a judgement on whether particular performances or the Rope Trick were 'real' or 'fake', but rather that the whole idea that anyone had ever seen even a 'fake' performance was itself a hoax. That is, even in their modern sense of magical performance, the Rope Trick was a hoax because all account of its performance were themselves fictions.

Finally, with little sign that factual exposure was overcoming Orientalist fantasy, the Magic Circle issued its famous 'challenge' to anyone who could successfully perform the Indian Rope Trick in full and in natural conditions in 1933.[25] The challenge was orchestrated by the Circle's (newly re-established) Occult Committee, which, as we've seen, had been started by John Nevil Maskelyne in 1914 as a body to investigate and expose fraudulent Spiritualists and to combat investment in the supernatural.

The real point of contention in 1933 appeared to remain whether an Indian fakir or yogi could actually perform magic that a Western stage magician could not: was there really a mystical or magical secret accessible only to these mysterious and exotic men of the East? Or, were the stories of past performances and alleged eye-witnesses simply folk stories or blatant lies? Were the mechanized, modern performances of versions of the trick (such as those by Thurston) really all that was possible? The Magic Circle offered 200 guineas to find out; the Magic Circle sought to unmask Orientalism publically.

This high-profile public challenge was seen by many as a necessary move to explode a dangerous myth that 'gave the appalling impression that Indian jugglers were superior to Western conjurors', or even that modern magic (and modernity itself) was simply wrong about its stance on the unified nature of *real magic*. That is, if Indian jugglers were better than Western conjurors, that would be humiliating enough for imperial magicians; but if Indian fakirs really had access to counter-physical supernatural causation when modern magic was founded on

---

[24] Thurston showed no particular concern for his role in the politics of knowledge or Orientalist discourse as he advertised his show as the WORLD'S MOST FAMOUS ILLUSION FIRST TIME OUT OF INDIA – the poster includes an image of Thurston ushering an Indian boy up a rope while a turbaned fakir watches in awe.

[25] The challenge stated that the rope must be thrown up into the air and defy the force of gravity while someone climbs it and then disappears.

Figure 4.1 Thurston, 'Indian Rope Trick', c. 1927, Stobridge. Courtesy of Nielsen Magic Collection. Thurston amazes an Indian audience with a Western version of the Rope Trick assisted by leprechauns and imps.

its impossibility, the delicate balance of dis-enchantment in modernity was in serious jeopardy.

On the other hand, not unpredictably given the persistent romance of magicians for the idea of magic that we saw in Chapter 1, some members of the Magic Circle felt that the Occult Committee's agenda was too aggressive, seeking as it did to place both mystery and the Orient itself on trial. Lamont quotes the melancholy of one member's response to the committee's challenge: 'why must we have our dreams shattered? The world would be dull, miserable and intolerable if we believed only what our step-mother Science would have us believe.... Science is already robbing us of our Romance.... We all love mystery and many of us would like to possess the mysterious reputation of the fakir, but [instead] we are always trying to expose him as a fraud.'[26]

In the end, there were various responses to the challenge. One man, 'His Excellency Dr. Sir Alexander Cannon', declared that he could arrange for a yogi to come over from India to perform the trick if the Magic Circle could also ship over sufficient, authentic Indian sand to fill the Albert Hall, and could also heat the Hall to tropical temperatures, at a total estimated cost of 50,000 pounds. One of the interesting implications of this offer was its presupposition that the trick relied upon material authenticity: if India could be brought to London, Indian magic could come with it.[27] Then, in 1935, an 'Indian' magician named Karachi accepted the challenge, claiming to have learnt the feat from a Gurkha soldier during the Great War. However, there was much controversy around both the man and the performance. Academic opinion was that it would be very unlikely for a Gurkha to have any such knowledge;[28] others questioned (rightly) whether Karachi was really Indian or just an imposter (his real name turned out to be Arthur Claude Derby from Plymouth); and finally it seemed that the trick he proposed to perform was not actually the complete version of

[26] Quoted in Lamont, *The Rise of the Indian Rope Trick*, p. 125.

[27] It is curious to reflect that Bram Stoker makes a similar case for the magical efficacy of authentic soil in *Dracula*, which was published in 1897. The Count must rest in his native soil, and so always takes it with him when he travels.

[28] Lamont suggests that an academic from Cambridge University went on record to assert this position. Lamont, *The Rise of the Indian Rope Trick*, p. 137. I have not been able to identify this figure.

the trick proposed in the Magic Circle's challenge, which was already a much more modest version of the legendary effect.[29]

In the end, the Magic Circle refused to accept the counter-challenge of Karachi. Firstly, he was not endeavouring to perform the legendary version of the Indian Rope Trick that the Magic Circle found so entrancing and dangerous – indeed, he was offering to perform something that stage magicians were already incorporating into their shows in Europe and the United States. Hence, his counter-challenge was much more in the spirit of the 'magical duel' between stage magicians that had been prevalent thirty years earlier, in which competing magicians tried to best each other in knowledge and technique, but neither made any pretence of esoteric or exotic mystery.[30] The stakes in a magical duel were about mastery of *modern magic* itself, not about a confrontation between the Orient and the Occident or between supernatural and natural magic; in such a duel the Magic Circle had nothing to gain and nothing to prove.

And secondly, it was increasingly obvious to everyone involved that Karachi's connection with India, fakirs, and yogis was almost wholly inauthentic. He was simply following in the wake of many other Western performers who adopted the guise of an 'Oriental' in order to add some extra glamour to his performance and persona. Hence, it was not clear what it would mean for him to defeat the challenge, even if he were able to do so. What would be the significance of a costumed white, European man from Plymouth performing a modest, technical version of part of the Indian Rope Trick? Karachi, a *fake Indian*, could not manifest the contrived confrontation between Orient and Occident or between supernatural and natural magic; he would simply represent an ongoing pantomime of Orientalist magic.

So, the Magic Circle, like all the modern magicians who went in search of the Rope Trick in India, never had to pay out its reward. Modern magic was not exposed as somehow inferior to Oriental magic; Western magicians were not exposed as ethnically inferior to Indian magicians; modernity (and modern magic) was not exposed as

---

[29] Karachi offered to make a rope rise vertically from his lap and then have someone climb it, as long as he could have forty-eight hours to prepare the staging and as long as the audience was not permitted within fifteen yards. He declined to attempt to make the boy vanish from the top of the rope.

[30] This convention is subverted wonderfully in the Christopher Priest novel, *The Prestige* (1995), which was made into a movie of the same name by Christopher Nolan (2006).

essentially flawed in its commitment to scientific reason. Instead, the Indian/Chinese Rope Trick was exposed as an Orientalist fantasy, invented from fictions in the late nineteenth century as part of the glamour of the mystic East, explicable only in terms of intoxication or mass suggestion. The Indian Rope Trick emerges as an intriguing example of a magical *effect* that has no *feat* – this, it seems to me, is the genius of Penn & Teller's performance in 2003 (Scene five).

Magic in India

The Indian repertoire

While there were various modern magicians in Europe and the United States who endeavoured to participate in the glamour of *Indian magic* by performing in the guise of Indian fakirs at home, there were also many who travelled to India in order to discover for themselves the magic actually being performed *in India*. In most cases, these magicians personified the conflicted and contradictory relationship between modern magic and the mystic East. They were caught between romance and lust, on the one hand, and disappointment, disparagement and disgust, on the other.

An indicative example would be the American magician Howard Thurston (The King of Cards), who recounts in his memoirs the details of his travels around the world, during which he performed in theatres all over Asia. He relates his excitement at the prospect of leaving Rangoon ('a city of enchantment to me') and travelling to India in 1906, 'the home of magicians, and the mecca of my travels'.[31] He explains how this excitement led him to engage a large room at the Continental Hotel and to lease 'a long corridor extending the full length of the building'. He then proceeds to hire 'twenty "boys," as servants are called in the East, with instructions to bring to me, early the next morning, all the magicians they could find in the streets. The following day the corridor was filled; more than a hundred magicians, snake charmers, animal trainers and street entertainers were present.'[32] However, disappointed with this large but motley assortment, Thurston continues to search with a little more discernment: 'My eagerness to witness the famous mysteries of the Orient

[31] Howard Thurston, *My Life of Magic*. Philadelphia: Dorrance & Co., 1929, p. 184.
[32] Thurston, *My Life of Magic*, p. 187.

was so keen that I asked the servants to bring in a troupe of the best performers of the city while I was having my coffee in bed.'[33]

Once again, rather disappointed by the 'weird incantations' and 'weird ceremonies' of these performers who performed famous Indian feats, such as the Mango Trick, Thurston 'finally . . . asked for the very best, whereupon three men dressed in gaily colored clothes entered, and presented their feature illusions', which turn out to be tricks they had learned in Chicago.[34]

Thurston reveals that he continued his disappointing search in this way for three days, hoping 'to find something worthy of the reputation of the Indian magician', but finding only some clever sleight of hand, some well-timed misdirection, and some 'highly developed personality'. As we saw in Chapter 3, Thurston joined his Western confreres by attributing these qualities of the Indian magician to the 'reason that some of the tricks performed by the Hindu conjurers have been handed down for generations; and they have the accumulated training of hundreds of years'.[35]

The only category of performers to which Thurston attributes any great enchantment were the snake charmers, whom he described as having 'combined the thrill of handling a poisonous cobra with some of the cleverest deceptions known in magic.. . . It was the first time in years that I had witnessed any magic that mystified me.' Nevertheless, his respect had limits: he went on to note that snake charmers form a special (low) caste of their own and that they make most of their money in disreputable ways, for instance, by hustling 'newly arrived British families . . . holding a snake in their hands, claiming they caught it as it crawled from under their house'.[36]

---

[33] Thurston, *My Life of Magic*, p. 187.

[34] Thurston, *My Life of Magic*, pp. 187–188.

[35] Thurston, *My Life of Magic*, p. 188. In more recent years, Lee Siegel has also observed that 'the magic has hardly changed at all.... They are born to what they do ... trained in magic from infancy.' (Siegel, *Net of* Magic, pp. 2–3). It should be recalled, from Chapter 3, that Elliot also emphasized the repetition and timeless lack of innovation in Oriental magic, when compared with the pressure for constant invention in Western magic (Elliot, *Myth of the Mystic East*, pp. 53–54). Less charitably, Lionel Branson declares: 'I have very little praise to give to the Indian conjuror as an artists, either in sleight-of-hand, in juggling, or as an illusionist. His tricks are as "old as my unpaid bills" and from time immemorial have been performed with the same monotonous patter and the irritating drone of the "bean" or so-called musical instrument.' Branson, *Indian Conjuring*, p. 9.

[36] Thurston, *My Life of Magic*, pp. 190–191. The relationship between caste and Western respect for Indian magicians is a study in itself. In his studies, for

In the end, Thurston decided to give a free afternoon performance of his own magic in the Theatre Royal especially for all the magicians of Calcutta. He claimed that he had been playing to full houses of Europeans, but that he more than doubled the 1,400-seat capacity for this special performance. While he had them captive, he used the opportunity to enquire after the fabled Indian Rope Trick, only to discover that 'not one of the three thousand fakirs, conjurers and magicians had ever heard of it'. So, instead, Thurston treated them to a performance of a Levitation (which was presumably a variation on Maskelyne's 'The Enchanted Fakir'):

> Among the mysteries I presented was the Levitation act in which a girl is apparently hypnotized and placed on a couch in the centre of the brilliantly lighted stage. I command her to rise slowly in the air to the height of six feet. On this occasion I invited a score of magicians from the audience to come on the stage, and led them around the suspended lady. They put their hands over her and under her, and I passed a hoop back and forth over her body. To my astonishment the magicians fell on their faces. There was a general murmur in the audience and I was told that they were declaring I had supernatural powers.[37]

The reasons for Thurston's astonishment in this scene will become readily apparent in the next section, when we explore the history of the Levitation in detail. It is such an important illusion and so centrally

instance, Harry Kellar is dismissive of 'low caste' magicians for being of dubious talent and morality but reserves high praise for the apparently superlative accomplishments of 'high caste magicians' (Harry Kellar, 'High Caste Indian Magic'. *The North American Review*, 156:434 (Jan. 1893), pp. 75–86). In recent years, this low/high distinction is also observed by Siegel, who recognizes it as both a sociological phenomenon and as an indicator of magical training and performance. For instance, Siegel notes that the 'low caste' magicians of the street are 'blood members of a Muslim low caste, Maslets, bound together by a secret language and secrecy itself.... The boys perform with their fathers until they are old enough to out on their own, taking a little brother or cousin along – no one plays the magic show alone. The girls perform – handle the snakes, are stuffed into baskets, have swords passed through their necks – until they are women; then they are expected to bear new conjurers, nourish them, and teach them ancient secrets' (Siegel, *Net of Magic*, p. 3). Meanwhile, the 'high magic' belongs to the magician with a patron – a religious, sacred, or courtly figure, rather than a *jādū* of the streets – it embodies the 'mystic kitsch' of grandly Orientalized Maharajas of Magic.

[37] Thurston, *My Life of Magic*, p. 192.

associated with India that Thurston's performance to such a shocked audience of Indian magicians in Calcutta has the poetic aura of irony. Presumably that was Thurston's intention in telling the story as he did. In general, though, Thurston's memoirs serve to illustrate a trend in the writings of modern magicians of the Golden Age, who sought to expose the alleged superiority of Indian magic by revealing the 'truth' about how magic was actually performed in India and, sometimes, contrasting this with the shock caused to local audiences when they witnessed the wondrous modern magic of Westerners on their stages.[38]

Before taking a closer look at the Levitation as an exemplary case, it is worthwhile to look briefly at the other tricks and illusions associated with the inherited repertoire of the Indian magician. In particular, no account of the magic of India from this period could exclude mention of at least the Mango Tree and the Basket Trick.[39] Thurston himself referred to the Mango Trick rather dismissively in his account of the 'weird incantations' and 'weird ceremonies' that he witnessed in his hotel. He glosses it in this way: 'the mango was delicious; but the trick, to the eyes of a trained magician, was

[38] In fact, as we saw in Chapter 3, Thurston was particularly guilty of exploiting the 'glamour' of modernity, wasting few opportunities to communicate the impression that, as a representative of Western imperial superiority, he was the master of tremendous supernatural powers. We have already seen how this kind of ethic ran counter to the development of 'modern magic' as a moral movement, and it would have been deeply controversial had Thurston made similar claims to audiences in Europe or North America. The unevenness of this ethic is a clear symptom of an imperial political culture.

[39] In addition to the Levitation, snake charming, and the mythical Indian Rope Trick, these tricks are the most commonly mentioned in the travelogues of the modern magicians. They also feature in the most important manuals of Indian magic from the period and afterwards: Branson, *Indian Conjuring*; Elliot, *Myth of the Mystic East*; Will Ayling & Sam Sharpe, *Oriental Conjuring and Magic*. Exeter: Supreme Magic Co., 1981. Other important illusions might include the Dancing Duck, the Bamboo Sticks, the Egg Bag, and the Cut and Restored Rope. A number of manuals also include 'endurance illusions' such as being 'buried alive'. Maskelyne ('Oriental Jugglery') mentions this, together with the Basket Trick and Mango Trick, as the most important Indian feat. Some texts from the Golden Age also include the famous 'cups and balls' as a feat of Indian juggling, but it seems more likely that this trick is of Egyptian origin. In any case, the classic 'three cups' street performance was already so deeply embedded within European conjuring by medieval times that it had featured in European art, literature, and theatre for centuries before the Golden Age, leading many leading modern magicians (such as Houdini, Hoffmann, and Devant in particular) to refer to it as laying the foundations of all legerdemain.

disappointing'.[40] In fact, the Mango Tree Trick was one of the most beautiful and poetic illusions of the Golden Age, which was quickly appropriated by many magicians in Europe. Maskelyne published a method in 'Oriental Jugglery' in 1892. A similar method appeared in *Mahatma* in 1895, but it was given a much more comprehensive treatment by Charles Bertram (1853–1907) in 1899.[41] The basic effect is elegant and simple: a mango seed is planted and grows into a tree in a matter of a few minutes; the tree then sprouts fruit, which the spectator can eat. The effect is accomplished through the use of a tripod, in the middle of which is a pot where the mango seed is seen to be planted. A sheet is then draped over the tripod while the magician sits behind it. At various intervals, the sheet is removed to show the mango seed sprouting, growing into a stem, into a branch, and finally into a little tree with a fresh mango ready to be picked.

Of course, Thurston was already fully aware of how this trick was accomplished when he saw it in Calcutta. His trained and critical eye does indeed reveal the method, and also emphasizes the effective glamour of wearing long Indian robes when performing this trick:

> I clearly saw the fakirs, under cover the cloth, take the [successively larger] mango branches from under their clothing and place them in the [pot]. Despite the fact that three assistants gathered round to shut off my view, I saw the fakir deliberately substitute larger branches for the smaller. These branches were taken from his long robe, also from the robes of his assistants. It was a very awkward attempt, and a failure so far as mystery was concerned.[42]

The Indian Basket Trick is perhaps even more well-known today, since it has spawned many imitations and variations in modern magic. The basic effect is that a magician places a lidded basket onto the ground, removes the lid, and invites a young boy with a scarlet turban to step inside. The basket doesn't appear large enough to contain the

---

[40] Thurston, *My Life of Magic*, pp. 187–188.
[41] Charles Bertram, 'Are Indian Jugglers Humbug?' *Mahatma*, 3:6 (December 1899), p. 326 and 3:7 (January 1900), pp. 340–343. Bertram was an intrepid magician explorer, whose account of his travels through India, China, Japan, and the United States is an invaluable resource for understanding magic in this period. Charles Bertram, *A Magician in Many Lands*. London: Routledge & Sons, 1911.
[42] Thurston, *My Life of Magic*, p. 188.

boy. He stands in the opening with his feet inside. The magician covers the boy and the basket with a sheet, pushing down on the boy's head until he is squashed into the basket. Replacing the lid, the magician removes the sheet. The audience can see the basket with the boy presumably inside it. Reaching under the lid, the magician removes the boy's scarlet turban. He then proceeds to thrust swords through the basket at different angles; blood pours out through the weave. Then, recovering the basket with the sheet, the magician removes the lid once again and jumps into the opening, stamping around to show the basket is empty. Finally, the magician climbs out of the basket and the sheet immediately rises back up into the shape of the boy. Removing the sheet, the boy is standing there completely unharmed (but without his scarlet turban).

Many modern magicians on their tours of India witnessed this trick, but its method was already well known in the 1860s in Europe, when Joseph Stoddart (Colonel Stodare) was performing a version in the Egyptian Hall in London (1865). Maskelyne provides an explanation in 'Oriental Jugglery' in 1892, and by the time of Carrington's account in 1914 the various methods were relatively well-known.[43] In brief, the 'trick' is the basket itself, the sides of which are curved in such a way that a small boy can curl around the inside of it and leave the centre completely unobstructed, which allows swords or even the magician himself to plunge into the middle without harming him.

Ingenious, poetic, and grotesque as these effects might be they did not excite the public imagination as much as the miraculous stories of Indian Levitations (or the mythical Rope Trick). Well performed, the Mango Tree Trick did communicate an aura of enchantment and mystical power over nature, which is probably why Thurston and others took pains to debunk it (and also to appropriate it). But the main impact of the Basket Trick was to support popular opinion in the West that Indian conjurers were brutal and callous, as we saw in Chapter 3. Presumably this aspect of the Basket Trick also fuelled rumours about the more macabre versions of the Indian Rope Trick. However, in terms of *Indian magic* that was also *magic in India*, it was the feat of Levitation that most enchanted the Western imagination, and it is to that we turn in the second half of this chapter.

[43] Carrington, *Hindu Magic*, pp. 19–26.

Scene six: buried alive?

12 April 1999 was a rain-drenched, overcast day in New York City, but only David Blaine was buried six feet beneath three tons of water. For the previous week he'd been lying in a transparent plastic coffin, squashed beneath a transparent tank of water, and packed in by gravel. On the 5 April, when he had been sealed in, only a few people even knew what he was doing. 75,000 visitors and dozens of film crews later, he was a global superstar. The media carried the story that Marie Blood, Harry Houdini's niece, had visited on behalf of her legendary uncle, commenting that not even the great Houdini ever attempted such a feat.

Blood was only partially correct. In fact, Houdini attempted three variants of the famous 'buried alive' stunt, inspired apparently by stories of the fakirs of India and Egypt. The first attempt might (or might not) have been in Santa Ana, California, in 1915. Houdini himself related versions of this story on a number of occasions, not always consistently, but it was consistently important to him that people believed he attempted to bury himself alive. Apparently, having heard that a yogi had accomplished a similar escape, Houdini was buried six feet underground without a casket. He then proceeded to attempt to dig his way back to the sunshine; when his hand finally broke the surface, he was so panicked and exhausted that he lost consciousness and he had to be dug out by his assistants.[44] He reported that this was the most dangerous feat he'd ever tried.

A few years later, on 5 August 1926, Houdini once again took aim at an allegedly mystical Oriental magician, Rahman Bey, who had let it be believed that supernatural powers enabled him to be submerged in a sealed casket in the swimming pool of New York's Dalton Hotel in July for a full hour, setting a world record. Houdini himself duplicated the feat in New York's Hotel Shelton, but managed to remain underwater for ninety-one minutes, claiming that there were no trickery or supernatural powers involved – he just breathed calmly and concentrated on the certainty of his safety. He thought this should inspire miners trapped in restricted spaces with little oxygen.

---

[44] Attempts to recreate the feat as described by Houdini have concluded that it would not have been possible for him even to move his fingers under the pressure of six feet of compacted earth. Hence, either there were other conditions or the feat was different from this description.

Unwilling to let go of being 'buried alive', Houdini also planned an elaborate stage escape for his 1927 season, billed as 'Egyptian Fakirs Outdone!' The feat would have involved Houdini being straight-jacketed, sealed in a casket, and then buried in a giant, sand-filled tank. Sadly, he died on 31 October 1926, and the casket planned for 'buried alive' was used to carry his body back to New York City.

In interviews following his own burial, Blaine has been quite explicit about his debt to Houdini and, in particular, to the way that Houdini didn't *pretend* to be buried alive or locked into caskets, but was *actually* buried alive and locked up. He trained hard to become able to endure the unendurable and escape the inescapable. Rather than performing tricks or appealing to supernatural causation, Houdini strove to demonstrate what a normal, everyday man could accomplish. Talking about his own burial, Blaine explains to *Time Magazine*, 'I'd always wanted to do these types of things – pieces of magic I could put out not as illusions, but really doing it. Which is really in the tradition of Houdini, who was an escape artist but who was really doing things: training hard, keeping a serious regimen.'

However, while Houdini was inspired by stories of Indian and Egyptian fakirs performing apparently impossible feats, seeking to debunk their spiritual claims, Blaine was inspired by the fakirs in different ways, seeking to re-enchant what Houdini had exposed as mundane.

'For the coffin, I read about an Indian fakir who was buried alive for a month', explains Blaine, presumably referring to the incredible story of Sadhu Haridas in 1880, who was apparently buried alive in box for forty days, during which time he entered a trance state of suspended animation, only to revive himself after being dug up and presumed dead. The *London Telegraph* (22 August 1880) saw the feat of Haridas as clear evidence of superhuman (if not supernatural) physical control due to rigorous and mysterious ascetic conditioning. However, Blaine must be aware that Haridas and his many imitators were attacked by modern magicians such as Maskelyne, who revealed secret underground passageways that allowed the sadhu out of their burial sites and back again before they were dug up.[45] So, 'I thought instead of burying myself under dirt, I'd bury myself under water so everybody could see that you're there.'

In other words, Blaine isn't interested in producing the *effect* of being buried alive, he's interested in performing the *feat* itself. And

---

[45] Maskelyne, 'Oriental Jugglery', pp. 178–181.

this is not because such a performance exposes the normality of the feat, but rather it's because the act manifests an ascetic accomplishment. He's not trying to debunk the Oriental mystic, he's seeking to become one. 'I do a lot of research on what people have done in the past. I started to become interested in ascetics, the great monks, San Simeon. Reading *Siddhartha* as a kid got me interested in fasting.... '

As the three-ton tank of water is lifted off Blaine's plastic coffin, the magician struggles to sit up and squints in the dim glare of an overcast sky. Cheers and screams whirl around in eddies of appreciation. Weak with fatigue, Blaine clutches a microphone and manages to get his message across: 'I saw something truly incredible: people of all kinds all banding together and smiling. That made all of this worth it.' In his voiceover, watching himself being draped in robes and sunglasses and photographers, Blaine adds his own footnote, 'That's when I realised that this is what magic is all about; it's about bringing people together that normally don't come together. And that's when I realised that this is what I want to do with the rest of my life.'

A few years later, in 2003, Blaine effectively buries himself alive in the air, spending forty-four days in a transparent plastic box above the Thames in London. And then in 2006 he was 'Drowned Alive' in front of the Lincoln Center in New York City. Reflecting on these variations on yogic asceticism, Blaine explains that 'the most pleasurable one was London. There was just a whole heightened sense of everything: taking everything away like that really sharpens colors, tastes, senses, smells, hearing. Even though the taste is you digesting your own muscle tissues and fats, you still taste this sweet pear-drop in your mouth. Every time you taste water, it's so sweet – at least for the first twenty-eight days, until you shift to digesting your organ walls, and then it begins to taste like sulphur and becomes horrific. I got liver and kidney failure from that one.'[46]

The miraculous Indian levitation

Remarkably, one of the most influential voices in the establishment of the modern fantasy of Levitation was that of the great fourteenth-century Moroccan explorer, Ibn Battuta, who is widely regarded as

[46] Quotations from *Time* in this scene are from the interview by Alex Altman, 1 May 2008.

the greatest traveller of all time.[47] Battuta claims to have witnessed an Indian yogi levitating in a crossed-leg position in Delhi, somewhere between 1332 and 1347. His account became central to debates in the Golden Age of Magic, although his credibility as a reliable witness was by no means certain. Just as we saw a resurgence of interest in the travel accounts of Marco Polo in the nineteenth century, as travel to Asia became more thinkable for more people, so there was a boom of interest in Battuta.[48] His written account of twenty-nine years of travelling, *A Gift to Those Who Contemplate the Wonders of Cities and the Marvels of Travelling*, known simply as the *Rihla* or 'The Journey', was completed in the mid-1350s (almost entirely from memory, since there are no records that he took notes on his travels). But it was not known in Europe until the nineteenth century, when abridged sections of the manuscript were discovered by various European scholars and explorers during the boom of interest in the Islamic world. Extracts were published in German as early as 1818 and an abridged Arabic text was translated into English in 1829, using copies bequeathed to the library of the University of Cambridge about a decade earlier.[49] The National Library of France obtained copies in the 1830s, following the French occupation of Algeria, and translations started to appear in the 1840s, with a major four-volume edition in French in the 1850s, which has formed the basis of many subsequent translations into other languages, including another abridged translation into English in the 1920s.[50]

[47] Battuta's place in the history of travelling and exploration is analysed with great sophistication in Roxanne Euben, *Journeys to the Other Shore: Muslim and Western Travelers in Search of Knowledge*. Princeton: Princeton University Press, 2008.

[48] Separate new editions of *The Travels of Marco Polo* appeared in 1844, 1854, and 1874, for the first time since the sixteenth century. Marco Polo recounts witnessing great feats of magic (such as controlling the weather) in Kashmir, and seeing Indian conjurers perform miracles at the court of the Great Khan between 1270 and 1290 (Sidney Clarke, 'Oriental Conjuring', p. 373). Hugh Murray, *The Travels of Marco Polo*. Edinburgh: Oliver & Boyd, 1844; Thomas Wright, *The Travels of Marco Polo, the Venetian*. London: Henry Bohn, 1854; Henry Yule, *The Book of Ser Marco Polo, the Venetian, Concerning the Kingdoms and Marvels of the East*. London: John Murray, 1873/1903.

[49] Cambridge University received its abridged Arabic texts from Johann Ludwig Burckhardt (1784–1817) as part of the 800 manuscripts he left to the university, where he had studied Arabic. The Swiss explorer is most famous for his 'discovery' of Petra.

[50] The four-volume edition from the 1850s is now reprinted in a scholarly edition: Charles Defrémery & Beniamino Sanguinetti (trans.), *Voyages d'Ibn Batoutah*

It is notable that Battuta's work was not mentioned in any detail by Maskelyne in his book of 1892, but it was sufficiently well known to feature prominently in the work of Sidney Clarke in 1928,[51] which suggests that it arose into public consciousness precisely during the period of the Golden Age of Magic, paralleling the rise of the Indian Rope Trick, which Battuta claims to have witnessed in Hangzhou, China. Already in 1928, however, Clarke is aware of the controversy about whether Battuta really visited the 'Flowery Kingdom'.[52] Indeed, like Maskelyne and Elliot, who both doubted the credibility of travel writers in general, Clarke was healthily sceptical about the reliability of Battuta's accounts. He asks whether Battuta can 'be accepted as a credible witness, and did he in fact see what he says he saw?' Pointing to some of the dramatic devices of Battuta's account, such as his persistent shock at witnessing the apparently miraculous, Clarke suggests that 'his naïve confessions of faintings, palpitations, and need of restoratives do not point to acuteness in the perception of trickery or to accuracy in description. Is he not merely stating as an actuality something he had been told had happened at some time or other (a very common failing of the narrators of marvels)?'[53]

At about the same time that Clarke asked these questions about Battuta's credibility, SOAS (School of Oriental and African Studies) Professor Hamilton Gibb (1895–1971) asked similar questions in the introduction to his English-language translation of *The Journey*. Indeed, Gibb notes that Battuta gave unusual credence to the esoteric powers of dervishes and Sufis, suggesting in particular a sympathy for the 'severe bodily and mental training undergone by a darwísh as he advances to the higher grades of initiation', which is often presented as being

Texte Arabe, accompagné d'une traduction, vols 1–4. Cambridge: Cambridge University Press, 2012. The 1929 English version by Hamilton A.R. Gibb was also published in an abridged form that included selections from all four volumes covering the period 1325–1354. It was originally published by Routledge, which has subsequently reprinted it: Hamilton Gibb (trans.), *Ibn Battuta: Travels in Asia and Africa*. London: Routledge, 2013.

[51] Sidney Clarke, 'Oriental Conjuring'. *The Magic Wand*, 17:138 (June 1928). Reprinted in Sidney Clarke, *The Annals of Conjuring*. Seattle: Miracle Factory, 2001, pp. 373–400.

[52] The term 'Flowery Kingdom' appears to have entered common usage in the 1910s (it first appears in *Webster's Dictionary* in 1913). It is popularly associated with the autobiography of Carl Crow, *Foreign Devils in the Flowery Kingdom*. New York: Harper & Bros., 1940.

[53] Clarke, *The Annals of Conjuring*, pp. 376–377.

'accompanied by an expansion of mental powers, beginning with simple telepathy'. Rather than expressing the same level of scepticism as the magician Sidney Clarke, however, it is noteworthy that Professor Gibb seems to be keen to move past what he saw as the 'naturalistic and mechanistic mind' of the nineteenth century, which tended to dismiss the accuracy of Battuta's observations of the mysterious and miraculous as 'wholesale invention',[54] preferring instead a more progressive faith in 'the powers of God and man' that he saw as typical of the emerging twentieth century. Indeed, in ways that we saw as characteristic of this 'modern' period in Chapter 1, Gibb expresses a faith in the possibility that science will eventually uncover the empirical truth of phenomena that it is as yet unable to explain. Hence, he suggests that 'the only prudent course, it would seem, is to suspend judgement, and in the meantime give Ibn Battuta the credit for relating what he at least believed to be the truth'. Indeed, for Gibb, Battuta's credibility is actually enhanced because he professed to disbelieve some of the things he claims to have seen and heard: 'His powers of belief are not … entirely unlimited, as may be seen from the doubts which he expresses on more than one occasion in regard to extravagant claims.'[55]

> The stories of miracles which he relates at second hand do him no discredit; the power of saints to perform miracles was and still is believed by the mass of Muslims, and such tales interested both narrator and audience. It is when he tells of miraculous events directly associated with himself that the problem of their truth must be definitely faced.[56]

In a manner that we have already seen as familiar to the discourse of Orientalist magic in Chapter 3, Gibb goes on to suggest that it 'may be possible to explain [these magical events] by hypnosis (if that in fact "explains" them)', or perhaps 'we may suspect the arts of the conjurer', but in the end, unlike the magician Clarke, the professor tends

---

[54] Gibb notes that 'all European commentators of Ibn Battuta have referred to his credulity, his fondness for the miraculous and uncritical acceptance of reported miracles worked by the famous shaikhs and saints whom he met'. Gibb, *Ibn Battuta: Travels in Asia and Africa* (1929/2013 ebook edition – 'Introduction', no page numbers).

[55] Gibb, *Ibn Battuta* ('Introduction', no page numbers).

[56] Gibb, *Ibn Battuta* ('Introduction', no page numbers).

towards the acceptance of the possibility of a 'miraculous element' at work.[57]

Of course, as we saw in Chapter 3, Clarke and the other modern magicians who read *The Magic Wand* were already unimpressed by the 'hypnosis' argument and were dispositionally predisposed to discount any explanation that relied on a 'miraculous element'. Rather than looking for evidence of miracles, modern magicians sought to debunk any alleged instances of supernatural magic by demonstrating how anything that was really witnessed could be explained by a combination of technical processes and artistic performance. Hence, Clarke and his peers poured over the text of Battuta's account trying to understand whether any of the feats he documented could be legitimate instances of the 'arts of the conjurer' or whether he had simply made them up under the influence of the 'glamour of the Mystic East', under the licence of the 'far far away', or even simply under the influence of opium.

From the standpoint of the present day, it is interesting to reflect on the kind of events in which Battuta (and presumably Gibb) was willing to invest his belief and those that troubled his sense of reason sufficiently to drive him to doubt. In general, the boundaries of his reason and thus the parameters of his magical belief were radically different from those of Clarke and the modern magicians. In some ways, his text emerges as a testing ground for the contradictory modernity of the mystical revival. For instance, Battuta recounts the incident that sparked his intention to explore Indian magic in this way:

> There are many tigers [in Parwán], and one of the inhabitants told me that a certain tiger used to enter the town by night, although the gates were shut, and used to seize people. It killed quite a number of

---

[57] Gibb, *Ibn Battuta* ('Introduction', no page numbers). These different types and levels of credulity between magicians and scholars as investigators into magic and the supernatural were constantly contested and tested by both magicians and scholars. Later on, in *Magician Among the Spirits* (1924), for instance, Houdini would lament *both* the credulity (and pomposity) of academics who were not magicians *and* the credulity of magicians who thought (naively) that being a magician meant that you could naturally see through the tricks of all charlatans, when experience revealed very clearly that magicians were very good at tricking other magicians as well as the muggles. In the end, Houdini appears to want to maintain the position that only *he* was really able to reveal the truth.

townsfolk in this way. They used to wonder how it made its way in.
Here is an amazing thing; a man told me that it was not a tiger who
did this but a human being, one of the magicians known as *Júgís*
[Yogis], appearing in the shape of a tiger. When I heard this
I refused to believe it, but a number of people said the same, so let us
give at this point some account of these magicians.[58]

Presumably this astonishing account of a man who could turn himself
into a tiger is an example of the kind of incident that Gibb suggests
does Battuta 'no discredit' because he is simply relating a story that
others (who believed in its truth) had told to him. Nonetheless, this
incident also doubles as an example of the kind of story that leads
Clarke to question Battuta's claim to being a 'credible witness': his
views on the nature of the incident are too intimately conditioned by
other people's stories rather than by any rational analysis (which would
have revealed to him immediately that nobody can turn himself into
a tiger). In short, following Maskelyne's lead, for Clarke Battuta is not
a *modern* witness, which means his testimony lacks credibility. From
this standpoint, allowing him to get away with this suggests that Gibb is
an Orientalist in the ideological as well as the scholarly sense.[59]

In fact, Battuta's story about the tiger does not even make it into
Clarke's discussion of 'Oriental Conjuring'. While the story contributes
to Western society's general representation of the Orient as a place of
mystery and magic, hence forming part of the 'glamour of the Mystic
East', presumably Clarke found nothing in it worthy of serious consideration in a study of Indian magic *per se*. This was just a story; nobody
turned themselves into a tiger, and (as far as we know) nobody even
witnessed someone performing such a transformation as a *magical
effect*.[60] The feat and the effect both seem impossible; they are of poetic
interest only.

[58] Gibb, *Ibn Battuta* ('Chapter 7', no page numbers).

[59] As we saw in the last chapter, since about the 1970s it has become very difficult to
talk about representations of the Orient without being sensitive to the possibility
that it is (also) an ideological and romantic construction of scholars at the turn of the
twentieth century. In this instance, Gibb, who was an accomplished orientalist (a
scholar working on the study of the Orient) might appear to allow for Battuta's
magical belief structure because of his own romantic ideas about the associations
between the Orient and magic.

[60] Battuta's explanation of the possibility of this transformation comes in the form of a
discussion of the ascetic practices of yogi, who could apparently go for months
without eating or drinking, be buried alive for long periods, concoct magical elixirs;

However, Clarke pays considerable attention to the details of the next incident, which Battuta claims to have witnessed personally. It is colourful in the original, and I quote it in full:

> The sultan sent for me once when I was at Delhi, and on entering I found him in a private apartment with some of his intimates and two of these *Júgis*. One of them squatted on the ground, then rose into the air above our heads, still sitting. I was so astonished and frightened that I fell to the floor in a faint. A potion was administered to me, and I revived and sat up. Meantime this man remained in his sitting posture. His companion then took a sandal from a bag he had with him, and beat it on the ground like one infuriated. The sandal rose in the air until it came above the neck of the sitting man and then began hitting him on the neck while he descended little by little until he sat down alongside us. Then the sultan said, 'If I did not fear for your reason I would have ordered them to do still stranger things than this you have seen.' I took my leave, but was affected with palpitation and fell ill, until he ordered me to be given a draught which removed it all.[61]

At first glance, this account could be a description of a Levitation fantasy from any of various religious traditions. Clarke is quick to point out that the 'hallucination of Levitation is common among ecstatics of all religions', and that the 'power to raise themselves in the air has always been a popular attribute of holy men both of the East and of the West'. In other words, Clarke suggests that Battuta was already predisposed to interpret events in this manner, particularly coloured by stories of Buddha in India as the archetype of 'the ascetic of the East [who] is still believed to attain "perfection" whereby he is able to rise in the air at will'.[62]

and also there are among them 'some who merely look at a man and he falls dead on the spot'. This kind of mixture of rural legend and legitimate yogic practices is typical of the romantic text of Orientalist magic.

[61] Gibb, *Ibn Battuta* (Chapter 7, no page numbers). I note that Clarke quotes a different translation, which differs in some details. For instance, the levitating man is said to resemble a 'cube'. He notes only that translations into English appeared in the early nineteenth century, but does not specify a source for his quotations. It appears to me that he has drawn his account from the unattributed (perhaps by Clarke himself) article 'Aerial Suspension' in *Magic Circular*, 9 (1914), pp. 282–287.

[62] Clarke, 'Oriental Conjuring', p. 377.

Yet, there is something irreligious about Battuta's scene that plays with the idea that this kind of magical power is an everyday experience for the sultan and his court, rather than an extraordinary moment of revelation. While Battuta himself is shocked to the point of fainting, the other people at the court appear to have found nothing remarkable in the accomplishment of the yogi. The story suggests that this kind of occurrence is endemic to India: yogis float into the air all the time, and nobody looks twice. Indeed, the sultan is explicit that there is a whole world of magic waiting to be revealed to Battuta (or any other traveller from the non-Indian world), if only they could cope with experiencing it. This Levitation is not performed as a remarkable demonstration of the power of the yogi, but rather it takes the form of a test of Battuta himself: can he cope with learning the truth about a larger and more magical world? Sadly, Battuta fails this test completely; he collapses from shock and disbelief, forcing the sultan to administer medicine to revive him, and resulting in any further demonstrations of supernatural power becoming unthinkable. One of the fascinating features of this 'test' is that the sultan explicitly describes this as a test of reason, or perhaps as a threat to rationality, which is certainly something that would have resonated with a twentieth century reader of Gibb's translation.

A number of commentators on this scene have expressed their suspicions about the nature of the 'potion' imbibed by Battuta, suggesting that (to the extent we should believe that his account genuinely conforms to his recollection of events) the potion was really a form of hallucinogenic. This theory would not only explain why Battuta thought that he saw someone levitating and being repeatedly struck by a flying slipper, but it would also explain why nobody else seems to participate in the vision (but are instead mostly interested in his reactions), and also why he experiences a series of neurophysiological side effects that necessitate the application of a tonic to calm his nerves.

Whatever the historical or even autobiographical veracity of Battuta's account, it is clear that it forms part of the contested and contradictory cultural context of Orientalist magic during the *fin de siècle* mystical revival. Not only that, however, Clarke and others also recognized in the description of this early Levitation a number of characteristics that would become features of stage Levitations in the modern period. Hence, while modern magicians may have dismissed Battuta's general claims, they saw evidence in his narrative that there could be another (more educated and reliable) version of the story that could explain what really happened.

One of the ambiguities, for instance, resides in the nature of the environment in which the Levitation was performed, about which Battuta says almost nothing. We learn from his account that the episode occurs in the sultan's 'private apartment', but we are not told whether the space in question was inside a room or outside in a courtyard.[63] At the same time, Battuta makes no observations about the presence (or absence) of nearby equipment (or furniture that could obscure equipment).

The significance of this missing data is immediately obvious to the modern magician, who is familiar with various ways to accomplish a Levitation using mechanical contrivances, especially in an interior space. In other words, the absence of these details from the account disables the modern critic from reaching a reasoned conclusion about the veracity of the story itself (hence, leaving space for interpretations involving counter-physical supernatural causation). Even accepting the likely influence of the 'Asiatic Soma' and the vagaries of memory, the real problem with this account of a Levitation is simply that Battuta was not himself a magician and so had no idea how to document or understand what he saw. For the magicians of the Golden Age, this kind of account was as woefully naïve as a fourteenth century account of gravity might be to a modern scientist. Indeed, as we saw in Chapters 1 and 2, it was precisely this kind of inadequate account of ostensibly occult events that led modern pioneers such as Maskelyne and Houdini to educate the public in the devices and techniques of magic, so that audiences could be more sophisticated and more critical of charlatans of various forms.

In his narrative of the history of this Indian Levitation, Clarke skips ahead nearly 300 years before encountering an account that provides a more helpful amount of data. He cites the travelogue of François Valentijn (1666–1727), who travelled around much of South and Southeast Asia with the Dutch East India Company and was one of very few agents of that company to be permitted to publish his memoirs (in 1724). Valentijn's work is not noted for its conscientious scholarship, and Clarke quotes a passage in which Valentijn reports on an incident that was described to him rather than directly witnessed by

---

[63] The translation used by Clarke renders 'private apartment' as 'palace'.

him. Nevertheless, the account begins to resemble something that a modern magician would recognize as plausible:

> A man will go and sit on three sticks put together so as to form a tripod; after which first one stick, then a second, then the third shall be removed from under him, and the man shall not fall, but shall remain sitting in the air!
>
> Yet I have spoken with two friends who had seen this at one and the same time; and one of them, I may add, mistrusting his own eyes, had taken the trouble to feel about with a long stick if there was anything on which the body rested; yet, as the gentleman told me, he could neither feel nor see any such thing. Still, I could only say that I could not believe it, as a thing manifestly contrary to reason.[64]

There are a number of important differences between Valentijn's and Battuta's descriptions. First of all, in terms of the typology of magic, they are describing two related but different feats: Battuta describes a *Levitation*, while Valentijn describes a *suspension*. The former involves a figure rising from the ground to take up a position in the air, where he resides suspended. The latter involves an already elevated figure remaining in the air after his support is visibly removed.

To the modern magician (and even to a modern audience), the feat of suspension described by Valentijn does not beggar belief. Indeed, it could be a description of a feat seen in a Golden Age theatre. The use of the tripod, and then the gradual removal of that tripod to leave the performer (or his assistant) suspended in the air, apparently unsupported, admits of mechanical explanation. Checking around the suspended body with a stick would also not be inexplicable in the early twentieth century. In this context, it is important that Clarke quotes Valentijn's disbelief about the possibility of a 'thing manifestly contrary to reason'. Clarke's point does not seem to be that his readers should find this story incredible, but instead that they should be aware of the

---

[64] Quoted by Clarke, 'Oriental Conjuring', p. 377. Unfortunately, Clarke does not provide a reference for this quotation. I have been able to locate the original Dutch text, François Valentijn, *Oud en Nieuw Oost-Indiën*. Dordrecht: Van Braam, 1724. I have not been able to find this exact passage, nor have I found the source of Clarke's translation. However, since my interest in this passage is largely in terms of its historical context in the 1920s, not the 1720s, I quote it from Clarke.

inexpert witnesses on whom they rely for their information. Valentijn's disbelief contrasts with Battuta's credulous shock and Gibb's generosity towards the latter. Valentijn had the right attitude but lacked the education in modern magic to reach the most plausible conclusion; he simply did not understand the importance of the presence of the tripod to the accomplishment of the *feat*, even if the *effect* involved taking it away.

In fact, Valentijn's (probably inadvertent) revelation about the tripod quickly becomes a standard feature of accounts of elevations (Suspensions and Levitations). We see it reappearing in travelogues throughout the eighteenth and nineteenth centuries, all the way through into the Golden Age of Magic itself. Indeed, it features in one of the most influential books for modern magicians, *Le Spiritisme dans le monde, L'initiation et les sciences occultes dans l'Inde et chez tous les peuples de l'antiquité* (1875), by the French lawyer, Louis Jacolliot (1837–1890).[65] Jacolliot lived for a number of years in India in the 1860s, where he was especially interested in what he assumed were the Indian roots of Western occultism and esotericism.[66] In this belief, as we saw in Chapter 3, he was firmly in the spirit of the mystic revival. During his time in India, Jacolliot claims to have encountered a fakir called Covindasamy, with whom he developed a friendship of sorts. On a number of occasions, he seems to have requested that the fakir demonstrate magical effects for him. One such instance involves an 'Elevation'.

> Taking an ironwood cane which I had brought from Ceylon, he leaned heavily upon it, resting his right hand upon the handle, with his eyes fixed upon the ground. He then proceeded to utter the appropriate incantations, which he had forgotten to favour me with the day previous.
>
> From the elaborate preparation he made in my presence, I formed the opinion that this was to be only another instance of what I had always regarded as an acrobatic trick. My judgment refuses, in fact, to attach any other name to such phenomena as this:
>
> Leaning upon the cane with one hand, the Fakir rose gradually about two feet from the ground. His legs were crossed beneath him,

---

[65] Louis Jacolliot, *Le Spiritisme dans le monde, L'initiation et les sciences occultes dans l'Inde et chez tous les peuples de l'antiquité*. Paris: Lacroix, 1875.

[66] Jacolliot collected and translated many Sanskrit and Hindi legends, myths, and fantasies, with a particular focus on the macabre. One of his most influential translations was of the *Manusmṛti* (The Laws of Manu).

and he made no change in his position, which was very like that of those bronze statues of Buddha that all tourists bring from the Far East, without a suspicion that most of them come originally from English foundries.

For more than twenty minutes I tried to see how Covindasamy could thus fly in the face and eyes of all the known laws of gravity; it was entirely beyond my comprehension; the stick gave him no visible support, and there was no apparent contact between that and his body, except through his right hand.[67]

While Clarke is rather dismissive of this episode, since he finds it 'so lacking in important details and ... so self-contradictory', there is much here of interest and value.[68] Most obviously, in terms of its continuity from Valentijn, this account also makes mention of a staff or rod as a potential device of the trick. Second, like Battuta, Jacolliot is keen to describe the unusual sitting position of the levitator and to tie this position to the popular imaginary of the Buddha. Finally, however, Jacolliot is able to admit that he cannot understand how Covindasamy accomplished this effect without either collapsing into shock, resorting to supernaturalism, or reacting with naïve scepticism: the fakir has no *visible* support and no *apparent* contact; he refuses to call this anything other than acrobatics, despite the performance of mystical incantations; and he is refreshingly sardonic about the beliefs of Western tourists about Indian esotericism (when they buy statues made in England).

In fact, Jacolliot has Covindasamy perform many feats during his stay, and the name of this fakir becomes very well known amongst magicians of the Golden Age, some of whom even claim to have met him themselves on their trips to India (although some also appear to have witnessed him performing exactly the same feats and described them in very similar words – magicians of this period are not noted for

[67] Louis Jacolliot, *Le Spiritisme dans le monde* was quickly translated into English in 1884 as Louis Jacolliot (trans. William Felt), *Occult Science in India and Among the Ancients, with an Account of Their Mystic Initiations, and the History of Spiritualism*. London: William Rider & Son, 1884/1919. Clarke's unattributed quotations appear to be based on this translation, but they show evidence of some selective editing. Here I quote the 1919 reprint, pp. 237–238.

[68] Clarke, 'Oriental Conjuring', p. 378. Clarke hypothesizes various solutions to the puzzle of how Covindasamy accomplished this effect, noting that this particular fakir had visited a number of times and so knew the environment and the house servants, suggesting that collusion in preparation of the ground (for instance, by making a hole into which the rod could be slotted for vertical strength) was entirely possible.

respecting copyright).[69] Because of the lyrical tone of Jacolliot's descriptions, Covindasamy becomes something of a poster-boy for Orientalist magicians, who see him as an instance of the 'real and potent' magic of India and the Ancients. However, the content of Jacolliot's account also provides ample data for the modern magicians who sought to maintain that any accurately described incident must be explicable to a properly educated and trained modern magician.

For instance, Jacolliot offers the following description of another (apparently spontaneous) Levitation by Covindasamy:

> As the Fakir was about to leave me, to go to his breakfast and obtain a few hours rest, of which he stood in urgent need, having had no food nor sleep for the last twenty-four hours, he stopped in the embrasure of the door leading from the terrace to the outside stairs, and, crossing his arms upon his chest, lifted himself up gradually, without any apparent support or assistance, to the height of about ten to twelve inches.
>
> I was able to determine the distance exactly by means of a point of comparison which I had fixed upon during the continuance of the phenomenon. Behind the Fakir's back there was a silken hanging, which was used as a portiere, striped in gold and white bands of equal width. I noticed that the Fakir's feet were on a level with the sixth band. At the commencement of his ascension I had seized my chronometer; the entire time from the moment when the Fakir commenced to rise until he touched the ground again, was more than eight minutes. He remained perfectly still, at the highest point of elevation for nearly five minutes.[70]

This passage is quoted in various forms by different authors, depending on their agenda in the politics of knowledge of the mystical revival. Strangely, Clarke (who quotes this passage without comment) omits the first half of the second paragraph, in which most of the data relevant to explaining the likely mechanisms being deployed are explained: vertically striped wall-hangings are extremely useful for effects involving vertical motion. That said, authors who were keen

---

[69] Perhaps the other most influential account of Covindasamy appears as one of the adventures of Baron Hartwig Seeman (1833–1886), 'the Emperor of Magicians', as recounted by Hardin Jasper Burlingame (1852–1915), *Around the World with a Magician and a Juggler: Unique Experiences in Many Lands.* Chicago: Clyde Publishing Co., 1891, especially chapter 7, 'Experiences with a Great Fakir'.

[70] Jacolliot, *Occult Science in India*, p. 257.

to emphasize the possibility of supernatural agency (or to more fully evoke the atmosphere of the mystic East itself) in stories of Covindasamy were keen to emphasize the passages that preceded and followed this one. Immediately prior to his apparently spontaneous 'street magic' Levitation, the fakir had rendered a servant incapable of speech with a hand gesture (and caused him to recover it again similarly), and had also caused a palm-leaf fan to rise from a table and fan Jacolliot to ease his discomfort in the heat. And then immediately after the Levitation:

> As Covindasamy was making his parting salaam, I asked if he could repeat the last phenomenon whenever he pleased.
> 'The Fakir', answered he, emphatically, 'can lift himself up as high as the clouds.'
> 'What is the source of his power?' I do not know why I asked him the question, as he had already told me, more than twenty times, that he did not regard himself as anything more than an instrument in the hands of the Pitris.
> He answered me with the following lines:
>
> Swadyaye nityayoukta' syat
> Ambarad avatarati deva'.
>
> 'He should be in constant communication with heaven, and a superior spirit should descend therefrom.'[71]

In fact, Jacolliot introduces this entire sequence by saying that he does not 'undertake to decide' whether or not the effects he witnessed were 'purely a matter of skill or whether the performers are really inspired'. Instead, he claims that he's merely trying to observe and record 'the circumstances under which the facts occurred ... accurately'.[72] While Jacolliot's sympathy for Orientalist magic is clear from his endeavour as a whole, it is to his credit as (what Maskelyne calls) a 'modern witness' that he includes a number of observations that are of genuine use to the skilled modern magician in reaching a scientific understanding of the events being described. His accounts perfectly capture the contradictory and paradoxical modernity of the mystical revival: he is a romantic

[71] Jacolliot, *Occult Science in India*, pp. 257–258.
[72] Jacolliot, *Occult Science in India*, p. 255.

Orientalist in search of 'real and potent magic', but he has learned the legitimacy of positivism and sound empirical observation.[73]

With this in mind, it is important to realize that, by the time of Jacolliot's writing, Levitations were already being performed on the Western stage; he was not naïve about their impossibility. Indeed, it seems likely that the first European versions of Levitations were performed in the late 1840s, with Robert-Houdin in Paris, 1847, and Alexander Herrmann (Herrmann the Great) and John Henry Anderson (The Great Wizard of the North) in London, 1848. Furthermore, it appears that these early European performances closely resembled the descriptions of Valentijn and Jacolliot, specifically in the use of vertical rods as props. Indeed, it is conventional in the history of magic to suggest that Robert-Houdin, who is usually credited as the inventor of modern Levitation, turned his attention to the problem of 'suspension' after reading articles in the European press about 'two conjurers in India' who could suspend themselves in mid-air.[74]

It is certainly the case that interest in aerial suspensions ballooned in the 1830s, spurred on by a number of stories in popular magazines, such as *People's Magazine* and *Scientific American*. However, arguably the first of these was the piece that appeared on 28 July 1832 in *Saturday Magazine*, which included an account of a Levitation by Sheshal, the so-called Brahmin of the Air.[75] According to that account, Sheshal performed his Levitation in Tanjores, Madras, where he had emerged following the death of an 'old Brahmin' who had accomplished the feat with 'no better apparatus than a piece of plank, which, with four legs, he formed into an oblong stool; and upon which, in a little brass socket, he placed, in a perpendicular position, a hollow bamboo, from which projected a kind of crutch, covered with a piece of common hide. These properties he carried with him in a little bag, which was shown to those who

---

[73] However 'modern' he may have been in this respect, Jacolliot was not a magician and so was not fully aware of the significance of many of his observations. This enables him to conclude, for instance, that '*materially speaking*, I do not think it possible that any fraud could have been committed'. Jacolliot, *Occult Science in India*, p. 255.

[74] Milbourne Christopher, *The Illustrated History of Magic*. London: Robert Hale & Co., 1973, p. 143.

[75] 'The Air Brahmin', *Saturday Magazine*, 28 July 1832, p. 28.

went to see him exhibit.'[76] The article of 1832 offers the following description of Sheshal himself:

> He exhibited before me in the following manner he first allowed me to examine a stool, about 18 in. in height, on the seat of which were two brass stars inlaid, a little larger than a dollar; he then displayed a hollow bamboo, 2 ft. in length, and 24 in. in diameter. The next article was a roll of antelope skin, perhaps 4 in. in circumference and 2 ft. in length. The man then concealed himself in a large shawl, with these three articles and a large bag; after a delay of five minutes, during which he appeared very busy under the shawl, he ordered the covering to be taken off him, and he was discovered actually sitting cross-legged in the air, but leaning his right arm on the antelope skin, which communicated horizontally with the hollow bamboo, which again was connected perpendicularly with the stool, directly over one of the brass stars.
>
> He sat for more than half an hour counting his beads in his right hand, and without once changing the expression of his countenance, which was quite calm, and as if this new mode of sitting was no exertion to him. I saw him exhibit four times, and each time tried my utmost to discover the secret, but without success. A large bribe was offered to induce him to reveal his mode of performance, but he declined the explanation. I account for it thus. The brass stars in the stool conceal a socket for a steel rod passing through the hollow bamboo, the antelope skin conceals another steel rod which is screwed into the one in the bamboo; other rods pass through the (man's sleeve and down his body, which support a ring in which he sits).[77]

Many of the features of this feat are readily familiar from previous descriptions, but this account is notable for its level of mechanical detail, which would certainly be sufficient for an engineer-innovator like Robert-Houdin to start planning how to accomplish this illusion himself. Indeed, in his memoirs, Robert-Houdin relates his development of a technologically similar (albeit much more refined) version in 1847. For instance, he quickly dispenses with the (rather suspicious) shawl that

---

[76] 'Aerial Suspension'. *Magic Circular*, 9 (1914), p. 285, quoting Thomas Frost, *The Lives of the Conjurers*. London: Tinsley Brothers, 1876, pp. 206–207.

[77] This account is reproduced in a letter by C. Mostyn in *The Spectator*, 28 April 1894, p. 31. Mostyn adds, 'This solution appears to be applicable to most of the recorded performances of this feat.'

Sheshal apparently used to conceal his actions. He describes how he conducted his 'experiment' in three stages, making use of his youngest son, Auguste-Adolphe Robert-Houdin, who was then about six years old.

In the preliminary stage, the boy is invited to stand on a stool on the stage. Whereupon he stretches his arms out to the sides and upright poles are placed underneath them close to his body. In the first stage of the illusion, the magician reaches down and removes the stool, leaving the boy apparently suspended by his arms, which remain outstretched with triceps resting on the poles. In the second stage, the magician bends his son's right arm so that his cheek rests upon his hand and then moves over to the left and removes the pole on that side completely, leaving the boy suspended by one elbow. And then, in the final stage, the magician carefully and effortlessly lifts the boy's feet with the strength of just one finger, tilting him until he is lying horizontally, supported only by his right elbow on the pole, his head propped casually on his hand.[78]

As a technical accomplishment, this feat was impressive in the 1840s, although its debt to the Indian fakirs is very clear. Indeed, in his controversial *The Unmasking of Robert-Houdin*, Harry Houdini not only seeks to demonstrate that other modern magicians had accomplished this illusion in Europe before Robert-Houdin, but also to show that its real origin lay in 'an Oriental annual' that detailed the devices of the fakirs, which was compiled by officers from the Indian army.[79] In fact, as we saw in Chapter 3, the idea that Oriental magic was more advanced or more powerful than magic in the dis-enchanted West was pervasive in this period. In his influential account of Sheshal, for instance, Thomas Frost explains that 'while the conjuring art seemed to be declining in Europe, Indian conjurers were exhibiting in their own land the marvels which have since attracted wondering crowds to the temples of magic which their imitators have set up in the capitals of the West'.[80]

Presumably it was for reasons such as this that even the 'father of modern magic', Robert-Houdin, could not avoid surrounding his grand version of the aerial suspension with some Oriental incense.

---

[78] Jean Eugene Robert-Houdin, *Memoirs*. 2nd ed. London: Chapman & Hall, 1860. p. 239.

[79] Harry Houdini, *The Unmasking of Robert-Houdin*. New York: The Publishers Printing Co., 1906/8. Chapter 7, especially p. 233.

[80] Frost, *The Lives of the Conjurers*, p. 206.

In particular, despite the modern, scientific tone of the (inconclusive) inquiries into the aerial suspension that typified the articles in the popular press, Robert-Houdin must have been sensitive to the pervasiveness of more esoteric explanations, which still featured in the romantic, Orientalist accounts of Jacolliot and others much later. In particular, it remained a popular view that the Indian fakir could accomplish remarkable (and magical) feats through disciplined control of their breathing and creative control of unconscious states (such as trances).[81]

In his own performance, Robert-Houdin gave a modern twist to these Orientalist conceits, navigating between the suggestion that modern science could *explain the means* deployed by Indian fakirs, and the suggestion that (therefore) modern magic had *better means* available to accomplish the apparently impossible. Building on the twin notions of altering breath and consciousness, Robert-Houdin claims to have been inspired by recent advances in medical science and, in particular, by the discovery (in 1847) of the anaesthetic and sense-altering properties of ether: 'all the world talked about the marvelous effect of this anaesthetic, and its extraordinary results. In the eyes of many people it seemed much akin to magic.'[82]

In this context, Robert-Houdin dressed his illusion in the glamour of science and Orientalism at the same time, calling his new illusion, 'The Ethereal Suspension', and pretending to administer a magico-medical ether to his son at the start of the performance.[83] Holding a vial of steaming, yellowish liquid beneath the boy's nose, the magician explained that a deep breath of this substance would cause the boy to lapse from normal consciousness and to become as light as a balloon. Meanwhile, from backstage, the unmistakable scent of ether was wafted into the auditorium. After a moment, the boy's head

---

[81] For instance, in his account of the legend of the 'old Brahmin', Frost details how (especially local) explanations of his accomplishments tended to diminish the importance of his props (which were too simple to be of any great assistance) but instead suggested that they were 'effected by holding the breath, clearing the tubular organs, and a peculiar mode of respiration'. Frost, *The Lives of the Conjurers*, p. 207.

[82] Robert-Houdin, *Memoirs*, p. 238.

[83] It is noteworthy that Anderson's performances of the same illusion in London in 1848 were similarly titled. The advertising posters announce: EXTRAORDINARY NEW SCIENTIFIC WONDER: SUSPENSION CHLORIFOREENE. Poster is reproduced in Houdini, *Unmasking*, p. 234.

would sag distinctly, as he apparently fell into another state of consciousness, and his knees would bend in such a way that his feet lifted off the stool on which he had been standing. So, even before the magician removes the stool, the boy is seen to be suspended impossibly. The rest of the illusion then proceeds as though the boy is completely unconscious of what is happening to him, suggesting indeed that his altered consciousness (chemically induced) is itself a factor contributing to his ability to levitate.

This kind of suspension, together with variants involving Levitations and descensions, would become increasingly popular throughout the Golden Age, until such effects gradually lost their magic. Noteworthy in the attempts to maintain and enhance the enchantment of the feat was the work of Alfred Sylvester (1813–1886), who became famous in London as the Fakir of Oolu.[84] He based his entire act around the Levitation attributed to Sheshal, but performed in the guise of a maharaja, in turban and full regalia, surrounding himself by an ostentatiously Orientalist set. His authenticity as an Indian fakir was never seriously maintained, but his attempt to participate in Orientalist magic as a way to re-enchant an effect that was so deeply associated with India was rather successful. Sylvester billed himself as the Fakir of Oolu, 'Denizen of the Air'. It was at about this time that many modern, Western magicians travelled to Asia in search of secret techniques of magic; participation in the magic of Orientalism came in various forms, as we saw in Chapter 3.[85]

Sylvester's innovation was not only in the Oriental glamour of his *effect*; he also implemented two technical advances in the *feat* itself: in the first, his performance showed the suspended figure revolving around the last supporting rod, apparently enhancing the impression that the figure was genuinely 'floating' in the air; and in the second, he was able to remove the last supporting rod itself, much in the manner described by Valentijn in 1724, but Sylvester gave the impression that he was supporting the floating figure with his hand.

[84] Alfred's son and grandson continued to perform under the name of the Fakir of Oolu for many years in Australia, where Alfred senior died in 1886.

[85] In his remarkable book about Indian magic, *Net of Magic: Wonders and Deceptions in India* (Chicago: University of Chicago Press, 1991) Lee Siegel relates some of the details of Sylvester's performance and notes that Harry Kellar was amongst the Western magicians to travel to India in search of secret teachings in 1875 (p. 211). Kellar was just one of many to make this trip.

In fact, in this period we see modern magicians looking further and further back through the story of Levitation in the endeavour to produce the fantastical effects ascribed to the earliest (and least reliable) accounts. In the end, it was the arch-debunker of Spiritualism and Oriental Jugglery, John Nevil Maskelyne himself, who returned to the incredible description provided by Ibn Battuta of a man who rose from the ground at will, without any visible support, held himself suspended in the air at leisure, and then descended again in perfect control. Maskelyne's ingenious method for this effect was a great success at the Egyptian Hall in August 1894 (forming the core of his magical sketch, 'Modern Witchery'). It was then improved still further in 1901 in his stunningly successful play *The Entranced Fakir*. Of course, his methods required that the feat be performed under rather precise conditions on a modern stage, which enabled modern critics to reconstruct something similar about the conditions of the performance of Battuta's fakir (to the extent they were keen to believe even elements of his story), despite the absence of such details in his account.[86] Hence, one side effect of Maskelyne's accomplishment was the establishment of the possibility that Battuta did in fact see what he thought he saw more than 500 years earlier. Ironically, then, despite his deep commitment to modern magic, Maskelyne's inventive genius and performative brilliance also contributed to the perpetuation of the 'myth of the Mystic East'. The Entranced Fakir effectively re-enchanted the idea of Indian magic.

After Maskelyne's triumph, there were really only two more developments in this form of illusion. The first was enacted by

[86] 'Modern Witchery', which was really a parody of Theosophy, included the Levitation of 'Koot Houmi', who was presented as a mystical mahatma. The innovative Levitation took place when Houmi lay on a plank supported by the backs of two chairs, which were then removed one at a time, allowing the mahatma to float and descend. This was one of the first times that fine, steel wires were used for a suspension, and required very careful lighting and staging. The Entranced Fakir, includes the Levitation of George Cooke (in the guise of the fakir 'Dryanard Boo Sing'), who rises from a sarcophagus that is held away from the stage by two trestles. In bright light, Maskelyne was able to walk around the stage and pass a ring along the length of the fakir's body to show there were no wires or supports. In fact, there were no wires. Maskelyne had developed an ingenious metal 'gooseneck' that could support the fakir from behind without being seen, the shape of which allowed for a ring to pass almost along his entire body (Jim Steinmeyer, *Hiding the Elephant*, pp. 162–165). It is noteworthy that in both cases the person who levitates is in the guise of the Indian fakir, while the Western magician takes the role of observer, facilitator, or demonstrator.

Maskelyne's son, Nevil, who developed the technique of passing a ring around the levitating figure in order to demonstrate that it was apparently not supported by anything. This refinement evoked ideas from the account of Valentijn, who had described the way that a staff was passed beneath the levitating fakir to demonstrate that there was no hidden support. And finally, drawing on ideas from the fabled Indian Rope Trick, by the 1910s it had become possible to cause the levitating figure to vanish from under a sheet rather than to make it descend back down to the stage.

In the end, it is clear that the competing cultures of explanation, exposure, mystification, and enchantment that informed the formation of modern magic in this period, enabled and required a form of mystical Orientalism. The space of ambiguity that Jacolliot and others readily occupied during and after their travels around India was cultivated by magicians in the West who, on the one hand, sought 'to assert the immutability of Western laws of physics', but who were, on the other hand, 'motivated to maintain the mystique of the mystic East'. This was not only because this was 'a mystique which would draw audiences to their own Indian-styled reviews', but also because the literature of Indian magic was such a rich source of inspiration for magicians and public alike, provoking critical as well as poetic agendas.[87]

Street Levitation

Before leaving the problem of Levitation behind, it is worthwhile to reflect on one of the most important (but largely neglected) legacies of this feat as an instance of Orientalist magic in the contemporary period. In particular, as we saw in Chapter 3, there is a strong sense in which modern Street Magic owes a debt to the idea of the fakir – the 'magic man', who has cultivated himself through ascetic practice and arduous self-discipline to *become a magical creature*. There is no single feat more associated with this idea than the Levitation, precisely because it has been seen as a goal (or as a result) of spiritual discipline in many religious traditions for centuries and millennia.

[87] Quotations from Siegel, *Net of Magic*, pp. 211–212.

The romantic Western encounter with Indian fakirs during the Golden Age seemed to represent the idea of a meeting with extant magical creatures capable of performing this fabled feat. Many of the magicians and occultists (and tourists) who visited India in this period came away with the idea that they could transform themselves into magical creatures if only they lived their lives in more ascetic, disciplined ways. We have seen how ideas about breath control and trance states were always and already intermixed with more 'modern' explanations for the accomplishment of Levitation, and it was these ideas about self-cultivation and meditation as spiritual *devices* for the accomplishment of magical *effects* that permeated popular culture in Europe and the United States. After all, these were the elements of the travellers' tales that readers in search of magic in the world found enchantingly different from their everyday experiences.

In fact, these tales were quickly supported by photographs showing levitating yogis in Madras and Banaras. Such 'evidence' in the 1930s and 1940s, especially in the aftermath of World War II, was 'widely published in Europe and America, [and] convinced many readers that there were indeed Indian yogis who, through spiritual means, could defy known physical laws'.[88] This form of magical belief in the West edged into the growth of the Transcendental Meditation movement in the 1950s and 1960s, in which training centres 'offered courses in which one could enrol to learn the techniques of Levitation – not of *performing the trick*, but of *experiencing the miracle*'.[89] Indeed, the practice of 'yogic flying' was introduced in the mid-1970s in the context of the Transcendental Meditation movement, wherein it was presented as 'the ability of the individual to enliven the total potential of natural law in all its expressions – mind, body, behaviour, and environment'.[90]

---

[88] Siegel, *Net of Magic*, p. 213.

[89] Siegel, *Net of Magic*, p. 213, emphasis added. In it worthwhile to note that the Transcendental Meditation (TM) movement, which involves a specific form of mantra meditation, was created in India the 1950s by Maharishi Mahesh Yogi (1918–2008), who taught it worldwide in the 1960s. TM is now one of the most widely practiced and most frequently studied forms of meditation.

[90] Maharishi Mahesh Yogi, *The Complete Book of Yogic Flying*, Part 1. Maharishi University of Management (Issuu Publication, accessed January 2015), p. 13. While 'yogic flying' (which involves a form of bouncing) has generated a great many photographs of alleged Levitation, it is clear that it has very little to do with the Levitations apparently witnessed by Battuta, Valentijn, and Jacolliot (none of whom mentioned

For our purposes, it is important to reflect on two of the major performative differences between these Orientalist Levitations and the Levitations of modern magic during the Golden Age. In the first, while the Indian fakir of these stories cultivates the power to levitate himself (as a symbol of his cultivated harmony with nature), the modern magician educates himself in techniques that empower him to levitate others (as a symbol of his power over nature). And in the second, while the Indian fakir appears able to perform his Levitation spontaneously in 'unstaged' locations (such as outside in the street), the modern magician tends to perform his Levitation in a controlled, staged environment (such as in a theatre).

This combination of factors establishes a context for modern street Levitations, such as those performed by David Blaine in his landmark TV shows of 1997, 'Street Magic' and 'Magic Man'. In the context of the Vegas spectaculars of the 1980s and 1990s, Blaine's Levitations were ostentatiously modest and low-key. Indeed, in terms of television performances, Blaine followed the elaborate and grandiose Levitations of David Copperfield, who was one of the first major magicians to transition from levitating other people and objects (such as a Ferrari in 1980) to levitating himself (over the Grand Canyon in 1985, and, in one of the most astonishing Levitation-effects ever, around the stage in 1992).[91] However, Copperfield's fabulously contrived stagings and Vegas melodrama place his performances into an entirely different magical tradition from Blaine, who appears in his 1997 show out of the heat-haze in the Mojave Desert or emerging from a tunnel into Manhattan, walking slowly and simply in a T-shirt. Blaine's show opens with him standing in Times Square, where he

bouncing, and all of whom were specific that the suspension lasted for many minutes). As Lee Siegel observes of the latter, 'the trick, alas, is easier than the miracle – all the magicians of Shadipur can do it; but ... they rarely perform it because the gaff, the metal harness that must be worn, is cumbersome' (Siegel, *Net of Magic*, p. 213). Siegel also relates the story of a 'one-trick magician' in Calcutta who used to sit or lie with his eyes closed hoping that his audience would believe he had entered into a kind of *samādhi* before levitating.

[91] The levitating Ferrari was part of 'The Magic of David Copperfield, III', screened 25 September 1980. Floating over the Grand Canyon featured in 'The Magic of David Copperfield, VI', screened 6 April 1984. And the remarkable 'Live the Dream' flying illusion was the centre-piece of 'The Magic of David Copperfield, XIV', 31 March 1992.

says simply: 'This is Times Square. Here there're no boxes, no stages, no sets, nothing. Just people. And me.'

Unlike the modern magicians of the Golden Age, and unlike Copperfield, Blaine very deliberately cultivates a persona that blurs the lines between magic and reality, seeking to establish himself as a magical creature whose nature is magical, rather than as a Professor of Magic whose task is to demonstrate some magical effects. Hence, it is unthinkable that he would levitate someone else: like the Indian fakir or guru, the conceit is that he has conditioned himself to be able to levitate as an expression of his existential harmony with magical powers; he is not in the business of exercising power over other people's bodies. And likewise, like the mystical fakir, Blaine apparently has no need for elaborate stagings and equipment – he walks the streets *being magical*.

One of the most powerful features of that 1997 show was the response of the people for whom he performed on the street, many of whom could have had no idea that street magic in this Oriental tradition was even thinkable. Much to his gratification, I'm sure, Blaine received astonished feedback, very similar to the kind of reactions we saw from Western travellers who witnessed Indian fakirs for the first time in the streets of Delhi or Calcutta. Audience attention was focussed on *him* and on the fact that he didn't seem like a *normal person*: the conceit was that, divorced from the contrived setting of the stage or theatre or television studio, the magic must be emerging from the magician rather than from artificial or technological contrivances. He was not demonstrating magical effects; he was *doing magic*.

For instance, after Blaine sprinkles ash into his own hand and then transposes it into the hand of a woman on the street, she responds: 'That's not right. *You're not right. He's* not right.' Later, after performing a relatively simple card exchange, he receives the perfect endorsement: 'That's amazing. *You're* amazing. Are you a guru of some kind? Are you a guru?' And then, after witnessing Blaine throw a card through the window of a diner, a man remarks with all apparent sincerity: 'I think he's not natural – *for real*.'[92]

---

[92] David Blaine's NBC Special, *David Blaine: Street Magic*, screened on 19 May 1997.

In other words, consciously or not, Blaine's street magic evokes the idea of fakirs and gurus and the tradition of Orientalist magic. In fact, Blaine reserves his big guns for the second half of the show, in which he performs his street Levitation in cities across America. By this stage, Blaine is deliberately suggesting that he is performing a feat that requires his disciplined focus and attention. He clears people away from him, just as the fakirs needed space around them, cautioning them that he needs space for concentration, warning them that he might fall on them, suggesting that he might not be able to do it this time. And then, when he descends back to the ground, he slumps slightly as though physically exhausted by the ordeal, his face weary with fatigue. He performs for celebrity football players (including Deion Sanders) at their training ground and for people in the street. The responses are worth quoting:

> *Two women in NYC:* This man is not . . . he's not right. He floated. Maybe he's from another planet. He floated. He left the ground. His feet were off the ground.
> *Three women on a pier:* I mean, like, I've read up on this stuff . . . and I guess he's just really gifted, spiritually gifted. You know, meditation wise, he can do it. Because that was just unbelievable. There's, like, no strings attached <gestures to the open sky above> and he just came up off the ground. And then he came back down and he's all like . . . <mimes the face of someone drained by psychic effort> . . . Wow![93]

The point here is not that David Blaine has psychic powers, but simply that his performance participates in the tradition of Oriental magic that first inspired Orientalist fantasies about the possibilities of 'real and potent magic' by fakirs and gurus who disciplined themselves into transformed, magical beings. Rather than seeking to locate his work in the tradition of modern magic, which constructed this kind of 'magic man' discourse as illegitimate and morally dubious during the Golden Age, Blaine has re-evoked this kind of Orientalism as a counter-current in contemporary magic.

Indeed, leaning on the kind of existential commitment exhibited by famously Orientalist performers, such as Chung Ling Soo,

---

[93] *David Blaine: Street Magic*, screened on 19 May 1997.

whom we will consider in the next chapter, Blaine has built his life around his commitment to this persona.[94] His career has developed self-consciously towards establishing himself as an 'endurance artist' as much as a magician: amongst other things, he was buried alive in Trump Place for seven days in 1999, stood a pillar in Bryant Park for thirty-five hours in 2002, sat in a plexiglass box suspended over the River Thames for forty-four days in 2003, and held his breath under-water for over seventeen minutes in 2008 (which was a world record at the time). As we saw in Scene one (in Chapter 1), he has also impaled himself with metal skewers in 2013, a feat common to the yogis and fakirs of India. In each case, Blaine made a point of stressing the amount of physical conditioning required before each event (and similarly clear about the medical attention he apparently needed after them), in much the way that the fabled Indian fakir is reputed to be able to perform mystic feats of endurance and Levitation after extended periods ascetic training. When asked about this, Blaine has typically responded that he does not perform these feats for the audi-ence, but rather because they are steps along his own spiritual journey of discovery. Hence, it doesn't matter to him that, for instance, the British public were completely mystified by (and generally disparaging of) his epic forty-four days in a plastic box suspended over the Thames.[95]

One of the fascinating things about Blaine is the question of the extent to which the public is supposed to take him seriously. Are we supposed to believe that he is, in the words of that woman in LA in

---

[94] Amongst other things, Chung Ling Soo (William Robinson) has become famous for setting new standards for commitment to character. Robinson did his very best to live his entire public life in the guise of a fictional 'Celestial', on the basis that the enchantment of his stage performances relied (at least in part) on the credibility of his performances off-stage. To some extent, as we saw in Chapters 1 and 2, we might see this as an extreme implementation of Robert-Houdin's eighth principle of modern conjuring: the conjuror not only plays the part of a (great) magician, but also 'the performer must sufficiently enter into the part he plays, to himself believe in the reality of his fictitious statements. This belief on his own part will infallibly carry a like conviction to the minds of the spectators' (Robert-Houdin, Secrets of Conjuring and Magic, p. 33).

[95] Like the British public, the British media seemed unsure how to understand Blaine's performance in London. Coverage in the influential periodical, The Scotsman, might be representative of the mystification. While maintaining a generally disparaging tone, The Scotsman featured stories about Blaine consistently throughout his feat, noting the amount of fascination and provocation he was causing.

1997, a guru? Should we believe that he's on a journey? Are we even supposed to believe that *he believes* he's on a journey of spiritual discovery, and that his magic/endurance is just something he has to do along the way?[96] Does he suffer the criticisms and disbelief of a cynical British public as a test of his faith, embracing it as an opportunity to better himself? Is he really aspiring to *become magical*, in the mysterious manner of the Indian fakir? Or is the whole thing just a giant publicity scam, since in these modern times we know that people *can't be magical*; they can just perform *feats* that communicate magical *effects*? Is there something morally wrong with creating this uncertainty? Or is he a moral inspiration in a popular culture devoted to quick fixes and cheap thrills?

The point here is that Blaine has done something powerful with the legacy of Orientalist magic, taking the idea of ascetic cultivation as a *spiritual device* for the accomplishment of *magical effects* and detaching it from the aesthetic paraphernalia of theatrical Orientalism. In the language of Harry Kellar, Blaine has abandoned the pomp and glitz of Oriental 'high magic' and instead adopted the faerie glamour of Indian 'low magic'. He has moved Western magic away from what Siegel calls the 'mystic kitsch and melancholy glitz' of high Orientalism, and immersed himself in the idea of the '*jādū* of the streets'. Nobody could be more distant from Blaine than Ali Bongo (see Chapter 3). Because of this, Blaine suggests a deracialization of Oriental magic and its reform as a type of discipline and a way of life.[97] And in this way, Blaine has preserved elements of Indian magic after the collapse of Orientalist magic in the 1970s, when its fantastical

---

[96] Famously and visibly, Blaine has a shoulder-to-shoulder tattoo of Dali's Crucifixion of the Christ of St. John and Primo Levi's concentration camp number tattoed on his arm. As we saw in Scene six, he has likened his pillar stand in Bryant Park to St. Simon of the Desert and his starvation in a box to the Hunger Artist of Kafka. To some extent, we might ask whether Blaine's apparently existential immersion in a form of Oriental glamour is a form of adherence to Robert-Houdin's eighth principle of modern magic even more extreme than that of Chung Ling Soo. Here, Blaine appears to take literally (rather than performatively) Robert-Houdin's maxim that 'the performer must sufficiently enter into the part he plays, to himself believe in the reality of his fictitious statements' (Robert-Houdin, *Secrets of Conjuring and Magic*, p. 33).

[97] In fact, Blaine's position in racial and ethnic politics is very complicated and deeply contested. Indeed, his own ethnic background is a mixture of Puerto Rican and Italian (on his father's side) and Russian Jewish (on his mother's side).

aesthetics came to be seen as camp, shallow, and offensive. Blaine calls our attention to the idea that Indian magic is not necessarily about flowing robes, turbans, or even Levitations; Indian magic can be about living with magic on the street and committing to it as a performer.[98] In this context, magic is a vocation.

---

[98] It should be clear that not all modern street magic works in this register. For instance, the remarkable Dynamo (Stephen Frayne) performs street magic with great authenticity. He is an urban trickster drawing upon traditions of cheeky street performers and hustlers in European and North American cities. In this spirit, he even performs the Levitation (and famously a Matrix-like partial Levitation) and walks on the River Thames, but there is never any indication that his accomplishment of these *effects* is premised upon any ascetic training or spiritual *feat*. Indeed, the assumption is that Dynamo is a *modern magician* who is performing in the street: he does not court ambiguity about the naturalness of his devices or techniques. Hence, Dynamo is a modern street magician in the sense that Maskelyne *et al.* would have recognized. In contrast, Blaine's relationship with Maskelyne's modern magic is much more problematic. His attempt to *be a street magician* is existentially different from Dynamo's endeavour to perform modern magic in the street.

5 CHINESE MAGIC AND MAGIC IN CHINA

Chinese magic

As we saw in the last chapter, India was unchallenged as the apparent focus and origin of magic and mystery, especially in Britain and the United States, but also on the European continent. Nonetheless, China and then Japan gradually became more prevalent in the magical imagination of the West, especially after the second half of the nineteenth century. Indeed, until that time, European magicians would have seen very little *technical* difference between the performance of Indian and Chinese magic on the stage, and audiences would have differentiated mainly (and perhaps exclusively) by aesthetic issues: a 'Chinese' performer would be clothed in flowing silken robes, while an 'Indian' would be more scantily clad and less ostentatious; a 'Chinese' magician was dramatically theatrical, while an 'Indian' appeared more esoteric and occult.[1] There was a different kind of Oriental *glamour* involved. However, these apparently cosmetic differences did have some implications for the kinds of feats that were possible for magicians: for instance, the flowing robes of a 'Chinese' magician enabled the production (and disappearance) of larger objects from the person of the magician himself, such as the famous goldfish bowl. The aesthetics facilitated technical feats.

---

[1] As we saw in Chapter 4, there was some variation in the representation of 'low' and 'high' Indian magic, where the latter tended towards the more dramatic burlesque of Orientalist magic in general.

Sidney Clarke suggests that audiences might have associated Indian conjurors with greater expertise with the Cups and Balls and Chinese with the Linking Rings, but suggests that this was a matter of degree rather than absolute identification.[2] The origins of such tricks were hazily 'Oriental' in the public imagination. It was not until later, in the early years of the twentieth century, that audiences would become accustomed to seeing the Basket Trick and the Mango Trick on the stages of Europe and North America; while modern audiences would associate these with 'Indian Magic', the same basic *feats* were also performed in China (where the basket might be a lacquered box and the mango might be a melon), such minor technical changes produced concomitant changes in *effects*. As we saw in the last chapter, there remains some historical confusion about whether certain 'Indian' tricks really originated in China – such as the fabled Rope Trick – but the opposite is also true, with some modern commentators attributing the origins of the 'Chinese Rings' to Indian street magic.[3]

The confusion in representations of Indian and Chinese Magic on the Western stage was partially a result a romantically muddled media and public ignorance, but partially because the first really talented Chinese performer to be recognized as a 'magician' did not perform in the West until 1898, when Zhu Liankui (aka Ching Ling Foo, 1854–1922) began his international tour. Zhu's show was a great success in North American and Europe, where the 'Conjurer to the Dowager Empress of China' spurred a surge of imitators who assumed Chinese names, titles, and costumes, with varying levels of commitment and burlesque. Indeed, Zhu Liankui, who was born in Beijing and was well established as a performer in China, is often cited as the first Asian magician to achieve worldwide success: in the years between 1898 and his mysterious death in 1922, Ching Ling Foo became a household name in New York and London, as well as in Beijing and Shanghai; he played to packed houses and even toured with the 'Dean of American

---

[2] Sidney Clarke, 'Oriental Conjuring'. *The Magic Wand*, 17:138 (June 1928). Reprinted in Sidney Clarke, *The Annals of Conjuring*. Seattle: Miracle Factory, 2001, p. 398.

[3] Will Ayling is sufficiently convinced about the Indian origins of the Linking Rings that he simply calls the effect the 'Indian Link Trick'. Will Ayling & Sam Sharpe, *Oriental Conjuring and Magic*. Exeter: The Supreme Magic Co. 1981, pp. 60–61. As we'll see later, there is also a case to be made that the Chinese/Indian Link Trick was originally Japanese.

Magicians' Harry Kellar, who famously declared him a world-class magician.

Before the emergence of Zhu, however, the exposure of Western audiences to 'Chinese magic' was largely in the form of juggling, opera, acrobatics, and carnival conjuring. Hence, the aesthetics of Chinese theatre arrived substantially before anything that the modern magicians of the time recognized as 'magic'. To some extent, as we'll see later, this was because before the arrival of modern Western magic in China, the allied arts of juggling, conjuring, tumbling, and so forth were all considered to be part of the same entertainment milieu. As we will see in the next chapter, this pattern of blended popular entertainment was also common in Japan (which had inherited much of its conjuring heritage from China). Indeed, the separation of magic as a distinct discipline was as much as a feature of modernity in East Asia as in the West; part of the reason for Zhu Liankui's great success in the West was precisely his modern disciplinary focus on magic as a distinct art.

The emergence of 'Chinese magic' from the world of Chinese theatre, opera, and circus immediately placed it into a different representational frame from 'Indian magic' in Europe and North America. As we have already seen, the image of Indian magic was inextricably intertwined with various forms of occultism and magical beliefs, which placed it (and its imitation) into discourses about 'real and potent magic', especially those that emphasized 'the darker or even macabre aspects of magic. In India, magic was invariably associated with religious rites and holy persons, and often attended with fear and superstition.'[4] Indian magic was popularly entwined with Spiritualism and Theosophy. However, as we will see was also the case with Japan, Chinese magic was largely associated with entertainment from the start – the lush, ostentatious, and exotic costuming of the Chinese circus lent this magic 'a poetic beauty unlike the style of the East Indian magicians'.[5] Hence, the aesthetics of 'Chinese magic' were fabulous and colourful (and rippling with silk) even before audiences had any conception of what kinds of feats of magic might fall into this category.[6]

---

[4] Edward Claflin & Jeff Sheridan, *Street Magic: An Illustrated History of Wandering Magicians and Their Conjuring Arts*. New York: Dolphin Books, 1977, p. 40.

[5] Claflin & Sheridan, *Street Magic*, p. 35.

[6] As we will see, it was not until much later, after the so-called Kung Fu Boom that followed the global emergence of Bruce Lee in the 1960s and 1970s, that China would become more readily associated with esoteric magic and self-cultivation, which is now

To some extent, 'Chinese magic' of this period manifested itself as a form of *pure glamour* – re-enchanting feats and renewing effects that had only been seen in other styles before. It was a magic of defamiliarization. Hence, while the presentation and style were fresh and exciting, Clarke notes that the performances of the first Chinese troupes in Britain in the 1830s were full of feats (if not effects) that 'were no novelties to English audiences'.[7]

The first documented performances of magic by Chinese performers in England were part of the 1830 'Court of Pekin', who performed at Saville House in Leicester Square, London.[8] Their show contained a number of effects that would come to be synonymous with Chinese magic, including fire-eating and the production of colourful ribbons from the mouths of the performers. These feats did not seem innovative in themselves, but their presentation was novel enough to strike a chord in London. Together with other tricks, such as the Chinese (or East Indian) Needle Trick (in which the performer swallows numerous needles, takes a drink of water, shows his mouth empty, and then extracts the needles in a perfect chain neatly threaded on white cotton),[9] sword-swallowing, various kinds of dismemberment, and the 'torn and restored paper' trick (in which a sheet or ribbon of paper is

---

a commonplace association with China and the martial arts. The Boxer Rebellion of 1900 provided an early episode in this future history, with the European press paying considerable attention to the claims of the Boxers to be able to shield themselves from bullets by magic. It was also at this time that ideas about 'magic boxing' started to circulate in Europe and North America. Cashing in on this, as we shall see, William Robinson (aka Chung Ling Soo) started to incorporate a 'bullet catching' effect into his stage show at the time of the Rebellion. In itself, a bullet catch had no particular 'Chineseness', but the glamour of Chinese magic re-enchanted the feat not only through silken robes and exoticism but also via association with the 'magic armour' of the Boxers.

[7] Clarke, 'Oriental Conjuring', p. 397.

[8] This performance is cited by both Sidney Clarke and James Randi (who is presumably leaning on Clarke) as the earliest recorded company of 'Chinese jugglers' in England. Clarke, 'Oriental Conjuring', p. 397; James Randi, *Conjuring: Being a Definitive History of the Venerable Arts of Sorcery, Prestigitation, Wizardry, Deception, & Chicanery*. New York: St. Martin's Press, 1992, p. 247.

[9] This needle trick is simply one of many whose origins between India and China are hazy and disputed. It is entirely conceivable that such tricks have been performed in both countries (and elsewhere) for so long that they have become embedded into local heritage. One of the most impressive performances of the needle trick in recent years was that of Teller during the 'China' leg of the *Penn & Teller Magical Mystery Tour* (CBC/Channel 4, 2003), where Teller performs the needle trick to a community of local magicians in rural China.

torn into shreds and then restored to its previous, undamaged form), these were quickly revealed as the staples of the Chinese magical repertoire.[10] Again, qua *feats*, these were not new to the London audience, and many would have been associated with Indian magic had they been performed in a different style and atmosphere. However, they were presented intermixed with colourful feats of juggling, acrobatics, and 'quick changes' of masks and clothing, giving the shows a sumptuous, energetic, and glamorous atmosphere that bordered on pantomime or burlesque. In this respect, theatrical China and theatrical Japan tended together and distanced themselves from India. Indeed, the aesthetic similarities between such shows and the emerging aesthetic of comic opera, as presented by Gilbert and Sullivan's hugely popular classic of Victorian Orientalism, *The Mikado; or, the Town of Titipu* (1885), were clear to many commentators at the time.[11]

However, the 'Court of Pekin' also exhibited two important effects that caught the public imagination and triggered professional interest from magicians in London. The first of these was the 'Chinese' Linking Ring trick, for which the troupe used eight metal rings, linking and unlinking them into various configurations and patterns. And the second appears to have been a version of what came to be known as the Goldfish Bowl Trick, in which a large bowl of water is impossibly produced by the magician on an otherwise empty stage.

[10] This impression was bolstered by travel accounts of the magic witnessed in China by missionaries, such as the American Reverend Justus Doolittle (1824–1880), whose popular book, *The Social Life of the Chinese* (2 vols., 1867, published as two volumes in one: *Social life of the Chinese: With Some Account of Their Religious, Governmental, Educational, and Business Customs and Opinions. With Special but not Exclusive Reference to Fuchchau*. New York: Harper & Bros., 1876), included accounts of witnessing acrobatics in the streets, impossible feats of juggling and balance, fire eating and sword swallowing, as well as the needle trick, the Mango/Melon Trick, and a whole variety of tricks involving dismembering young boys and putting them back together again (along the lines of the Indian/Chinese rope trick). Doolittle also includes an account of the so-called Chinese Linking Rings trick (a variety using three or five rings, rather than the eight most often seen on the stage at that time in the United States or Europe) – see especially pp. 79–83.

[11] The representation of China on the London stage is well discussed in Dongshin Chang, *Representing China on the Historical London Stage*. London & New York: Routledge, 2015; see also, Laikwan Pang, *The Distorting Mirror: Visual Modernity in China*. Honolulu: University of Hawai'i Press, 2007. A valuable account of an earlier period from the standpoint of performativity is Chi-Ming Yang, *Performing China: Virtue, Commerce, and Orientalism in Eighteenth-Century England, 1660–1760*. Baltimore: Johns Hopkins University Press, 2011.

(Chinese) Linking Rings

The Linking Rings has become such a commonplace of conjuring and magic in the contemporary period that it is almost impossible to imagine modern magic with this iconic effect. The long-running journal of the International Brotherhood of Magicians (IBM, est.1922) is titled, *The Linking Ring*. Almost every box of magic tricks for beginners or for children includes a set of linking rings of varying sizes and number. Indeed, the 'trick' of the Linking Rings is now so well known by the general public that it is extremely difficult for a performance to express anything close to enchantment or magic. Nothing is more likely to induce yawns or groans of resignation than an amateur magician brandishing a series of steel rings and attempting to behave as though the audience is going to be astonished. In many ways, the Linking Rings have become emblematic of what we previously identified as the death of magic in the second half of the twentieth century: they are as closely associated with clowns and balloon animals as they are with a sense of mystery and wonder. When not farcical, the Linking Rings have come to be seen as simple, routine, mundane, and mechanical, rather than mystifying, enchanting, or magical.[12]

On the China-stage of their *Magical Mystery Tour* (2003), for instance, Penn and Teller visit a circus school in Wuzhou provincial city (which they suggest is the 'birthplace of magic and the cradle of acrobatics in China') where students are trained in various forms of tumbling and juggling, and where the 'magic master' drills a classroom of students in the correct performance of the Linking Rings. Students sit diligently mimicking the same ('correct') routine in a mechanical manner. Penn comments wryly that it resembles the Communist dream of a magic school (having already noted that magic was persecuted and props destroyed in China during the Cultural Revolution); however, my point here is not an ideological one (to which we will return later) but instead a magical one – it is specifically the Linking Rings that has become the focus of this conveyor-belt magical training, just as it is the Linking Rings that appear in every children's magic set.[13]

---

[12] For readers who missed out on their childhood magic sets: the 'secret' of the Linking Rings is that one of the rings has a small gap in it (sufficient in size to allow another ring to pass through it), and some of the other rings are permanently linked together.

[13] In fact, the contemporary mundanity of the Linking Rings is reinforced by Penn & Teller when they segue from conveyor-belt magical training (the secrecy of which the master magician seems to take very seriously) to a shopping mall where a market

Nonetheless, the decline of the Linking Rings as a highlight of magical performance is a relatively recent development. Some of the great magicians of the last few decades made exciting, innovative, and often beautiful routines using the Linking Rings, including Al Koran (1914–1972, who used three rings), Dai Vernon (1894–1992, who used six), and even the Bizarre Magician Jeff McBride (who also uses six rings). To some extent, precisely because of the saturation of the Linking Rings into the public sphere, performance of this classic effect places even greater emphasis on the ability of the magician to transport the audience into a space of magic – the artistry is the enchantment. This is why the conveyor belt imagery is so antithetical to magic in this case (as in most others).

For example, in 1989, the contemporary Japanese magician Yanagida Masahiro performed a striking variant of the Linking Rings that he called the Ninja Rings at the Magic Castle in Hollywood.[14] Yanagida made use of unusually small rings (about 10 cm in diameter) and blended the presentation with the idea of ninja heritage and skill, placing an emphasis on the mythical skill and precision of the mystical ninja to bring a new dimension to his performance. Part of the conceit of Yanagida's performance was that he was making use of traditional Japanese methods (in which he had apparently trained in a traditional Japanese way for thirteen years) to bring about a revolution in this classic effect of modern magic. In this way, Yanagida capitalized on the 1980s boom in martial arts Orientalism in the West and, in particular, on the myth of the ninja as mystical 'shadow warriors'.[15]

---

vendor has dozens of cheap sets of Linking Rings for sale to anyone interested, complete with printed instructions for the secret routine.

[14] The Magic Castle is the headquarters of the Academy of Magical Arts (AMA) in the United States. Despite being one of the younger magic associations (the AMA was incorporated in 1961, and the Castle opened in 1963), it has quickly developed a strong reputation for excellence and exclusivity. It runs classes and gives lectures for members. For many years, it was the home of the late, great Dai Vernon. Its proximity to and associations with Hollywood connect it with a high-profile constituency.

[15] Yanagida Masahiro has since passed on his routine to Shoot Ogawa (Ogawa Makoto), who maintains many of the same elements and conceits, and who was awarded the prestigious title of close-up 'Magician of the Year' in 2003 and 2006 by the AMA, partially on the basis of his handling of the Ninja Rings routine. Although I have not been able to verify claims about an ancient tradition and special method of performing the Linking Rings in Japan (although a version does appear in the *Hōkasen* magic manual by Hirase Hose in 1764), it does not seem implausible that the Linking Rings would have arrived in Japan from China very early in history (along

In the nineteenth century, though, the Linking Rings were state of the art. The success of the 'Court of Pekin' troupe was sufficient that 'after these performances there was a run on Chinese jugglers, real and imitation'.[16] This was the first time that Europeans had seen the trick, and thus it was immediately associated with Chinese magic. However, it is an intriguing thought experiment to ask whether we would be talking about the Japanese Linking Rings had Japanese conjurors arrived in Europe before the Chinese (instead of being forbidden to leave Japan until the second half of the century). Clear methods and routines for the Linking Rings appear in Japan's oldest extant manuals of magic, including the *Hōkasen* of 1764.[17]

One of the first Europeans to perform the Linking Rings in his own show was Joseph Jacobs (1813–1870, who performed as M. Jacobs), who apparently included the effect as early as 1834.[18] At this stage in his career, Jacobs was a provincial magician (billing himself as a wizard and ventriloquist, and sometimes as a mesmerist and electro-biologist), but his success with the Linking Rings eventually

with various other aspects of Japanese magic and culture more generally), but the plausibility of this is also beside the point – the association with the ninja *mythos* is simply part of the presentation of the trick and an effective way to generate enchantment.

The conflation of the martial arts and magic is a feature of Chinese popular culture, especially in the modern period, and also of the invention of the ninja in modern Japan; it becomes an intriguing feature of contemporary magic in the West later.

[16] Clarke, 'Oriental Conjuring', p. 398.

[17] Sadly, we do not have such reliable old records of magical techniques in China, following their widespread destruction in the Cultural Revolution. However, conventional wisdom is that many techniques (including the Linking Rings) probably travelled to Japan from China. A magic manual known as the *Shenxian xishu* was reputedly compiled during the Ming dynasty (and possibly published later, in 1696); the received knowledge about this manual is that it contained more than twenty tricks, including the famous Butterfly Trick, and that it was transported to Japan, where the Butterfly Trick has become a part of the national heritage. However, the manuscript of *Shenxian xishu* has been lost. The oldest extant magical manuals in China is the Qing dynasty manuscript *E huan huibian* (1889) by Tang Zaifeng, which contains references to hundreds of traditional Chinese tricks and many 'foreign tricks'. It does not elaborate on all of the tricks listed, and does not contain a guide to the Linking Rings. On the other hand, the Japanese book *Hōkasen* (1764) by Hirase Hose includes a double-page image of a Linking Ring performance (using seven rings) and then later an elaborate, illustrated instruction guide.

[18] Randi, *Conjuring*, p. 247.

took him to London in 1841 for several successful seasons and then to the United States and Australia. During this time, however, the influential French conjurer Jacques Noel Talon (1802–1878, aka Philippe) also incorporated the Linking Rings into his high-profile show as early as 1836, claiming to have learnt the routine from a troupe of travelling Chinese magicians in Britain.[19] Philippe, who occupies an intriguing place on the cusp between 'old' and 'new' magic, became renowned (and controversial) for performing in the guise of a medieval sorcerer. In fact, part of his reason for doing this was to find a way to perform Chinese tricks without wearing Chinese robes, thus allowing him to maintain his European identity and an aura of traditional enchantment.

Part of the importance of Philippe was the impact he had on the 'father of modern magic', Jean Eugene Robert-Houdin, who credits his countryman with being 'my immediate predecessor in the conjuring art, whose success in Paris at that period was most brilliant'.[20] Robert-Houdin recounts the mysterious transformation of the confectioner Talon into the magician Philippe during his stay in Aberdeen, his rising reputation as a magician in Scotland that led him to build his own theatre of magic in Glasgow, and then his trip 'over to Dublin, where he acquired two new tricks, which were the foundation of his future reputation'.[21] In Dublin, Philippe met a Chinese performer (whose troupe had apparently failed to impress in Paris and so had disbanded and scattered) who taught him the Linking Rings and the so-called Goldfish Trick. Robert-Houdin immediately recognizes the essential technical connection between the latter and the adoption of a Chinese costume – since the production of the goldfish bowl requires long, flowing robes – but he also notes with approval the moral concerns that Philippe exhibited about adopting this guise. He explains that had Philippe attempted to dress as a 'mandarin' despite the fact that 'his face had none of the distinguishing features', the 'public would not have

[19] Talon's claims to meeting a Chinese troupe are not well substantiated. Some versions include him meeting them in Scotland (where he was a confectioner after leaving Paris), and others have him meeting them in Dublin. As we have seen, it was not uncommon in this period for magicians to make spurious claims about their connections with the Orient and 'Oriental' teachers.

[20] Jean Eugene Robert-Houdin, *Memoirs of Robert-Houdin: Ambassador, Author, and Conjuror* (2nd ed., trans Lascelles Wraxall). London: Chapman & Hall, 1860, p. 165.

[21] Robert-Houdin, *Memoirs of Robert-Houdin*, p. 168.

endured such a slight'. He talks about costuming as a 'responsibility' that a magician must take seriously.[22]

In fact, Robert-Houdin's moral concerns on this issue were far in advance of the audience of his day: by the time of Philippe's return to Paris in the summer of 1841 he was performing the second half of his show as 'A Festival at a Palace in Nankin', with the dark staging of the first half replaced by 'brocades glistening with gold and precious stones'; Philippe changed from a black outfit into a 'costume which, in the public admiration ... must have exhausted the riches of Golconda to buy'.[23]

In one of the earliest accounts of a performance of the Linking Rings in Europe, Robert-Houdin describes how Philippe opened this part of the show:

> Philippe took up several rings about eight inches in diameter, and intertwined them into chains and knots with the greatest possible ease. Then suddenly, when it seemed impossible for him to unravel his handiwork, he blew upon them, and the rings fell apart at his feet. This trick produced a charming illusion.[24]

'A Festival at a Palace in Nankin' included a few other feats of almost no connection with China, but the headline effects were the Linking Rings, which opened the show, and the Goldfish Bowl, which closed the show. The sumptuous costuming and glamorous presentation, together with this top-and-tailing of the show with signature Chinese effects, gave the overall impression of Chinese magic being performed.

Just as we saw with the appropriation of Levitation effects into the canon of modern magic, so the Linking Rings were quickly adopted. In fact, the rings so clearly matched the emerging ideas about 'modern' magic that they rapidly became symbols of modern magic itself. There

---

[22] Robert-Houdin, *Memoirs of Robert-Houdin*, p. 168. It seems that Philippe's compromise was to wear the flowing costume of a medieval magician or sorcerer, rather than the flowing robes of a 'Celestial'. Given Robert-Houdin's principled opposition to this mode of presentation, as part of the construction of modern magic (as we saw in earlier chapters), his condoning of Philippe's sorcerous persona as an alternative to Oriental dress is fascinating, suggesting that a recourse to the imaginary of 'old magic' in Europe was morally preferable to the embrace of 'Chinese' representations.

[23] Robert-Houdin, *Memoirs of Robert-Houdin*, p. 171. Golconda is presumably a reference to the capital of the Golconda sultanate near Hyderabad in India (not China!), which was (and remains) famous for its affluence in gem stones, including as the origin of the Hope Diamond.

[24] Robert-Houdin, *Memoirs of Robert-Houdin*, p. 171.

was no supernatural ambiguity about the performance, as there often was with so-called Indian magic or with Spiritualism. The rings did not seem to be embedded in any grand ideological or occult system of exotic knowledge – they were not a challenge to the moral imperatives of modern magic – rather, the exoticism resided almost entirely in the aesthetics of the performance itself. The Linking Rings could be dressed as an 'experiment' in the scientific properties of metal, and a performance of the Linking Rings *qua* Chinese magic added a new level of enchantment through a theatrical exoticism that did not under-cut the cleanness of this basic position. Indeed, the idea of 'Chinese magic' was already being pulled away from its reference to feats of magic *from China*, and instead it was being pushed towards the perfor-mance of any feat of magic in a 'Chinese style', where the aesthetics of this style were not necessarily rooted in China itself.

The Linking Rings became such an accepted part of the reper-toire of modern magicians that instructions on its performance were included in both of the great, foundational texts of modern magic: Robert-Houdin himself devotes a chapter to 'The Chinese Rings' in his seminal work of 1868; and Professor Hoffmann includes a detailed section in his book of 1876. Aside from the name of the trick, neither Robert-Houdin nor Hoffmann make much reference to the 'Chineseness' of the routines, but instead focus on the practical skills and techniques that are needed to perform them, emphasising them as effective parts of a modern magical performance. Hoffmann's illustra-tions clearly show the routines being performed by a man in a dinner-jacket, while Robert-Houdin showcases a theatrical 'Chinaman' flourishing a twelve-ring chain at the start of the chapter – an image that is reproduced on the front cover of the 1878 English translation.[25] Hence, without the accompaniment of any explicit cultural or ethnic commentary, the Chinese Linking Rings take pride of place on the cover of the foundational text of modern magic. Their 'Chineseness' has already become an (partially fabricated) aesthetic choice for Western performers, rather than a signifier of ethnic origination or authenticity.

---

[25] Jean Eugene Robert-Houdin, *Les Secrets de la Prestidigitation et de la Magie*, 1868– translated by Professor Hoffmann as *The Secrets of Conjuring and Magic, or How to Become a Wizard*. London: Routledge, 1878, pp. 291–300. Professor Hoffmann, *Modern Magic: A Practical Treatise on the Art of Conjuring*. 1876, U.S. edition reprinted Philadelphia: David McKay, 1910, pp. 401–409.

As we saw in the last chapter, the situation with Indian magic was very different.

The Goldfish Bowl

The second iconic piece of Chinese magic introduced by 'The Court of Pekin' seems to have been a version of the so-called Goldfish Bowl Trick. Our records of this performance are not very detailed, but the programme notes contain this basic description:

> From under a green carpet, on which the performers walk, and where it appears impossible that anything can be concealed, an immense Flower Pot is produced, and afterwards a large Basin is exhibited (as if by magic) full of Water.[26]

Just like the Linking Rings, this effect excited the imagination of audiences and magicians in the West, and for some time it seemed genuinely baffling. However, as with the Linking Rings, the bafflement was not framed in supernatural terms but rather in terms of admiration for the cleverness and dexterity exhibited by these Chinese 'jugglers', amplified by the glamour of the exotic. Like the Linking Rings, and somewhat unlike the Indian Levitation, the Goldfish Bowl was immediately framed as a genius feat of theatrical entertainment and superior dexterity. And also like the Linking Rings, these early performances in the West quickly sparked mimics and imitators of various kinds. Once again, Robert-Houdin provides an account of Philippe's landmark performances of 'A Festival at a Palace in Nankin' in Paris:

> Philippe usually ended the evening's performance with the famous Chinese trick, to which he had given the pompous name of 'Neptunes's Basins, or the Gold-Fish'.
>
> The magician, clothed in his brilliant costume, mounted on a sort of low table, which isolated him from the stage. After a few manoeuvres to prove he had nothing about him, he threw a shawl at his feet, and, on lifting it up, he displayed a glass basin filled with water, in which gold-fish swam about. This was thrice repeated, with the same result; but, in his desire to improve on his

---

[26] The programme is cited in Randi, *Conjuring*, p. 247. I have been unable to find an original version of the theatrical programme to verify this quotation, but the description is certainly plausible for that period. The same (unsourced) quotation appears in Clarke, 'Oriental Conjuring', p. 397.

brethren of the Celestial Empire, the French conjuror had added a variation to their trick, which gave an amusing termination to the performance. Throwing the shawl on the ground for the fourth time, several animals, such as rabbits, ducks, chickens, etc., emerged from it.[27]

Philippe was only one of the first of a profusion of 'Chinese magic' acts that emerged in Europe and the United States at this time. Some, such as the troupe leader Tuck Quay, brought entire Chinese-themed shows on world tours in the 1850s, often incorporating a mixture of Chinese performers and performances in the 'Chinese style'.[28] Others adopted a Chinese style for their own acts or themed one of the acts of their show on China, sometimes blending it into a hybrid Orientalist aesthetic, as did Philippe himself.

As early as 1853, in Ponsin's *Nouvelle Magic Blanche Dévoilée*, methods for the performance of the Goldfish Bowl Trick were already circulating in Paris and London. Robert-Houdin includes a version in his 1868 *Secrets*, and Hoffmann's *Modern Magic* provides an explication in 1876.[29] Jean Nicholas Ponsin (1801–1863), whose work Sam Sharpe considers the 'first really practical treatise on conjuring to appear in any language' and suggests that Professor Hoffmann's seminal

---

[27] Robert-Houdin, *Memoirs of Robert-Houdin*, p. 172. In fact, ending this trick with 'surprise productions' of various kinds is a conventional feature.

[28] Milbourne Christopher includes a poster depicting Tuck Quay, describing his troupe: 'Tuck Quay, Wan Sing, and Yan Yow were among the Chinese magicians who showed their Oriental wonders at the Walnut Street Theatre in Philadelphia in 1853.' He also includes a bill describing the implausibly named Tuck Quay, Whangnhoo, Tin-kee, and Amoy as 'The Chinese Magicians from the Court of his Celestial Majesty'. *Magic: A Picture History*. London: Constable & Co., 1962/1991, p. 124. According to Claflin & Sheridan, Tuck Quay was also billed as a 'chief performer of the Court of Pekin'; the highlight of his show at the Drury Lane Theatre in London was his performance of a knife-throwing act. Claflin & Sheridan, *Street Magic*, p. 38. As we will see in the next chapter, knife-throwing was an intriguing example of an effect that was more of a juggling act or stunt in China and Japan, but which became a 'trick' when it was incorporated into Western magic acts. Instead of actually throwing the knives, 'modern magicians' contrived a backboard with spring-loaded knives in it, so that the magician could feign the throws and the knives would spring into the correct places.

[29] Robert-Houdin (1868), *The Secrets of Conjuring and Magic*, pp. 362–368. Hoffmann, *Modern Magic*, pp. 371–373. Hoffmann appears much less interested in this trick than Robert-Houdin; his description offers little more (indeed less) detail and relies on Robert-Houdin's modern method.

Modern Magic owes a substantial debt to it,[30] devotes a section of his book to 'The Fish-Bowls, or The Unexpected Appearance of Vases Full of Water'. Ponsin's enthusiasm for the trick is clear:

> I wish to explain this famous trick of the fish-bowls to you, a trick which, for more than two years, was the talk of Paris; a trick which you could see so many times with admiration without understanding it; a trick, in short, so wonderful that ... Ah! You think I am jesting![31]

Like Robert-Houdin later, Ponsin was also concerned to balance the success of the effect against the need for it to appear as a feat of *modern* magic. Indeed, Ponsin makes no mention of the Chinese origins of this particular effect and so makes no reference to the need for flowing Chinese robes to obscure the fish bowl. By focusing exclusively on the mechanics of the trick, Ponsin demonstrates a clear lack of interest in questions of nationality, ethnicity, or culture; Ponsin's priority is in exploring how the modern magician can accomplish this amazing effect. With this in mind, it is somewhat predictable that he, like Robert-Houdin, would lament the way that Philippe resorted to the costume of a sorcerer to make the performance possible:

> This is the method used by M. Philippe. But it is rather embarrassing as it requires a special costume. You have to dress yourself up like a [fantasy] magician, which I find ridiculous, since the prestidigitateur who takes the title of physician ought at least to dress decently, so as not to fall into inconsistency.[32]

According to Ponsin, Philippe's miraculous fish-bowl production was accomplished through the use of a *gibeciere* suspended beneath his robes and behind his legs. The triangular *gibeciere* was shaped into

---

[30] Sam Sharpe, 'Translator's Preface', in S.H. Sharpe, *Ponsin on Conjuring*. London: George Johnson, 1937, pp. 7-10, being a translation of Jean Nicholas Ponsin, *Nouvelle magie blanche dévoilée: physique occulte, et cours complet de prestidigitation*. Reims & Paris, 1853.

[31] Ponsin in Sharpe, *Ponsin on Conjuring*, p. 113.

[32] Ponsin in Sharpe, *Ponsin on Conjuring*, p. 113. Ponsin is here referring to the modern convention for magicians to present themselves as 'doctors' or 'professors' conducting experiments, rather than as supernatural agents manipulating supernatural counterphysical causation. Like Robert-Houdin, he is using the term 'magician' to contrast with the term 'conjuror', which he identifies with the role of physician.

a kind of pouch, with the corners threaded by cords, in which the bowl could safely be placed. He suggests that multiple pouches could be arranged behind the magician's legs without seriously encumbering his freedom of movement, and that the bowls could be laid – rather like golden eggs – by crouching and releasing the appropriate cord. 'You now see that the wizard's robe is essential. A riding-coat would do, but this costume is not a suitable one.'[33]

For Robert-Houdin, the great challenge of this trick was how to accomplish it without compromising the modernity of the magician performing it. Admirable, successful, and unusual as his performance may have been, Philippe's medievalism risked 'inconsistency' with the requirements of modern magic. Philippe may have learned his method from a Chinese magician in Dublin, and Ponsin may have accurately related that method, but that method was not deemed appropriate for the modern magician in the West. Robert-Houdin was clear that two things were unacceptable for modern magicians: the first was that an audience would find it unacceptable for a modern European magician to dress as a Chinese magician (although this was not, *per se*, an affront to modernity, the 'public would not have endured such a slight'); and the second was that the modern magician himself should find it morally unacceptable to resort to the imaginary of old magic by presenting himself in the guise of a sorcerer (which could be an affront to modernity). Hence, if the Goldfish Bowl Trick was to form a legitimate part of the modern repertoire, Robert-Houdin had to find a new way to accomplish it. In this respect, the trick's 'Chineseness' represented a moral as well as a technical challenge for modern magic, even if this 'Chineseness' could simply be reduced to wearing a flowing robe. In this intriguing ethical dilemma, we can see the foreshadowing of modernization theory, in which the Oriental and the Medieval are constructed as tending together.

> I have recorded in my Memoirs that the gold-fish trick had been introduced into France by certain Chinese performers, and that the conjuror Philippe, having become acquainted with the secret, had assumed the conventional costume of a magician, in order to have, like his Celestial brethren, a flowing robe wherewith to hide the famous bowl.
>
> ... I myself had a strong desire to exhibit this trick on my own stage, but where and how could I conceal about my person an

---

[33] Ponsin in Sharpe, *Ponsin on Conjuring*, p. 115.

object so bulky as the bowl in question, with no other aid than a mere dress-coat?[34]

In the end, Robert-Houdin suggests that the dilemma is overcome by technical progress and concerted reason: modernity provides the technical solution that simultaneously resolves the ethical and aesthetic dilemma. 'By dint of much mental exertion, however, I at last managed to solve the difficulty, and even to produce a bowl larger than those of my predecessors.'[35] The chapter devoted to 'The Miraculous Fishery' opens with a triumphant illustration of Robert-Houdin (in a dinner jacket and bow tie) flourishing a shawl from under which appear goldfishes swimming in a bowl of water.

In fact, Robert-Houdin's 'improvement' on the Goldfish Bowl Trick represents the opposite compromise to the one made by Philippe. While Philippe was willing to sacrifice aesthetic elements of the modernity of magic (by wearing the flowing robes of a Merlin) in order retain mechanics that accomplished a reliable feat of magic, and while other performers were willing to risk 'affronting' their audiences by dressing as 'Celestials' for the same reason, Robert-Houdin compromised the mechanics of the feat in order to maximize the aesthetic modernity of the effect. The 'compromise' was also a technical innovation: Robert-Houdin devised a new way to seal the bowl so that it could hang vertically without spilling while suspended and obscured under the tails of his dinner-jacket; this enabled the production of a goldfish-filled bowl, but also introduced new restrictions on acceptable lines of sight from the audience, making the presentation rather more stilted and formal.

It is an interesting thought experiment in the normative history of magic in the modern period to ask which of these compromises accomplished the most magical *effect*. As we have already seen in some detail in earlier chapters, it seems that Ponsin was probably correct to find Philippe's medievalism 'ridiculous' – performance magic in the complex age of scientific modernity struggled to retain even symbolic associations with the 'old magic' of Europe, at least to the extent that it invested in the idea of *modern magic*. It also seems that Robert-Houdin's remake of the Goldfish Bowl Trick would have been the most cleanly and ethically modern, folding it neatly into the emerging field of *modern* magic. However, even if his instincts on this seem to

---

[34] Robert-Houdin, *The Secrets of Conjuring and Magic*, pp. 362–363.
[35] Robert-Houdin, *The Secrets of Conjuring and Magic*, p. 363,

Figure 5.1 Chung Ling Soo, 'A Name to Conjure With', c. 1905. Courtesy of Nielsen Magic Collection. Soo was playful about the magical manipulations involved in his stage name.

resonate with critical opinion in the post-colonial present, Robert-Houdin seems to have been wrong that audiences in the nineteenth century would be affronted by the sight of a Western magician adopting the guise of a 'mandarin' in order to perform magic – indeed, as we've seen, there were clear associations between the Orient and magic during this period that offered the possibility of enhancing the impact and effect of any magical feat.[36]

The arrival of Ching Ling Foo

A landmark moment in the development of the representation of Chinese magic in the West was the arrival of Zhu Liankui in the United States in 1898. His first performance in the West was as the lead in the Ching Ling Foo Troupe of Oriental Wonder Workers at the China Pavilion of the Trans-Mississippi Exposition in Omaha. Although Western audiences were already accustomed to 'Chinese style' performances, this was the first time that a complete Chinese magic act had been shown to the public. The show included staples of Chinese magic, including fire-breathing, various productions from his mouth (including ribbons and a long pole), and decapitations. However, Ching Ling Foo's signature trick was a version of the Goldfish Bowl Trick: he produced a huge bowl of water (weighing upwards of 40 kg)[37] from beneath a cloth in the middle of the stage, without the use of trapdoors. The size and weight of the bowl was so astonishing that it made instant headlines and catapulted Ching Ling Foo to fame. In various versions of the trick, the bowl might also contain

[36] As late as 1923, somewhat in the wake of the Chung Ling Soo episode, practitioners of magic were visibly wrestling with these problematics. James Elliot and Houdini even went so far as to raise the question of whether 'Caucassian [sic]' magicians made Oriental magic better, by 'Occidentalizing' and 'Modernizing' what they called 'Asiatic modes of thought'. For them, this was a matter of technical (and technological) development and excellence, having nothing to do with esoteric or mystical powers (on the topic of which, Houdini was an outspoken detractor). In other words, the question was whether Oriental magic could be improved by moving it into modernity, rather than leaving it 'closely wedded to mediaeval interpretations'. Such a question might have been a paraphrasing of the Magic Circle's Rope Trick challenge a decade later, as we saw in Chapter 4. J. Elliot (Houdini, ed.), *Elliot's Last Legacy: Secrets of the King of all Kard Kings*. New York: Adams Press Print, 1923, pp. 43–49.

[37] Ching Ling Foo sold postcards of himself next to the bowl, with a prominent label declaring the weight of the bowl to be 100 pounds.

a clutch of apples or swimming goldfish; sometimes it would be replaced by a small child. Robert-Houdin's method of obscuring a shallow dish under the tails of his dinner-jacket seemed inadequate to the task![38] Unable to speak much English, Ching Ling Foo's act was conducted without patter – the silence of the magician combining with the sumptuous aesthetic of flowing silken robes to bolster his Oriental mystique. More than any other act, Ching Ling Foo and his apparently impossible Goldfish Bowl Trick came to emblemize Chinese magic in the West.

Somewhat ironically, it was Ching Ling Foo's adoption of a modern, Western magical convention that triggered one of the most remarkable stories of twentieth-century magic, which ends with a magical duel in London in 1905. During a publicity event in New York, Ching Ling Foo issued a challenge to any magician, saying that he would pay the princely sum of one thousand dollars to anyone who could perform his Goldfish Bowl Trick. As Dexter remarks:

> These, you must know, were the days of challenges. Right and left they flew almost daily. There were a score of Kard Kings, dozens of Koin Kings.... There were Handcuff Kings, Billiard Ball Kings ... [and] contests between the members of these monarchies of magic.[39]

[38] In fact, the 'secret' was not very different, since Ching Ling Foo relied upon his long robes to hide whatever he was planning to produce. However, the size and weight of the objects he produced remained astonishing to magicians (who knew how it must be accomplished) and to audiences (who seemed genuinely baffled), not least because he appeared to move so naturally around the stage before the productions. In fact, the 'secret' was Ching Ling Foo's commitment and training: he would practice holding large, heavy objects suspended beneath his robes constantly, integrating this into his daily life as much as possible to normalize the impediment so that he would move as naturally as possible when performing.

[39] Will Dexter, *The Riddle of Chung Ling Soo*. London & New York: Arco Publishers ltd., 1955, p. 42. Dexter also notes that these challenges tended not to extend into the field of mentalism until William Robinson's challenge to the spiritualist medium, F.P. Evans, to whom he proposed a 'slate writing' challenge on 29 January 1900 after Ching Ling Foo withdrew his challenge when Robinson accepted it. In fact, Robinson's skill at slate writing was already widely admired and respected; his much sought-after little book on the subject was published by the Office of the *Scientific American* in 1898: William Robinson, *Spirit Slate Writing and Kindred Phenomena*. New York: Munn & Co., 1898. An enthusiastic and erudite discussion of the convention of the 'magical battle', focussed around the figure of Howard Thurston, is the excellent Jim Steinmeyer, *The Last Greatest Magician in the World: Howard Thurston vs. Houdini, and the Battles of the American Wizards*. New York: Tarcher, 2012.

In a fateful move, an accomplished, experienced, and ambitious professional magician who was struggling to find his own place in the limelight, William Robinson (1861–1918), accepted Zhu's challenge. As it happens, Zhu seems to have been surprised that someone would have accepted his challenge; perhaps he had envisioned the 'challenge' as a hollow cultural and commercial convention of Western magic (which was often the case), and so may have found Robinson's response a rude awakening to American culture.[40] Whatever the case, Zhu withdrew the challenge, and it promptly vanished from the press, leaving an unhappy and resentful Robinson holding a large bowl of water instead of a thousand dollars – a considerable amount of money for a struggling performer (or anyone else) at that time. Dexter suggests that Robinson went as far as 'turning up at Keith's one night with a large suitcase, containing a Chinese robe – and a large bowl'.[41]

---

[40] In fact, the magic press seems to have attributed his reversal to his Chineseness, referring to it as his 'Chinese bluff'. The *Mahatma* notes how successful Ching Ling Foo continues to be, and then reported the event:

> Upon Ching Ling Foo offering a reward of $1,000 to any person duplicating his bowl trick, Robinson, the 'Man of Mystery', now with the Herrmann show, offered to duplicate the trick, but very funny to state his offer was not accepted. It was a Chinese game of bluff. It is stated by those who have seen Robinson do the trick, that he does it just as good as the Chinaman.
>
> (Mahatma, *3:3, September 1899*).

A couple of months later, Mahatma confirms the 'wiliness of the Chinese' in its news 'Flashes':

We hear from good authority that Robinson, the Man of Mystery, accepted the challenge of Ching Ling Foo of $1,000 to any person duplicating his tricks. The wily Chinaman backed out and his challenge was taken out of the papers (*Mahatma*, III:V, November 1899).

[41] Will Dexter, *The Riddle of Chung Ling Soo*. London & New York: Arco Publishers Ltd., 1955, p. 42. Dexter also notes that his sources for this story may be unreliable. Nonetheless, the image is evocative of the impact the event seems to have had on Robinson. Keith's was the theatrical venue in Union Square, in New York, at which Ching Ling Foo was performing: Benjamin Franklin Keith (1846–1914) was an entertainment entrepreneur and vaudeville theatre owner in the eastern United States, famous for (amongst other things) embracing the Gilbert & Sullivan operetta boom and attempting to make it available to the masses for only a quarter. It is reputed that *The Mikado* was a particular favourite. Following his success at the Exposition, Ching Ling Foo followed the so-called Keith Circuit of vaudeville bookings to New York.

There are various interpretations of the way in which this event impacted on Robinson. Dexter's influential account, which is framed rather self-consciously as a defence of Robinson against his detractors, suggests that Robinson took Zhu's conduct personally and that the affront caused by this scenario justifies (and, to some extent, explains) Robinson's subsequent orientation towards Ching Ling Foo in particular and towards Chinese magic in general. It is certainly true that Robinson appears to have been annoyed by this incident. Perhaps in order to vent his frustration, in the same year he collaborated with Thomas Edison to produce a short, silent film entitled, *Ching Ling Foo Outdone*, in which Robinson appears to perform the Goldfish Bowl Trick, producing a washing barrel (instead of a bowl), geese (instead of ducks), and then a young boy.[42] The exaggerated effects in the film, which Robinson manages in formal, Western evening wear, are accomplished by camera tricks rather than any feats of prestidigitation, which might be interpreted as giving the one-upmanship a mocking tone. Not only was Ching Ling Foo *matched* by an American in a dinner jacket (i.e., a 'modern magician' in Robert-Houdin's tradition), but he was also *outdone* in scale, and he was also *outdone* in terms of the technological devices of magic – Ching Ling Foo could never match the effects produced by camera trickery on stage, no matter how long and flowing his silken robes.

This little-regarded film can be seen as important in many ways, not only in terms of the biographical development of Robinson, who famously went on to develop a 'Chinese magic' act under the *nom-de-théâtre* Chung Ling Soo (which included the Goldfish Bowl Trick as a signature effect), but also in terms of the negotiation between modern and Oriental magic. The film might be seen as Robinson's (rather embittered) response to the refusal of the great Chinese magician to bear witness to his ability to mimic the Goldfish Bowl Trick on-stage in the guise of a Chinese magician; Robinson's desire to become the exotic had been denied by the very object of his exoticism, sparking an extended, elaborate, seriously committed, but deeply conflicted form of identity tourism for Robinson for the rest of his life. However, the film might also be seen as an instance of the intimate relationship

---

[42] Thomas Edison (1847–1911) developed his 'Kinetoscope' in 1891, and his short films rapidly became staples of the penny arcades. 'Ching Ling Foo Outdone' – at less than one minute in duration – is now freely available online.

between modern magic and technological progress: the dinner jacket serves merely as a symbol of the real issue – the development of moving film was perhaps the single most transformative moment in modern magic, for better or worse. For some, motion picture technology rapidly became the cutting-edge in magical devices; for others it was the beginning of the death of magic itself.[43] Critical in the Robinson film is the way that Ching Ling Foo (*qua* Chinese magic) is 'outdone' by the technological advances of modernity, not by opting out of that modernity and adopting the guise of a 'Celestial' or a medieval sorcerer, but by the technology itself. Hence, Robinson's film might be seen as the inheritor of Robert-Houdin's attempt to modernize Philippe's medievalized mimicry of Chinese magic: *Chinese magic outdone by modern magic.*

However, even if this is a compelling and interesting reading of the scenario, it is clear that Robinson himself was not content with it. Indeed, as we have seen over and over again, Robinson exhibited the typically conflicted relationship between magic, modernity, and Orientalism. He may have been able to 'outdo' Ching Ling Foo in *feats* of magic, but in the end it seems that this was not really his goal. His true goal, it seems, was to accomplish the magic of *becoming* Ching Ling Foo, of appropriating the magical *effect* of his Chineseness. More than any other magician of the modern period, Robinson personified the Orientalist desire to become Oriental, even in the face of his concrete, technical knowledge that his own modern magic was already more potent. The romance of Chinese magic – the opulence, the silken robes, the spectacular sets, and the astonishing theatrical aesthetics – was simply enchanting. Robinson was bewitched by Ching Ling Foo.

The unnatural birth of Chung Ling Soo

(and the appearance of Ching Ling See, Ching Ling Sen, Chung Ling Sen, Chung Ling Fee, Ching Ling Fee, Ling Lang Hi, Li Chang Hi, Ching Foo Soo, Chung Ling Hee, and Little Chung Ling Soo)[44]

---

[43] Important discussions in this area include Matthew Solomon, *Silent Film, Houdini, and the New Magic of the Twentieth Century.* Chicago: University of Illinois Press, 2010; James Cook, *The Arts of Deception: Playing with Fraud in the Age of Barnum.* Cambridge: Harvard University Press, 2001.

[44] In his influential biography of Chung Ling Soo, Dexter lists these and other acts that were playing in European music halls in the early years of the twentieth century. He

Although it may have been a catalysing factor, it is not good enough to argue that Zhu's affront to Robinson was all that it took to trigger Robinson's quest to 'outdo' Chinese magic by becoming a Chinese magician. In fact, Robinson's existential Orientalism had already begun many years earlier. In his excellent biography, Jim Steinmeyer carefully reveals the younger Robinson as a technically talented and ambitious magician (who spent much of his early career as assistant or manager to some of the great magicians of the nineteenth century, including Alexander Herrmann and Harry Kellar), but also as a mediocre performer lacking in the natural charisma and powerful stage presence needed for him to launch a successful independent career.[45] In this light, Robinson's attraction to Oriental magic as the source of a new stage persona that might liberate him from his personal insecurities begins to make psychological sense, as well as to fit into a general cultural Orientalism associated with magic at that time.

Indeed, as early as 1886, while he was visiting Germany, Robinson witnessed the 'Black Art' of Max Auzinger (1839–1928), who performed in the guise of a generic 'Oriental magician' called Ben Ali Bey, manoeuvring eclectically between Indian and Egyptian modes of presentation. Robinson was apparently so impressed by this early glimpse of the power of an Oriental stage persona as a device to enchant an audience that he adopted the guise of 'Achmed Ben Ali' upon his return to New York. His show at the vaudeville theatre, New Century Museum, Rhode Island, not only attempted to conjure an Oriental aura of enchantment but also attempted to mimic the 'Black Art' of Auzinger.[46]

For our purposes here, there are three noteworthy elements to this episode. First, Robinson recognized the theatrical value and artistic liberty afforded by the adoption of a stage persona recognizably different from his own – a basic principle of stage performance. Second, Robinson

notes a similar profusion in North America. Dexter, *The Riddle of Chung Ling Soo*, p. 56.

[45] Jim Steinmeyer, *The Glorious Deception: The Double Life of Chung Ling Soo*. New York: Carroll & Graff, 2005. Steinmeyer's meticulous and balanced book replaces Dexter as the definitive biography of Robinson. I gratefully confess my debt to him for the historical details in this section.

[46] 'Black Art' was a technique that involved the use of black drapes on stage to obscure anything that should not be seen, together with the careful positioning of intense lighting directed towards the audience rather than onto the stage.

appears to have intuitively connected the emancipation associated with such a persona (specifically in the performance of magic) with the guise of Orientalism (in the sense that it was a fashion redolent with exoticism at the time). And third, Robinson (like many magicians of his age, before and since) establishes a precedent of unashamedly 'borrowing' the effects of inspirational or successful competitors, complete with the spirit and atmosphere of their acts. In fact, Robinson's performance as the 'Egyptian mystic' was certainly his most successful performance until that time; his discomfort about speaking in front of audiences was mitigated by the pantomime of foreignness that he performed.

Intriguingly, when Robinson started to work with Harry Kellar, Kellar is reported to have insisted that Egyptian mystics were inferior to Indian fakirs, and hence that Robinson's persona should not be Egyptian but Indian, and thus his stage character was changed to Nana Sahib,[47] who was billed as the 'East Indian Necromancer in Oriental Occultism' on posters which portrayed him as a wild-looking, white-bearded Indian fakir or yogi.[48] Then again, when Robinson returned to the employ of Herrmann, he was advised that neither Egyptian nor Indian magic could match the Oriental conjuring found in Constantinople, so his identity was changed once again, this time to Abdul Khan.[49] Like other magicians of the time, as we've seen, both Kellar and Herrmann professed direct and intimate knowledge of the Orient (from travels that are not properly substantiated) and Oriental magic.

Hence, by the time Robinson and the American public encountered a real Chinese magician in the 'Ching Ling Foo Troupe of Oriental Wonder Workers' in 1898, Robinson had already been through various Oriental stage personas, and Western audiences were already in the

---

[47] It is not clear whether Kellar or Robinson were aware that Nana Sahib was a famous rebel leader who played an important role in the Indian Rebellion of 1857, mysteriously vanishing without a trace after inflicting two bloody defeats on the British and then suffering a complete defeat himself. However, in 1880 Jules Verne published his novel, *La maison à vapeur* (The House of Steam), which features Nana Sahib (indeed, one of its alternative titles is 'The End of Nana Sahib'), and it seems plausible (given their interests in automata and mystery) that Kellar and Robinson would have been familiar with the novel's representation of a steam-powered, mechanical elephant carrying a house around India and with its romanticization of the mysterious adventures of Nana Sahib.

[48] Steinmeyer, *The Glorious Deception*, p. 92.

[49] Steinmeyer, *The Glorious Deception*, p. 118.

thrall of Oriental conjuring and magic as a genre of performance. The stage was already set, then, for William Robinson to show more than passing interest in the act of this talented Chinese magician: it contained an unusual, spectacular effect previously unseen in the United States (the Goldfish Bowl Trick); it was an act performed in the aura of Orientalism; and it was an act that didn't require Robinson to develop or deploy the charming, witty patter with which he was so uncomfortable, but instead required a mysterious, enigmatic silence.

In fact, even before the ill-fated challenge in Union Square in New York, 1900, Robinson had already met Zhu at the Boyd Theatre in Omaha in 1898, where Robinson had been performing together with Alexander Herrmann (1844–1896). The first of two encounters saw the great Herrmann himself (somewhat naively) perform the Chinese linking rings for Zhu, perhaps as a tribute to the Chinese visitor. The second encounter saw Zhu perform the linking rings with such virtuosity that he seemed to shame Herrmann; he then cast the rings aside as though in disgust at their simplicity, moving on to more spectacular 'Chinese' effects, such as the Goldfish Bowl Trick and spitting fire. The next year, Ching Ling Foo was the talk of New York; his show at the Union Square Theatre was a tremendous success, and it seems that Robinson attended at least some of those performances and studied him closely. For a while, Zhu was the highest paid performer on the vaudeville circuit. Reviews were consistently excellent. In other words, there was a sense in which the magical feud between Robinson and Zhu was already underway (at least for Robinson) when Zhu declined Robinson's offer to meet his challenge and duplicate the Goldfish Bowl Trick.

Magic feuds and magic duels: Foo vs. Soo

Just as he had done after witnessing the Black Art of Ben Ali Bey, Robinson resolved to adopt and then outdo this Oriental wonder-worker. Following the abortive challenge in New York, Robinson hastily made plans for a tour of continental Europe. The conjuror's journal, *Mahatma*, carried notice of a 'rumour' from its correspondent in Paris that Robinson, 'the man of mystery, the late Herrmann's assistant, is coming over to present the Ching Ling Foo act'.[50]

---

[50] *Mahatma*, 3:10, April 1900 (pages un-numbered). I note that Dexter attributes this notice to the March issue, which gives the impression of great haste on the part of

Indeed, at that time, the idea that the 'Ching Ling Foo act' could and would be presented by all kinds of people other than Ching Ling Foo himself was already very normal. The apparatus and workings of his Goldfish Bowl Trick were for sale in the trade press even before he issued the challenge that Robinson tried unsuccessfully to accept; the method was exposed in the pages of *Mahatma* itself in July 1899.[51] Hence, the rumour that Robinson (already noted for his Orientalist performances) was bound for Paris to perform the Ching Ling Foo act was not so remarkable; indeed, it probably meant little more than that he was planning to include the Linking Rings, the Goldfish Bowl, and some Chinese-styled aesthetics in his act. This put him in

---

Robinson. Dexter, *The Riddle of Chung Ling Soo*, p. 43. The March 1900 issue contains a number of interesting references to Ching Ling Foo (although none to Robinson). The 'Notes' explain that 'Ching Ling Foo presented his novel act for several weeks, at Shea's Garden Theatre, Buffalo', and later also explain that he had to cancel his show in Toronto because of complications with his visa, which would have led to him being deported were he to cross the Canadian border. In addition, the 'Notes' show how influential Foo's act had become, highlighting that 'Hewes, the White Yogi, is touring the New England States. He is presenting the Ching Ling Foo act with American improvements, together with his original illusions.' (The so-called White Yogi was the American Frank Hewes (1862–1917), who made a successful Oriental-style act and achieved a measure of fame after innovating a method for the Sword Suspension in 1899). That is, Robinson would not be the first (only or last) to mimic Foo's act. Indeed, the January 1900 issue of *Mahatma* carries a half-page advertisement (on the back cover) for the apparatus and method of 'Ching Ling Foo's Bowl Trick', suggesting that 'anyone can do it'. The power and pervasiveness of Ching Ling Foo's act in this period is evidenced by the note in the column 'Flashes' (March 1900), which suggests that only the arrival of Houdini himself at Keith's Theatre provides any competition for the Chinese magician: 'he proved the first formidable rival Ching Ling Foo has yet encountered'.

[51] In a piece titled, 'Ching Ling Foo's Marvelous Feats Exposed', George Browne relates that:

> Ching Ling Foo has been mystifying New York for six weeks. He is a Chinaman of huge stature and a magician of wonderful skill. He has been at Keith's. It is not too much to say that his marvelous tricks have been the sensation of the vaudeville season.
>
> Night after night large audiences have watched him do these apparently impossible things, but no one, not even the stage attendants, has been able to detect how he performed his remarkable feats.
>
> (Mahatma, III:I, *July 1899*).

Browne goes on to explain the Water Bowl Trick, the Three Plates Trick, and finally the Wonderful Fire Trick.

the company of dozens of magicians in the United States at that time.[52]

    In the end, Robinson adopted the stage name of Hop Sing Loo for his Paris appearance at the Folies Bergère in April 1900. According to the Paris correspondent of the *Mahatma*, the show was not a success:

> Hop Sing Loo, otherwise Mr. Wm., E. Robinson, so well and favorably known in the United States, opened at the Folies Bergere, on the 15th April, and assisted by Miss Dot Robinson and a clever Chinese equilibrist gave a very good imitation of Ching Ling Foo. For want of rehearsals, it went somewhat slow at first, but has improved greatly since. Still your correspondent who knows Robinson's capabilities, feels assured he would have made a greater success had he given an evening dress performance and exhibited some of his admirable hand and mechanical illusions, as he is out of his element in Chinese business and the French people are difficult to please.[53]

---

[52] Already in 1899, the *Mahatma* reports that:
    An imitator of Ching Ling Foo, calling himself "Clung Ling Too," under the management of Chas. Carter, duplicates Ching Ling Foo's tricks. Any person with the necessary apparatus can easily perform these tricks (*Mahatma*, III:IV, October 1899).

[53] *Mahatma*, 3:11, May 1900 (pages unnumbered). On the very same page, the Boston correspondent reports on the great success of the German magician Sigmund Neuberger (1871–1911, who adopted the name The Great Lafayette in London earlier in 1900 when he began his career as a Ching Ling Foo imitator) 'in his remarkable Impersonation of Sousa and Burlesque of Ching Ling Foo's conjuring. The appearance of the magician, his mongolian assistant, his clucks and exclamations and the "properties" were reproduced amusingly, and then instead of showing how the tricks were done, Lafayette went on producing not only Ching's bowl of water, but other large bowls of pigeons, ducks, a dog, and a pickaniny dressed for the bath. He is certainly a strong headliner.' The contrast with the review of Robinson's performance is damning. Intriguingly, the cover story of this issue of *Mahatma* is about the American 'White Yogi', Frank Hewes, who was mentioned in April as one of the (many) Ching Ling Foo mimics doing the circuit. The editorial tone is in stark contrast with the account of Robinson's first attempts to perform Foo's show. Of Hewes the *Mahatma* reports:

> Shortly after the close of his engagement at the Chicago World's Fair, he devoted much time to the study of Oriental Magic, realizing that many of the principles underlying the feats of the eastern wonder-workers might well be adapted to suit western tastes. His success in this line encouraged him to seek a more appropriate title, and thus for the first time he adopted the Nom de Theatre of 'The White Yogi'. The success of Ching Ling Foo, the Chinese conjuror, raised oriental magic to a high place in popular favor.

What is particularly interesting about this review (from an apparently affectionate and supportive pen) is its focus on Robinson's failure to inhabit the theatrical Chineseness of his act. There is no doubt that Robinson could perform the *feats*; he simply failed to give them the enchantment of Chinese *effects*.[54] Indeed, the critic reveals that Robinson would have affected greater magic had he assumed the guise of a modern American gentleman; in this case, then, the attempt to appropriate the magic of Chineseness had resulted in the *disenchantment* of the show. While it is possible that Robinson's failure in Paris was at least partially attributable to what Robert-Houdin had predicted as the distaste of the French audience for a European pretending to be Chinese, this is a clear instance of the importance of meeting the Orientalist expectations of an audience. However, it also seems to speak to the need to respect Robert-Houdin's dictum that not only is a conjuror 'an actor playing the part of a [real] magician', but also that his success in this performance relies on the magician's ability to 'sufficiently enter into the part he plays, to himself believe in the reality of his factitious statements. This belief on his own part will infallibly carry a like conviction to the minds of the spectators.'[55] In short, no matter what the Orientalist preferences of the Parisian audience, it seems that Robinson failed as the hastily produced Hop Sing Loo at least partially because he didn't really believe in this identity for himself: Robinson the

> His bowl trick was the only feat The White Yogi did not at that time possess, and immediately adding that trick to his repertoire, he commenced a tour of the New England States. His success attracted the attention of prominent managers and resulted in a three months contract, for the summer months in one of our leading New York theatres. Mahatma's good wishes go with him.

By December 1900, *Mahatma*'s Boston correspondent notes: 'A unique feature in the bills of the Proctor theatres in New York City for the week of Nov. 19th, is the fact that there are three different performers presenting the Ching Ling Foo bowl trick, namely:—Lafayette, Henri French, and Aldrich, the tramp juggler.' The Goldfish Bowl Trick, now known colloquially as the Ching Ling Foo Bowl Trick, is no longer a rare or exclusive feat. The advertisements inside the back cover include: 'THE CHING LING FOO BOWL TRICK. The marvelous production of an immense bowl, fifty-four inches in circumference, containing several gallons of water; as performed by Ching Ling- Foo, Lafayette, Chung Ling Soo, Henri French, Hewes the White Yogi, Aldrich, etc.'

[54] That said, reports suggest that Robinson spilled some water on the stage, which upset the theatre manager.

[55] This proposition is discussed at length in Chapter 1. It is the eighth of Robert-Houdin's fifteen 'General Principles'. Robert-Houdin, *Secrets of Conjuring and Magic*, p. 33.

conjuror may have been an actor playing the part of a Chinese magician, but did not *believe* that he was a Chinese magician (and neither did anyone else).[56]

This failure in Paris encouraged Robinson to cross the channel, where he was immediately booked at the Alhambra, arguably the most prestigious venue in London at that time. When his new show opened three months later, he had transformed himself into Chung Ling Soo (which he claimed was a real Chinese name, meaning Double Good Luck).[57] At this time, the name of his nemesis Ching Ling Foo, 'The Marvellous Chinese Conjuror', was well-known in London, but the Chinese magician had not yet performed extensively in Europe himself; indeed, he had been forced to return to China in June 1900 where, if the *Mahatma*'s reporting is accurate, as a Western-sympathizer he lost his wife and two children to violence at the hands of the Boxers.[58]

[56] Dexter suggests that the theatre manager believed that Hop Sing Loo was a real Chinese magician. Indeed, he quotes a conversation in which the manager dismisses Robinson after a bad performance and then declares: 'And then tomorrow, I shall engage to myself another prestidigitateur who is in Paris – William Robinsons [*sic*], the Man of Mystery ... Ah! What a magician is this William Robinson! He shall drop no bowls of water on my stage! No ducks shall he bring to my theatre! Tomorrow this Man of Mystery shall take the place of Hop Sing Loo!' Dexter, *The Riddle of Chung Ling Soo*, p. 53. It's not clear how Dexter could have a transcription of this conversation, but the twin ideas of confused identity and of Robinson's magical credentials are motifs in the Chung Ling Soo story.

[57] Despite claiming various meanings for his made-up name (and trying to write it with various different Chinese characters, some of which were also made up), the name Chung Ling Soo is basically gibberish in Chinese. In any case, the *Mahatma*'s London correspondent dutifully reported in June 1900 that 'William E. Robinson has crossed the Channel with his Chinese act, and scored a tremendous success at the Alhambra, London.' That is, the magic community in the United States, at least, was under no illusion about the fact that Chung Ling Soo was William Robinson in 1900.

[58] *Mahatma*, 4:7, January 1901 (pages unnumbered).

In this respect it was ironic that Robinson exploited his freedom to manipulate and participate in Orientalist fantasies at this time, entering self-consciously into the discourse around the politics of knowledge at the turn of the century. As the British public started to hear about the Boxer Rebellion in China and public opinion started to turn against the Chinese in London, he toyed with the legends of Boxer 'spirit soldiers' who were invulnerable to bullets but neatly subverted the narrative so that he could perform a bullet-catching routine in which he pretended to be executed *by* the Boxers (Condemned to Death by the Boxers). Hence, Robinson both managed to appropriate the mystique of Chinese magic (including emerging, occultist ideas about the 'supernatural counter-physical causation' commanded by the Boxers) *and* managed to position himself as sympathetic to Western interests in China! In fact, the bullet catch is closely associated with the idea of Chinese magic largely because of Robinson, not least because he died during its performance at the Wood Green Empire in London, 23 March 1918. (See Scene four)

Hence, the name Chung Ling Soo resonated with the public but carried very little concrete public memory.

It is conceivable that the British audience of Chung Ling Soo's first-ever performance at the Alhambra Theatre in London, April 1900, actually thought that they were seeing Ching Ling Foo. The names are so close as to be confusing even today, and in 1900 they would have seemed exotically indistinguishable, especially as Robinson billed Chung Ling Soo as 'The Great Chinese Magician', a phrase that would immediately have been associated with the famous magician from China.[59] The public would have heard of the wonders of Ching Ling Foo (and seen pictures of his Chinese act), but would never have heard of Chung Ling Soo (and would have found his appearance very similar to that of Foo). Whatever the case, the potential for confusion was certainly one of the reasons that Robinson chose this name and launched in London rather than back in New York.

---

[59] So effective was this illusion that confusion persisted for many years about who was who, when it came to Chung Ling Soo and Ching Ling Foo. In 1940, the periodical *Genii* made a list of 'Ten Questions You Should Be Able To Answer', number five of which was: 'Which was the real Oriental, Chung Lung Soo, or Ching Ling Foo?' (Frank Stratton, 'Ten Questions You Should Be Able To Answer', *Genii*, 4:7 (March 1940), p. 218). It should be noted that *Genii* got Chung Ling Soo's name slightly wrong, reflecting exactly the kind of confusion that Robinson had aimed for from the start. In 1905 the leading magic journal *The Sphinx* carried a short poem in the centre of its front cover, apparently etched into a stone monument between the figure of the devil, an English gentleman-magician, and beneath the sphinx itself. The poem confused nearly all the syllables of the two 'Chinese' names, but it didn't seem to matter:

> THE MAGICIAN.
> The magician's a man who wonders does work;
> He's sometimes an Englishman, sometimes a Turk,
> But always with wand and magic words, too.
> He produces enjoyment for me and for you.
> There's Ching Ling Soo and Chung Lung Foo,
> Both produce fire and water for you.
> There's Houdini, who from handcuffs escapes,
> And Ten Ichi, who gets out of tapes.
> There's Downs and Thurston and others galore
> Who have puzzled many and will more.
> But on the top, there stands by far
> The king of magicians, Harry Kellar.
> *By Frederick Roche, 'The Magician', The Sphinx.*
> *4:6 (1905)*

The proximity of the names and speed with which Robinson's Chung Ling Soo act appeared in Europe in mid-1900 after the establishment of Zhu Liankui's Ching Ling Foo act in the United States in 1899/1900 led to a widespread conflation of the two as a single emblem of Chinese magic. Indeed, the history of Golden Age magic is unclear about the extent to which the deluge of imitators that flooded the scene after 1900 were copying Ching Ling Foo or Chung Ling Soo.

In fact, it seems quite likely that the crowd of popular imitators were imitating the imitation, since it turned out to be Robinson who really knew how to sell 'Chinese magic' to Western audiences. As Dexter asserts in his rather partisan account, 'Soo's performance was immeasurably superior to Ching Ling Foo's. The Mongolian, in capable hands as he may have been, lacked the basic knowledge of Western vaudeville, and presented a programme almost entirely traditional and Chinese.'[60] Many magicians and historians would dispute the claim that Zhu was immeasurably inferior as a magician – indeed, Zhu was demonstrably an outstanding magician of global importance. However, it was certainly true that his show was composed almost entirely of authentically Chinese magic and that Robinson's show contained a mixture of feats borrowed from Ching Ling Foo and other feats that were simply performed in 'Chinese style'.[61] This mixing of the unfamiliar and the defamiliarized appeared to be the secret of Robinson's tremendous success in London: 'Soo ... *invented* most of *his* show.... Soo put on a show that was Chung Ling Soo and nothing else. He dressed it in Oriental trappings and perfected his style until it became accepted as the real thing.'[62]

---

[60] Dexter, *The Riddle of Chung Ling Soo*, p. 56. I have not been able to verify whether Zhu was Chinese of Mongolian descent or whether Dexter is following the vulgar convention of the press at the turn of the century by using various ethnic appellations interchangeably as though the various ethnic groups of East Asia were the same. Some sources suggest that Zhu was of Manchu ancestry.

[61] One of the various ironies regarding this was the emerging fashion for magicians to imitate Chinese magic 'in evening dress'. For a while, this was the way that the magical press talked about modern, Western magicians who followed Robert-Houdin's dress code but who performed some of tricks associated with Chinese magic, such as the Linking Rings and the Goldfish Bowl. The likelihood that some of the 'modernized' Chinese magic was originally Western magic that had been 'Orientalized' for a 'Chinese' show and then retranslated back into a Western context is tantalizing.

[62] Dexter, *The Riddle of Chung Ling Soo*, pp. 56–57 (emphasis in the original). Dexter seems begrudgingly to acknowledge that Robinson at least imitated Ching Ling Foo's name, although he suggests that Robinson deserved to take this name in recompense

As we saw in Chapter 3, there is a sense in which invention and originality were prized as critical characteristics of modern magic, and Oriental magicians were often accused of failing to inhabit this modernity because of their emphasis on preserving a traditional repertoire and cultivating a specific set of inherited skills. Indeed, by the end of 1900, the excitement about the Goldfish Bowl Trick (by then known as the Ching Ling Foo Bowl Trick or sometimes the Chung Ling Soo Bowl Trick) was already beginning to wane.[63] Western audiences wanted to see new, previously unknown feats of magic, not only the performance of familiar tricks with increasing levels of perfection and polish. In fact, it is at least debateable whether Robinson's creativity with the meaning of 'Chinese magic' and its repertoire saved it from becoming passé, even if this process of saving it also transformed it into something different.[64]

To some extent, this is a powerful example of creative, cultural, and artistic hybridity driven by capitalism. However, there is an important sense in which this apparently progressivist reading is politically and ethically naïve. For Dexter, there was no problem with Robinson/Soo's appropriation of Chinese magic: 'If the public went out of the theatre believing that this was genuine Chinese magic, nobody was any the worse for that.'[65] However, at the very least, we might suppose that Zhu Liankui was the worse for that and, arguably, that China was the worse for that. By extension, we might also argue that Robinson's audience were also the worse for that misrepresentation, whether they were happily entertained or otherwise.

Dexter's position on the ethical neutrality of this situation is largely consistent with the way it was seen in the early years of the twentieth century. At that time, the neutrality was partially sustained by bracketing out the Chinese magician as a moral agent; Zhu Liankui was

---

for the $1000 that Foo would have been forced to give him had he not reneged on the challenge in New York.

[63] After consistently laudatory reviews and notices for months, *Mahatma* (4:1, July 1900) already reports: 'At the beginning of the season the oriental act of Ching Ling Foo was no doubt the sensation of the hour, but of late his star is on the wane.'

[64] Sidney Clarke notes how audiences grew tired of Oriental magic in the nineteenth century precisely because 'the conjuring tricks [of one company] were practically the same as those presented by the earlier company'. Clarke, 'Oriental Conjuring', p. 398. The advent of Ching Ling Foo was crucial in the reinvigoration of Oriental magic in the West, and perhaps the creative enlargements of Chung Ling Soo were similarly important.

[65] Dexter, *The Riddle of Chung Ling Soo*, p. 56.

Figure 5.2 Chung Ling Soo, 'Studying Ancient Chinese Mysteries', c. 1910. Courtesy of Nielsen Magic Collection.

literally a silent figure, both on stage as Ching Ling Foo and off stage as a visible-minority immigrant with poor English and a vulnerable residency status. For instance, in his biography of Robinson, Dexter asks rhetorically about the profusion of Ching Ling Foo imitators: 'Heaven knows what the staid old Mongolian who started it all thought!'[66] Later, when discussing the emerging magical duel between Soo and Foo, when Zhu had finally come to London to perform in January 1905 and had found the city full of advertisements for Chung Ling Soo 'The Original Chinese Conjuror', Dexter reports: 'What old Foo thought about it himself nobody knows, for his English was confined to just a few words.'[67]

And yet Zhu Liankui was not a black box or a hollow man; he was simply Chinese, and all that would have been required to discover his thoughts on these issues would have been to ask him (in Chinese or through a translator). Protestations that 'heaven knows!' or 'nobody knows!' would not be morally acceptable today, and they're indicative of a more generally racist culture at the time. This remarkable Chinese magician is revealed as an archetype of powerlessness with regard to his self-determination; his account of himself was a silenced voice at the time. As a public figure, his silent stage persona, Ching Ling Foo, is either conflated with his everyday identity, and he is thus historically silenced by his discomfort with English, or his faltering English is conflated with the gibbering of fake-Chinese (as eventually spoken by Chung Ling Soo and his Japanese 'translator'), and his voice is ridiculed as meaningless, nonsensical, or comedic.

In fact, as we will see, even without access to Zhu Liankui's personal correspondence or memoirs, it is very clear from the historical record of events how he felt about the imposture of Chung Ling Soo. It is clear that he would not have agreed that 'nobody was the worse for that'. At the very least, he felt damaged personally and also felt that China (and Chineseness) was being disrespected and ridiculed. Indeed, he felt the injustice so strongly that he effectively engineered a (doomed) public show trial to reveal the truth.

One of the most intriguing and unique features of this scenario was that Robinson's transformation into Chung Ling Soo played

---

[66] Dexter, *The Riddle of Chung Ling Soo*, p. 56.
[67] Dexter, *The Riddle of Chung Ling Soo*, p. 63.

with the edges of what we might now call 'identity tourism'. That is, Robinson was not content to adopt a Chinese-style stage persona and trappings simply in order to add glamour and faux authenticity to his Chinese magic act. Had he done only this, he would have been little different from the other burlesque Ching Ling Foo imitators, such as the Great Lafayette or even Fu Manchu later on.[68] Instead, Robinson seems to have evolved a more existential will to *become* a Chinese magician. Indeed, while the readers of *Mahatma* may have been well-aware that Chung Ling Soo was Robinson imitating Ching Ling Foo in 1900, over the next few years Robinson studiously culti-vated the identity confusion that was facilitated by the intimate proxi-mity of these *nom de théâtre*, gradually allowing his persona as Chung Ling Soo to spill out off the stage and into the public sphere around it. He would make public appearances as Chung Ling Soo, in his elabo-rate 'Chinese' costume, affecting an inability to speak English and so communicating through a 'translator' while mumbling gibberish that he claimed was Chinese.[69] He brought a travelling exhibition of 'Chinese' artefacts (i.e., random Orientalia) with him on tour, show-ing them off in the theatres where he performed; he even published a book of 'Chinese Fairy Tales' that carried his own picture on the

[68] Fu Manchu was the nom-de-théâtre of David Tobias Bamberg (1904–1974), who played a world tour as this Chinese magician in the 1930s. While in the United States, he played as Fu Chan in order to avoid (legal) confusions with the fictional Dr. Fu Manchu – the villain of Sax Rohmer's hugely successful novels. It is Dr Fu Manchu, not Bamberg's Fu Manchu, who becomes the villainous archetype of cinema, televi-sion, and graphic novels in the second half of the twentieth century.

Bamberg was the son of the magician Tobias Bamberg (1875–1963), who per-formed as the Japanese character Okito. Tobias was the son of David Bamberg (1843–1914), who was also a magician. In fact, the 'Bamberg Dynasty' ran for six (or perhaps seven) generations, beginning with the alchemist Jasper (1698–1780) and ending with the Orientalist magician David (Fu Manchu). This Dutch dynasty is one of the most famous and long-running in history, although it was only in the modern period that it turned to Orientalized magic.

There is some disagreement about whether Jasper was really part of the same family. And it's notable that H.J. Burlingame (1852–1915), who trained under David (Tobias's father, not his son), performed under the name Jasper Bamberg in the United States.

[69] One of the many ironies of this performance was that his translator after 1904, Fukuda Kumetaro, 'Frank' (1874–1946) a Japanese acrobat who, like Robinson, could not speak Chinese. From the vantage point of today, it is shocking to reflect that the public could not recognize this linguistic deception, but in 1904 very few people in London would have heard any real Chinese – the Chinese community was small.

cover.[70] This is not to say that William Robinson disappeared altogether – he did not – but rather that Chung Ling Soo emerged as a new member of London society with a life of his own (modelled rather clearly on the life of Zhu Liankui, while he was overseas and unable to intervene).

It remains an unresolved question whether Robinson's desire to *be* a Chinese magician (rather than merely to *play* a Chinese magician on stage) arose from his participation in the romantic Orientalism of his day (and thus the fantasy that being Chinese would make him more magical) or whether it evolved as a consequence of his personal animosity towards Zhu after the New York incident (and thus a desire to prove that he could do and be anything as well as the Chinese magician). Given the background, it seems likely that both motivations were at work, and it's interesting to see how they reflect the familiar ideological dimensions of Orientalism: the lust for the Orient, and the drive to subordinate it.

While it is clear that Robinson's approach to becoming a Chinese magician was very different from that of his confreres in magic at the time (and since), contemporary magicians and historians remain unclear about how to understand this becoming. For magicians, it reveals an intriguing and powerful tension in the performative and ethical foundations of modern magic: Robinson found himself caught in the lacuna between Robert-Houdin's call for magicians to be actors and his insistence that they must not only pretend but also believe in their pretence. As we saw in part one of this book, there is a sense in which this is an endorsement of a form of method acting that emerged with Stanislavski at the turn of the twentieth century. However, given the particular context of magic – an art of deception – this space of committed pretence is unusually slippery.

Robert-Houdin's principles sit alongside the moral maxims of Maskelyne and Devant, who argued that modern magic must carefully control its interventions into magical belief. In particular, the legitimate

[70] I have not been able to locate this book, although a 1910 advertising flyer shows a full-length portrait of Soo with a seated Soo on the verso under the title *Chinese Fairy Tales – Compliments of Chung Ling Soo*. Presumably, this publication was an attempt to associate Soo with the interest in Chinese folklore that followed the publication of Pu Songling, *Strange Tales from a Chinese Studio* (1740), which includes an early description of the 'Indian' Rope Trick, suggesting its Chinese origins. Herbert Giles (trans.), *Pu Songling: Strange Stories from a Chinese Studio*. London: T. De La Rue, 1880.

modern magician must seek to contain and limit the realm of magical belief in the space of his performance. In this framework, when a magician seeks to extend his deception of the audience off the stage into everyday life, he surrenders his status as a modern magician and becomes a charlatan. Of course, Maskelyne and Devant were principally concerned to condemn Spiritualists who sought to con the public into believing that their tricks were not stage performances but results of their magical being. But the moral principle is clear: legitimate modern magic must be circumscribed by the stage (wherever and howsoever that is constructed as a place of performance).

In this context, how are we to understand the way that Robinson's commitment to his pretence overflowed from the stage into a very public life off stage? He jealously guarded the public separation of Robinson and Soo, seeking to enable both to live their lives in London. Robinson would reflect on the moments at which he would lose his identity and become Soo, and vice versa. Most importantly from the ethical standpoint of modern magic, however, is the question of whether Robinson deliberately engaged in the deceit of the general public (off stage) in order to manipulate their magical beliefs in way that misled them about his performance of magic. By *becoming* Chung Ling Soo rather than merely *playing* him on stage, was Robinson engaged in illegitimate or 'black' magic, deceiving people *about* magic not only *with* it. Or, conversely, by inhabiting this space of committed pretence unlike any other magician of his time (or since), was Robinson accomplishing the most 'glorious deception' of all time, setting new standards for artistic commitment and the possibilities of magic in the modern period?[71] Is it conceivable that Robinson was alive to the

---

[71] The 'glorious deception' line is the one most often encountered in the literature of magic. It is pushed very hard by Will Dexter, and it is eloquently presented by Jim Steinmeyer in his book of the same name. Whatever the case, Chung Ling Soo is certainly one of the most important magicians of the twentieth century.

One of the fascinating possibilities about this 'glorious deception' interpretation is the way that it connects with, for instance, the apparently existential and spiritual mission of contemporary magicians like David Blaine. In the last chapter, we saw how Blaine appears to invest in magic as a means to self-transformation, modelled on the Indian archetype. If Blaine is insincere about this (and I certainly do not assert that), it represents a public deception very similar to that accomplished by Robinson: Blaine would be seeking to deceive the public about who he is in everyday life in order to transform the effects produced by his magic on stage. That said, if Blaine is sincere about this process of self-transformation, this raises many additional questions! Sadly, I have not been able to talk with Blaine about this.

possibility that Robert-Houdin was correct to think that modern audiences would find it offensive to see a European magician pretending to be Chinese, and so resolved to find a way not to pretended but simply to be?

In a broader perspective, the idea that Robinson could become Chung Ling Soo raises a host of complicated questions. Perhaps core to this constellation of issues is the question of what it means to *become* someone else, either psychologically or culturally. In fact, this is a central problematic in the Orientalist discourse, which includes the desire to become the romanticized Other. In the case of Robinson, it seems clear that he *wanted to become* the Chinese magician Chung Ling Soo, and there is a sense in which he succeeded in this. However, there is also a very powerful sense in which this was a trick – a feat of magic; Chung Ling Soo was an *effect*, not a real Chinese magician. An insoluble issue remains: no matter how much he wanted to be a Chinese magician, Robinson could not become Chinese.[72] Indeed, the impossibility of this is exactly why he needed to accomplish it with magic.

The challenge of Chinese magic

By the time of the famous 'magic duel' between Foo and Soo in January 1905, it was already clear that Zhu's objection to Robinson was not that he was yet another Ching Ling Foo imitator, but rather that Robinson was claiming to *be* Soo and that Soo was claiming to manifest an authentic China (and that this deception was facilitated by a shamelessly ostentatious and deliberate imitation of Foo's name and identity). The public were clearly confused, and many seemed to think that Soo was Foo. The situation resembled a form of magical identity theft, in which Zhu had lost control of his identity itself, both personally and culturally, while Robinson had been establishing himself in London in his absence. Indeed, the dispute between the two magicians appears to

---

[72] This statement raises many questions about what it means to be Chinese (or perhaps what it means to be a member of any ethnic or national grouping). It is, of course, conceivable that an individual can change her nationality and in that sense become that national. However, this was clearly not the sense in which Robinson wanted to be Chinese. We can deduce from his actions (i.e., from all the things he faked) what it meant to him to become Chinese: first and foremost, it meant transforming himself ethnically in a man of Manchu ancestry; it meant speaking Chinese; and it meant mastery of Chinese heritage.

have pivoted around the appellation, THE ORIGINAL CHINESE CONJUROR, which appeared emblazoned on both sets of posters while Chung Ling Soo appeared at the Hippodrome and Ching Ling Foo appeared across the street at the Empire. Indeed, the design and imagery of the posters were almost identical, with only two letters distinguishing the exotically Oriental names. Londoners of the time would not have been aware that Ching Ling Foo was a real Chinese name and Chung Ling Soo sounded strangely incoherent; they were not aware that Ching Ling Foo was the Chinese magician on whom the character of Chung Ling Soo had been modelled; and they were not aware (in general) that Chung Ling Soo was William Robinson.[73] They were aware, however, that Chung Ling Soo had been astounding audiences in London for five years and that this 'other' Chinese magician had just shown up in the city.

Jim Steinmeyer suggests that it was Zhu's manager, Leon Mooser, who issued the fabled challenge to Chung Ling Soo on behalf of his client.[74] The wording of the challenge, which was posted into the *Weekly Dispatch* (1 January 1905), reveals the constellation of issues that had offended Zhu:

[73] It is one of the persistent surprises of this story that the general public and the magical confraternity managed to form fairly discrete epistemic communities on the question of Robinson's identity. Somewhat akin to the culture of secrecy that surrounds knowledge of magical feats and mechanisms in the magic community, there was a clear discrepancy of knowledge between magicians (who knew Soo was Robinson) and the muggles (who did not).

The lead story on the front cover of *Mahatma* (6:7, January 1903) carries the following story, two years before the fabled 'magic duel' in London:

It is indeed a pleasure, to be able, to present to our readers an old friend in a new guise. Chung Ling Soo is no other than William E. Robinson, 'Man of Mystery'.

Those who have had the good fortune to see Chung Ling Soo, 'The Marvellous Chinese Conjurer', and have also known Robinson, can hardly convince themselves that both are one and the same individual. It is claimed, by those who are well able to judge, that his impersonation of a Chinaman is so realistic that one fails to realize that he is only acting the part but actually looks like a high caste celestial. In fact, Robinson himself says: 'The moment I step upon the stage I lose my own identity and become in fact, what I am to be, Chung Ling Soo.'

[74] Steinmeyer's account of the events around the challenge is excellent, meticulous, and reliable. I cannot do better than to acknowledge my debt to him here. Steinmeyer, *The Glorious Deception*, p. 255.

> I, CHING LING FOO, am the original Chinese magician. There is no other native-born Chinese sorcerer in London at the present time.
>
> I offer £1000 if Chung Ling Soo, now appearing at the Hippodrome, can do ten out of twenty of my tricks, or if I fail to do any of his feats.[75]

First and foremost, the challenge drew immediate and stark attention to the question of authenticity and origination. Zhu focussed on Robinson's claim to be the 'Original Chinese Conjuror', and interpreted 'original' to signify a claim to origination in China.[76] Even worse, in an interview, Zhu scoffed at Robinson's claim to be called the 'Royal Court Magician' of the Dowager Empress, instead calling him a 'foreign devil' and stating emphatically (and correctly) that he is 'not a Chinaman at all but a Scotch-American of the name Robinson'. He mocked Robinson's attempts to appear Chinese: 'Him wear robes him have him head chop off if he go China. He wear woman's dress – him one big fool' (*Weekly Dispatch*, 1 January 1905).[77]

For his part, Robinson/Soo declared himself unable to talk to the press about these accusations, since his English was not adequate to the task. Instead, the journalist spoke with his 'Chinese secretary' (the Japanese acrobat and Robinson's assistant, Fukuda Kumetaro, who spoke no Chinese). Fukuda reported that 'Chung Ling Soo is wroth with the street sorcerer who has slandered him, but his rank as a Mandarin of the one button precludes him from entering into any controversy with one of an inferior class.' In other words, 'the dignity of Chung Ling Soo is too sublime to permit him to enter into any discussion with a slave who has sat at street corners juggling for "cash"' (*Weekly Dispatch*, 1 January 1905). Fukuda related a story of Chung Ling Soo's

---

[75] 'Chung v. Ching: One of the Greatest Encounters of Modern Times. Battle of the Sorcerers, Who Will do Magic on Either Side of a Glass Screen', *Weekly Dispatch*, 1 January 1905, reprinted in Todd Karr (ed.), *The Silence of Chung Ling Soo*. Seattle: The Miracle Factory, 2001, p. 87. Karr's compilation is an invaluable resource.

[76] There are at least two other ways in which 'original' could have been interpreted in this debate: 1. Original = first (which would have been Foo rather than Soo, but there were plenty of Chinese conjurors in the West in the nineteenth century); 2. Original = novel or creative (which would have been Soo rather than Foo, since Soo's act was certainly more creative and dynamic than the more traditional Foo).

[77] From today's standpoint, it is also revealing to see the way that the reporter represents Zhu's English in this comedic way.

emergence as a famous magician in China, how he came to the attention of the Dowager Empress and was promoted to Celestial Honours, and ultimately to the rank of Mandarin.

This wondrous (and entirely fictional) story deeply impressed the media and the public, for whom this was exactly their fantasy of a Chinese magician from 'a land where every little boy is an expert conjurer'.[78] For good measure, the reporter added that Chung Ling Soo *looks* Chinese: 'his skin is yellow, his eyes are black and oblique, and his teeth are absolutely inky' as though he'd spent a lifetime chewing opium. Such stereotypes were typical of the time, especially after the Opium Wars (1838–1842, 1856–1860). Remarkably, despite having being identified as a Scottish-American magician called Robinson, Soo emerged from this initial exchange as the public's darling, and nobody even bothered to check the facts. But, of course, the facts were not necessarily the point for the Londoners of 1905: 'The public can have cared little whether the complaints were justified. All they wanted – and expected and got – was good entertainment'.[79] Indeed, Steinmeyer and others have suggested that Mooser originally hoped that the challenge would work as a publicity stunt, ironically catapulting Ching Ling Foo into the London limelight through his association with his imitator Chung Ling Soo!

By all accounts, Zhu was deeply angry about Robinson's verbose and culturally outrageous response to his challenge, seeing the American as attempting to appear more 'inscrutably Chinese' than the actual Chinese magician. Soo seemed to have been fashioned as a parody, glorification, and super-Orientalization of Foo.[80] Even worse, Robinson's public performance as Soo seemed to work; the London public were entranced by his deception, despite (or because of) its ridiculousness.

---

[78] Ironically, it seems likely that Zhu Liankui's real story was not very different from this fiction; he had actually performed for the Dowager Empress.

[79] Dexter, *The Riddle of Chung Ling Soo*, p. 64.

[80] The spectacular costumes of Chung Ling Soo were still attracting attention and setting a particular kind of standard for magicians into the 1950s and beyond. In his survey of appropriate magical costuming, John McArdle notes approvingly that because of their 'association with the mysterious East, Chinese costumes have long been popular with magicians'. However, he goes on to point out that many Western performers adopting the role of a Chinese magician prefer the flamboyance of clothing reserved for Mandarins, while authentic Chinese performers tend to wear the typically less flamboyant clothes permitted to their station. John McArdle, 'Costumes to Conjure With'. *The Linking Ring*, 31:7 (1951), p. 13.

In the end, the second half of Ching Ling Foo's challenge, which addressed Chung Ling Soo's competency as a magician, was almost irrelevant. Even though the methods of signature tricks were jealously guarded (Robinson even attempted to patent his entire act), there were probably dozens of magicians in Europe and the United States who knew the methods, owned the equipment, and could perform the tricks exhibited by Foo and Soo. As we've seen, professional journals and limited-print books constantly 'exposed' magic to magicians in the name of advancing the art. Hence, it's reasonable to assume that Foo could perform many of Soo's tricks and vice versa. As we saw in Chapters 1 and 2, the secret to modern magic was in the artistic ability of the magician to enchant his performance, not in the mechanisms being deployed *per se* (although the *invention* of new mechanisms was highly valued). And this was entirely the point of Foo's challenge: the key to the magic of his act was that he was the 'Original Chinese Conjuror'; his originary Chineseness was foundational to his ability to enchant. In this light, his challenge was not a technical one of the kind that was pervasive amongst magicians of this period, but rather it was a challenge of identity *qua* magic. What mattered was whether Soo could really claim to inhabit the ostensible magic and mysteriousness of the Orient, or whether his magic was fake in some important sense. Was he deceiving his audience *about* his magic as well as *with* it?

In many ways, consciously or otherwise, it was the Chinese Zhu Liankui rather than the American Robinson who seemed to be upholding the moral principles of modern magic *qua* legitimate magic or white magic, as established in London by Maskelyne and Devant. At the very least, Zhu's challenge further reveals the problematic nature of the ethical parameters of magical legitimacy at this time. As we've seen, it would have been considered ethically irresponsible for Robinson to perform magic in the guise of, say, a Spiritualist medium or a medieval wizard and then to attempt to convince audiences that this persona was really him (i.e., that it was not a performance), but it seems that it was acceptable for him to perform in the guise of a Chinese magician and then to attempt to convince audiences that this persona was really him (i.e., that it was not a performance). While the modern magicians would have considered the former charlatanism, as we have seen, it seems that they were less clear about the latter. Zhu was adamant.

Of course, there are a number of differences between pretending to be Merlin and pretending to be Chinese, not the least of which is the fact that Merlin is a fictional character while China is a real place full of real people. On the face of it, though, this should intensify rather than mitigate the moral implications of pretence in the case of the latter. However, it is not at all clear that the 'Chinese magician' constructed by Robinson was any more factual than Merlin; they were both fictions, but the former was also a caricature of a real, living person. Perhaps the critical difference, then, at least from the perspective of the theory of modern magic, was that Robinson might have been pretending to be a Chinese magician, but he was not making any strong claims about the innate magical power of such a magician as a magical being. That is, his deception was not intended to con the audience into believing that he had mastery over 'supernatural, counterphysical causation'. Instead, his deception was intended to con the audience into believing that he was Chinese and so to associate his performance with the glamour of mystical Orientalism. While this is a form of intentional enchantment, it is not the kind of deception about magic that worried Maskelyne and Devant. Unlike the popular imaginary of much Indian magic and so-called Old magic, Chinese magic already operated in an explicitly theatrical arena.

In other words, from the standpoint of the theory of modern magic, it was clear that Robinson had crossed a line with his personal transformation into Soo – a line that is made even clearer by the multiple instances of magicians who adopted Chinese stage personas without taking this extra existential step. However, it is less clear that Robinson's step was a move into illegitimate magic, since he did not make use of his deception to claim 'real and potent' magical powers, even if his deception did enhance his ability to enchant audiences. At the same time, from a broader social and political perspective, Robinson's deception constituted a powerful intervention into the politics of knowledge at the start of the twentieth century, and seems to indicate the double standards of a generally racist polity.

In fact, the terms of Foo's challenge changed slightly as the date drew closer, drawing more and more attention to the question of Chineseness rather than magical skill. The *Express* reported that, in addition to the £1000, Foo would pay Soo £100 if he could prove that he was Chinese. The same article carries a new accusation from Soo that Foo had plagiarized his tricks, and then a £500 counter-challenge from Foo to Soo asking him to prove this.[81] Of course, had he been Chinese, it would have been an easy thing for Soo to demonstrate this, perhaps by talking with the Chinese community in London, but since Soo was Robinson this was not going to happen. Thereafter, Steinmeyer reports that Robinson became very worried that Zhu would lunge at him when they met, 'ripping off his braided queue and exposing him as a fraud'.[82] Thus, he made the organizers promise that the two magicians would be separated by a glass partition and would not come into direct contact with each other. This is a remarkable image of the metropolitan Orientalist literally seeking to be protected from direct exposure to (and by) an actual Oriental by a transparent barrier. And then finally, Zhu reformulated his original challenge in a way that placed even more emphasis on the question of Chineseness. Steinmeyer relates the new challenges:

> They stipulate first, that Chung Ling Soo prove before members of the Chinese legation that he is a Chinaman. Second, that Ching Ling Foo will perform any ten Chinese tricks performed by Chung Ling Soo, and third, that Ching Ling Soo cannot perform ten out of twenty tricks performed by Ching Ling Foo.[83]

---

[81] 'Chung Ling Soo Declines Ching Ling Foo's Challenge: Dignity Too Sublime', *Express*, January 1900, reprinted in Karr, *The Silence of Chung Ling Soo*, p. 89. Of course, the accusation from Robinson that Zhu had copied his show was unsustainable, not least because Robinson had copied the Chinese elements of his show from Zhu. However, the psychology of this move is entirely consistent with his earlier attempt at one-upmanship by claiming that Soo is a higher-ranking Chinese subject than Foo. The idea that Soo was the original (first) Chinese conjuror in London was true (even if he were not Chinese), so the claim that his material was original would have some public resonance. Making this claim also enabled Robinson to edge the terms of the debate away from a sense of 'original' tied to 'Chinese' and towards a sense of 'original' tied to 'magician'.

[82] Steinmeyer, *The Glorious Deception*, p. 257. In an editorial note added to James Elliot's book of 1923, Houdini explains the fear of his friend William Robinson that his identity as a 'Caucassian' could be revealed in this way, and that the public was largely unaware of this fact. Never one to miss an opportunity for self-promotion, Houdini goes on to explain how Robinson asked him to come down to London to teach him the Needle Trick (which he thought Foo might perform as part of the challenge), apparently because Houdini's method for the trick was superior to that of Foo. James Elliot (Houdini, ed.), *Elliot's Last Legacy: Secrets of the King of all Kard Kings*, New York: Adams Press Print, 1923, p. 44.

[83] Steinmeyer, *The Glorious Deception*, p. 257. The strength of the first clause speaks for itself, but the subtle change in the second requirement (to stipulate Chinese tricks) is also very powerful, not least because Robinson's entire Chinese repertoire was taken from Zhu's act.

As it turned out, the *Weekly Dispatch*, which was hosting the challenge in its offices, did not see any value in supporting these new terms, and they were ignored. The media and public debate were already alive with the story, and the *Dispatch* simply needed the 'battle' to occur. Perhaps the editors sensed (or were told) that the question of Chineseness could be a deal breaker for Chung Ling Soo, and they hastily swung coverage to emphasize 'the question of whether Ching Ling Foo or Chung Ling Soo is the better man at juggling, conjuring, wizardry, sorcery, and the kindred arts and sciences'. Indeed, they went so far as to state categorically that 'it has been sought in some quarters to change the issue into one of the nationality of the rivals. This is a mistake.' Of course, this was a mistake if the interests of Robinson (and metropolitan Orientalism in general) were prioritized, but it was essential for Zhu. The reporter goes on to draw a clear line between issues of ancestry and issues of conjuring, claiming that the public is interested in the latter only.[84] However, it was (and remains) far from clear that this line can be sustained or that the challenge was not primarily about the question of ancestry (and its apparent importance for the art of enchantment). In the absence of the question of ethnicity, the challenge had no bite and no point: it was just two magicians doing ten random tricks. In a clumsy move, the *Dispatch* then reprinted the text of Foo's original challenge but omitted the whole of its first clause, hence attempting to delete the centrality of ancestry in the public record.[85]

This partisan move by the *Weekly Dispatch* reflects a more general turn against Foo in the press after Foo failed to show up for the magic battle on the morning of 7 January 1905.[86] Chung Ling Soo proceeded down the Strand and Fleet Street in his ostentatious red Daimler,

---

[84] 'Soo and Foo: Hippodrome Wizard's Feats at the WD Office. Foo Invisible, Although He was the Issuer of the Original Challenge', *Weekly Dispatch*, 8 January 1905, reprinted in Karr, *The Silence of Chung Ling Soo*, p. 92.

[85] The *Weekly Dispatch* also changed the way they referred to the magicians for the first time, omitting any mention of China in reference to Soo: 'Ching Ling Foo, the Chinese Sorcerer Appearing at the Empire Theatre, London, Challenged Chung Ling Soo, the Hippodrome Magician.' 8 January 1905.

[86] The reasons for Zhu's failure to participate in the challenge are not fully understood. There is evidence to suggest that he did not feel that the challenge had been finalized (after his conditions were ignored) and hence was not aware that it was happening at that time or place. There is also an argument that Mooser saw no value in conducting the challenge without the question of ancestry on the table, and so cancelled it, but that the *Weekly Dispatch* was not willing to let the story die in that way.

resplendent in his 'Chinese' finery. It was a publicist's dream. Once he arrived, he waited for a while and then performed ten impressive tricks, causing the press to laugh at the ridiculousness of the challenge. But Foo was nowhere to be seen. The *English News* ran a headline that captured the mood: 'Made Invisible! Chung Ling Soo Causes Ching Ling Foo to Vanish. Uncanny Victory at the Great Battle of the Rival Chinese Magicians.'[87] Indeed, the eventual disappearance and marginalization of Zhu Liankui and the issues of importance to him (such as public acknowledgement of and respect for questions of ethnicity, ancestry, and heritage) is a remarkable instance of the struggle for the Other to be heard in a colonial and Orientalist polity. In fact, Zhu left England within a month, never to return, and Robinson emerged as the victorious 'Original Chinese Magician'.

It is an intriguing historical counterfactual to posit that the *Weekly Dispatch* had taken Zhu's position more seriously and so had upheld his requirement that Robinson must prove his Chineseness on 7 January 1905. We must suppose that either Robinson would have failed to show up (and thus Foo would have caused Soo to vanish!) or that he would have taken the gamble that the public would still side with his super-Orientalized faux-Chineseness, even if it were exposed in this way, and so he would have turned up that morning and just carried on as usual. Given the atmosphere of the time, it's not obvious that the latter would not also have resulted in a victory for Soo and the humiliation of Foo.

Magic in China

Unlike the magicians who travelled to India, those who ventured to China during the Golden Age did not generally go in search of mysterious and ancient Chinese magic. Notwithstanding the fact that the image of China in the West competed with that of India as the home of magic itself, there was much less of a sense that China held lost esoteric knowledge or hidden communities of master sorcerers and necromancers. Instead, as we saw in reports around the contest between Foo and Soo, China was seen as a place of expert jugglers and circus performers ('a land where every little boy is an expert conjurer'). It was

---

[87] *English News*, 7 January 1905, reprinted in Karr, *The Silence of Chung Ling Soo*, p. 91.

not until the emergence of the Boxer 'spirit warriors', together with legends of their magical invulnerability to bullets, that Chinese magic developed a darker image in the West.

In general, Western magicians in China seemed respectful of the long history of magic in that country, even when they were not entirely sure of what that history might be. The sense of China as an 'ancient and mysterious civilization' to rival not only India but also Europe was powerful. Early travel accounts by magicians, such as the delightfully unreliable *Adventures of a Strange Man* (1873), typically veer between disdain and amazement. Dr Lynn (Hugh Simmons, or Washington Simmons, 1835–1899) found the Chinese 'habitually dishonest', dirty, deeply superstitious, and incomprehensible as performers.[88] And yet, he also confesses to moments of wonder and amazement at their skill:

> The Chinese, like the Japanese, are extraordinary performers.
> I have seen Chinese jugglers cut a man in half with a sword, and the
> man has then danced about the stage. I used to walk about in
> Shanghai with my head under my arm, to the astonishment of the
> natives, but I have not succeeded in discovering how the division of
> the body was accomplished.[89]

Hence, by the time the great Howard Thurston made his way to Hong Kong and Shanghai in 1906, 'eager to see the strange land of the Chinaman', he already had a strong sense of (and respect for) Chinese magic. After all, this was the year after the infamous Foo-Soo battle in London, and many decades after the first troupes of Chinese conjurors

---

[88] One of those magicians particularly struck by dirtiness and cruelty in China was Charles Bertram, who carefully illustrated his book with photographs of 'slow strangulation' of criminals in Canton (pp. 154–155) and who describes how 'offal and filth of the most revolting nature is carted about in open tubs in these narrow thoroughfares which literally teem with human beings'. And yet, Bertram is also alive to astonishment; he visits a 'native conjuror ... [who] was remarkably clever in his particular style, and far eclipsed anyone I had previously seen'. He even 'tried to induce him to come to Europe' (p. 167). Charles Bertram, *A Magician in Many Lands*. London: Routledge & Sons, 1911.

[89] H.S. Lynn, *The Adventures of a Strange Man, with a Supplement Showing How It's Done*. London: Egyptian Hall, 1873, p. 8. One of the things for which Lynn became famous was for an early piece of trick photography that showed him standing in a dinner jacket with his head missing from his shoulders and tucked neatly under his arm.

had started touring the West. In this context, it is perhaps unsurprising that he should have viewed himself as a child amongst his elders:

> They followed my tricks with a gravity that charmed me, and an attention for detail that put me on my mettle. They were so imperturbable, so wise with the ancient wisdom of their race, that at first I felt as if I were a child showing off before my elders. Sometimes in the midst of a trick or an illusion I caught myself wondering what was going on behind those bland, inscrutable countenances, what they, who were old when the pyramids were new, thought of my little bag of tricks.[90]

In fact, the records of the peripatetic Western magicians of this period are rather focussed on how they were received by the Chinese; the accounts linger over cultural and racial observations of amateur ethnography. Unlike those who travelled to India, there were no elaborate quests or investigations attempting to reveal the secret and potent magic of local sages or mountain ascetics. No rewards were offered to local magicians should they prove able to perform the Rope Trick or a mysterious Levitation, and certainly no rewards were offered for the Linking Rings or Goldfish Bowl Trick. In some ways, this orientation towards magic in China reflects the way in which Chinese magic was received in the West, where the meaning of 'Chinese magic' tended towards an aesthetic or cultural styling rather than particular magical cosmologies or feats of power. After all, it was Chung Ling Soo not Ching Ling Foo who was crowned the 'Original Chinese Magician' in London.

In other words, with the admixture of a new form of glamour derived from cultural differences in styles of performance, China seemed to have been accepted within the emerging world of modern magic already at the turn of the century. As we will see, while Chinese-style magicians performed modern magic in an Orientalized guise in London and New York, Chinese magicians *in China* in this period (and thereafter) made a deliberate attempt to embrace the modernity of magic precisely as a way to participate in this incipient international regime. Similar to the case of Japan, modern magic in China became rapidly and (apparently) inextricably associated with the magic performed by Western visitors, like Thurston. Indeed, this is what it meant to perform

[90] Howard Thurston, *My Life of Magic*. Philadelphia: Dorrance & Co., 1929, p. 152.

magic in modernity, even (and perhaps especially) if you were Chinese. In short, modern magic was part of the package deal associated with modernization.[91]

In this context, magicians visiting China tended to describe 'the Chinese' rather than performances of magic; Chineseness (not feats of magic *per se*) was the magical commodity in which Western magicians were interested. Of course, as Edward Said argued so persuasively, travel writing rarely consists 'simply of individual or disinterested factual accounts. Rather, travellers have already been influenced, before they travel, by previous cultural representations that they have encountered.'[92] Hence, the accounts of magicians in the early twentieth century show the clear impact of Western Orientalism, and demonstrate the resilience of this ideological structure in the face of direct experience. Upon arriving into Hong Kong harbour, for instance, Thurston reports being concerned about how to make himself understood. Confronted by an official who bows at him gravely, Thurston blurted out:

> 'Hello, John, I wantee go theatre', imitating as closely as possible the Chinamen I had heard talk in America. He looked at me placidly, a smile wriggling across his moonlike face. I pulled out a few coins. 'How muchee cost – you showee theatre?'[93]

The 'Chinaman' in question, Mr. Tam, a graduate of Cambridge University in England, remained unperturbed and replied to Thurston in perfect English. For his part, Thurston seems to have been suitably embarrassed about how he had spoken to Tam; he even apologizes for having been rude. Nonetheless, it is relatively clear that the idea that Chinese people speak pidgin English (even in China) was a central and resilient feature of their popular identity in the West, buoyed by Britain's imperial presence in Hong Kong and Shanghai. Indeed, the perception that pidgin English could confer a level of authenticity upon

---

[91] As we will see, an interesting implication of this was that performances of traditional or 'old' magic in China by the Chinese were seen as ideologically conservative. Unlike Western magicians, such as Robinson, who were at liberty to indulge in a burlesque of traditional Chinese performances from within the parameters of modern magic, Chinese magicians performing in such a manner would occupy a very different political and ethical space. This was especially true after the May Fourth Movement.

[92] Tim Youngs, *The Cambridge Introduction to Travel Writing*. Cambridge: Cambridge University Press, 2013, p. 9.

[93] Thurston, *My Life of Magic*, p. 151.

a faux-Chinese magician was one of the factors that enabled the creation of Chung Ling Soo. Charles Bertram went so far as to recall that a Chinese usher had explained the popularity of his magic act in this way: 'Every man plenty too much come magic man's pidgin.'[94] Like Thurston, we must assume that many people realized this was offensive and had perhaps even experienced the shame of being offensive, yet the representation persisted.

The other aspects of 'Chineseness' that attracted Western magicians in China were similarly recognizable from the image of the Chinese magician in the West. Some of these seem unpleasantly racist today, such as Bertram's description of Chinese people as having a 'sameness of facial expression [that] is remarkable ... they are as alike as "peas in a pod" – indeed, monotonously alike'.[95] Others struck a more appreciative tone: Thurston describes his delight at the view that greeted him when he stood on the stage and looked out into the theatre, a vision that 'was one that few white men have been privileged to behold'.

> The tables on the ground floor were surrounded by Chinese gentlemen in rich silks of many different colors, yellow and purple predominating. Some wore gorgeous mandarin coats. Pretty little sing song girls, as colorful as hummingbirds, flitted in and out among the tables, pouring tea into rose-leaf cups or filing tiny silver pipes. In the boxes above set the wives of wealthy merchants and officials. They wore embroidered tunics of yellow and purple and were weighted with jewelry and precious gems ... I could see a mountain of yellow faces.[96]

In common with other visiting magicians, Thurston notes how dirty and chaotic Chinese cities were at the time, but it is with descriptions of sumptuous silks, glorious colours, and romantic femininity that his account comes alive. In the context of such descriptions, it is little wonder that the public perception of Chineseness in the West tended towards Chung Ling Soo rather than the more austere Ching Ling Foo.

---

94 Bertram also provides a short vocabulary list for those who'd like to learn pidgin and cites the poem 'Excelsior' as an instance of good practice. I will not reproduce it here. Charles Bertram, *A Magician in Many Lands*. London: Routledge & Sons, 1911, pp. 147–148.
95 Bertram, *A Magician in Many Lands*, p. 146.
96 Thurston, *My Life of Magic*, p. 166.

And although Thurston was quite right that very few Western men had seen such things with their own eyes at that time, these were precisely the visions that floated before the eyes of the magicians who had not been to China, such as William Robinson himself.

Thurston, who expresses great warmth and affection for the Chinese people in his account, goes on to relate some of the cultural problems he encountered when performing magic to this audience, thus providing an account of his perception of the different conventions of magic in China at that time. First, Thurston explains that the Chinese audience preferred their magic to be performed slowly, rather than in the rapid-fire manner of the modern magician in London, Paris, or New York. They expected to have time to contemplate the effect and perhaps even to discuss it. To facilitate this, Thurston developed the practice of leaving the stage for a cigarette after each trick; he suggests that the audience's appreciation of an effect was proportional to the amount of time they were allowed to consider it in this break.[97] Charles Bertram and others also opined that they were discomforted by the noises made by Chinese audiences instead of applause and by their tendency to want to climb up on stage to examine the magician's apparatus.[98]

Secondly, Thurston expressed great surprise at the behaviour of his translator, who appeared on stage next to him and was supposed to repeat his words in Chinese. Instead of simply repeating the words, 'he began a fusillade of outlandish sounds, the spectators eagerly listening, and raised his voice gradually until he became blustery. He contorted his face and used many violent gestures, after the manner of the Chinese actor.'[99] Leaving aside the implication that Thurston thought Cantonese a 'fusillade of outlandish sounds', the great magician seems to have found himself in a living moment of cultural encounter. Rather than merely translating word for word, his interpreter had done his best to convey the force of Thurston's patter in a manner that would retain its magic for the Hong Kong audience. Indeed, when challenged about his translation, the translator (an editor from a Chinese newspaper) explained that he was simply following the customs of his country.[100]

---

[97] Thurston, *My Life of Magic*, p. 167.
[98] Bertram, *A Magician in Many Lands*, pp. 171–172.
[99] Thurston, *My Life of Magic*, p. 167.
[100] Thurston relates that these customs involved giving salutations to each rank and social group present in the audience, being respectful to the nobility, absent parents,

How wonderful it would be if we were able to compare the transcripts of the English and Chinese speeches from those evenings – but, sadly, such transcripts do not exist.

It was precisely these theatrical customs that so fascinated Western magicians about Chinese magic – the conventions of the Chinese stage were radically different from those of the West. While modern magic in Europe and North America was forming itself around the rather austere, professional, and gentlemanly guise of a doctor performing experiments in evening wear, stage magic in China seemed to remain an explosion of colour and dramatic expression. In Thurston's words, the 'Chinese are natural pantomimists'. As the inimitable Dr Lynn put it many years earlier: 'The Chinese performances are simply incomprehensible to an European, and consist mainly in beating a gong or tom-tom, and tumbling about the stage.'[101] In this context, it is little wonder that the image of Chinese magic in the West became a stark juxtaposition with the dinner jackets endorsed by Robert-Houdin; the grandiose, flamboyant, burlesque of the Great Lafayette, Chung Ling Soo, and others represented the dramatic appropriation of this process of translation. Ironically, Ching Ling Foo just didn't measure up to the Western ideal of Chinese magic.

It's curious to reflect that Thurston seems to have been alive to some of these issues of cultural translation. Indeed, he freely engaged in a form of what we might call Occidentalism, which significantly impacted on the construction of modern magic in China, which was in turn modelled on perceptions of Western magic. When he caused great offence to his audience by making use of female assistants (which he claims were forbidden from the stage in China), he argues that only women could be put into the 'necessary degree of hypnosis' for his illusions to work – he suggests that it would be entirely normal in the

and deceased ancestors. This is probably an exaggerated account, but the principle remains sound: Western visitors were often not very sensitive or respectful about the cultural customs of the countries they 'invaded'. (Thurston himself talked about his trip around the Far East as an 'invasion' – p. 172), and so this kind of 'translation' represented an act of generosity. The translator assumed that Thurston meant no offence to his audience, and so translated these intentions into Chinese. And, to be fair, Thurston does seem to have apologized for 'offending one of the customs of the country' later on, after 'grossly defying one of their oldest and most cherished traditions' by parading his female assistant on stage (pp. 168–169).

[101] Lynn, *The Adventures of a Strange Man*, p. 5.

West for fully half of his regular programme to include hypnotized women. This stance on gender roles in modern magic is further reinforced when Thurston attempts to douse the uproar caused by someone kissing his assistant on stage: 'I assured the spectators that kissing was a very important custom in my country, that, in fact, no play could be successful unless the women in it were kissed every few minutes.'[102] In other words, even while Thurston was experiencing a particular sense of Chineseness, China was experiencing a particular vision of Americanness in the interaction with modern magic.

Magic and modernity in China

The development of something resembling 'modern magic' in China moves hand in hand with the complicated social and cultural matrix of modernization, which in turn was accompanied by the imperial thrust of Westernization.[103] Before the mid–nineteenth century, there was already a long and intricate tradition of magic in China, intermixed with religious rituals and folk practices just as was the case in Europe. In the case of China, this kind of 'old' magic was associated with Daoist magic, alchemy, and various forms of supernatural belief, including in witches, wizards, spirits, and daemons.[104] This 'old magic' was variously referred to as *wushu*, *huanshu*, *xifa*, or sometimes *fangshu*.[105] However, at the turn of the twentieth century with the arrival of modern magic from Europe and America, a new term (derived from the English word 'magic') was coined: *moshu*. Indeed, Laikwan Pang suggests that the word *moshu* (magic) and *modeng* (modern) were linked in the popular imagination because of their homophonic first syllables (which, nonetheless, have no etymological connection):

---

[102] Thurston, *My Life of Magic*, pp. 169–170.

[103] The literature on the emergence of modernity in China and its relationship with a process (or threat) of Westernization is so vast that I cannot begin to summarize it here.

[104] The historical reach and depth of magical belief in China finds a powerful illustration in Liang Cai, *Witchcraft and the Rise of the First Confucian Empire*. Albany: SUNY Press, 2014; and then concerning a much later period, Philip Kuhn, *Soulstealers: The Chinese Sorcery Scare of 1768*. Cambridge: Harvard University Press, 1990.

[105] Seminal works on the history of magic in China include Zhen Guozheng & Yang Xiaoge (eds), *Zhongguo moshu*. Tianjing: Tianjing kexue jishu, 1981; and Xie Guai'an, *Zhonghua zaxu*. Taipei: Wenjing, 1995.

> Modern Western magic's arrival coincided with the advent of
> modernity in China, and the two parallel events heralded the arrival
> of a new era of sensation in which magic was modern and the
> modern was magical.[106]

Unlike in Europe, where much of the battle over the meaning of modern
magic was staged around the confusion that arose from the ambiguity of
the term 'magic' itself, as we saw in Chapters 1 and 2, in China this new
word enabled the construction of clearer symbolic boundaries around
'old' and 'new' magic. Modern magic was *moshu*. Old magic was something else. According to Pang, the idea that *moshu* was at least partially
(and perhaps completely) foreign to China helped to validate it *qua*
magic. She argues that part of the power of magic has always resided
in its alienness and marginality. In other words, immersion in magical
culture is rarely a conservative act – it is not a reaction against foreign
encroachment or progressivism, as it is often depicted. Instead, Pang
argues that 'people are enchanted by magic not because of its association with their cultural heritage but because of its modern eccentricity
and unpredictability'.[107] So, just as Western magicians were entranced
by the idea of Oriental magic as a way to bring the periphery into the
centre, so Chinese magicians 'understood new magic cultures to be
"Western"'.[108] Part of the power of magic is its essential intertwinement
with the Other.

The relationship between *moshu* and the Chinese people
evolved rapidly during the late years of the Qing dynasty. In the period
between the supposed trip of Dr Lynn in 1862[109] and the tour of
Howard Thurston in 1906, much changed. One important change was
that *moshu* shifted from being an art performed by and for foreigners in
international compounds, broadening to include rich groups of Chinese
patrons, and then eventually a wide public. Thurston, for instance, took
great pride in his insistence that his show must be open to locals as well

---

[106] Laikwan Pang, 'Magic and Modernity in China'. *positions: east asia cultures critique*, 12:2 (Fall, 2004), p. 300. Pang places her argument into a more general one
about visual culture and Chinese modernity: Laikwan Pang, *The Distorting Mirror:
Visual Modernity in China*. Honolulu: University of Hawai'i Press, 2007.

[107] Pang, 'Magic and Modernity in China', p. 303.

[108] Pang, 'Magic and Modernity in China', p. 303.

[109] Dr Lynn claims to have left the navy in 1862 in order to pursue magic, and then to
have travelled for hundreds of days to various places, eventually arriving in Hong
Kong.

as expats. In this period, Chinese magicians also rose to prominence, perhaps the most famous of which was Zhu Liankui himself (Chung Ling Soo), who developed a sufficiently impressive repertoire and reputation to launch his own world tour in 1898, mixing traditional Chinese feats with Western feats to produce a truly innovative and exciting form of transnational modern magic. The groundwork for Zhu's innovation was laid by the work of (the slightly mysterious) Tang Zaifeng ten years earlier, when he compiled the *E huan huibian* (1889) – China's earliest extant manual of magic, which includes a mixture of 'foreign' techniques, puzzles, lock-boxes, and supernatural ideas.[110]

By the time of Zhu's return to China, magic was witnessing the 'increasing popularity of modern Western magic among ordinary Chinese urbanites'.[111] Zhu continued to perform in Beijing throughout the 1910s, incorporating his act into the Chinese Opera. Spurred by high-profile, Chinese (and international) successes like Zhu Liankui, and buoyed by the wider availability of manuals like the *E huan huibian*, 'a large number of local magicians started to give modern magic shows among the urbanites' in 1920s Beijing.[112] It was at about this time that the first modern magical societies started to appear in China, either mirroring those in London and New York or sometimes being established as branches of them.[113]

Local magicians started to become celebrities in their own right, often performing shows that closely imitated the style and content of the Western magic they had seen.[114] Traditional Chinese tricks became

---

[110] Although she doesn't mention the *E huan huibian*, Pang does cite a host of books about magic from the 1930s that combined ideas about modern magic with more traditional, supernatural practices and ideas drawn from Taoism. Pang, 'Magic and Modernity in China', p. 318.

[111] Pang, 'Magic and Modernity in China', p. 305.

[112] The importance of the availability of literature about magic in China cannot be underestimated. Translations of Western works were also appearing in this period, and performers who had done the European or American tour would invariably return with resources and knowledge and training. Pang also argues that the commodification of magic in the 1920s and 1930s, when tricks and books became more commonplace, served as a form of democratization, making magic into something 'purchasable and possessable' by anyone with a few coins. Pang, 'Magic and Modernity in China', p. 318.

[113] Perhaps the most famous of these was *Wanguo moshu xiehui*.

[114] Pang lists the following as notable Chinese magicians of the period: Han Jingwen, Xu Jingyun, Mo Wuqi, and Zhang Huichong. Pang, 'Magic and Modernity in China', p. 305.

decreasingly popular on stage; they didn't seem to fit in with modern magic in China, where a burlesque of Chinese magic *qua* modern magic would simply have been bizarre. Such tricks (which typically involved jugglery, manipulation, sword-swallowing, and fire-spitting) remained in urban (and especially rural) culture, but largely as entertainments in markets or on the streets.

Chinese magicians also adopted the convention of 'magical duels' from modern magicians in the West. Just as magicians in New York duelled with each other to prove their superiority, so Chinese magicians in Beijing, Hong Kong, and Shanghai did the same thing, feeding into an existing culture of competition between artistic studios and martial arts schools in the cities.[115] Not only that, but in a curious cultural inversion of the Soo vs. Foo battle of 1905, in Shanghai in 1923 the Chinese magician Zhang Huichong 'became instantly famous ... because he managed to successfully copy all the performances of Nicola ... but also adding one more "Escaping from Water" ... to show that Zhang was a greater magician than Nicola. Both the Chinese magicians and the audience were anxious and elated to see how the Chinese could perform better Western magic to claim superiority over Westerners.'[116]

Other than Zhang Huichong (1898–1962), who became famous for his magical duel with 'the Great Nicola' and went on to become a movie star in the emerging *wuxia-shen'guai* (martial arts and magic) genre, I have been unable to find details about these interesting figures. Zhang was apparently attracted to magic after seeing a performance by Horace Goldin (1873–1939), whose signature trick was to saw a lady in half (which he is often mistakenly credited with having invented). Following his career as a magician and moviestar, Zhang wrote three important magic books following the founding of the People's Republic in 1949; for many years these were the best (and sometimes only) texts available for aspiring magicians.

[115] The association between martial arts and magic is powerful in China. In this period, the association emerged most strongly in the form of the *wuxia-shen'guai* (martial arts and magic) movies, in which Zhang Huichong frequently starred. The association has persisted and even recent movies such as the 2011 Derek Yee film, *The Great Magician*, starring Tony Leung Chiu-Wai, make use of traditional structures from the wuxia genre but simply replace the martial arts with magic. Themes of quests for secret scrolls of power (illustrating lost techniques), duels between rival schools, and competition with Japan (and the West) are staples to the genre.

[116] Pang, 'Magic and Modernity in China', p. 306.

Nicola (William Mozart Nicol, 1880–1946) was an American magician on the vaudeville circuit who performed as 'The Great Nicola' in Shanghai at least twice, once in 1910 (when he also visited Egypt and India) and once in 1923. It is an intriguing historical coincidence that his break into vaudeville occurred after he appeared at the same Exposition in Omaha as Zhu Liankui in 1898. It is interesting

This idea that Chinese magicians should aspire to perform 'Western magic' better than 'Westerners' persisted through the twentieth century. It both affirmed China's place in a modern international regime, and it expressed an aspiration towards China's predominance in that international space. As was also the case in Japan, this kind of cultural pattern was common to many aspects of China's engagement with modernity and its engagement with the West. Also as in Japan, China's relationship with its own culture was deeply controversial during these years, especially around the May Fourth Movement and the so-called New Culture Movement of the 1910s and 1920s, in which the value of Chinese traditions were questioned against the demonstrable power of Western modernity. In such a context, it is unsurprising that performers and audiences embraced the modern magic associated with the West rather than the traditional magic of China. The irony is that this was happening at exactly the moment when the West was enthusiastically imitating Chinese magic as an emblem of magical potency and poetry.

In fact, the idea of establishing China as the global centre of an international regime of modern (Western) magic has remained a feature of magic in China until the present day. In recent years, China has made moves to institutionalize itself as a magical hegemon, as interest in magic (and the market for magic) has exploded.[117] In 2012, The First China Beijing International Magic Carnival was held at Changping Stadium, where government plans were announced to build a 'Beijing Magic City' in the Changping district around the stadium, and to launch a systematic programme of education in magic for the Chinese youth. It was an event to rival Las Vegas in glitz, with dozens of international guests, celebrities, and advisors. Due to open in 2016, Magic City will include a theatre, a school, a museum, and a research & development

to consider the possible influence of the Chinese magician on Nicola's ambitions to perform in China. It seems conceivable that Nicola chose his name to associate his modern, equipment-oriented magic with Nikola Tesla (1856–1943), whose remarkable work with electricity was already in the public eye and was often associated with magical theatre; *Pearson's Magazine* (May 1899) called Tesla 'The New Wizard of the West', and he was certainly an appropriate poster-boy for the ideal of magic driven by modernity.

[117] At the same time, confidence in Chinese traditions in the new era of the market economy in China has blossomed. Many Chinese magicians today make at least some aesthetic use of their 'Chineseness'. Parasol productions appear to be a particular favourite.

centre for the creation of new equipment and apparatus.[118] The poster boy was the emerging star of Chinese (and international) magic, the Taiwanese magician Lu Chen. In fact, the *International Magic Carnival* is not even the only show in town; it is forced to share the stage on a biennial cycle with the *China Beijing Asia College Magic Convention*.

At the second International Magic Carnival in 2014, plans were announced for the use of this platform as the foundation for an International Magic Cooperation and Promotion Association under the supervision of the Chinese Ministry of Culture and the Ministry of Civil Affairs.[119] Of course, there is already a basic architecture for the international magical regime, albeit one heavily biased towards Europe and the United States. There are numerous national and international magical associations of varying ages, levels of exclusivity, and standing. And the Fédération Internationale des Sociétés Magiques (FISM, est. 1948) is an independent organization designed to facilitate coordination, communication, and the promotion of mutual interests amongst all the other clubs and societies in the world. Indeed, FISM also organizes the prestigious, triennial World Championship of Magic, which was held in Beijing in 2009.[120] Hence, the creation of a new international association sponsored by the Chinese government, which has similar goals regarding the (re)formation of an international regime, appears to some to be a competitive move.[121]

Despite its remarkable enthusiasm for modern magic today, the modern Chinese government has not always been so supportive, although it has always played a much more central role in magical affairs than other governments. The complicated relationship between magic, the supernatural, and superstition has taxed Chinese politics throughout the modern period. Perhaps the most dramatic manifestation was the Cultural Revolution itself, in which magic books and equipment of all kinds were burned. The 'socialist spiritual civilization' rests upon a radically disenchanted worldview 'in which magical belief

---

[118] Dale Salwak, 'China's Grand Plans'. *The Linking Ring*, 93:2 (February 2013), pp. 32–35.

[119] Dale Salwak, 'A Letter from Beijing'. *The Linking Ring*, 94:9 (September 2014), pp. 52–53.

[120] China is not well represented amongst the winners of this competition. Their single winner in the last ten years was Chun Daibin, who won in the manipulation category in 2006.

[121] FISM presently incorporates approximately 50,000 magicians from 32 countries, including many in China.

appears to be a misguided understanding of reality'.[122] Magic appears as a heretical 'false science'.

Just as we saw in the discourse around the establishment of a recognizably *modern* magic in the West, in which it was so important to open some clear water between modern magic and so-called old magic, so the ambiguity about the parameters of *moshu* in China have been even more politicized in the twentieth century. In particular, it has been vital to isolate the idea of 'magical belief', which we discussed at length in Chapters 1 and 2, since heresy resides in a form of belief that tends to towards confidence in 'supernatural counter-physical causation'. Hence, magic that professes to make use of such powers (and thus attempts to persuade its audience to believe in them) is heretical. In formal terms, it constitutes either religious superstition (which is tolerated but suspicious), folk superstition (which tends to be private and so less threatening to social order), or feudal superstition (which includes temple cults, magical healing, and myriad other beliefs, and is the most dangerous because it amounts to counter-hegemonic dissent).[123] In London, as we've seen, Maskelyne and Devant called these kinds of magic 'illegitimate' and denied their modernity.

Intriguingly, then, we find that the Chinese government seems to have pursued a more politically and ideologically charged version of Maskelyne and Devant's moral mission to modernize magic into a practice that could reside within the worldview of scientific modernity. While Maskelyne and Devant declared that 'old' magical beliefs should be denied and actually exposed by modern magicians as part of the process of making modern magic respectable and legitimate, in China 'magical belief itself becomes an evil to be exorcised through science and ideological work'.[124] One of the crucial differences, however, is that Maskelyne and Devant were deeply conflicted about completely shedding the association of magic with magical belief; indeed, they wanted to retain magic as an art of enchantment within modernity. In the case of China, on the other hand, even though *moshu* might self-consciously reside within and embrace a scientific worldview, and even if this

---

[122] Ann Anagnost, 'Politics and Magic in Contemporary China'. *Modern China*, 13:1 (January 1987), p. 41.

[123] Anagnost provides an excellent elaboration and discussion of these categories. Anagnost, 'Politics and Magic in Contemporary China'.

[124] Anagnost, 'Politics and Magic in Contemporary China', p. 44.

constituted a discrediting and even an exposé of superstitious or magical belief, *moshu* could never properly liberate the people from false consciousness or heretical thinking. This is precisely because *moshu* – modern magic – is still in the business of *performing* magical belief, even if this is designed to be a device to refute that belief. Modern magic does not seek to destroy the experience of enchantment or even of the magical; rather it seeks to be honest about how that sensation is created. So, *moshu* – modern magic – has a 'gravitational field' that naturally draws people back towards magical beliefs.[125] In earlier chapters, we talked about magic as intoxication; here it is constructed as a gateway drug.

In practice, modern magicians were not the main targets of this policy in China, but they were certainly not exempt. This orientation contributed to the way that Western magic became preferred over more traditionally styled Chinese magic, which was much more closely intertwined with 'old' Chinese magic. As early as the 1920s and 1930s, just as we saw in Europe earlier, the scientific credentials of various methods of modern magic became vital to its presentation. A powerful example would be the case of hypnosis, which was not only seen as an entertainment but also, 'along with the discourse of psychology and psychoanalysis ... was also considered a new scientific discovery that could reach the inner psyche of human beings'.[126] Magic became a form of super-science or science-plus. To co-opt Pang's lovely expression, modern magic in China became a 'transnational pseudoscience', locating China in an emerging global modernity.

[125] I have borrowed the term 'gravitational field' from Anagnost, who uses it to describe the way that exposé does not exclude belief, and how residual belief by some draws in others. Anagnost, 'Politics and Magic in Contemporary China', pp. 51–52.
[126] Pang, 'Magic and Modernity in China', p. 309.

6 JAPANESE MAGIC AND MAGIC IN JAPAN

Japanese magic

The mysteriousness of Japan in the Western imagination was already firmly embedded before the middle of the nineteenth century. This was partially because of its extreme distance from Europe and the haziness of distant geography at the time. It was partly because of a general confusion about the perceived difference, if any, between China and Japan. But it was largely because Japan's official policy of *sakoku* – isolationism – had severely restricted the flow of information and commerce between Japan and the Western world.[1] Although *sakoku* was far from watertight, it was a sufficient deterrent to make it unlikely that European powers would make the extra effort of travelling into the far, Far East, when India and China were open for business en route. Before the westward expansion of the United States reached California in the mid-1800s, there was very little chance that anyone would approach the Japanese islands from the east. Hence, Japan was

---

[1] The Shogunate imposed *kaikin* (maritime restrictions) ostensibly to block further incursions of European colonialism, especially Catholicism, which were destabilizing domestic order in Japan. These restrictions amounted to a policy of *sakoku* (locked country), a term coined in the 1800s. The Tokugawa or Edo Period that followed, which witnessed many social and political changes and restrictions in Japan, was a long era of peace and stability. Although the Tokugawa regime collapsed in the face of foreign power and domestic unrest, and Japanese historians in the late 1800s would question its impact on the dynamism of Japanese culture, the Edo period is usually seen as an era of great cultural richness and accomplishment in Japan.

mysterious largely because of Western ignorance about it, which made it fertile ground for the fantastical and magical imagination.

In fact, Jonathan Swift (1667–1745) famously included Japan as one of the fantastical lands in part three of *Gulliver's Travels* (1726/35). Gulliver finds Japan just to the west of Lugnagg and Glubbdubdrib, which is a land filled with necromancers, sorcerers, and magicians, but he notes with some resentment that only the Dutch were allowed to land there. Swift was correct that the Dutch maintained a small trading port near Nagasaki – the islet of Deshima – and the Netherlands was the only European nation permitted to trade with Japan, albeit with strict prohibition against any incursions onto any of the main Japanese islands.[2]

Hence, it was not until after the forced opening of Japan in 1854 that the populations of Western nations really became able to access information about the distant empire or actually to see Japanese people.[3] Even so, until at least the Meiji Restoration in 1868, access to the cities and interior of Japan was still very restricted: foreigners were limited to the international zones of port cities like Kobe and Yokohama. At the same time, Japanese subjects were not formally permitted to leave the country unless they were on official diplomatic missions.[4]

---

[2] Deshima is an artificial island built in 1634, originally as a base for Portuguese traders, but only the Dutch (and, in practice, some Chinese, Ryukyuans, and Koreans) were permitted between 1641 and 1853. The islet is tiny; approximately 120 × 75 meters. The islet was connected to the mainland by a single bridge, which was constantly guarded. Ships in the port had their sails confiscated until they could be searched prior to departure; any books or maps about Japan would be confiscated, and attempts to remove such materials from Japan could result in a death sentence for the smugglers. Conversely, the Dutch were not allowed to practice any religious activities on Deshima, and were not permitted to spread destabilizing cultural information into Japan. *Rangaku* (Dutch Studies) arose as a field of knowledge dedicated to understanding the West, particularly Western medicine. For some time into the nineteenth century, *rangaku* persisted as the term for Western studies.

[3] Japan's seclusion was ended by the (second) arrival of Commodore Perry's famous 'Black Ships' of the U.S. Navy in March 1854, when the Treaty of Kanagawa began the process of opening Japanese ports to Western traders and official missions. It is noteworthy that Russia was also exploring ways to open Japan in this period, and that treaties with the other European powers followed in short order.

[4] The first delegations were sent by the Japanese government to the United States in 1860, with two embassies to Europe in 1862 and 1863, and then a formal delegation to the 1867 World's Fair in Paris. The most famous and important mission of this period was the first undertaken during the Meiji era; the so-called Iwakakura Embassy, which was initiated in 1871, travelled to the United States, Europe, and parts of the Middle East and Asia, and then returned to Japan in 1873.

During this period, perceptions of Japanese magic in Europe and America were inspired by the early experiences of intrepid travellers and explorers like Lafcadio Hearn (1850–1904) and Percival Lowell (1855–1916), who were amongst the first Westerners to devote their attention directly to questions of magic and the supernatural in Japan.[5] Hearn's many books about Japan in 1890s provided one of the most popular lenses through which Western readers viewed this little-known county. He drew an unashamedly romantic picture of his adopted home, depicting it as a land of poetry, gentle beauty, and mysteriousness. In the late 1890s, beginning with *Japanese Fairy Tales* (1898), Hearn turned explicitly to supernatural themes. Indeed, his most popular and enduring work (both in the West and in Japan itself) was *Kwaidan: Stories and Studies of Strange Things* (1904), which showcases a Japan rich with animal spirits, ghosts, and supernatural magic.[6] Hearn's Japan fed directly into the aesthetic of *Japonisme*, which emerged in the 1860s and 1870s in Europe.

At the same time, in the general context of mystical Orientalism that we saw in Chapter 2, audiences were enthusiastic about travel accounts that engaged directly with the idea of Japan as living realm of real magic. Hence, Lowell's depiction of Occult Japan (1894) as

[5] Of Irish and Greek descent, Hearn travelled to Japan in 1890, where he became a teacher. He eventually married a Japanese woman, Koizumi Setsu, converted to Buddhism, and became a naturalized Japanese citizen under the name Koizumi Yakumo. This process of enchantment with an actual (as well as a fantastical and magical) Japan, leading to an authentic act of becoming Japanese, contrasts markedly with William Robinson's deeply ambivalent Orientalist drive to become a Chinese magician without ever approaching China itself. Through his many books about Japan, Hearn became one of the most important literary lenses through which the West viewed Japan in this period.

An American astronomer, Lowell travelled to East Asia in the 1880s, spending time in Korea and Japan on government business. Although most famous for his speculations about the origins of the canals on Mars and for setting in motion the research that eventually led to the discovery of Pluto, Lowell wrote a number of popular works on Korea, Japan, and the Orient more generally.

[6] Hearn produced a series of books on these topics: *Japanese Fairytales* (1898); *In Ghostly Japan* (1899); *Shadowings* (1900); *Kwaidan: Stories and Studies of Strange Things* (1904). *Kwaidan* (Ghost Stories) contains a selection of ghost stories that Hearn suggests are translations of folkstories, and an extended essay about insects. Today, Kwaidan is as well known for the prize-winning Kobayashi Masaaki film of the same name (1964). Most of his stories are collected into Lafcadio Hearn, *Writings from Japan: An Anthology*. London: Penguin, 1994. Not incidentally, given William Robinson's interest in Chinese fairytales in this period, Hearn also wrote *Some Chinese Ghosts* (1887).

a land riddled with esoteric practices and rituals spoke to a strong cultural tendency. Lowell characterized the Japanese as living 'the Way of the Gods', and practicing *kamiwaza* (spirit techniques); his enquiry into Japan embraced *Shintō* as its pervasive national culture, and rendered *Shintō* into a nationalized system of magic.[7] For instance, Lowell identifies a number of 'miracles' performed by *Shintō* priests, such as the Ordeal by Boiling Water (in which the adept submerges his hands into a cauldron of boiling water and sprays it at the observers), the Ordeal of Walking Barefoot over Hot Coals, and the Ordeal of Climbing a Ladder of Swordblades.[8] Such feats, and others, were connected to empowering chants and mystical actions, which either summoned a *kami* to assist the adept or directly empowered him to perform the miracles. Western magicians were already familiar with such feats, not only but also as instances of Indian magic.

Lowell is particularly interested in the *in-musubi*, which he calls 'seal bindings', and what he calls the *kūji*, or the 'nine characters'.[9] These appear in various places in his book, where they are connected with the performance of magic in much the way that an audible 'spell' might be associated with magic elsewhere.[10] Presumably, these are references to the symbolic hand gestures that find their origins in

[7] Lowell cites the term *kamiwaza* as 'god-arts', translating *kami* as god, which was conventional at the time. However, because of the ambiguity around the word 'god' in English, this is rarely the translation today. In fact, the force of *kami* is closer to 'spirit': the *kami* are multiple and diverse, inhabiting (or expressing) myriad natural features and creatures. *Waza* is a technique.

   Shintō – the Way of the Gods – is ostensibly the indigenous religion of Japan; through the *kami* (*shin*) it is closed tied to the land of Japan itself, since the *kami* reside there and the imperial family claims divine ancestry. However, its place in Japanese society has not always been rigorously demarcated or systematized until the modern period, and it was disestablished in 1945 following the defeat of Japan in the Pacific War.

[8] Percival Lowell, *Occult Japan: or, The Way of the Gods*. Cambridge, MA: Riverside Press, 1894, pp. 36–96.

[9] Lowell, *Occult Japan*, pp. 136–137.

[10] In his treatment of 'Oriental Fantasies', Claflin suggests that Japanese magicians use a chant that is the equivalent of 'hocus pocus' or 'abracadabra' in the West: 'Na myoho rege kyo'. He observes that this is very similar to a chant used in Buddhist temples to accomplish wish-fulfilment, which he says is, 'Na myo hoo renge kyo'. Edward Claflin & Jeff Sheridan, *Street Magic: An Illustrated History of Wandering Magicians and Their Conjuring Arts*. New York: Dolphin Books, 1977, p. 41. Presumably, Claflin is referring to the *daimoku* mantra of Nichiren Buddhism, *namu myōhō renge kyō*, which means to place one's faith in the Lotus Sutra, and the chanting of which is supposed to bring about merit along the path to awakening.

esoteric Buddhism.[11] In Japan, they are most closely associated with Shingon Buddhism, but their use has spread into wider culture, particularly in the form of the *kūji-in* and the *kūji-kiri*, which have been assimilated into the mythology of 'ninja magic' and the magic of *yamabushi* mountain ascetics. The *kūji-in* comprise a sequence of nine different hand configurations, in which the fingers are carefully and intricately intertwined; this practice is supposed to magically enhance the power of the practitioner. With similar goals, the *kūji-kiri* involves cutting a 'gate' (with five horizontal and four vertical bars) into the air with your finger, often to seal a visualization.

While this picture of Occult Japan contributed to the culture of the mystic revival and magical Orientalism during the Golden Age, this image of Japan as a land of occult power and mountain ascetics was too dark to catch the popular imagination in Europe or the United States at the turn of the century. In fact, just as we saw with changing perceptions of Chinese magic after the 'Kung Fu Kraze' of the 1970s, it was not until the 'ninja boom' in the post-war period that these ideas became contagious in the Western imagination of Japanese magic.[12] During the Golden Age, in contrast,

[11] Lowell recognizes that these gestures are not 'pure' Shintō, but he refuses to believe those who tell him that they are Buddhist, because 'I have never seen a Buddhist practice them.' Lowell, *Occult Japan*, p. 138.

In the yogic traditions of Indian Buddhism, the hand gestures are known as *Mudra*, and they can be seen in various forms on statues of Buddha and the Bodhisattvas. In general, though, the sequencing of these gestures into a type of physical mantra is associated with Shingon practices. And their rapid exercise before engaging in challenging activities is associated with Japanese folk magic. In recent years, they have become famous in ninja movies and especially in manga and anime like *Naruto*, in which particular sequences of gestures activate particular supernatural powers. Kishimoto Masashi, *Naruto* (manga: Weekly Shonen Jump) 1999–2014; the anime, directed by Date Hayato began in 2002 and is still ongoing.

[12] The invention of the ninja tradition in the post-war period is a fascinating and controversial topic. To some extent, it is the limit-case of the argument about the invention of the *bushidō* (the way of the warrior) tradition in the first half of the twentieth century. To be clear, in neither case is the argument that there were no warriors or covert operatives in Japanese history, nor is it that there were not various codes of conduct or rituals of power performed by some of those agents. Rather, the argument is simply that there was no coherent or unified *tradition* in either case, only multiple separate instances that were then used as the historical materials to build the idea of a tradition in the modern period. In any case, the 'ninja' first emerged into the Western consciousness in the James Bond film, *You Only Live Twice* (1967), in which Sean Connery endeavours to become Japanese through a combination of makeup and cosmetic surgery (in addition to have taking 'Oriental Studies at Cambridge'), with the

this kind of occult magic that seemed to rely upon religious or semi-religious self-cultivation was caught in the gravitational field of 'low' Indian magic. The impression of Japan was that it was more like China than India; indeed, if anything, that it was an even more courtly, refined, and civilized version of China.

The general representation of Japan in the context of Japonisme was of delicate beauty and sumptuous silks, drawn out of the *ukiyo-e* art of Hokusai (1760–1849) and others. As Claflin puts it, drawing on the influential essays of Ishii Black in *Magician's Monthly* in 1914, Japan resembled a '"Garden of Fantasy", a kind of mystical garden full of delicate creatures, blooming flowers, and sparkling fountains'.[13] In fact, the tremendously popular *Hokusai Manga* (1815) that circulated around Europe in the nineteenth century included numerous pictures of supernatural events, which were reproduced in books about magic to illustrate a peculiar blending of delicate beauty, formal society, mysterious tricks, and supernatural happenings.[14] One of the most famous of these images was the juxtaposition of a man swallowing a sword, which seemed like a conventional act of conjuring, and a man apparently swallowing a horse, which seemed less conventional. Unlike the mythical Indian Rope Trick, the impossible feat of swallowing a horse did not inspire Western magicians into decades of questing for the secret,[15]

---

goal of joining a group of ninja. This kind of becoming would have been familiar to the magicians (and audiences) of the Golden Age; it was relatively unexceptional to that audience in the 1960s; but following the post-colonial turn it has been widely interpreted as offensive, much in the manner of Mickey Rooney's character in *Breakfast at Tiffany's* (1961).

[13] Claflin & Sheridan, *Street Magic*, p. 40.

[14] Three such images are reproduced in Claflin & Sheridan, *Street Magic*, p. 39.

The Manga constitutes a collection of hundreds of sketches by Hokusai, ranging from landscapes, portraits, scenes of daily life, animals and plants. But perhaps the most famous images are those of supernatural scenes. The sketch books were assembled into fifteen volumes and published in 1814. Volume 10 contains many of the supernatural images.

[15] The *donba-jutsu* (horse-swallowing technique) is traditionally attributed to Shioya Chōjiro, a seventeenth-century magician. In a fascinating study about this technique, Matsuyama Mitsunobu suggests that because nobody has ever seen this legendary trick performed in real life, the mystery of it rivals that of the Indian Rope Trick. Mitsunobu Matsuyama, 'The Legend of Donba-Jutsu: Swallowing a Horse'. *Gibeciere*, 10:1 (Winter 2015), pp. 11–52. For some reason, however, the claim that someone has a trick that enables them to swallow a horse seems so incredible, and the act of swallowing a horse seems so disagreeable, that it seems unlikely to inspire the

although a number of other Japanese tricks did catch the imagination of modern magicians and audiences. Chief amongst these, as we will see, would be the Butterfly Trick and the Magic Fountain.

These images by Hokusai included pictures of feats of juggling, balancing, top-spinning, as well as conjuring, culminating in a representation of Japanese magic that included what the Japanese called *daikagura*, which is an eclectic performance tradition associated with *Shintō* rituals of protection. Indeed, to some extent, *daikagura* originated as a feat of juggling or balancing performed as a religious or magical rite. Some of the feats associated with *daikagura* were also features of *daidōgei* (street performance).[16] In other words, Japanese magic begins to emerge in this period as a mixture of different dexterities and delicate skills, including various conjuring tricks and feats of endurance, enwrapped in a mysteriously symbolic world of meaning. As Claflin describes it, Japanese magic was clearly different from Indian magic but may have shared some things in common with theatrical Chinese magic. However, it differentiated itself by a strong emphasis on 'symbolic gestures' within the theatrical mode. Japanese magic seemed to *mean* something.

> The magical effects of the Japanese seem to have required a calm, contemplative style analogous to that of the ancient tea ceremony, in which each gesture and motion was given considerable attention.[17]

As it happens, Japan was fully aware that its image in the West was somewhat confused, after centuries of relative isolation. Hence, during the second half of the nineteenth century it engaged in a concerted effort to (re)build its national identity through cultural exchange. Aside from the formal delegations, state-sanctioned troupes of performers left Japan in the 1860s. Perhaps the most famous of these were the Imperial Japanese Troupe, which set off east to the United States, and the Japanese Troupe, which travelled west to Europe in 1867, followed

same kind of search for a mythical secret technique. It is interesting to reflect on why this seems less likely than investigation of the Indian Rope Trick.

[16] The definitive guide to *daikagura* and *daidōgei* is probably the encyclopaedia, Miyao Yoshio, *Zusetsu edo daidōgei jiten*. Tokyo: Kashiwashobō, 2008.

[17] Claflin & Sheridan, *Street Magic*, p. 38.

by the Royal Tycoon Troupe, which headed into Asian and Oceania.[18] These troupes performed a range of acts, incorporating tumbling, acrobatics, balancing, juggling, and conjuring. In self-conscious moves to demonstrate the rapidly developing technological modernity of Japan, they also brought automata with them to the various Expos and World's Fairs.[19] These mechanical wonders demonstrated exquisite workmanship and intricate gearing to rival those of Robert-Houdin and others, for whom, as we have already seen, the automaton was one of the great symbols of magic's technological modernity.

Nonetheless, despite Japanese accomplishments with these mechanical wonders, it was not primarily their automata that caught the attention of Western magicians or audiences. In fact, by far the most resonant magical feat was the so-called Butterfly Trick, which was first performed in Europe by Asakichi (Yanagawa Chojurō) of the Japanese Troupe on 11 February 1867 at St. Martin's Hall in London.[20] At approximately the same time, Sumidagawa Namigoro of the Imperial Japanese Troupe performed this trick for the first time in the United States, in San Francisco on 8 January.[21] In fact, Sumidagawa also performed the Butterfly Trick months later, alongside no fewer than fifteen automata, at the Exposition Universelle in Paris in 1867; it was the Butterfly Trick and the other feats of acrobatics, balancing and juggling that stole the show.[22]

---

[18] The story of the Imperial Japanese Troupe is recounted in great detail by Frederik Schodt, *Professor Risley and the Imperial Japanese Troupe*. Berkeley: Stone Bridge Press, 2012.

[19] Both the Japanese Troupe and the Imperial Japanese Troupe appeared at the 1867 *Exposition Universelle* in Paris. In fact, Japan had a long history of automata, reaching back at least as far as the *karakuri* puppets of the seventeenth century, which inspired many developments in the Japanese puppet theatre. The term *karakuri* refers to the idea that the puppet generates a sense of enchantment or awe through secret mechanisms that cannot be seen. The classic, early picture book about *karakuri* by Tagaya Kanchūsen (who also published a famous magic manual in the Kyoho era) *(Jūchin otogi) karakuri kinmō kagami gusa* (1730), was republished at the start of the twentieth century, Tokyo: 1929. Japanese fascination with automata is often linked with a cultural affinity for robotics in the contemporary period, which has helped to make Japan the world's leader in this field.

[20] There is some evidence to suggest that a version of the Butterfly Trick was developed by Johann Hofzinser (1806–1875) in Vienna as early as 1860.

[21] The performer was Sumidagawa Namigoro.

[22] Matsuyama notes that accounts of the automata did not even make it into the press coverage of the event, despite (or perhaps because of) the closeness of fit between this type of modern, technological magic and the form of magic in Europe at that time, following the mechanical predilections of Robert-Houdin and John Nevil Maskelyne, who were both watchmakers. Mitsunobu Matsuyama, 'An Investigation into Magic

Scene seven: magic or manipulation?

In Japan the conjurer sits on the floor while he is performing this trick, but as the position would be rather inconvenient for an English magician, I will explain how the trick can be performed with equal effect when one is standing.

The performer should stand behind a small table without any covering. On the table are placed a small china bowl and a bunch of flowers, or, still better, a branch of blossom, and two folding fans. The performer, addressing the audience says – 'Ladies and gentlemen, perhaps of all the creatures of the insect world there are none so beautiful as butterflies. To see them flying about from flower to flower is a charming spectacle. Unfortunately, we cannot always have them with us, but I will endeavour to create a pair of these delightful creatures for your entertainment this evening.

'I have here a piece of tissue paper which I tear into shape and twist into the form of a butterfly. It quickly comes to life and flies and dances about in the sun – or rather the lamp light.'

The performer now fans the butterfly so that it flies about naturally.... Afterwards, the performer takes up the other fan, opens it in his left hand, saying – 'See, the butterfly is attracted by the flowers painted upon the fan, being imitation itself it fancies that the flowers are real. Its wings grow weary, it stops to rest upon the fan. In Japan the butterfly is the emblem of conjugal bliss. We will procure for him a wife, who shall be the darling of his life.'

Catching the butterfly in his right he places it upon the back of his right hand ... He now proceeds to tear a piece of tissue paper and make another butterfly.... Beginning to fan them gently, he continues –

'Ah, we have now a happy pair! How they dance and frolic. Let us hasten to give them some honey. Here, my darlings, come and enjoy the sweets I have provided for you.' Here the conjurer takes up the flowers, the butterflies approach and hover about them, now resting upon a flower, now flying above it in a most natural manner.... He puts down the flowers, and taking up the bowl – 'You must be thirsty, but alas I have not heaven sent dew to offer you, but come here is water, drink.' The butterflies hover about the bowl, now one then the other entering it. At last they both do so, and, although the performer continues to fan, they refuse to come out again.

in Japan after the Opening of the Country: The Butterfly Trick.' *Gibeciere*, 1:2 (Summer 2006), pp. 49–50.

'Hullo! How is this? I hope they are not drowned.' He peers into the bowl. 'Ha, ha! No, they are both asleep, lazy dears.'[23]

The Butterfly Trick

Just as we saw with the Linking Rings and the Goldfish Bowl Trick, the Butterfly Trick was immediately copied by Western magicians. Although better known for his Indian magic at the Egyptian Hall, Colonel Stodare performed the Butterfly Trick within a month of Asakichi's first performance in London, and Lizzie Anderson (daughter of the Great Wizard of the North, John Henry Anderson, 1814–1874) performed it a few months after that.[24] Records also suggest that the remarkable Dr Lynn (Hugh Simmons), who claimed to have learned the trick from a 'native juggler' in Nagasaki, performed this trick at the Egyptian Hall in London in 1873.[25]

Unlike the Goldfish Bowl Trick, which inspired all kinds of pontification and innovation in order to work out new ways to perform it, especially for those magicians who wanted to perform it in a manner

[23] This account is from Ishii Black, 'Japanese Magic: Simple Explanations of the Conjuring Tricks of Japanese Magicians'. *The Magician Monthly*, 11:X (October 1914), pp. 167–168.

[24] Much of the biographical information we have about Lizzie is recorded in Edwin Dawes & Michael Dawes, *John Henry Anderson: The Great Wizard of the North & His Magical Family*. New York: Conjuring Arts Research Centre, 2014. By far the best study of Stodare, Joseph Stoddart (1831–1866), is Edwin Dawes, *Stodare: The Enigma Variations*. Washington: Kaufman & Co., 1998. Clarke suggests that Lizzie was performing the Butterfly Trick as early as 1865, but provides no evidence for this, and it seems unlikely, given that this would be two years before the arrival of the Japanese Troupe. Sidney Clarke, *The Annals of Conjuring*. Seattle: Miracle Factory, 2001, p. 221.

[25] Lynn reveals that he was taken ill in Nagasaki and so 'held a reception every morning in my room, at which native jugglers came and taught me many interesting tricks, amongst others the top-spinning on a single thread, and the butterfly trick'. H.S. Lynn, *The Adventures of a Strange Man, with a Supplement Showing 'How It's Done.'* London: Egyptian Hall, 1873, p. 11. In his influential work on magic in the Meiji period, *Meiji kijutsushi* (Tokyo, 1952), Hata Toyokichi suggests that Lynn must have learned this trick from the famous Itchosai Yanagawa (to whom we will return later). Itchosai was certainly the most famous magician of this period in Japan, and certainly performed the Butterfly Trick, but this seems very unlikely. Given how unreliable Lynn's travelogue is in other ways, it seems plausible that he would have claimed to have met Itchosai and to have learned from this master, even if he had not; since he makes no mention of Itchosai at all, it's safe to assume that he had probably never even heard of the great magician. Matsuyama is similarly sceptical, 'The Butterfly Trick', p. 26.

consistent with a modern identity, the attraction of the Butterfly Trick was not the *feat* but the *effect*. It immediately became synonymous with the possibility of beautiful and even poetic magic, what Theodore Bamberg (aka Okito, 1875–1963) would later call 'romantic magic' that appeals to the senses.[26] In this way, it seemed to be expressive of the nature of Japanese (and, to some extent, Chinese) magic, 'which had a poetic beauty unlike the style of the East Indian magicians'[27] or the Western magicians.

The Butterflies were so intimately associated with Japan that for some commentators this trick seems to have been one of the ways to differentiate between Chinese and Japanese magic, even when they themselves were not quite sure what the actual difference was between China and Japan. Edwin Sachs (1850–1910), for instance, provides one of the earliest written explanations of the Butterfly Trick in English in his classic work on legerdemain in 1877; he includes it in a chapter on 'Chinese Tricks' but sees no contradiction when he calls it the 'celebrated and fascinating *Japanese* butterfly trick', as though Japanese were a subset of Chinese.[28] Indeed, the idea that Japan was an especially cultivated and refined (and hitherto hidden) part of China was not

[26] Theodore Bamberg, *Okito on Magic: Reminiscences and Selected Tricks*. Chicago: Edward O Drane & Co., 1952, p. 31.

[27] Claflin & Sheridan, *Street Magic*, p. 35.

[28] Edwin Sachs, *Sleight of Hand: Being Minute Instructions by the Aid of Which, with Proper Practice, the Neatest and Most Intricate Tricks of Legerdemain Can Be Successfully Performed*. London: The Bazaar, 1877, p. 45 (emphasis added). The description in this first edition is unchanged in the second edition of 1885, which is otherwise much expanded and is now the standard text. Curiously, his explanation of the trick (which is entirely consistent with the method traditionally used in Japan) ends with some thoughts about how similar are the methods of legerdemain developed in the West and in *China*, which he suggests is evidence that these are the best possible methods, since it would be very unlikely that two different civilizations would develop the same techniques independently if they were not the optimal techniques. He also dismisses the possibility that China learned the techniques from the West or vice versa, concluding that 'it is only during the present century that we have been sufficiently familiar with the Chinese to borrow their ideas on magic, did we wish to do so' (pp. 46–47). So, despite having just discussed the Japanese Butterfly Trick, he ends with this note about Chinese magic as though it subsumes Japanese magic. While that argument is retained into the expanded and revised second addition, the rather chauvinistic last lines on p. 47 are not: 'Although we certainly own many pretty modern tricks to the Pigtails, tricks of Oriental origin are not so numerous as one would imagine from reading the catalogue of a "Conjuring Repository." Everything is a "Chinese puzzle," "Arabian mystery," or an "Indian feat," when it is to be sold.'

uncommon at the time. Nonetheless, the delicate beauty of the butter-flies was certainly seen as Japanese.

In fact, the 'trick' of the Butterfly Trick is very simple. Sachs was not the first to explain it; it even appears in Hoffmann's *Modern Magic* in 1876.[29] It seems that magicians had hoped for a clever device or mechanical gimmick that would make the butterflies fly so beautifully, but in the end there were two simple 'secrets'. The first involved the use of a thin piece of silk thread (or human hair) to control the absolute range of movement of the butterflies (i.e., to prevent them from simply flying off). As for the second, in Hoffmann's concise words, 'the remainder of the trick is a matter of practice'.[30] While Hoffmann attempts to encourage his readers to try the trick by explaining that it's easier than they might think, he also confesses that the 'spectator naturally concludes that an extra-ordinary degree of dexterity must be necessary to enable the performer to keep them from diverging more widely'.[31] In his account, Sachs explains frankly that 'there is more skill required to perform this trick really neatly than is generally supposed', and he freely admits that 'when this trick was first brought out, "all the world wondered", for no one, even after long practice, could keep the paper butterfly hovering in a given space for a single moment'. But in the end, the 'secret' really does reside in commit-ment and practice:

> After a time, practice will enable the performer to cause the but-terfly to settle on a flower or on the edge of another fan, and also to sustain two in the air at one time, which has a very pretty effect indeed.[32]

As we saw in part one of this book, to varying extents, all magic relies upon dexterity and practice. The field of magic known as legerdemain (or

---

[29] Professor Hoffmann, *Modern Magic: A Practical Treatise on the Art of Conjuring.* 1876, U.S. edition reprinted Philadelphia: David McKay, 1910, pp. 397–398.

[30] Hoffmann, *Modern Magic*, p. 398. Hoffmann adds that 'it is less difficult than would be imagined by any one who has never attempted it'.

[31] Hoffmann, *Modern Magic*, p. 398. Hoffmann is talking about a version of the trick in which two butterflies fly around together, always remaining within a small distance of each other (because they're secretly connected by the thread), hence the performer appears to be not only keeping the butterflies flying but also keeping them swirling around each other. Other versions of this trick involve different numbers of butter-flies; the method explained by Sachs, for instance, which makes use of the thread in a different way, focuses on a solitary butterfly.

[32] Sachs, *Sleight of Hand*, pp. 46, 45, 46.

sleight of hand) is perhaps the most intense in this respect, while mechanical or 'self-working' tricks might be the least intense.[33] However, almost without exception, the emphasis in modern magic is on the perfection of technique so that it can be performed *without it being seen.* In the immortal words of the late Dai Vernon: *be natural!* Magicians practice passes, palms, forces, false-shuffles, and bottom-deals until they can be performed without an audience noticing. Indeed, as we have seen, the modern magician goes to great pains to represent the normality of a situation and his movements, precisely so that the apparently impossible feat seems genuinely impossible. Robert-Houdin's dinner jacket and the salon performances of Hofsinzer were all designed to establish this mundane foundation for modern magic. When an audience notices the skills being performed, the performance is no longer magical: the impossible becomes the improbable or the merely difficult. At worst, this simply represents a performative failure; at best, it's a successful performance of something other than magic – perhaps manipulation, juggling, or cardistry. It might provoke an audience's admiration at the skill demonstrated, but it will not generally provoke a sense of enchantment.

In this context, the Butterfly Trick represents something of an aberration in modern magic. Indeed, *prima facie*, it does not seem to be magic at all. While it seems to fit into the category of magic that Robert-Houdin called 'feats of dexterity', which meant tricks 'requiring much study and persistent practice', it seems to contradict the spirit of his tenth and twelfth 'general principles', which require modern magicians not to draw unnecessary attention to their techniques. Indeed, Robert-Houdin is clear that performing one's techniques in a manner that renders them undetectable requires 'a very much higher degree of dexterity'.[34]

---

[33] The title of the first edition of Sach's seminal work on legerdemain clearly draws attention to the importance of practice. But if this were not enough, his introduction spells it out. He declares that he intends to provide instruction, but that success will depend upon 'a due degree of attention [being] given and a reasonable amount of practice undertaken. Practice, indeed, is what is required in order to achieve success ... without it the best of instruction is given in vain. For this reason, I must exhort such of my readers as may seek to amuse their friends through the medium of what I shall impart to them to devote as much time as they can spare to practice.' Sachs, *Sleight of Hand*, p. 4.

[34] Jean Eugene Robert-Houdin, *Secrets of Conjuring and Magic*. Reprinted Cambridge: Cambridge University Press, 2011, pp. 30, 34, 35.

Yet, audiences during the Golden Age (as well as before and since) were enchanted by the Butterfly Trick, when it was performed well. It was universally presented and perceived as magical. So confident in its effect was Sachs, for instance, that he seems to advocate a direct breach of Robert-Houdin's tenth principle for this particular feat, despite pronouncing himself an admiring follower of the Father of Modern Magic:

> While cutting out and twisting up the paper, it is as well to call attention to the fact that the trick is performed by some people with the aid of a thread – an assistance which you will say you utterly despise, as will be perceived. This will totally disarm those people who may have bought the trick (it is sold universally), and are yet only tyros at performing it.[35]

In other words, for Sachs and others like him, the magic of the Butterfly Trick resided in the fact that it was (relatively speaking) an honest feat of skill and dexterity. It broke some of the conventions of modern magic, and it could be enhanced by breaking others (such as by exposing the possibility that something similar could be accomplished by deceptive means and thus awakening audiences to the possibility of deception). But it was magic because the *effect* was magical, whether or not the *feat* involved deception.

During the Golden Age of Magic, the Butterfly Trick came to emblemize Japanese magic precisely because it seemed to combine various kinds of performance skills in an atmosphere of mystery and beauty. The delicacy of the tissue-paper butterflies, the paper fans, and the apparently natural flight of these graceful creatures manifested

---

[35] Sachs, *Sleight of Hand*, pp. 3–4, 45.
  Robert-Houdin's tenth principle reads as follows:

> Many conjurors make a practice, in the course of their performances, of indicating such and such expedients of the art, and of boasting that they themselves do not employ the method in question.... It follows, as a natural result, that the spectator, being thus made acquainted with artifices of which he would otherwise have known nothing, is put on his guard and is no longer open to deception.

Robert-Houdin, *Secrets of Conjuring and Magic*, p. 34.

Figure 6.1 Okito, 'The Floating Ball – Panel', c. 1920. Courtesy of Nielsen Magic Collection. After learning the floating ball from David Abbot in 1913, Okito's remarkable routine became the standard version after 1920.

Orientalist fantasies of Japan as a land of daintiness, animism, and poetry, just as *Madame Butterfly* sought to capture this fantasy in opera.[36] In other words, the magical effect of the Butterfly Trick relies upon the conceits of mystical Orientalism, but also demonstrates the potentials of Orientalism to affect enchantment. Indeed, unlike the Goldfish Bowl Trick and various other feats of Oriental magic, the magic of the Butterfly Trick appears to have been almost entirely aesthetic, meaning that even if it was performed in the modern attire of a Western magician it still communicated something that seemed like *Japanese* magic to its audience. While Chinese magic came to be seen as a flamboyant visual style, Japanese magic came to be felt as a delicate quality of sensation.

Meanwhile, the Butterfly Trick also brings into focus the nuanced relationship between disciplined practice, performance, and the accomplishment of the magical. As we saw in the case of Indian magic and its appropriation as a form of existential commitment by some Western magicians, especially as a kind of post-modern movement, there is a place in the imagination of Oriental magic for the attainment of *magical being* through personal cultivation. While the Butterfly Trick does not go that far (since there is no pretence that arduous training or ascetic practice will enable the magician genuinely to transform the tissue-paper into animated, living butterflies), it does draw a link between iterated, routinized perfection and the achievement of a kind of magic that is not deception but is rather pure sensation. In many ways, then, far from being an aberration, the Butterfly Trick was at the forefront of modern magic in this period, precisely because it relied almost entirely upon the magician to enchant his audience with honest skill.

Rendering this approach to practice into a form of training and cultivation represents a transformation of the criticisms levelled at Oriental magicians by modern magicians in this period, who (as we saw in Chapter 3) typically argued that Oriental magicians showed little invention or creativity and instead simply spent their time repeating the same limited repertoire of tricks as their fathers and grandfathers. For the modernist magician, this criticism was tantamount to revealing that

---

[36] Puccini's famous opera, which premiered in 1904, was based on the 1898 short story of the same name by the American writer John Luther Long (1861–1927), whose sister has spent time in Japan as the wife of a missionary.

Oriental magicians do not participate in *progress*, which meant they were outside modern magic itself. However, the Butterfly Trick enabled a re-evaluation of repetition and training from the standpoint of artistic and even spiritual accomplishment: if the magic emerges from the poetry of a performance rather than from a successful deception, then the imperative for the magician is to ensure beautiful performances rather than to invent new deceptions for every performance. This conception of Japanese magic as a form of *practice* (in an almost spiritual sense) was supported by the idea of its ancient and mysterious history as well as by emerging ideas about the master-disciple relationship (*shitei seido*) in the Japanese arts as a whole.[37]

Nonetheless, during the Golden Age, the idea that Japanese magic communicated a methodological innovation (i.e., it was an approach to magic that emphasized seriousness of training and heritage) found less

---

[37] It would not be until the post-war period that this kind of iterated (and finally sublimated) practice would become associated with a more general 'Zen' aesthetic (largely thanks to the work of cultural ambassadors like D.T. Suzuki, 1870–1966) and tied to the popular imagination of Japan. As recently as 2015, a circular from the Conjuring Arts Research Centre in New York claims that some top card experts recommend Eugen Herrigel's *Zen in the Art of Archery* as 'a way of learning how to practice your sleight of hand effectively.... "The man, the art, the work – it is all one"' (email, 5 August 2015). In fact, the Butterfly Trick has a genuinely historical pedigree in Japan, reputedly having been performed at the imperial court for centuries. The method appears in many of the oldest extant magic manuals. I have been able to verify it in the *Zoku zange bukuro* (1727), the *Hōkasen* (1764), and the *Tezuma hayakeiko* (1862). Although street performers have always learned and performed magic on their own initiative in Japan, it is also true that, like many other arts in Japan, *tezuma* (magic accomplished by dexterity – legerdemain) has been passed down through generations of masters and disciples. Perhaps the most famous of these in the early-modern period was the Yanagawa family line of magicians, one of whom (under the *nom de théâtre* Asakichi) was the first Japanese magician to perform the Butterfly Trick in Europe. The first generation of this family, and the first to take the name Yanagawa Itchosai, is commonly credited with having elevated the Butterfly Trick to its modern level of artistry, and of starting the magical dynasty that would perpetuate this (although, as we've seen, rumours that he also taught it to Dr Lynn are probably exaggerated!). The first Itchosai was widely celebrated in Japan, was enlisted to entertain the shōgun, dignitaries, and foreign guests in the 1860s (before his death in 1870), and received the honorary title of *bungo daijo* (in 1847), marking his importance to the national culture. There followed at least three, perhaps more, generations of Yanagawa Itchosai, each of whom performed the Butterfly Trick, and a stylized butterfly became the family crest. The story of this dynasty is incredibly intricate and complicated, and I will not attempt to narrate it here; much of the detective work has been done by the meticulous Matsuyama Mitsunobu in his excellent, *Jisshō Nihon no tejinashi*. Tokyo: Tōkyōdōshuppan, 2010, chapter 3.

resonance than the simpler idea that it exhibited a delicate, beautiful, and poetic sensibility. Hence, some feats performed by the Japanese troupes of the period with the same ethos, such as knife throwing and using a sword to slice an apple that was balanced on someone's neck, did not catch on in the same way.[38] In this period, Japanese magic, like Japan more generally, was supposed to be effeminate, naturalistic, and beautiful not masculine, dangerous, violent, or threatening.

The Magic Fountain

In addition to the Butterfly Trick, a second classic of Japanese magic enchanted Western audiences during the Golden Age. It emerged on the Western stage slightly later than the Butterflies and was very closely associated with the breakthrough act of Shōkyokusai Ten'ichi (1852–1912) – the 'Japanese Father of Modern Magic'.[39] The so-called

---

[38] There is a long tradition of knife throwing in Japan (as elsewhere), in which knives are actually thrown with great precision around a person who is standing against a board. Such a feat requires great skill and commitment (and trust). One of the intriguing features of this was the way that vaudeville performers transformed this feat into an effect by using a gimmicked board from which knives would spring into place, creating the illusion they had been thrown. The sword-cutting feat is also traditional in Japan, associated with Shintō ritual. Like knife throwing, it is basically a test of skill and faith. The idea is that a swordsman will cut down at an apple balanced on the back of someone's neck, and will cut cleanly through the apple but leave the neck untouched. Rather than using a gimmicked apple, the sword genuinely cuts it. To the extent that there is a trick involved, there is a small iron bar (small enough to be imperceptible) placed under the apple, which would obstruct a blade that pushed too far. However, the assumption is that the swordsman's strike would always at least slice perfectly through the apple in line with the narrow bar. For understandable reasons, this 'trick' did not catch on, despite its consistency with Japan's attempts to represent itself as a warrior nation of 'samurai' at the turn of the twentieth century, including with publications (in English) such as Inoue Nitobe, Bushidō, the Soul of Japan (1900). In fact, the modern period has seen an ongoing tension in Japan about its self-identity, polarized between representations of the stoic, honourable samurai and representations of elegiac romantic courtly life of the Heian period. See Chris Goto-Jones, Modern Japan: A Very Short Introduction. Oxford: Oxford University Press, 2009, especially pp. 110–116.

[39] Of the numerous biographies of Ten'ichi, one of the most recent and entertaining is Fujiyama Shintarō, Ten'ichi ichidai, meiji no sūpāmajishan. Tokyo: NTT shuppan, 2012. Fujiyama is himself an accomplished magician (and director of the Japan Professional Magicians Association) – he is particularly renowned for his performance of traditional Japanese magic (wazuma) and for his work in protecting it as national heritage. Fujiyama maintains the master-disciple system (shitei seido) of the traditional arts. He has also helped to appropriate the more general term tezuma

Enchanted or Magic Fountain captured the public imagination for many of the same reasons as the Butterfly Trick – it seemed to express something elegant, beautiful, and poetic that could clearly be associated with the idea of Japan as a 'garden of fantasy'.

In fact, Ten'ichi is perhaps best known today as the originator of the Thumb Tie Trick (in which the magician's arms are wrapped around a pillar with his thumbs tied together, but then the magician is able simply to walk free of the pillar even though his thumbs appear to remain tied). Indeed, this trick is still often referred to as the Ten'ichi Thumb Tie – in the early years of the twentieth century, the method and apparatus was sold under this name.[40] Nonetheless, despite its strong association with Ten'ichi, who certainly elevated the performance of this trick to new heights sufficient to claim it as his own, it is reasonably clear that the Thumb Tie was not invented by Ten'ichi and was not even of Japanese origin. It does not appear in the Japanese literature until the Meiji period, when it seems likely that the method arrived from Europe.[41]

The press coverage of Ten'ichi's tour of the United States and Europe focussed almost exclusively on two of the troupe's tricks.

(legerdemain) as a label for traditional Japanese magic (*wazuma*), sometimes referring to it as *Edo tezuma*, thus affecting a shift in the convention of contrasting Japanese magic with magic in general and giving the idea of *tezuma* a more romantic force.

[40] For example, *Mahatma*, IX:VI (December 1905) was only one of many journals in that period to advertise:

> Ten Ichi Thumb Tie – Absolutely the correct method – just as performed by Ten Ichi himself. Performer's two thumbs are tied together, with two special strings (can be thoroughly examined) by a committee selected from the audience. A solid hoop is thrown toward him quickly. If desired, the knots can be sealed as an assurance that the performer does not tamper with them after they are once tied. Many surprising experiments can be done while the thumbs are still tightly tied together. Can be examined at any stage of the trick. No risk. Will create more talk than the rope tie or handcuff release. Sure and simple. With a pair of strings and full instructions, post free, only $1.00.

In fact, in the entire run of Mahatma, the term 'thumb tie' never appears without being associated with Ten'ichi.

[41] Versions of the thumb tie appear at least as early as the 1700s in Europe, including in Henri Decremps, *Supplément à la magie blanche dévoilée* (Paris, 1785).

During his stay at the Alhambra in London in 1904, for instance, the *Mahatma* describes the show concisely: 'Ten Ichi is introduced and performs the Thumb Tie. The act concludes with the magic fountain.'[42] Yet the centrepiece of Ten'ichi's act was certainly the fountain:

> Ten-ichi, a Japanese conjurer, gave a clever exhibition at Chase's Theatre, Washington, DC, a few weeks ago. His specialty consisted in producing jets of water from sword blades, fans, from burning torches, and from the heads of his assistants.[43]

Indeed, the Evansonia columnist of the *Mahatma* suggests that the novelty and value of Ten'ichi's show is almost entirely limited to this one effect; he calls it a 'unique specialty act'. Because of this, he argues that 'Ten'ichi's show cannot compare with that of Ching Ling Foo – he of the mighty porcelain water bowl'.[44] While this author's tone is generally sceptical about the relative accomplishments of what he calls 'these bizarre people the Oriental conjurers', he is appreciative of the astonishment they cause with 'pretty, graceful and fantastic conceits' such as the '"bowls of water," the "Chinese rings," ... "the butterflies"'. And, just as we saw in the debates about the Goldfish Bowl Trick in Chapter 5, the author laments the unmodern measures that seemed to be required: 'the Oriental costume is conducive to tricks of this character'. He suspects that Ten'ichi's robes hide pipes that run water to the various props.

One of the great ironies of this suspicion is that Ten'ichi chose to perform in elaborate Japanese costume in the West precisely because he thought this would satisfy the fantasies of the local audiences there. Indeed, Ten'ichi might be the first instance of an Asian magician who

---

[42] *Mahatma*, VIII:III (September 1904). A few months later a similar description is provided of Ten'ichi's performance in Pittsburgh: 'The Ten Ichi troupe of Japanese magicians played here week of Nov. 28th, at the Grand Opera House. They introduced their famous Ten Ichi Thumb Tie trick and the water illusion.' VIII:VI (December 1904). And then in Cleveland: 'The Ten Ichi Troupe of Japanese magicians were at the Keith Theatre week of November 28. Their principal hits were the Thumb Tie and the Water illusion.' VIII:VII (January 1905).

[43] 'Evansonia'. *Mahatma* V:VII (January 1902).

[44] It is interesting, not incidental, to observe that Evansonia correctly identifies Ching Ling Foo (rather than Chung Ling Soo) as the appropriate comparison.

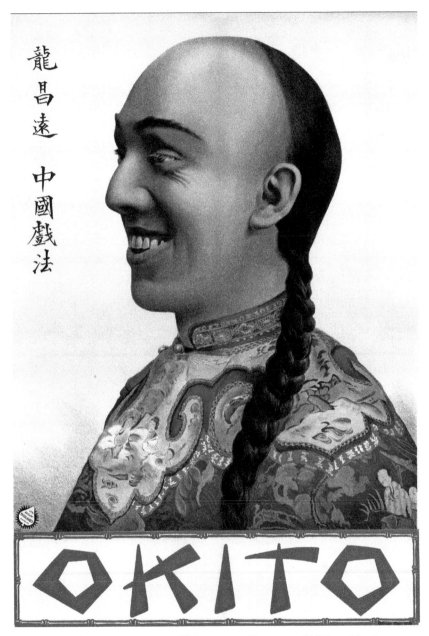

龍昌遠 中國戲法

OKITO

Figure 6.2 Okito, 'Portrait in Profile', c. 1925. Courtesy of Nielsen Magic Collection. To a contemporary audience, this portrait doesn't look very Japanese, but in the 1920s its imagery was effective.

made this aesthetic choice as a type of strategy. Although not the intention of Evansonia, this is where the comparison with Ching Ling

Foo is most interesting: while the Chinese magician performed Chinese-style magic in both the West and China (where he based his show in Chinese opera), Ten'ichi performed in the guise of a Japanese magician in the West and in the guise of a modern, Western magician in Japan. Indeed, part of the reason that he is considered the Father of Modern Magic in Japan is because he was one of the first Japanese magicians to perform in the modern manner of Robert-Houdin – in dinner-jacket and top hat. Aside from providing a clear demonstration of the powers of enchantment of Orientalism in the West and Occidentalism in Asia, the versatility of Ten'ichi in this respect marks the accomplishment of a form of *overcoming* these cultural tendencies by reducing them to devices or tools for use in his performance. There is a very real sense in which Ten'ichi's Orientalist performances in the West were as much pretence as his Occidentalist performances in Japan – both were guises or personas created and inhabited to maximize the magical potentials of his act in the context of specific audiences.

While numerous Western magicians, most notably William Robinson / Chung Ling Soo, played with the cultural and ethnic politics of magic in their own countries (attempting to enchant their performances by Orientalizing their shows), Ten'ichi was one of the first to play with this so strategically both inside and outside his home, and was probably one of the first 'Oriental magicians' to deliberately exploit the prejudices of the metropolitan centres in the West.[45]

This is a fascinating moment in cultural politics, since Ten'ichi was correct to feel that a Japanese magician performing in the West at this time would not only be more acceptable and popular if he did so in a traditional, Orientalist guise, but also that it might even be *unacceptable* to Western audiences to see a Japanese magician dressed in the attire of a 'modern' magician, as advocated by Robert-Houdin.[46]

---

[45] Of course, it is conceivable that other Asian magicians who performed in Oriental guise in the West were also participating in a similar form of self-Orientalist strategy for commercial reasons, but the case of Ten'ichi is particularly clear because of the contrast with how he performed in Japan.

[46] By the 1920s, some Japanese magicians were beginning to experiment with performing in Western dress in the West. Perhaps the most famous of these was Asahi Tomo, who performed with the 'Great Asahi Troupe' in the United States. Like Ten'ichi, his signature effects included the Thumb Tie and the Magic Fountain (which he called the 'Human Fountain'). He performed some of his shows in an innovative 'hybrid' dress style, which combined a dinner jacket and bow tie with black pantaloon-style trousers that ended at the knee, together with black slippers, giving the impression of a Western-Eastern fusion.

Perhaps, just as Robert-Houdin had opined that a European audience would feel affronted if a European magician pretended to be an 'Oriental magician', so that same audience would be affronted if a Japanese magician pretended to be a 'modern magician', thus exposing the racialist conceit behind this category and the everyday conflation of 'modern' and 'Western'?

Meanwhile, in Japan, debates about how to overcome the conflation of the modern with the Western had already started, and the Japanese were already talking about 'modernity' as a technical category that could be detached from its Western form and pursued authentically by Japan. Hence, Ten'ichi and others were increasingly able to perform in the guise of 'modern magicians' in Japan without (only) giving the impression that they were utilizing the enchantment of Occidentalism to enhance their magic – rather, Ten'ichi inhabited the process of becoming both Japanese and modern as a unified persona. Japanese audiences not only accepted this without being affronted by any apparent incongruity, but actually celebrated it as emblematic of Japan's own rapidly developing, authentic modernity.[47] In fact, contrary to Evansonia's lament, Ten'ichi did not require long flowing, silken robes to perform the Magic Fountain – he could perform it admirably in a dinner jacket (or sometimes in military uniform) in Tokyo. Ten'ichi seems to have inhabited a magical modernity of his own.

Even before he first ventured to the West, Ten'ichi was amazing audiences in Japan:

> The finest magic of all that [was] seen yesterday was Ten-ichi Shokyokusai's Water Fountain. Dressed in [W]estern style, wearing beautiful black suits, Ten-ichi appeared, put a cup onto a two-tiered table, poured water into it and then set a saber on a sword rack positioned to one side. He began an incantation. Suddenly, a stream of water blew out of the cup, reaching as high as twelve feet. He then gestured to send some of the water to the saber, upon which

---

47 The early twentieth century witnessed lively debates in Japan about the idea of overcoming modernity or of forging a modernity of one's own. Perhaps the most famous of these was the *kindai no chōkoku* symposium of 1942. The coherence of the thesis that modernity could be overcome has been challenged, notably by Harry Harootunian, *Overcome by Modernity: History, Culture, and Community in Interwar Japan.* Princeton: Princeton University Press, 2002. It is at least debatable whether these ideas provided some of the intellectual and culture energy for Japanese imperialism and ultimately its war against USA and Britain.

another stream spouted up from its blade. The effect of making
water travel back and forth between the cup and the saber was
repeated for a time. Then Tenhide and Koten came in holding small
flaming paddles. Ten-ichi again used his fan to send a little water,
causing it to spout from within the flames on the paddles. He
further sent it to the crown of his nearby assistant, upon which
water shot up from his head; and once Ten-ichi opened his fan,
another water jet appeared unexpectedly on its paper edge as well.
He concluded these truly extraordinary scenes of stage, and
received a thunderous ovation.[48]

The Magic Fountain has been performed in Japan for centuries. Its early
history actually appears in the context of the development of automata
rather than magic. The eighteenth-century doctor Tagaya Kanchūsen
included a number of mechanisms in his classic works that depict ways
to secretly transport pressurized water in order to make it appear in
surprising places, such as from the wick of a candle (which is illustrated
in the *Morokoshi hiji no umi*, 1733).[49] It is noteworthy that the classic
manuals of magic from that period make no mention of these mechanical feats, so presumably they were seen as curiosities rather than magic
per se. It seems that Ten'ichi's incorporation of the Magic Fountain into
his magic show was itself a modern innovation, but his greatest innovation was to make use of rubber tubing (of the kind used in Western
medical instruments such as stethoscopes) instead of a combination
of bamboo, wire, and oiled-paper. The result was a genuinely modern
mechanism that could transmit water under much greater pressures,
over longer distances (without leaking), and without requiring
such elaborate staging to hide the pipes. Indeed, far from relying on
the flowing 'Oriental' robes about which Evansonia complained,
Ten'ichi's Magic Fountain was innovative precisely because its use of
modern technology removed the need for any traditional staging or
costuming. His choice to present the feat in that traditional way in the
West was, in many ways, a choice to obfuscate the modernity of

[48] *Fukuoka niche-nichi shimbun*, 27 April 1890. Cited and translated in Mitsunobu
Matsuyama, 'An Investigation into Magic in Japan after the Opening of the Country:
Ten-ichi Shokyokusai, the Japanese Father of Modern Magic'. *Gibeciere*, 5:1 (Winter
2010), p. 95.

[49] Tagaya's major work from this period was *(Jūchin otogi) karakuri kinmō kagamigusa*
(1730), which was reprinted in the context of the modern interest in these effects by
Beisando in Tokyo, 1929.

Japanese magic and thus enable the perpetuation of the view that Japan was pretty and harmless.

The 'Japanese' magicians

In addition to Ten'ichi himself, various other magicians travelled from Japan to perform in Europe and the United States. Some of them sought to capitalize on Ten'ichi's name, such as the successful Ko Ten'ichi Troupe (of which there was more than one). But, just as there were many who imitated Chinese magicians like Ching Ling Foo, so there arose all kinds of 'Japanese' magicians. One of them, Ten-i-chi, who performed a very similar act to Ten'ichi (including the Thumb Tie and Magic Fountain), turned out to be Dutch rather than Japanese, and also claimed that his name was inspired from Chinese.[50]

In fact, the confusion of Chinese and Japanese into a generic Oriental burlesque continued into the twentieth century. Perhaps the most explicit in this regard was Okito (Theodore Bamberg), who was also Dutch. Bamberg made a deliberate choice to embrace what he called 'romantic magic' or 'the new magic, with its preponderant appeal to the senses', rather than the 'classical magic' of Robert-Houdin's 'drawing room entertainer'. Like William Robinson, Bamberg sought an act that could be performed in silence, although in Bamberg's case this was because he had become deaf in an accident. The device that he decided to employ was that 'I could pretend I was a foreigner who couldn't speak the language – such as a Japanese or a Chinese.' Either Chinese or Japanese would meet his requirements: romantic, new magic in the silence of the colonial periphery. In the end, Bamberg picked a Japanese persona – Okito – because he could find 'an authentic Japanese costume in Amsterdam', but his act contained very little magic from Japan (or China).[51] Eventually, Bamberg found it difficult to procure authentic Japanese costumes so he simply changed to Chinese costumes: 'for the next forty-five years I travelled throughout the world with a Chinese act – and a Japanese name'. Yet, Okito's act was Chinese (or Japanese)

---

[50] This was exposed by Geoffrey Buckingham, 'Magicana: Ten-i-chi'. *The Magic Circular* 59 (1964), pp. 65–66.

[51] Judging from the photographs of Okito, it seems that these 'authentic' kimonos were of the kind specially made for export in that period: much more elaborate and gaudy than would have been worn in Japan itself.

largely in the Orientalist sense that he dressed in silken robes (made especially for the Western market) and applied heavy make-up in a caricature of the visage of an East Asian; and his name was Japanese only in the sense that he had assembled it from the letters in the Dutch romanization of Tokyo (Tokio). In other words, it made little difference whether Okito was a Japanese or a Chinese magician: he was an Orientalized Dutch magician. Hence, when Okito's son became Fu Manchu, the world knew them as the Japanese/Chinese generations of the Dutch Bamberg Dynasty of Magicians.[52]

Unlike the Ching Ling Foo / Chung Ling Soo saga that we considered in the previous chapter, there was no great drama or rivalry between magicians from Japan and so-called 'Japanese' magicians in the West. Perhaps the closest was the colourful figure of the American Wellington King Tobias (1858–1910), who performed in the guise of Soto Sunetaro throughout the 1890s and the early 1900s. Like William Robinson, whose Chung Ling Soo act would not appear until Soto was already well established, Tobias performed in full 'Japanese' paraphernalia and, being unable to speak Japanese and unwilling to destroy the illusion of his Japaneseness, he performed in silence.[53] Like Robinson's Soo, Tobias's Soto was a super-Orientalized version of a Japanese magician, wearing a flamboyant silk kimono of a kind rarely seen in Japan (and probably specially made for the export market, as was common at that time); his show did not consist of feats of Japanese magic, but instead included an eclectic mixture of all kinds of 'Oriental wonders' (from India, China, and Egypt) and feats of modern magic, all unified by the aesthetic of the 'Japanese' performance. In short, it was a magic show clothed in made-for-export Japaneseness. And again, like Robinson, Tobias could have been easily exposed at a time in which there were either more Japanese people on the east coast of the United States or in which the voices of Japanese people could be equally heard. The importance of silence as a characteristic of Oriental magicians and (semi-) colonial subjects cannot be ignored.

---

[52] Bamberg, *Okito on Magic*, pp. 31–32.

[53] Matsuyama suggests the possibility that Robinson was inspired by Tobias's ruse (hence suggesting that it was known even in the 1890s that Tobias was perpetrating a ruse and was not really Japanese). Mitsunobu Matsuyama, 'An Investigation of Magic in Japan After the Opening of the Country: Unravelling the Ultimate Deception of Soto Sunetaro'. *Gibeciere*, 3:1 (Winter 2008), p. 21.

Nonetheless, 'Tobias's impersonation of a Japanese conjuror, Soto Sunetaro, was sustained for a longer time and more successfully than even Robinson's Soo would manage.... Almost everyone who remembers Sunetaro's name still believes him to be a Japanese magician.'[54] Part of the reason for his success in this regard, however, is probably because Soto was never as high profile as Soo. This in turn is partly because Tobias was not as talented or innovative as Robinson, who was a genuine giant of the Golden Age, and, somewhat ironically, partly because Tobias did not have an authentic Japanese nemesis attempting to expose him. Soto was a reasonably successful magician; Tobias maintained careful control of public information about himself; and nobody really looked too carefully. He features on the cover of *Mahatma* twice, once in 1898 and then again in 1906 – the articles about him are slightly evasive and contain almost no information about him personally. They skate around the issue of his ethnicity, observing that he is 'appearing in a Japanese garb' (1898) and that he is 'in the guise of a Japanese conjurer' (1906). Most remarkably, however, both these issues (eight years apart) show exactly the same photograph of Tobias in his 'Japanese' kimono. In other words, while Robinson exploded into the limelight with brazen deceptions and constant publicity, challenging China and the Chinese magicians to expose him (before actually exposing them as failing to meet the West's expectations of Chineseness), Tobias remained relatively unassuming and conducted his career without controversy at the time. The controversy about Tobias only emerges in the post-colonial present as we unpick the politics and ethics of his pretence.

A very different case was the incredible story of the Englishman William Peppercorn (1847–1891), to whom H.J. Burlingame devotes the entire second half of his book, *Around the World with a Magician and a Juggler*.[55] Peppercorn performed under the name D'Alvini, and became known as the 'European Jap' or the 'Jap of Japs', terms that sound intensely derogatory today. The story of how this English boy took an Italian name and then sought to convince the world that he was a Japanese magician is remarkable. Peppercorn was born in London, apparently cousin to 'the famous clown Governelli', in whose honour he

---

[54] Matsuyama, 'An Investigation of Magic in Japan After the Opening of the Country', pp. 20–21.

[55] H.J. Burlingame, *Around the World with a Magician and a Juggler*. Chicago: Clyde Publishing, 1891.

eventually took an Italian *nom de théâtre*. Even as a small child, people noted that he had 'a strongly marked Japanese face', despite having no connection with Japan. As a child, he trained in the circus, learning legerdemain and juggling.

It is then alleged that he travelled with Sanger's Circus to Japan (probably in 1865–1866), trained in Japanese conjuring and juggling, thought of the idea of bringing a Japanese troupe to Europe, and then actually obtained permission from the emperor to take the first Japanese troupe to the West. He called this the Tycoon Troupe. Burlingame related all of this as though it was accepted as historical fact in 1891. From today's vantage point, there is almost nothing about this story that makes sense (Sanger's Circus didn't visit Japan at that time; entry to Japan was very restricted; there's no way D'Alvini could have gained access to the emperor, even if he had been in Japan; D'Alvini did not organize or accompany the first troupes to leave Japan).

However, it is interesting to see how his story worked in the second half of the nineteenth century when, as we've seen, there was already so much ignorance about Japan and such confusion about the Japanese Troup, the Imperial Japanese Troupe, and the 'other' troupe (the Tycoon Troupe), which went into Oceania. It seems that D'Alvini capitalized on this confusion and appropriated the (name of the) Tycoon Troupe for himself. In addition, he genuinely seems to have learned feats of *daikagura* juggling and conjuring, which he performed in United States and Europe, constantly embellishing his already amazing biography as he went.

In the end, D'Alvini's outrageous stories about himself were just part of the atmosphere of the Golden Age and the plasticity of the Orient as a form of magic wand. His claims about his connections with Japan were matched by claims about performing to all kinds of royal families (including a number who didn't exist). Hence, his claim to represent Japanese magic must be seen in the context of the more general deployment of enchanting fantasies rather than as a serious assertion of Japaneseness; Japaneseness was a magical device, like pixie dust. Indeed, we might see a connection between the brazenness of his claims to representation with those of William Robinson, and this helps us to understand the nature of Robinson's attempts to *be* Soo.

On the occasion of his death, *Mahatma* carried two articles about D'Alvini by Henry Evans, who follows Burlingame and makes no issue of D'Alvini's origins or identity. Instead, Evans talks of a 'phantasmagoria of the Mikado's palace' and a man 'gorgeously robed as a Japanese thaumaturgist'. He accepts that D'Alvini was in Japan and suggests that 'it was while performing in Japan that D'Alvini decided to abandon the conventional attire of a Western conjuror and appear in Oriental dress'.[56] More important than any of these cosmetics, however, was the kind of magic that D'Alvini performed. Unlike the other pretenders to Japanese magic, who relied on these aesthetic embellishments to transform and defamiliarize familiar feats of Western magic, D'Alvini was one of the first Europeans to offer some authentic Japanese *daigakura* to the Western public. In this sense, despite his astonishing stories, he sets himself apart from the other imitators through his performative honesty. Indeed, to some extent, his faux-Japaneseness actually obscures the way in which his magic was sometimes authentically (and even impressively) Japanese:

> D'Alvini's feats were admirable. The Fairy Fountain was a triumph of balancing. In this act, he built a Japanese pagoda out of blocks of wood, the foundation resting on his chin. When the foundation was completed, a stream of water issued out of it, the structure revolving all the time. The climax was reached when, in place of water, streams of ribbon and showers of paper flew out of the fountain.[57]

Magic in Japan

A number of Western magicians made the journey to Japan. Like those who travelled to China, the purposes of their trips were largely commercial. They were looking for audiences and markets as much as for experiences of authentic Japanese magic. The earliest of these visitors, such as the creatively unreliable Dr. Lynn (Hugh Simmons), who claimed to have visited Japan in the 1860s and provided accounts that seemed inspired by the public imagination of Japan rather than by actual experiences of Japan itself. Hence, Lynn's remarkable visit included an immediate audience with the Prince of Satsuma, various incidents with swords, strange assertions about national customs (such

[56] Henry Ridgely Evans, 'Modern Magicians and Their Tricks'. *Mahatma*, 4:6 (December 1900).

[57] Henry Ridgely Evans, 'Modern Magicians and their Tricks'. *Mahatma*, 4:7 (January 1901).

as that the Japanese never eat meat), earthquakes, and eruptions of Mount Fuji. Lynn also set an early trend for Western magicians to note how clean, neat, elegant, and honest the Japanese were, especially in comparison with the Chinese.[58] In fact, Lynn was also one of the only visiting magicians who seemed to recognize Japan as the potential home of innovative magic that he could learn. Somewhat in the manner of those who visited India, Lynn claims to have 'held a reception every morning in my room, at which native jugglers came and taught me many interesting tricks, amongst others the top-spinning on a single thread, and the butterfly trick'.[59] By the time of Charles Bertram's visit at the turn of the century, visiting magicians would lament that 'I was anxious to see a Japanese conjuror, but he seems to be remarkable for his absence.' Instead, Bertram identifies jugglers and equilibrists as being skills in 'which the Japanese are unsurpassed'.[60]

Indeed, by the end of the nineteenth century, magicians visiting Japan were primarily preoccupied with the way that the country was so rapidly becoming modern. They were no longer confronted by the kinds of romantic images of traditional Japanese culture, nature, and mystical animism that Lynn claimed to have encountered. Some of the travel accounts narrate the struggle of Western magicians to juggle their romantic preconceptions about Japan and their actual experiences of a modern, constitutional nation-state. Unlike India and China, which continued to struggle with domestic unrest and colonial occupation, Japan was a unified, powerful, and independent nation. In a revealing turn of phrase, the great American magician Howard Thurston confronts this directly during his brief visit of 1906: 'Conditions in Japan, however, were different. For the first time since my invasion of the Far East I faced failure.' He explains that the Japanese public boycotted his show as part of a general boycott of 'foreign enterprises' after the Russo-Japanese war (1904–1905).[61] Consequently, Thurston abandoned his

---

[58] Lynn, *Adventures of a Strange Man*, pp. 9–15.

[59] Lynn, *Adventures of a Strange Man*, p. 11.

[60] Charles Bertram, *A Magician in Many Lands*. London: Routledge & Sons, 1911, p. 201.

[61] Howard Thurston, *My Life of Magic*. Philadelphia: Dorrance & Co., 1929, p. 172. In fact, the Russo-Japanese war was the second major war for Japan in ten years, following its world-historic victory in the Sino-Japanese war of 1894–1895. Japan's demonstrable military power and its victories in this period marked its emergence (and recognition) as the first modern 'non-Western' Great Power, culminating in a seat at the victor's table at the Versailles Peace Conference in 1919. However, despite

plans in Japan and left immediately; his visit warrants only a paragraph in his book.

Other accounts of the encounter between Western magicians and a modernizing Japan struggle to negotiate these issues. Charles Bertram, for instance, begins his chapters about Japan with a lyrical description of being 'enchanted with the varied and kaleidoscopic scenery'. He goes on to express admiration for a country 'well cultivated and neatly laid out'.[62] And thus he joins in the convention of appreciating the elegance and beauty of Japan, especially in contrast with China. However, in the middle of this romance, Bertram offers a conflicted passage regarding his need to obtain a licence to perform in Japan. This had not been necessary elsewhere in Asia, and Bertram is so struck by this that he even reproduces the license itself in his book (albeit upside down).[63] With a characteristically colonial sense of entitlement, Bertram explains that he had already been forced to pay a tax upon entry to the country, 'which I considered a great injustice', so requiring a license seemed like adding insult to injury.[64] In the end, he manages to subvert the licensing protocols, and thus presumably restores his sense of justice, by having himself licensed as a 'buffoon' rather than an actor. This story renders the situation and the outcome ridiculous, but in reality the licence issued to Bertram (when viewed the correct way up) clearly states that he has been licensed to perform magic or sleight of hand (*tejina*), revealing that the licensing system was sophisticated enough to accommodate him perfectly. Bertram conjectures that their military modernization has caused the Japanese (especially 'the lower orders') to 'become arrogant, and their treatment of Europeans is by no means improved'.[65]

This kind of encounter between Western magicians who were expecting to find a mysteriously pre-modern, exotic, and subordinated culture, but who found a functioning modern nation that expected to be

its remarkable technological, social, and political accomplishments during this period, Western racism set double standards in international society, and Japan's attempts to have 'racial equality' built into the Versailles Treaty were thwarted. It is generally accepted that Japanese frustrations about this duplicity contributed to a political and cultural reorientation in Japan that led into the Asia Pacific War.

[62] Bertram, *A Magician in Many Lands*, pp. 178, 181.
[63] Bertram, *A Magician in Many Lands*, p. 180.
[64] Bertram, *A Magician in Many Lands*, p. 179.
[65] Bertram, *A Magician in Many Lands*, pp. 183–184.

respected on an equal footing, is a common feature of accounts from the period. In fact, Bertram's response was rather typical. He goes on to recount the various transformations of Japanese society that accompanied (or symbolized) its modernization. He notes, for instance, that the Japanese people have taken to wearing 'solemn and sombre' clothing instead of 'the bright-coloured picturesque garments previously worn'. The longing for Japan to resemble the Western fantasy of Japan was clear:

> I regretted that it had not been my good fortune to see these interesting folk garbed as at the time of the old Kwazoku (nobility) and the Shizoku (warriors) when the warrior carried two swords, one to be drawn at the time of war, and the other with which he took his own life by the command of the Mikado.[66]

Like others of that time and since, Bertram attempts to reconcile his ideas about a mystical Japan with his experiences of a modernizing Japan by claiming that its transformation was at least partially an illusion. He talks about a 'veneer of prosperity' in the cities that hides 'misery of the worst form' that the tourist never sees. He conjectures that the transformations in Japanese society are mistakes; its concrete modernity comes at the price of its romantic ideal. 'Japan may become a big power, but by the adoption of western ideas the happiness of her children has gone forever.'[67]

Bertram concludes his account with sentiments that were shared by many, not only in the West but increasing in Japan as well:

> If I were asked how my impressions of Japan compared with my ideas preconceived of the country, I should very reluctantly have to admit that I was much disappointed. I found it overrated and far from realising the accepted picture formed in the minds of the untraveled majority. The beautiful colours, universal neatness and cleanliness, and simplicity one expects to find, of which one has learned to believe Japan is the 'beau ideal', is a myth. Neither are the people particularly original, although wonderfully imitative of occidental manners, customs and ideas. Pictures are drawn of Japan as a country where all is bright; gaily dressed folks living butterfly lives, the sun always shining, a land of swaying lanterns, goldfish,

[66] Bertram, *A Magician in Many Lands*, pp. 182–183.
[67] Bertram, *A Magician in Many Lands*, pp. 185–186.

over blooming flowers, and happiness reigning supreme ... Japan is suddenly becoming Anglicised; one false step may wreck her forever.[68]

The conceit of the colonial imagination is a well-documented feature of Orientalism as an ideology, as is the resentment felt in the metropolitan centres when the objects of their fantasies turn out to be subjective agents of their own histories. Hence, it is possible to understand the frustrations of modern magicians when confronted with a modernizing Japan that does not conform with the 'phantasmagoria of the Mikado's palace' or even with the guise of Japaneseness adopted by 'Japanese magicians' in London and New York. The idea that Japan's modernity was itself a kind of magic, a trick or an illusion that simply obscures the truth that it is a mystical land, has an enchanting logic of its own. The notion that Japan was simply wearing the clothes of modernity – much as Soto Sunetaro or Okito or Chung Ling Soo wore the clothes of the mystical Orient – enabled the Western public to maintain its imagination of Japan as the magical Other.

One of the most intriguing responses to this grand question of cultural deception was the one offered by Percival Lowell, who managed to fold the apparent modernization of Japan back into a fantastical worldview that maintained Japan as an icon of natural beauty, animism, and femininity. Investing into the structure of hypnosis as the exemplar of modern magic, as it was seen at the time, Lowell makes an elaborate argument that the Japanese nation has been hypnotized en masse:

> It is hardly exaggeration to say that Japan at this moment is affording the rest of the world the spectacle of the most stupendous hypnotic act ever seen, nothing less than the hypnotization of a whole nation, with its eyes open.[69]

[68] Bertram, *A Magician in Many Lands*, pp. 209–210. In fact, this idea of a 'lost Japan' was also prevalent amongst Japanese intellectuals, writers, and opinion leaders in this period. The notion that modernity was somehow ruining a romantic, rural ideal of Japan was prevalent in the work of the so-called Romantic School. An excellent study of this is Kevin Doak, *Dreams of Difference: The Japan Romantic School and the Crisis of Modernity*, Berkeley: University of California Press, 1994. Indeed, this kind of romanticism persisted into the post-war period in Japan; it can be seen as characteristic of the Nobel Prize winner, Kawabata Yasunari, or even of the popular anime maker, Miyazaki Hayao.

[69] Lowell, *Occult Japan*, p. 288.

Hypnosis, suggests Lowell, is the only explanation for Japan's sudden imitation of the West in its cultural and social development. He suggests that the 'combinations in costume as beautifully incompatible as any the hypnotized subject can be induced to adopt' are seen all over Japan, and that this is explicable only because the hypnotized subjects will accept the 'unreasoned' and the 'ludicrous'.

Furthermore, argues Lowell, Japan's enchantment is not arbitrary but rather inherent. 'Hypnotoidal imitation is no new trait of these people.... Susceptibility to suggestion lies at the root of the race.'[70] The reason for this would be readily recognizable by magicians and audiences of the Golden Age: first, within Japanese magic there is only the precedent of influence by the natural world and animal spirits, which means that when the Japanese are subject to human suggestion they are unable to resist it; second, 'Japan is the feminine half of the world' recognized for her 'delicacy, her daintiness, and her dignity', and 'very different as are femininity and far-orientalism in most things, there is strangely enough in both a relative absence of self'. Hence, because of their relatively submissive and harmonious personalities, 'in spite of authoritative statements to the contrary, women are actually more hypnotizable than men', and thus Japan can be easily hypnotized.[71]

In this incredible way at the turn of the century, Lowell manages to make use of modern magic to construct an argument that flattens Japan's emerging modernity back into a romantic account of a mystical Japan alive with animism, animal spirits, natural beauty, and delicate femininity – the garden of fantasy. From our vantage point today, Lowell (an accomplished mathematician and astronomer) looks to be enmeshed in a form of magical thinking, but it's important to remember that hypnosis was at the cutting edge of modern, scientific magic during the Golden Age.

As we have already seen with the case of Ten'ichi, Japanese magicians in Japan were also wrestling with these questions of tradition and modernity in their performances and approaches to magic. Indeed, this has one of the core cultural problematics in Japan since

---

[70] Lowell, *Occult Japan*, p. 289.

[71] Lowell, *Occult Japan*, pp. 293, 283, 295. In fact, Lowell suggests that 'the Japanese are the French of the Far East', and hence that this argument might also be true of the French, which is why hypnosis and mesmerism succeeded in Paris but failed in Vienna (pp. 283, 297).

the opening of the country in 1854. The idea that the Japanese identity became somehow split or layered during its emergence into modernity was common: slogans such as *wakon yōsai* (Japanese spirit, Western technology) captured the notion that Japan could adopt the material and technological trappings of modernity without sacrificing its traditional soul.[72] Philosophers at this time started to develop 'dual-layered' theories of the self that could accommodate a foundational identity that was both modern and traditional simultaneously.[73] In the early years of the twentieth century, in the lead-up to the Pacific War, the idea that Japan could retain its traditional spirit and master the trappings of modernity gave way to the ideological discourse that came to be known as *kindai no chōkoku* (overcoming modernity).

In his discussion of the state of magic at the turn of the century, the third-generation Yanagawa Itchosai (Aoki Jisaburō) attempted to explain some of these dilemmas, which he presented under the potent title *konketsuji tejina* (mixed-race magic)[74] in the national newspaper, the *Yomiuri Shimbun*. The view that Western magic represents a materialist Western civilization is clearly expressed, as is the idea that Japanese magic is more nuanced, skilful, and elegant. Such an imaginary was common at the time in Japan, and shares a number of features with the Western imaginary that we have already considered. Unlike in the West, though, where the implications of adopting the guise of an Oriental magician were not seriously debated, except instrumentally, Yanagawa seems genuinely interested in trying to understand the significance of this meeting of magical traditions, not only for the traditions but also for magic itself:

> The Western magic shown these days is mostly Japanese, rather than genuinely Western magic. In most cases, the magic has simply been modified, for instance, by changing the prop from wood to

[72] This slogan is usually attributed to the progressive intellectual and cultural leader, Fukuzawa Yukichi (1835–1901), who was one of the driving forces between Japan's intellectual modernity. He wrote extensively on the meaning of progress, culture, and civilization, attempting to do so from a global perspective. And he founded Japan's first private university, which continues today as Keiō University.

[73] This concept is most closely associated with the work of the Kyoto philosopher Watsuji Tetsurō (1889–1960).

[74] *Konketsuji* also carries the meaning of a child, hence *konketsuji tejina* is the magic of the child of mixed blood.

metal, or by wearing Western clothes instead of traditional
Japanese costume. So, this should be called 'mixed-race magic'.
Generally speaking, Western magic operates by physical secrets, so
any layman could perform it easily, once learning how it is done.
Japanese magic, on the contrary, requires great practice to master
the sleight-of-hand, similar to the feats of acrobats and jugglers.
Even if one learned its secret and method, no layman could perform
it in a short time. Since Japanese magic requires considerable
sleight-of-hand and secret actions, it is difficult to perform in an
open area like a garden party, because our secret movements would
be observed from all directions. Similar difficulties exist in vaudeville theatres.... So, once a magician can perform everywhere,
regardless of various difficult situations ... he is considered one of
the master magicians.[75]

Of course, this description takes considerable liberties with the dimensions and content of Western magic in this period, but this in itself
provides a fascinating lens through which to reconsider Western constructions of Japanese magic. Yanagawa's image is not without merit,
and it is certainly the case that the mechanistic and technological aspects
of magic that accompanied the advent of modern magic in the West
were those that made the deepest impression on Japanese magicians and
audiences, just as it was the graceful skill and beauty of Japanese magic
that really impacted in the West.

In the Japanese context, it seems relatively clear that the magicians who were perceived to have 'true skill' (*shinko no gei*) at this time
would have been those, like Ten'ichi, who could perform in Japan and
in the West to equal acclaim, adapting their style and techniques to
meet (and confound) the expectations of different audiences. This magician of 'true skill' transcended the characteristics of both Japanese
and Western magic, assimilating the modern and overcoming it. In
Fujiyama's words, Ten'ichi was the 'super-magician'![76] Hence, the
acclaimed Western magicians who came to Japan to perform the same

---

[75] *Yomiuri Shimbun*, 25 February 1902. Reproduced in Matsuyama Mitsunobu, *Jisshō
Nihon no tejinashi*. Tokyo: Tōkyōdō shuppan, 2010, pp. 217–218. Matsuyama also
provides a translation of this passage, which I have amended slightly, 'An Investigation
into Magic in Japan after the Opening of the Country: Some Japanese Entertainers of
the Westernized Meiji Era.' *Gibeciere*, 6:1 (Winter 2011), p. 65.
[76] Fujiyama Shintarō, *Ten'ichi ichidai, meiji no sūpāmajishan*. Tokyo: NTT shuppan,
2012.

shows that they performed in New York and London were inferior to these emerging master magicians of mixed-magical race. Indeed, this shape of argument (about the historical superiority of global hybridities that incorporate and then transcend the conventions of modernity) would come to be seen in numerous sectors of Japanese society in the 1920s and 1930s.[77]

Nonetheless, Yanagawa's emergent philosophy of the history of magic (which pushed into a hybrid future of master magicians) was only one response to what Thurston called magic's 'invasion of the Far East'. As in China, this period also witnessed the creation of Japan's first magic societies, such as the *Tokyo kijutsu kenkyūkai* (est. 1930) and then the *Nippon kijutsu kyōkai* (est. 1936),[78] which served to democratize access to magic by shifting it away from the traditional apprentice system. The emergence of modern magic as a commodity that could be purchased transformed access to tricks; indeed, it was in this period that we saw the rise of department store magic in Japan. The amateur magician emerged. Leading professionals such as Shōkyokusai Tenyo (1888–1980), who had made his name performing with the great Ten'ichi, started to give demonstrations and sell magic props in leading stores, such as Mitsukoshi in the 1930s. After the war, Tenyo re-established his magic business and held popular performances in the Mitsukoshi Theatre. Today, the Tenyo Magic Company is a world-leading name in research, development, and production of magical apparatus. An intriguing extension of this high-street magic presence in post-war Japan is the prevalence of 'magic bars' in the major cities, where waiters will serve close-up magic with your drink.

One of the unique and noteworthy features of this embrace of 'modern magic' in Japan was the rise of female magicians. As we've seen, female magicians were only on the margins of the scene in the West. But in Japan the 'queen of Japanese magic', Shōkyokusai Tenkatsu (1886–1944) emerged from the Ten'ichi troupe and started her own

---

[77] This form of the philosophy of history is now associated with the work of the so-called Kyoto School of Philosophy. Chris Goto-Jones, *Political Philosophy in Japan: Nishida, the Kyoto School, and Co-Prosperity*. London: Routledge, 2005.

[78] The *Nippon kijutsu kyōkai* would later become the premier association for professional Japanese magicians, *Kōeki shadanhōjin nihon kijutsu kyōkai* (Japan Professional Magician's Association, JPMA), established by the Agency of Cultural Affairs in 1993.

troupe in 1911.[79] Tenkatsu was a gifted magician, performing a variety of feats from the Ten'ichi period, and often dressing and performing in Western attire (sometimes even the attire of a Western male). Tenkatsu represents a remarkable moment of cultural and political progressiveness in the development of modern magic globally.

However, as also in China, the democratization and commodi-fication of modern magic, either in a hybrid or a Western form, also provoked conservative reactions, especially from magicians who identi-fied closely with magic as it was practiced in Japan before the arrival of the West – what came to be called *wazuma*, originally in contrast with *yōzuma* (Western magic), both of which are regional specifications of *tezuma*. Unlike in China, where textual sources for indigenous magic are rare, *wazuma* benefits from the preservation of a cluster of classic texts from the Edo period (and is sometimes referred to as *Edo tezuma*): *Shinsen gejutsu* (1696), *Zoku zange bukuro* (1727), *Haiseki tama-tezuma* (1780), *Hiji hyakusen* (1827), and *Tezuma hayakeiko* (1862). Partly thanks to the efforts of the innovative impresario of Japanese magic, Ton Onosaka, perhaps the most famous of these today is the *Hōkasen* (1764). The 'three jewels' of *wazuma* are the classic effects of Japanese magic that came to represent it in the West during the Golden Age: *chō no tawamure* (Butterfly Trick), *mizugei* (Water Arts), and also the apparently universal classic *owan to tama* (Cups and Balls).

In comparison with China in this era of the Golden Age, where a new category of magic (*moshu*) was created for modern Western magic at least partially to demarcate it from 'feudal superstitions' that were devalued and sometimes persecuted, Japan's period of insecurity about its own traditions in the face of the West was much shorter. Hence, while Japan very quickly started to mix and match Japanese and Western magic into its own form of modern magic – *tejina* or *kijutsu* – it also sought to identify its own traditional arts in order to value and preserve them. Rather than creating a term to signal the progressive value of Western magic, then, Japan moulded a term to enshrine the value of Japanese heritage – *wazuma*. In the modern period, it was associated powerfully with the Yanagawa Itchosai lineage. Eventually, in 1997, the Agency of Cultural Affairs designated *wazuma*

---

[79] An excellent biography that explains the emergence of Tenkatsu (and Tenyo) from the Ten'ichi troupe is Marukawa Kayoko, *Kijutsushi tanjō – Shōkyokusai Ten'ichi, Ten'ni, Tenkatsu*. Tokyo: Shinchosha, 1984.

as 'intangible cultural heritage' to be preserved, placing it alongside other traditional cultural forms such as *Noh* drama, *Bunraku* (puppet theatre), and *Kabuki* theatre.

Perhaps ironically, one of the ways in which *wazuma* was preserved was through the interest of Western magicians in Japan as a 'garden of fantasy'; one of the most complete (albeit imperfect) manuals of *wazuma* in the early twentieth century was compiled by Black Kairakutei (Black Ishii, or Harry Black, 1858–1923) for serialized publication in the British journal, *The Magician Monthly* in 1914–1915.[80] In many ways, as we've seen, Black Ishii's articles were not describing magic as it was being performed in Japan in 1910s (although they certainly contributed to this impression in the Orientalist West), but instead was engaged in a form of cultural preservation of Japanese magic from an earlier period.[81]

---

[80] Harry Black was an Australian who became Japan's first foreign-born performer of *rakugo* (story-telling) and *kabuki*. He became a naturalized Japanese citizen. His articles in *The Magician Monthly* (September 1914 – November 1915) are certainly the most comprehensive guide to *wazuma* from that period, and they are definitely the only non-Japanese source to provide any details on tricks other than the Butterfly Trick, Thumb Tie, or Magic Fountain.

[81] It is fascinating to note that Black Ishii saw his task as something akin to translating a piece of literature. Before noting the various differences in modes of presentation between Japanese and Western magic (such as that Japanese magicians perform sitting down, Westerners standing up; Japanese use a fan where Westerners use a wand etc.), he explains his rationale for the series of articles:

> In writing these articles about magic as practiced in Japan, I have endeavoured, as far as possible, to retain the real Japanese character of each trick which I have explained. All magicians will appreciate my meaning when I say that I wanted to impart a sense of the Japanese atmosphere which surrounds the performance of these tricks when they are presented by native magicians. At the same time, in order to make the articles of practical use to English and American magicians, I have adapted many of the tricks to their requirements. It goes without saying, of course, that to see a trick presented properly, with the intentions of the inventor duly respected, one must see it in the land of its birth. However, just as one may get to know something of the literary value of a book by reading a translation of it, so I hope, will the tricks I have explained be appreciated by magicians who may never have an opportunity of seeing any one of the tricks performed by a Japanese magician.

Ishii Black, 'Japanese Magic: Simple Explanations of the Conjuring Tricks of Japanese Magicians'. *The Magician Monthly*, 11:IX (September 1914), p. 156.

CONCLUSION: MAGIC IN THE WORLD

Looking back on this project, I find that I am relieved to see that it involved so few balloon animals or card tricks. Having said that, it's worth taking a moment to reflect on the absence of the latter: while they have become such a staple of modern and contemporary magic (including in Asia), playing cards have played almost no role in this story of Oriental magic. Indeed, this absence is one of the simplest historical observations about these categories. The absence of balloon animals seems less interesting, at least to me.

One of the ideas that I have tried to keep in focus throughout this book is that 'modern magic' can be a meaningful category, not only historically but also theoretically and performatively. When I say it's a meaningful category, I'm also saying that it's not a universal category – some magic isn't modern magic. Indeed, 'modern magic' can be seen as a critical category, both in terms of its engagement with ethics and aesthetics.

A powerful characteristic arises from the contradictory relationship between its two essential components: modernity and magic. While modernity appears to push in the direction of the scientific disenchantment of the world and the eradication of magic, modern magic seems to absorb this tendency and transform it into a form of creative tension. Within this tension seems to reside a basic human desire to live lives of enchantment – lives with non-material meanings. Modern magic embraces this desire while denying its object; it maintains that magic can be meaningfully experienced even within the parameters of a disenchanted modernity. This is an ethically delicate balance, and magicians have played with it in various ways, sometimes successfully, and only sometimes deliberately.

A curious outcome of this tension has been the modern magician's paradoxical fear of magic and the concomitant tendency towards self-ridicule. The modern magician embodies *both* the desire to bring magic into the world *and* a cultural nexus that declares this juvenile or primitive. During the so-called Golden Age of Magic, as part of the relegation of magic to the margins and peripheries of society, some magicians recognized the possibilities inherent in the geographical margins of empire – in the so-called Orient – as a potential space for squaring this circle. The Orient was constructed as a fantastical place in which 'real magic' was possible because it was outside the immediate pressures of Western modernity. Oriental magic represented the desire by modern magicians (and audiences) to live in a world of enchantment, even when it was ideologically outlawed from Europe and the United States.

If anything, the idea of Oriental magic was even more conflicted than the idea of modern magic in the West. In addition to the tension between the drive for scientific progress and a desire for an enchanting life, Oriental magic provoked issues of imperial politics, power relations, and racism. The desire for magic to be 'real' in this world was no longer only in metaphysical tension with the desire for scientific control of the world, but also in political tension with the desire for colonial superiority and the conceit of the 'white man's burden'. Oriental magic was both a lifeline and a threat, a hero and a villain, a master and a slave.

In this complex space, Oriental magic becomes intertwined with all kinds of ethnic and racial stereotypes. Even 'old' magic had the racially charged categories of 'black and white', but we see the emergence of 'yellow' magic during the Golden Age, sometimes in the guise of European or American men in thick make-up, swaddled in flowing, silken robes, and speaking pidgin English. At the same time, magicians from Asia faced complex choices about how to present themselves on the stages of London, Paris, and New York, with many adopting a form of self-Orientalism that effectively (and sometimes literally) silenced their voices.

Despite the magnitude of the ethical and political dilemmas of Oriental magic, the encounter between Western and Asian magic was also genuinely and profoundly constructive and exciting. Many of the most popular and enchanting effects of modern magic arose from this interface. Not only that, but Oriental magic probed at the frontiers of modern magic in myriad ways, not only expanding its repertoire of tricks but also testing its presuppositions about ways to accommodate the magical in modern societies. Oriental magic opened up possibilities for the contemporary renaissance of magic in the form of Bizarre Magic and Street Magic; it enabled and encouraged new ways for magicians to exhibit a form of commitment to magic that resembled a process of *becoming a magical being*. In other words, while Oriental magic arose as a core component of modern magic, it also proved to be a radical force within it, undermining and creatively transforming some of the foundational assumptions of magic in the modern West (such as that a magician is only an actor).

In this way, it's possible to see the global spread of modern magic as the emergence of an international regime. Like many such regimes that developed in the twentieth century, it began with a very clear hegemonic focus in Europe and then the United States, and it spread quickly into the so-called non-Western world together with imperial power and (semi-) colonialism. This brought modern magic into contact with local magical traditions outside the metropolitan centres, where those local magicians suddenly had to negotiate the relative status of this magical invasion and their own traditions of practice. We have seen that, not unlike modern medicine, modern magic rolled over the traditional magics of Asia, either replacing them or requiring a new cultural category in which Asian magicians could participate.

Ideological and practical responses to this situation were diverse: they included, at one extreme, movements to identify and preserve this new 'modern magic' as a respectable way to maintain enchantment within a rapidly modernizing and alienating society, which simultaneously involved turning away from local traditions as regressively superstitious; and at the other extreme, they included the perception of this modern magic as a form of cultural imperialism that needed to be controlled, thus provoking movements to more clearly identify, preserve, and value local traditions of magic.

In the contemporary world, then, we find a fascinatingly diverse world of magic. The modern magic regime remains firmly in place, bolstered by the establishment of various national and international organizations in the West as well as in Asia. Yet the content and meaning of modern magic have been modified and changed through its interaction with Oriental magic and magic in/from Asia. In the spirit of the words of Yanagawa Itchosai (the third): the days of modern magic being simply Western magic have gone; even while the term 'modern magic' retains its roots in the ideological and ethical commitments of the Golden Age, through its interaction with Asia it has developed into a more *worldly modern magic*, which blends elements from all over the world. Modern magic is beginning to overcome the idea that modernization and Westernization need to be identical. Perhaps as evidence of this, there seems to be an ongoing shift in the centre of gravity in the international regime; we are witnessing a hegemonic shift from Europe and the United States to China and Asia more generally.

At the same time, a consequence of the consolidation of this international regime of modern magic in Asia is that those traditions of Asian (or other) magic that do not fit comfortably into this regime need to find other spaces to perform. Hence, we can see the emergence of the idea of *world magic* – echoing world music or world philosophy – in which magical practices that don't clearly subscribe to the ideals of modern magic can find themselves. This category participates in debates about heritage studies and cultural preservation in an age of global capitalism; the term 'ethnomagicology' has been used to indicate its study. Perhaps the clearest and most institutionalized instance of this is in Japan, where modern magic predominates, but where *wazuma* has been recognized as cultural asset to the nation in need of protection.

For myself, I have been constantly amazed and deeply gratified by the way that magicians all over the world have given their time and opinions on this little project. Oriental magic still excites controversy. I am particularly grateful to a talented young magician I met in Hong Kong in 2012, who explained to me very patiently that I was clearly right that there was a lot of misunderstanding about Oriental magic. Indeed, he lamented that this term had become so muddled and polluted that it had almost lost all meaning. To my great surprise, however, it gradually transpired that he was of the opinion that modern magic had systematically sought to discredit the power of real Oriental magic in order to assert the dominance of Western materialism. After a long discussion about this, I read him a passage from an astonishing book by Claude Alexander (1880–1964, aka 'The Man Who Knows'), whose picture adorns the cover of this book.

Alexander was an American vaudeville magician who performed in the guise of a generic 'Oriental seer' in the 1920s, when he allegedly became the highest-paid magician in the world. 'The Man Who Knows' could apparently answer any question posed to him by clairvoyance. Unlike William Robinson, Alexander did not claim to *be* an Oriental

Figure C.1 Alexander, 'Mental Mystics Panel', c1915. Courtesy of Nielsen Magic Collection.

magician, but he was deeply committed to propagating the idea of the reality of Oriental magic. He was an exemplary instance of the con man magician – the charlatan so disdained by Maskelyne and Devant.

In his incredible book, *Oriental Wisdom, Its Principles and Practice*, Alexander attempted an ambitious and bizarre reconstruction of Hindu mysticism as a 'self-exposé' and instructional guidebook, encouraging his readers to practice meditating on a crystal ball in order to attain powers of clairvoyance like his and thus become rich and famous like him. He insisted that the wondrous stories of Oriental magic were true and that they did not require his readers to believe in the supernatural. Instead of the super-natural, he elaborates a theory of the *super-normal*, which defends the scientific veracity of clairvoyance and telepathy on the grounds that they are consistent with laws of nature that the West has not yet understood. But because laws of nature are universal, he reasons, they must be just as valid for his readers as for Oriental magicians.

In many ways, Alexander's amazing book is as shameless as Chung Ling Soo's makeup and costume. Yet, it still seems to enchant readers today, and we should learn something from the incredible resilience of this imagery. My friend in Hong Kong endorsed the following passage wholeheartedly, and so I assume he'd include my little book amongst the 'rubbish' mentioned. I have to confess, part of me still hopes he's right:

> The Orient has always been the great centre, and, in fact, the great source, of Magic. Careful students of the subject have discovered that, although the practice of magical arts and science is found in almost all parts of the ancient and modern world, the real original source of Magic is to be found in the Orient, from which it spread and flowered by innumerable streams and channels into other lands. The great Masters of Magic always received their instruction, directly or indirectly, from the great Fountain of Magic in the Orient.... Even unto this day, amidst all the rubbish that has accumulated around the principles and practice of Magic, in the Orient, is still to be found the highest and most advanced forms and phases of the magical art.[1]

---

[1] Claude Alexander, *Oriental Wisdom, Its Principles and Practice*. Los Angeles: C. Alexander Publishing Co., 1924, p. 69.

Index

Page numbers followed by "n" and an additional number indicate a numbered footnote